Philip James Bailey
Festus

Edinburgh Critical Editions of Nineteenth-Century Texts

Published titles
Richard Jefferies, After London; or Wild England
Edited by Mark Frost
Marie Corelli, A Romance of Two Worlds: A Novel
Edited by Andrew Radford
Sensation Drama, 1860–1880: An Anthology
Edited by Joanna Hofer-Robinson and Beth Palmer
Agriculture and the Land: Richard Jefferies' Essays and Letters
Edited by Rebecca Welshman
Maxwell Gray, The Silence of Dean Maitland
Edited by Julian Wolfreys
Jane Porter, Thaddeus of Warsaw: A Novel
Edited by Thomas McLean and Ruth Knezevich
Hubert Crackanthorpe, Wreckage: Seven Studies
Edited by David Malcolm
Catharine Sedgwick, Redwood: A Tale
Edited by Jenifer B. Elmore
Philip James Bailey, Festus: An Epic Poem
Edited by Mischa Willett

Forthcoming titles
William Barnes, Dialect Poems in The Dorset County Chronicle
Edited by Thomas Burton and Emma Mason
Geraldine Jewsbury, Critical Essays and Reviews (1849–1870)
Edited by Anne-Marie Beller
Hartley Coleridge, The Complete Poems
Edited by Nicola Healey
George Gissing, The Private Papers of Henry Ryecroft
Edited by Thomas Ue
William Morris on Socialism: Uncollected Essays
Edited by Florence Boos

Visit the Edinburgh Critical Editions of Nineteenth-Century Texts
website at: edinburghuniversitypress.com/series/ecenct

Philip James Bailey

Festus: An Epic Poem

Edited by Mischa Willett

EDINBURGH
University Press

Edinburgh University Press is one of the leading university presses in the UK.
We publish academic books and journals in our selected subject areas across the
humanities and social sciences, combining cutting-edge scholarship with high
editorial and produ ction values to produce academic works of lasting importance.
For more information visit our website: edinburghuniversitypress.com

Edinburgh University Press Ltd
The Tun – Holyrood Road, 12(2f) Jackson's Entry, Edinburgh EH8 8PJ

First published in hardback by Edinburgh University Press 2022

Typeset in 11/ 12.5 Baskerville and Times New Roman by
IDSUK (DataConnection) Ltd, and
printed and bound by CPI Group (UK) Ltd,
Croydon, CR0 4YY

A CIP record for this book is available from the British Library

ISBN 978 1 4744 5 781 1 (hardback)
ISBN 978 1 4744 8468 8 (paperback)
ISBN 978 1 4744 5782 8 (webready PDF)
ISBN 978 1 4744 5783 5 (epub)

Contents

Acknowledgements

Philip James Bailey

I'd like to express my deepest gratitude to Charles LaPorte at the University of Washington, who first introduced me to this magnificent poem, and in so doing, gave me one of the aesthetic highlights of my career. I'm also grateful to the University of Tübingen, especially Christopher Harvie, for a fellowship during which much of my work on Bailey and the Spasmodics took shape.

Thanks are also due to Seattle Pacific University, particularly to my department chair, Mark Walhout, to librarian Steve Perisho, to the Faculty Life Office, especially Margaret Brown, and to my colleagues in the English department, especially Traynor Hansen, Jeffrey Overstreet and Peter Moe, who kept me encouraged and engaged throughout a long project.

Furthermore, I am indebted to my student research assistants for bonhomie and for sharing in this work: Robert Banks, Pierce Papke, Edison Cummings, Joshua Ulrich, and above all to Abby Rogers, *ne plus ultra*. The work of editing this text was made massively more lively by your voices.

The North American Victorian Studies Association (NAVSA), the Modern Language Association (MLA) and the North American Society for the Study of Romanticism (NASSR) staged the gatherings at which I first floated the critical and textual ideas contained in this volume. Many thanks to the tireless organisers of those conferences, which are themselves exercises in optimism.

Without the wonderful editorial team at Edinburgh University Press, this volume would not exist and this poem would have remained inaccessible to readers and scholars alike. I'm grateful for their care, grace and enthusiasm for the project.

Thanks finally to my family, who had to listen to me say things like 'this Lucifer is amazing' more times than is theologically advisable.

A portion of this research was made possible by a travel grant from the Conference on Christianity and Literature.

Introduction

Having received at Princeton University Library a donation of some documents 'of great interest for the literary history of the nineteenth century in England and America', Morse Peckham set out to discover what he could about the figure with whom they were concerned.[1] It turned out to be a difficult task because the editions, manuscripts and correspondence were related to Philip James Bailey's *Festus*, a poem Peckham found 'the literary world' had both 'misinterpreted' and 'underestimated'. More shockingly for Peckham, scholars had been ignoring it, leaving questions 'still unanswered', such as 'what is the nature of the appeal of a long, complex, and to many people, heretical poem'? Where was the record of scholarly commentary a poem of *Festus*' reach and complexity warranted?

Calls for rejuvenation, based either on the poem's staggering popularity among Victorians, or on its influence on other authors, proliferate. The whimsically named F. B. Money-Coutts pleads, for example, in *The Academy* (1901), 'not from any audience chamber ought this great, this conscientious prophet-poet to be dismissed without being fully heard' and 'Mr. Bailey's life-work deserves, not an ephemeral comment, but a volume of earnest analysis.'[2] *The Athenaeum* (1876) avers that 'in the study of English poetry, it is always necessary to consider the influence of . . . *Festus* . . . upon most subsequent poetry'.[3] For some readers, the poem's obvious quality all but guaranteed it a place in posterity. *The Saturday Review* (1889), for instance, contends, 'the fact remains that schools of poetry rise and fall, one influence yields to another influence, and Mr. Bailey's . . . poem rides every storm and survives every revolution of taste'.[4]

Yet the poem's importance for the Victorians and for literary history has failed to secure its endurance. If it was not true in 1876, when W. M. Rossetti lamented that '*Festus* is, at present, but little read,' and was chastened by an angry correspondent who argued that, far from being a forgotten work, *Festus*' readership had widened in the 1870s

1. M. Peckham, 'A Bailey Collection', *Princeton University Library Chronicle*, 7:4, 1947, p. 150.
2. F. B. Money-Coutts, 'Bailey's Festus', *The Academy*, 25 May 1901, p. 448.
3. T. Watts, 'Festus and Recent English Poetry', *The Athenaeum*, 1 April 1876, p. 465.
4. *The Saturday Review*, 18 May 1889, pp. 617–18.

rather than contracted, it is certainly true now that *Festus* is little read.[5]
No editions of the poem have been printed since 1903 and, despite its
influence, ambition and breadth of appeal, *Festus* has never inspired
an academic monograph, nor a biography of its author.[6] It is, however,
often treated in period surveys, and nearly always mentioned in over-
views of the aesthetic movement to which it gave birth: the Spasmodic
School.[7] In that company, Herbert Tucker tackles the poem as an ego-
istic turn in the history of epics,[8] Jason Rudy uses it to describe electric
sensation and metrical irregularity,[9] and Mark A. Weinstein casts *Festus*
as a target in a discussion of W. E. Aytoun's satirical criticism,[10] but for
the most part, Peckham's accusation, that 'no scholarly attempt has yet
been made to find out what is even in the poem', stands.[11]

There are at least two reasons for this lack. Partly, it is due to the
unavailability of reliable editions. Over a dozen official editions were
printed in England, each substantially different from the last, and as
many again in America, which sometimes, but not always, kept pace
with the changing British versions. Additionally, scores of pirated edi-
tions were published, which vulgarised the already fluid and difficult
text. Because of Bailey's practice of expanding the text in successive
editions, when someone refers to *Festus*, it is difficult to say what they
mean exactly: the 8,100-line poem from 1839 or the 39,160-line poem
from 1889? Another possible reason why the poem fared less well after
the turn of the century is its strangeness. *Festus* is amorous, even sen-
sual, but also deeply devotional. It features an offbeat metaphysic,
wherein Christ spends eternity saving the many populated and fallen

---

5. See the exchange in W. M. Rossetti, 'W. B. Scott and the Course of Modern Poetry',
   Macmillan's Magazine, 1876; Watts's reply in 'Festus and Recent English Poetry', p. 465;
   and Rossetti's retort in 'Festus and Recent Poetry', *The Athenaeum*, 15 April 1876, p. 533.
6. The most recent official edition was P. J. Bailey, *Festus: A Poem* (London: Routledge,
   1903). For the most complete publishing history of *Festus*, see M. Peckham, 'American
   Editions of "Festus": A Preliminary Survey', *Princeton University Library Chronicle*, 8:4,
   June 1947, pp. 177–84.
7. See, for example, R. Cronin, 'The Spasmodics', in *A Companion to Victorian Poetry*, ed.
   Richard Cronin, Antony Harrison and Alison Chapman (Malden: Blackwell 2002),
   pp. 291–304.
8. H. Tucker, 'Glandular Omnism and Beyond: The Victorian Spasmodic Epic', *Victorian
   Poetry*, 42:4, 2004, pp. 429–50.
9. J. R. Rudy, *Electric Meters: Victorian Physiological Poetics* (Athens: Ohio University Press,
   2009).
10. M. A. Weinstein, *William Edmondstoune Aytoun and the Spasmodic Controversy* (New Haven:
    Yale University Press, 1968).
11. *Festus* has, however, been treated in graduate school dissertations. See N. Brown, *Devo-
    tional Cosmology: Poetry, Thermodynamics and Popular Astronomy, 1839–1889*, University of
    Glasgow, PhD thesis, 2017.

planets, each through different means, but is steeped in recognisable literary traditions from Goethe, Edward Young and Byron. Its prayers and sermons are expressions of Christian piety to such a comforting degree that some preachers read from *Festus* in church, but its underlying theology, especially Lucifer's redemption at the eschaton, were sufficiently troubling that other preachers warned congregations to stay away from it.

Yet the poem remains an important nineteenth-century literary achievement for many of these same reasons. Even after the rise of science fiction as a genre, its metaphysical inventiveness is engaging, even startling. Its theological daring broadens conceptions of Victorian religious practice. Its aesthetic mechanisms are so varied and so generous that readers are tempted to say with Ebenezer Elliot, the Corn-Law Rhymer, that 'it contains poetry enough to set up fifty poets'.[12] Above all these concerns is the bare fact of the poem's popularity. *Festus* appeared on the literary horizon with a reach the English-speaking world had not seen since Byron and has rarely seen since. As Richard Cronin writes, *Festus* 'was recognized . . . rather widely, as the great poem of the age'.[13] *Festus* was undeniably a cultural force, imitated *ad infinitum* by other writers, and an acknowledged influence on many writers considered major.

The present Introduction situates *Festus* in a range of literary, scientific, theological and cultural contexts, providing an outline of Bailey's life and work, and a sketch of *Festus'* reception in England and America. An explanation for the choice of text, a critical apparatus and a bibliography for further reading are included. In addition, a selection of responses to the poem from authors and from periodicals is included in the Appendix, to provide a view to the actual level of excitement caused by its publication.

Most importantly, this volume is meant to take Bailey's contribution to Victorian poetry seriously, rather than as evidence of 'the vagaries of Victorian taste'.[14] Though the poem is usefully read as the founding document of a later school of writers, and as a successfully mass-marketed cultural product, it is yet more usefully considered as what it was to its first readers: the most dynamic, energetic, metaphorically rich poem most of them had ever seen. An attempt to understand that enthusiasm should recognise the audacity of Bailey's attempt to rein in

12. J. Searle, *Memoirs of Ebenezer Elliott, the Corn Law Rhymer* (London: Whitaker, 1852), p. 160.
13. Cronin, pp. 291–304.
14. C. LaPorte, and Jason Rudy, 'Spasmodic Poetry and Poetics', *Victorian Poetry*, 42:4, 2004, pp. 421–8.

Byronic ethical excess while creating an aesthetic excessiveness all his own, of his attempt to write the drama of the world's end as the first work of a young writer, of his attempt to marry devotional reflections on holy scripture and God's goodness and strength with an outlandishly heretical narrative overdrive. *Festus* is an unusual book, but one that, considered rightly, has prompted many to say, with Tennyson, that they cannot be trusted 'to say how much [they] admire it, for fear of falling into extravagance'.

Bailey's life and career

Philip James Bailey was born on 22 April 1816 in Nottingham, to newspaper editor and sometime poet Thomas Bailey and his first wife, Mary Taylor. Interested in literature and speculative metaphysics from an early age and brought up on Byron, he entered the University of Glasgow at sixteen but left before completing a degree, not wishing to enter the Scottish clergy. After some travels, he entered Lincoln's Inn as a barrister and began composing *Festus* the next year, when he was nineteen years old. The first version was published anonymously in 1839 by William Pickering, who had recently published works of similar imaginative metaphysical reach by Coleridge, Cowper, Milton and Young.

Instantly, it was a hit. The poem 'enjoyed an almost uproarious state of success', all across the social spectrum.[15] Even before its official release, the printers and binders – 'the gentlemen engaged in the mechanical execution of the work' – gathered at the Manchester home of its first printer, Wilmot Henry Jones, to stage a reading.[16] Entranced by the staggering quality of the book they themselves were assembling, these rude mechanicals recalled decades later the precise time the last pages were printed and had their names inscribed on the bookplate, as if joint partners in creating a monument for the ages. The anecdote gives some sense of the poem's appeal for working-class figures, and also the rare enthusiasm it stoked. Readers took to referring to the author himself as 'Festus' in the absence of an alternative, and to the end of his life the author was known in some circles as 'Festus Bailey'.

Bailey lived a long life after *Festus*, working continually to perfect – or at least, to expand – his youthful masterwork, entertaining illustrious visitors and admirers, and making trips to the continent. His home

15. The most complete summary of *Festus*' popularity can be found in Tucker, 'Glandular Omnism and Beyond', pp. 429–50.
16. The early printing story is recounted in 'The First Edition of *Festus*', *Book-Lore*, May 1885, pp. 23–5.

became a stop on tourist maps and encounters with the mysterious author appeared in books of literary reminiscence, such as those by William Winter, Joseph Knight or Mary Watson. When Ralph Waldo Emerson visited England, he dined with 'Festus Bailey' at least twice, telling him 'that his appreciation for *Festus* was great', and that 'Philip Bailey was the first of the Trancendentalists & its founder.'[17] Attracted as ever to cataclysm, and with a knack of being present at historical events such as Lord Byron's funeral, Bailey witnessed the major eruption of Vesuvius in 1872. The poet died in Nottingham in 1902, spawning obituaries and career remembrances from across the literary spectrum.

Bailey's corpus and the reception of *Festus*

The poem was more than just a popular success; critics responded with an enthusiasm that can only be described as 'breathless'. An Appendix to the present volume contains a sampling of these critical effusions. Early reviewers noted the social diversity of *Festus*' readership, as though it were unusual to have spanned such divides: 'both cultivated and uncultivated . . . [feel] a . . . passionate sympathy with Mr. Bailey's poem'. They noted further its ubiquity, 'Bailey['s] . . . volumes sell by the thousands and are on all tavern and parlor tables.'[18] Authors particularly rushed to embrace *Festus*. When naming the six greatest poets then living, Elizabeth Barrett Browning identifies R. H. Horne, Tennyson, Macauley, Browning, Heraud and 'the author of *Festus*' as 'the only men of genius who are poets at all at the present day'.[19] Further praise would come from Tennyson, Dante and William Michael Rossetti, Owen Meredith, James Montgomery, W. M. Thackeray and Ebenezer Elliot, to name only the most prominent. Reviewers recommended for Bailey a place beside Shakespeare.[20] One went so far as to stake the very notion of genius on Bailey's qualifying as one.[21] The Scottish critic George Gilfillan called *Festus* 'the greatest work of our generation'.[22]

---

17. This anecdote is featured in unpublished memoirs related to Bailey in the Princeton Library, and is recounted in Peckham, 'A Bailey Collection', p. 150.
18. W. P. Atkinson, *A Lecture* (Boston: Crosby, Nichols, and Lee, 1860), p. 29.
19. E. B. B. to Mary Russell Mitford, 9 October 1843, London, in *The Brownings' Correspondence*, 7 (Kansas: Wedgestone Press), pp. 361–4.
20. See '*Festus* and the Literary World', *The North British Review*, 23 June 1849, for example.
21. 'Bailey's *Festus*', *Dublin University Magazine*, July 1847, p. 100 has 'Genius itself may despair, if Mr. Bailey be refused his title to a place in its temple.'
22. 'Two of the greatest poems in English of this century are, in our judgement, Wordsworth's "Excursion" and Bailey's "Festus"', in G. Gilfillan, *Second Gallery of Literary Portraits* (Edinburgh: James Hogg, 1850), p. 11.

In America, the embrace was, if possible, still more rapturous. Margaret Fuller wrote in 1841 that, 'in inspiration, in prophecy, in those flashes of the sacred fire which reveal the secret places where time is elaborating the marvels of nature, [Festus] stands alone'.[23] Emerson went still further, listing Bailey among 'the excellent men of [England]', and claiming that only Tennyson stood beside him.[24] Thoreau memorised large sections of the poem that he recited on walks, quoting Bailey in both letters and journals. Walt Whitman became, in the words of one critic, '[Bailey's] American disciple'.[25]

Not all of the responses were positive, of course. A Whig journal attested that 'Festus violates all the laws of character and passion, and exemplifies all the vices of a conceited and opinionated author' – that, in short, 'the whole thing is false – false to truth, false to nature, false to itself, false to everything it purports to be'.[26] Some objected to its theological positions. *The New York Evangelist*, for example, while noting 'without question' its 'intellectual riches' and 'wealth of imagination', cautioned: 'let none admire the riches of genius alone', for this book '[gives] scope to every wild and crude thought that can come into [a] mind . . . sacred or blasphemous'.[27] But most complained about Bailey's meddling from version to version: 'Festus, as it has come down to us, expanded by numerous additions, fattened, as it were, upon choicer morsels of younger and less successful brethren, is likely to remain an essentially unreadable poem.'[28]

Often, critical opinions broke along the political and religious lines of the journals wherein reviews were hosted. It is not surprising, for example, that *Blackwood's Magazine*, infamous as the enemy of Keatsian and Shelleyan Romantic excess, accuses Bailey of lacking sufficient control over his mind. He allows, they write, 'the fervor of imagination to carry him wide beyond the pale of common sense' and 'his passion to bear him away from the sympathy of all other mortals'.[29] Likewise, the Whig-oriented *Edinburgh Review* hosted a piece by Coventry Patmore, who, it

23. M. Fuller, review of 'Festus: A Poem by Philip J. Bailey', *New-York Daily Tribune*, 8 September 1841, p. 1.
24. W. H. Gilman and Ralph Waldo Emerson, *The Journals and Miscellaneous Notebooks of Ralph Waldo Emerson: 1848–1851* (Cambridge, MA: Belknap Press of Harvard University Press, 1975), p. 50.
25. Tucker, 'Glandular Omnism and Beyond', p. 347.
26. Unsigned, 'Festus', *The American Whig Review*, January 1847, p. 59.
27. Anonymous, *New York Evangelist*, 16:47, 20 November 1845, p. 186.
28. Edward Mortimer Chapman, *English Literature in Account with Religion 1800–1900* (Boston: Houghton Mifflin, 1910), p. 425.
29. Anonymous, review of *Festus*, *Blackwood's Magazine*, 67, April 1850, p. 422.

should be noted, harboured a personal animus against the Spasmodics, which argues that *Festus* (and works like it) have 'attracted far more than their proper share of attention', and that Bailey 'rushes in where Milton stumbled, and Dante feared to tread'.[30] On the other hand, *The Eclectic Review*, a non-denominational religious–intellectual journal specifically aimed at literate readers across classes, argued 'we suppose no poem of our time . . . has had a larger acceptance', calling *Festus* 'an infinite-sided beauty' while also cautioning readers about Bailey's admixture of heresy and devotion: 'in the same page, the brightest gleams of faith and aspiration are shaded off by dark, rolling clouds of dark suggestion'.[31] In America, while *Harvard Magazine* opined that, 'as a literary production, *Festus* richly merits the favor and commendation it has received' due to the 'beautiful thoughts to be met with on almost every page', they quibble about its 'rattle-brain style' and its lack of 'reverential propriety of expression' with regard to things divine.[32]

What subject marshalled such a host of opinions? The poem's inaugural scene takes place in heaven, where seraphim and cherubim adulate God. They are joined by a fallen Lucifer, who, after voicing a hymn of his own, seeks divine permission to tempt a youth named Festus. God consents without hesitation, while guaranteeing the futility of Lucifer's temptation. The next scene introduces a disenchanted Festus, whom Lucifer offers 'to crown . . . with liberty and joy, / And make . . . free and mighty even as I am!'. Festus yields to Lucifer's offer, assured that '[God] will not let thee harm me.' And so, whether soaring above the nations on black steeds or mixing with humanity in settings like 'A Metropolis' and 'A Large Party', the pair tour the globe, all the while dialoguing on metaphysics. Scenes of courtship dot their escapade, as Festus indulges in amours with several mistresses, and even Lucifer dabbles in romance. Eventually, their journey transcends Earth, as, with the command 'Body and spirit part!', Lucifer disembodies Festus to take him on an interstellar voyage. Visiting Venus, Festus discourses with spirits who reside there, including that of Angela, a deceased lover. Later, Lucifer escorts Festus heavenward to meet God himself, though the mortal glimpses 'nothing but dazzling darkness'. While in heaven, however, Festus finds his name inscribed in the Book of Life, a guarantee of his salvation. In time, the duo also survey the flames of hell, where the Son of God joins them and proclaims the redemption of 'both men

30. Coventry Patmore, 'New Poets', *Edinburgh Review*, October 1856, p. 182.
31. Anonymous, 'The New Edition of Mr. Bailey's Festus', *The Eclectic and Congregational Review*, June 1865, p. 545.
32. Anonymous, 'Bailey's Festus', *The Harvard Magazine*, 1:7, July 1855, p. 315.

and devils'. After completing Festus' 'every quest', Lucifer endows his companion with 'the power which thou dost long for', and so, at 'A Gathering of Kings and Peoples', Festus is crowned 'monarch of the world'. His reign, however, is curtailed by the apocalypse, and Festus dies along with the rest of the world, entrusting himself to God. The hero's eternal fate is unveiled at 'The Judgment of Earth', when, as foreshadowed from the poem's start, the Son of God declares that 'he too is saved' along with all men. Laying claim to Festus' soul, Lucifer objects, 'Is he not mine?', but is dismissed by God, who reaffirms Festus' salvation. As Lucifer prepares to depart heaven, he entreats Festus, 'Forgive me that I tempted thee,' and – in all editions that follow the first – an ambivalent God then recants Lucifer's banishment, restoring him 'to archangelic state'. With heaven's throng made complete, the poem closes.

Despite the fact that Bailey worked on *Festus* intermittently for most of his life, he also found time to compose several other books. *The Angel World and Other Poems* was released eleven years after *Festus* to a public holding its breath in anticipation, but, as one reviewer phrased it, 'Not one quality that had won admiration in *Festus* was evident in *The Angel World*.'[33] As Tucker details, Bailey folded much of the text of that latter, mostly failed poem, into the next edition of *Festus*. *The Angel World* was followed by *The Mystic* (1855), which is as nebulous as it sounds, giving full voice and free rein to the spiritualised abstractions that punctuated his earlier works but without the relative coordinates of plot and plan. Bailey's next book was a satire, no doubt intended as a follow-up to Hazlitt's *The Spirit of the Age* (1825), entitled simply *The Age* (1858). In it, the poet issues directly many of the criticisms of contemporary letters that his Lucifer utters obliquely throughout *Festus*' growing editions, many of which were probably conjured in response to the critical reception of the poet's later two books. Abandoning all aesthetic indirection due to the immediate importance of the subject, he next published a treatise on 'The International Policy of the Great Powers' (1861), not this time on the powers of heaven and hell, or of earth and air, but on the politics of Britain, France, Prussia, Germany and Russia in the aftermath of the Crimean War. More mysticism appeared in *The Universal Hymn* (1867) and then finally, true to abstruse form, Bailey's last publication: the privately printed 'Causa Britannica' (1883), a small octavo in Latin hexameters. The range of these documents is important because Bailey is often considered a dreamer, an aesthete *avant la lettre*, apolitical and egotistical – in short, a Spasmodic – when, for at least half his working life, his concerns were very much this- rather than otherworldly.

33. Anonymous, review of *Festus*, *The Athenaeum*, 11 August 1877, p. 170.

However great *Festus* may or may not have seemed to its first readers, it became the spark that lit a literary movement: the Spasmodic School. When modern critics mention Bailey, they do so in the context of the Spasmodic phenomenon. The term was coined by William Edmonstone Aytoun in 1854 to criticise poets writing in the style of Bailey and was sometimes referred to simply as 'the school of Bailey'. Alexander Smith in *A Life-Drama* (1853), Sydney Dobell in *The Roman* (1850) and *Balder* (1854), J. Stanyan Bigg in *Night and the Soul* (1854) and others attempted to write verse in the Festonian style, many successfully. It may be hard to discern at this vantage, but when *The Scottish Review* writes that 'Tennyson can scarcely be said to have founded a school; Bailey has,' the writer is bragging about a figure he sees as clearly the more significant of the two.[34] Whether we think of the Spasmodics as a Victorian aberration, or as integral to the history of English poetry, as Rossetti, Tennyson and others did, we have Bailey to thank for them.

But there are also reasons to keep them distinct. For one, *Festus* predates other Spasmodic productions significantly; if he also outlived the other Spasmodics, his life-work was already a bestseller by the time any of them had taken up a pen. The Spasmodic craze is generally thought to be a feature of the 1850s, coming to a head in 1853–4 with Smith's *A Life-Drama*, at which point *Festus* was entering its fourth official edition. That is, he ought not be considered part of a movement so much as the instigator of one. Moreover, Bailey himself spurned the association, writing, 'I have no sympathy with their works specially, nor with their ways.'[35] If Bailey eventually accrued to himself orbitals, even so many that they began to resemble a system after the fact, he was still the star.

The school of Bailey is even broader than the world-spanning reach of the Spasmodics. Suzette Henke has shown convincingly how James Joyce took *Festus* as a model for *Ulysses*.[36] Florence Boos has argued for its influence over psychologically charged novels such as those of the Brontës.[37] Charles LaPorte has shown its implications for the work of Elizabeth Barrett Browning and Arthur Hugh Clough.[38] Herbert Tucker mentions its importance for Walt Whitman's poetry and for Matthew Arnold's criticism.[39] Emily Dickinson wondered if she herself counted

---

34. 'Bailey and Tennyson', *The Scottish Review*, 3:12, October 1855, p. 348.
35. 'A Letter from the Author of *Festus*', *The Bookman*, May 1893, p. 50.
36. *James Joyce Quarterly*, 9:4, Summer 1972, pp. 445–51.
37. Florence Boos, 'Spasm and Class: W. E. Aytoun, George Gilfillan, Sydney Dobell, and Alexander Smith', *Victorian Poetry*, 42:4, 2004, pp. 553–83.
38. Charles LaPorte, 'Spasmodic Poetics and Clough's Apostasies', *Victorian Poetry*, 42:4, 2004, pp. 521–36.
39. Herbert F. Tucker, *Epic: Britain's Heroic Muse 1790–1910* (Oxford: Oxford University Press, 2012), p. 347.

as a Spasmodic writer.[40] Even the modernist poet Conrad Aiken is indebted to Bailey, paying a sincere compliment of flattery via imitation in his fragmented, imagistic, metaphysical work *The Pilgrimage of Festus* (1924), which covers much of the same ground as Bailey's masterpiece.[41]

Orientation to critical topics

Festus is a boundary-breaking poem, considered radical, heretical and disjointed at the same time that it was also thought to 'play to the era's tastes'. When reading such a dense and complex work, it pays to keep in mind the features of the poem that made it so electrifying for its first readers: namely, its mixed theology, its daring aesthetic, its uses of science and sensuality, and its unique marketing programme.

Theology

Some have attributed *Festus'* attractiveness to its religious impulses and sentimental reassurance, a sort of broad appeal enjoyed earlier in the century by Keble's *Christian Year* (1827). Dorothy F. Donnelly, for instance, claims that *Festus* offers 'no real challenge to the intellect or to the emotions' and that its favourable reception is due to a 'predisposition' on the part of Victorian readers toward 'vaguely suggested but easily recognized beliefs'.[42] But if that is so, why did others list Bailey among 'the Satanic School'?[43] Why did preachers speak out against it? The fact is that, far from simply playing to the choir, or flattering readers' Christian piety, *Festus* challenged readers deeply and seriously, and much of the challenge was theological. Its use of biblical texts is highly nuanced, its figuration of Lucifer and the angelic cosmology daring, and its sentiments of Christian devotion genuinely moving.[44]

In *Festus*, spirituality and theological reflection hold a central place. Whatever else ostensibly happens in the poem, its *raison d'être* is to provide occasions for intellectual engagement with the Bible and theological literature. *Festus* teems with allusions to scripture, evincing Bailey's

---

40. See Jonathan Morse, 'Emily Dickinson and the Spasmodic School: A Note on Thomas Wentworth Higginson's Esthetics', *The New England Quarterly*, 50:3, September 1977, pp. 505–50.
41. Conrad Aiken, *The Pilgrimage of Festus* (New York: A. A. Knopf, 1923).
42. Dorothy F. Donnelly, 'Philistine Taste in Victorian Poetry', *Victorian Poetry*, 16:5, 1978, p. 107.
43. R. B. Steele, 'Bailey's "Festus"', *The Sewanee Review*, 17:1, 1909, p. 27.
44. For more on poem's theology, see Hoxie Neale Fairchild, *Religious Trends in English Poetry IV: Christianity and Romanticism in the Victorian Era* (New York: Morningside Heights and Columbia University Press, 1957), pp. 200–12.

intimacy with biblical texts. The poem's likeness to Job is foremost; as one reviewer acknowledges, 'Festus is the argument of Job applied . . . to the whole human family.'[45] Yet the poem's kinship with biblical narratives does not end there. In fact, it is likely that, while retaining a phonetic tie to the legend of Faust, the name 'Festus' is meant eponymously to suggest a New Testament passage. *The New York Evangelist* attributes the poem's title to biblical influence: 'And this poem is under the very plain title of *Festus*, we scarcely know why, except it be because Festus in the scriptures heard Paul, and trembled before him, but to do the Jews a pleasure, left Paul bound.'[46] But this reviewer fails to recall the biblical narrative correctly, confusing Festus with his predecessor, Felix. In Acts 25–6, the apostle Paul, indicted by Jewish authorities, stands trial before Porcius Festus, a Roman provincial.[47] Mid-trial, Paul appeals to the court of the Emperor, suspending his hearing and thus releasing Festus from making a legal judgement. Though a relatively obscure point within the biblical narrative at large, Festus' cameo features a great deal of thematic overlap with Bailey's poem.

Like *Festus*, the biblical passage is undergirded by uncertainty, asking who has authority and in which spheres. Moreover, the Acts passage begins with a figure being handed over from the care of one potentate to another, more nefarious one, essentially mirroring the motivating action of the poem. As the Governor fails to identify Paul's legal guilt, his indecision infuses the passage with a sense of instability. In fact, grappling with the question of Paul's innocence, Festus quintessentially declares, 'I have nothing definite to write to my lord [Caesar] about him.' Correspondingly, Bailey's *Festus* wants solidity, typified by scenes set 'Anywhere', 'Everywhere', 'Air' and 'Elsewhere'. As reviewers were often quick to point out, ambiguous theology characterises the poem, and even *Festus*' form, largely unstructured, contributes to its unanchored air. Moreover, just as the Acts passage revolves around culpability, with Festus ultimately neglecting to condemn his defendant, an issue of guilt also threads *Festus*, which, in keeping with its universalistic message, presents a Final Judgement devoid of condemnation.

References to insanity also colour both texts. When Paul passionately recounts a heavenly vision of a resurrected Christ in Acts 26, an exasperated Porcius Festus deems him insane, concluding, 'Your great learning is driving you out of your mind.' *Festus* also features a scholar

45. George Gilfillan, *Modern Literature and Literary Men; Being a Second Gallery of Literary Portraits* (New York: D. Appleton and Co., 1860), p. 342.
46. *New York Evangelist*, p. 186.
47. Acts 26: 24 (ESV).

whose great learning has driven him mad, pulsing with an insanity
often noted by Victorian readers; the *American Review*, for instance,
growls that half the poem comes 'from Bedlam'.[48] Lastly, it is notable
that, according to extra-biblical records, death cut short Porcius Festus'
tenure, a fact mirrored by Bailey's Festus, who dies shortly after assum-
ing his promised throne.[49]

From its first publication, *Festus* was prefaced with a dedicatory
poem in honour of the poet's father. It begins 'My father! unto thee
to whom I owe / All that I am, all that I have and can'. Certainly,
Thomas Bailey was a colossal figure in his son's life, and there is a literal
sense in which the poet owes his existence to his father, and also that
the poem owes its existence to him as well, since Bailey's father had first
introduced him to poetry. But on another level, it makes more sense to
think of the poem as dedicated to God. 'My father' echoes the 'Our
father' prayer, and it is to that greater father that Bailey really feels he
owes his existence. The dedication then continues to ask pardon for the
poet's excesses. After all – 'not twenty summers had imbrowned my
brow' when he began – he was just a boy when he wrote it. A reading of
the poem as dedicated to his Thomas Bailey interprets the final lines,
'hope that I may earn that love / More unto me than immortality', as
meaning that his father's approval is more important to the poet than
fame, that earthbound immortality. But read as a dedication to God,
the poet's having 'strang [his] harp with golden strings' implies a heav-
enly state to which he dare not aspire; God's blessing is enough for him.

Despite its use of biblical texts, *Festus* presents an offbeat meta-
physic. The cast of characters includes an array of unorthodox other-
worldly figures. In the poem's course, Bailey gives voice to 'the Muse'
– who inhabits Venus – 'Genius' and a personified 'Death'. Guardian
angels are assigned to both individuals and planets, as is a Recording
Angel who documents the fates of men; both mingle with biblically
traditional seraphim, cherubim and archangels. In another unusual
feature, allusions to extra-terrestrial life thread the poem, which cast
the Earth as one of many populated orbs, some of which have already
undergone apocalypses of their own: 'Worlds have been built, and to
their central base / Ruined and rased to the last atom.' For Bailey,
planets also act as holding places for the deceased; Festus finds that
Venus, called 'Another and a Better World', harbours spirits of the
pure, whom Lucifer equates with angels. Evidencing what Wheeler

---

48. Edwin Percy Whipple, 'The Poets and the Poetry of England', *American Review*, 2, 1845,
    p. 55.
49. Craig S. Keener, *Acts: An Exegetical Commentary* (Grand Rapids: Baker Academic, 2012),
    p. 1180.

terms Bailey's 'confused theology',[50] heaven holds still other spirits who, moreover, have posthumous agency: 'for God hath made it lawful for good souls / To make souls good; and saints to help the saintly'. In a similar vein, Bailey's hell is ultimately purgatorial, its flames refining marred spirits (a fact that seems unknown to Lucifer, however).

Bailey's Lucifer, moreover, is not an orthodox Satan who happens to be forgiven by an overly gracious omnipotent. Rather, he is an agent of God, working destruction and death in the world when it is called for by the Almighty. Unlike in Goethe, or Milton, for whom Satan might have figured in some original plan but is now a fallen rebel, Bailey represents a Satan who freely acknowledges God's sovereignty and who works for him, causing death when it is called for, and war when necessary. Even sin is constructive, according to Bailey's spiritual vision. Lucifer volunteers:

> God! for thy glory only can I act,
> And for thy creatures' good. When creatures stray
> Farthest from Thee, then warmest towards them burns
> Thy love . . . . (1.240–4)

As *Festus*' 'Proem' explains, echoing Milton's 'fortunate fall', 'Evil and good are God's right hand and left. / By ministry of evil good is clear.' For Bailey, evil is not a threat to God's sovereignty but an expression thereof, a force that nudges all spirits into heaven's fold.

Though it is beyond the scope of this Introduction to detail the history of universalism, a brief outline of its main tenets will be useful for readers of the poem. It is important to realise that *Festus*' denouement is not the piece of aberrant poetical heresy that some readers surely saw it as, but a theological system that the poet had thought through in intellectual community with other writers and theologians, developed largely in response to the sceptical tradition of Kant and Lessing. The universalism that Herbert Tucker dismisses as 'the big hug of a no fault apocalypse' contains several important doctrines.[51] The first of these is an emphasis on solidarity with other humans. Universalists in the early part of the nineteenth century believed that dividing people into the blessed and the damned put an impossible strain on their practice of charity. 'The development of God-consciousness', they maintained, coevolved with 'a race-consciousness', or fellow-feeling.[52] That Bailey

---

50. Michael Wheeler, *Heaven, Hell, and the Victorians* (Cambridge: Cambridge University Press, 1994), p. 98.

51. Tucker, *Epic*, 341.

52. Murray Rae, 'Salvation-in-community: The Tentative Universalism of Friedrich Schleiermacher (1768–1834)', in Gregory MacDonald, ed., *'All Shall Be Well': Explorations in Universalism and Christian Theology from Origen to Moltmann* (Eugene, OR: Cascade Books, 2011).

held this universalist doctrine is evident in the following prayer, placed
in the mouth of Festus, wherein this fellow-feeling is used as an argu-
ment for the abolition of slavery and for unity among the classes. After
asking that education might lift the nations 'to loftier and more liberal
ends', he entreats the Almighty thus:

> We pray
> Above all things, Lord! that all men be free
> From bondage, whether of the mind or body;—
> The bondage of religious bigotry,
> And bald antiquity, servility
> Of thought or speech to rank and power; be all
> Free as they ought to be in mind and soul
> As well as by state-birthright. (7.535–42)

Another important universalist doctrine evident in the poem is pre-
destination. At first these two doctrines might seem incompatible: how
are some predestined to eternal life and others not, if all are eventually
saved? It is important to remember, however, that in *Festus*, universal
salvation is a great surprise at the end of the poem; the angels rejoice
at God's largesse because they could not have assumed it. This means
that, for all practical purposes, both the angels and individual believ-
ers act in a system that ascribes to them predestined categories before
God obliterates that system, along with the universe, at the apocalypse.
In the poem's metaphysic, every person, like every planet, is assigned
a guardian angel who prays for and watches over their charge, unsure
of his or her eternal destiny. This is why the angels rejoice when, in the
first scene, Festus is revealed to be among the elect: for them, it is won-
derful and surprising news.

We should also note that, for Bailey, these theological positions
are not staked out in support of some general permissiveness in con-
trast to the harder teachings of scripture; they simply take literally
1 Tim 2: 4, which says that 'God our Saviour . . . will have all men
to be saved, and to come unto the knowledge of the truth.' This tri-
umphalism, a third universalist doctrinal pillar, probably comes to
Bailey from Friedrich Schleiermacher, who speculated that, at some
point, either within the bounds of time or outside of them, Christian-
ity will triumph so completely that no other religion will effectively
exist. Thus, in *Festus*, Buddha and Brahma are welcomed into the
heavenly fold not because the systems they represent are thought by
the poet to be correct, but because, Christ having come again in
power, they arrive like the wise men from the East in a nativity scene
to do him honour.

All these doctrinal interactions take place against the background of Victorian debates about the authority of scripture, the nature of salvation and the mechanics of eschatology. There is one point at which Bailey differs from Schleiermacher's universalist speculations. For Schleiermacher, the idea of 'unbroken fellowship with Christ' must necessarily take place 'under conditions wholly unknown and only faintly imaginable'.[53] Bailey appears to have taken the caution as a challenge; imagining those conditions is the work of the poem. With those imaginings, he invited censure from several conservative reviewers, who took issue with the poet's daring to imagine lines that the Holy Spirit could have spoken.

More compelling, if less memorable, than the trope of a submissive and reinstituted Lucifer, however, are the poem's devotional expressions of orthodox Christianity, a devotional thinking not limited to the metaphysical structure in which the drama plays. Often, a character will see something beautiful – a woman, a sunset – and fall into rhapsodies about God's power and goodness, many of which are genuinely moving. Bailey's heterodox Satan certainly shocked audiences, but the poem still manages to read as worshipful. The most striking examples of this devotional style are found in the angelic songs and hymns. A typical example is the following:

> Thee God! We praise
> Through our ne'er sunsetting days,
> And Thy just ways
> Divine:
> In thy hand is every spirit,
> and the meed the same may merit;
> All which all the worlds inherit
> Are Thine! (1.396–403)

The poem's piety also includes sermonising. Lucifer delivers some of the most effective sermons. In one, the fallen angel approaches a crowd with 'I am a preacher come to tell ye truth' (6.200). Given who is speaking, there is a pleasant irony in the claim. Is he capable of telling the truth? Does he want to? As it happens, Lucifer is serious, and he is appalled at how unseriously the crowd takes his call to repentance, lamenting,

> The world must end. I weep to think of it.
> But you, you laugh! I knew ye would. I know

---

53. Friedrich Schleiermacher, *The Christian Faith* (Edinburgh, T. T. Clark, 1928), p. 698.

Men never will be wise till they are fools
For ever. Laugh away! The time will come.
When tears of fire are trickling from your eyes,
Ye will blame yourselves for having laughed at me. (6.205–10)

Lucifer's homily smacks of a Puritanical sensibility, emphasising the smallness of people in the hands of a supreme and all-powerful God, but its earnestness and force are compelling still. Why, he asks, do people who begin to seek salvation so often fail? 'It is that ye have sucked corruption from the world / Like milk from your own mothers,' he explains (6.224–5). Following the sermon in the marketplace, *Festus* offers up a sincere prayer:

May [humanity] mingle into one, like sister trees,
And so in one stem flourish: — that all laws
And powers of government be based and used
In good and for the people's sake; — that each
May feel himself of consequence to all,
And act as though all saw him . . .
We pray thee for the welfare of all men. (7.464–75)

The prayer evokes a sense of longing for human flourishing that is not class-based or political. In fact, so compelling were *Festus*' pieties that some congregations adapted sections thereof for ecclesiastical use, some preachers quoting the poem in sermons.[54] Regardless of what were sometimes considered heresies in Bailey's theology, the piety of *Festus* remained one of its popular aspects.

Aesthetics

Whether *Festus*' theological components flattered or offended Victorian readers' religious sensibilities, their presence (and the debates they conjured) certainly augmented the work's popularity. For most, however, *Festus* was read and adored not for its metaphysical musings, but for its poetry. Readers encountered here what they took to be a new kind of writing altogether, and one that showed more genius, however they interpreted this, than nearly anything in British literary history. Reactions from early readers, though they run a gamut from disgust to adoration, nearly always acknowledge a unique poetic power. The poem's influence upon its first readers was 'almost electrical', writes one review, written, not in the first flush of that excitement, but at a remove of some

---

54. See A. J. Lyman, *Preaching in the New Age* (New York: Fleming H. Revell, 1902), p. 58.

sixty-one years: 'the hearts of many were stirred to their depths by this strange weird rhapsody, blending so curiously together poetical exuberance, optimistic aspirations, and fanciful and sometimes nebulous speculation'. 'Strangeness', however, was not the chief appeal so much as the work's 'poetical exuberance': that is, its metaphorical richness.[55] Wrote another observer, 'I know no poem in any language that can be compared with it in copiousness and variety of imagery.'[56] However we may estimate *Festus* now, it is clear that the poem's first readers were overwhelmed.

One such stunning aesthetic technique of *Festus*, which read to most as 'new', was Bailey's use of stacked metaphors. Rather than using a point of comparison to illuminate a single line, an image, Bailey piles these up, 'load[ing] every rift with ore', as Keats recommended to Shelley.[57] His metaphors have metaphors to explain them, muddling the contours of the images, as one symbol gives rise to, and blurs with, another. Sometimes over twenty lines pass before the reader arrives even at the subject of the comparison, as seen in the following passage:

> Now,
> So light as not to wake the snowiest down
> Upon the dove's breast, winning her bright way
> Calm and sublime as Grace unto the soul
> Towards her far native grove; now, stern and strong
> As ordnance, overturning tree and tower
> Cooling the white brows of the peaks of fire —
> Turning the sea's broad furrows like a plough, —
> Fanning the fruitening plains, breathing the sweets
> Of meadows, wandering o'er blinding snows,
> And sands like sea-beds and the streets of cities,
> Where men as garnered grain lie heaped together;
> Freshening the cheeks, and mingling oft the locks
> Of youth and beauty 'neath star-speaking eve;
> Swelling the pride of canvas, or, in wrath,
> Scattering the fleets of nations like dead leaves;
> In all, the same o'ermastering sightless force,
> Bowing the highest things of earth to earth,
> And lifting up the dust unto the stars;

---

55. Anonymous, review of *Festus*, *The Athenaeum*, 11 August 1877, p. 169.
56. J. W. Marsten, recalled in Alfred Henry Miles (ed.), *The Poets and the Poetry of the Nineteenth Century*, 4 (London: Routledge, 1905), p. 520.
57. J. K. to P. B. S., 16 August 1820, in *Selected Letters of John Keats* (Cambridge, MA: Harvard University Press, 2005).

> Fatelike, confounding reason, and like God's
> Spirit, conferring life upon the world, —
> Midst all corruption incorruptible;
> Monarch of all the elements! (4.370–92)

Bailey describes the wind as 'monarch of all the elements', but in doing so makes so many qualifications that the qualifications themselves become the point rather than the actual syntactic sense. In the above, the wind is shown to be so gentle that it fails to ruffle a dove's feathers as the dove makes her way home, but her way-making is itself like God's grace to the heaven-bound soul. But sometimes, the wind is strong, the poet continues, as strong as a law that overturns towers as easily as the wind does trees. That strong wind is shown to cool 'the white brows of the peaks of fire', in which metaphor we see mountainous peaks, snow-capped, but aflame when pink sunset hits them and thereby in need of cooling, but also those same snow peaks as a feverish forehead, white and high, that likewise requires cooling. And all of this before the wind is shown to turn over the sea as though wind were plough and the sea land, to act as a fan, as a lover's breath, as a personified wanderer who visits the aforementioned snow peaks, the great 'sands', which are themselves like the beds of the sea, and the various cities in which men are stacked up like sheaves of wheat, presumably from the windswept plains.

This technique drove Victorian readers mad, either with delight or with frustration. For most, it was the former. They had simply never read anything so richly metaphoric. This is the feeling – of exhaustion, of sublimity – to which early reviewers are referring in comments such as that 'in point of brilliancy, [*Festus*] has no rival in our language'.[58] The sheer accumulation of poetic gold dazzled. Of course, other readers found such concentrations vexing. One – still acknowledging the quality of Bailey's proverbial jewels – decries their fecundity, arguing that too many diamonds make a ring tough to look at; it is blinding.[59]

To readers familiar with Percy Bysshe Shelley this sort of poetry would have been less startling.[60] It may have been conducted at a higher pitch than anything the Romantics attempted, but it took the same image-based, over-driven approach to searching out apt metaphors and

---

58. Anonymous, *The Eclectic Review*, June 1865, p 547.
59. *The Eclectic Review*, June 1865, p. 547 has 'to gaze upon a mountain of spar beneath the sunlight would be painful work for human eyes'.
60. As a *London Society* article, '"Festus" and its Author' (June 1897, p. 617), acknowledges, 'In the luxuriance of the descriptive passages, the reader is reminded of the poetic imagery of Shelley's writings.'

made it, rather than an occasional sublimity, the whole poetic game.[61] But then, in 1839, when *Festus* super-novaed over the firmament, few ordinary readers had read Shelley, his reputation not having been sufficiently rehabilitated by then. To them, Bailey's poetry seemed almost unbearably bright; hence the rhapsodies into which so many of them fell. Some pointed out the poetic resemblance. One reviewer, though he disagrees with the comparison, notes that 'some, indeed, have called [*Festus*] a mere canto from Goethe, Byron, and Shelley'.[62] For us, Bailey's sinuous lines and fraught determination, even his subject matter in the passage above, recall the opening of 'Mont Blanc', or 'Ode to the West Wind', wherein Bailey's 'scattering the fleets of nations like dead leaves' would be at home in a poem that enjoins the wind to 'drive my dead thoughts over the universe like leaves'. The point here is not that Bailey was some kind of acolyte in the Church of Romanticism, rather that his poem took an aesthetic approach that germinated therein and brought it to full flower.

Almost as important as the Shelleyan nature of *Festus*' multi-tiered metaphors are thematic similarities between *Festus*' Lucifer and Mary Shelley's monster in *Frankenstein*. The woeful sole member of his race, Bailey's Lucifer is a force for widespread destruction and ruin. Like *Frankenstein*'s monster, Bailey's disfigured Lucifer constitutes his entire species, his uniqueness excluding him from community. Lucifer offers a self-description strikingly evocative of the monster's lament: 'I have no kind. No nature like to me / Exists.' The two terrors share not only an exclusionary individuation, but a pervading sense of melancholia, as Lucifer in *Festus* laments,

> I might rejoice; and that
> To me by Nature is forbidden. I know
> Nor joy nor sorrow; but a changeless tone
> Of sadness . . . I am not
> As other spirits, but a solitude
> Even to myself. (3.152–8)

The trope of the outsider was, of course, known to readers long familiar with Byron's brooding figures, but in *Frankenstein* (1818), the monster is an outsider not only from the community and country, but even from the species. A force of pure destruction, *Festus*' Lucifer cries, 'Let ruin bury ruin. Let it be / Woe here, woe there, woe, woe, be everywhere!'

---

61. This is one of the similarities Tucker has in mind when he writes that 'Spasmodic poetics writ very large certain Romantic tenets that persist'; Tucker, p. 340.
62. Gilfillan, *Modern Literature and Literary Men*, p. 343.

Here, his glee at the idea of a havoc-wreaking rampage echoes that of Frankenstein's monster: 'I . . . wished to tear up the trees, spread havoc and destruction around me, and then to have sat down and enjoyed the ruin.'[63] In *Festus*, Bailey amplifies Shelleyan aesthetics and trades in Mary-Shelleyan themes.

Another element of *Festus*' aesthetic daring that helps to account for its popularity among Victorians is structural. Readers not only were surprised at the poem's plot, theological intrigue and metaphorical richness; they were affected – positively and negatively – by its experimental epic mode. In an era of daring epics, *Festus* stands apart among English poems for its hybrid of lyric impulse and epic form. While epics generally employ grand – often historical – subjects and consistent tone, *Festus* operates by placing the Romantic – lyric, introspective, effusive – into a dramatic setting. The drama, importantly, is not meant to be performed, but read. Meter is taken up and dropped, longer scenes are punctuated by arias, and some scenes seem to exist only in order to provide an occasion for the characters to launch into song.

This experimental form became one of the chief markers of Spasmodic verse. It popularised the idea that an epic might not be restricted to a metrical commitment but could expand to include any number of rhythms and modes. When Alexander Smith employed it in *A Life-Drama*, he was accused of 'spasmody': an inability to hold still, to restrain his style. But Smith was merely following the freedom he had learned from Bailey. This expansive technique had the practical effect of making the poem easy to break apart, a textual malleability Bailey epitomised with *Festus*. One reason why Bailey was able to expand the poem so capaciously over decades is that it was possible to do so without upsetting the overall design. More lyrics could always be added so long as a pretext was offered for the new songs.

Science

Additionally, *Festus*' extraordinary popularity among different types of readers is due in part to its scientific sensibility. The poem knowingly participates in scientific discourse, commenting in the opening pages that 'the world hath made such comet-like advance / Lately on science'. Rife with such references, *Festus* twines the realms of science and art. The poem makes pervasive mention of matter's atomic nature, for example. Envisaging the apocalypse, Bailey has Festus note, 'River and mountain melt into their atoms; / A little time, and atoms will be all,' and even

63. M. Shelley, *Frankenstein, or The Modern Prometheus* (London: Penguin, 1985), p. 138.

God, mingling science and metaphysics, declares that 'Suns are made up of atoms. Heaven of souls.' Again, he touches on the sun's composition in further detail:

> They tell us that the body of the sun
> Is dark, and hard, and hollow; and that light
> Is but a floating fluid veiling him.
> Ah! how oft, and how much, the heart is like him!
> Despite the electric light it lives and hides in. (26.171–5)

Bailey also shows an awareness of geological developments. In the poem, he theorises about the origin of gemstones and sends characters to the Earth's core, which he imagines to be a 'marble-walled immensity o'erroofed / With pendant mountains glittering'. This awareness of scientific trends and language made *Festus*, for some, a record of the age in which it was written. As one critic observed, 'We confidently declare there is no poem in existence, which makes such glorious use of the physics and metaphysics of the universe as *Festus*.'[64] Poeticising the technicalities of science, Bailey projects a sense of not only poetic, but also scientific innovation that captivated Victorian readers.

But over all the poem's other scientific concerns, astronomy rules. *Festus* is spangled with celestial allusions. At times oddly technical, these references to the cosmos are more than the quaint reveries of a stargazer; the poem speaks, for instance, of 'the white nebulous matter between stars' and 'Saturn's double rings'. In some instances, Bailey's cosmological language simply describes the physical universe, usually with an eye to the apocalypse: 'The stars / Which stand as thick as dewdrops on the fields / Of heaven, and all they comprehend, shall pass'. Most often, however, Bailey's references to outer space function metaphorically: 'Great thoughts are still as stars; and truths, like suns, / Stir not; though many systems tend round them,' an angel comments. Moreover, extra-terrestrial settings frame the poem, drenching the work in a cosmic aura. In later editions, Lucifer and Festus tour the moon, the 'Martian Sphere' and Venus, and ultimately traverse 'Space' to reach heaven, a journey that Festus recounts to a lover – 'When the stars come, thou shalt see / The track I travelled through the light of night' – promising her that the journey was not merely mental but mappable.

Early critics of the poem were quick to point out Bailey's astronomical emphasis. One reviewer in *The Dublin University Magazine*, attempting to show just how complete was Bailey's stellar obsession,

---

64. 'Festus, a Poem', *Macphail's Edinburgh Ecclesiastical Journal and Literary Review*, 3, 1847, pp. 419–33.

tried counting the references to stars used as images: 'we stopped after counting five hundred; and a large section of the poem was to come'.[65] A later critic of J. Stanyan Bigg's *Night and the Soul* writes 'The subject [of Bigg's poem] is the . . . stars . . . already sufficiently treated by Mr. Bailey,' as though after *Festus* the stars were extinguished of inspirational fire.[66] Michael Crowe has claimed, 'Among all Victorian poets, none was more interested in astronomy, none more intent to assay its significance than Tennyson,' but in terms of either the number, variability or cultural impact of its astronomical allusions, surely that celestial crown belongs to Bailey, whose evident knowledge of the cosmos dominated his poetic imagination.[67]

Sensuality

But when *Festus* seeks to induce our swoon over heavenly bodies, these are not only of the astronomical kind; if the poem is star-struck, it is also girl-crazy. As in *Faust*, *Festus'* action centres on romantic prospects of the pure soul, but Bailey shares the love more broadly, since, over the long poem's course, his hero woos not one beloved, but four: Angela, Clara, Helen and Elissa. In addition to the theological dissonance, aesthetic newness and astronomical contemplations, its effusions of ardour help explain the poem's massive appeal in the nineteenth century. One example of such amorous lyricism occurs while Festus praises Helen:

> To say sooth,
> I once loved many things ere I met with thee,
> My one blue break of beauty in the clouds;
> Bending thyself to me as Heaven to earth. (20.1608–11)

In such exchanges, the beloved occasionally breaks into songs that can act as stand-alone ditties, typical of Victorian love-making. Helen, for instance, rhapsodises:

> Like an island in a river
> Art thou, my love to me;
> And I journey by thee ever
> With a gentle ecstasie. (20.905–8)

These love scenes allow Bailey to practise his stock-in-trade of overripe encomium on mortals as well as on the lauded deity, and, in addition

---

65. *Dublin University Magazine*, July 1847, p. 91.
66. *The Athenaeum*, 1854, qtd in S. Gilpin, *The Songs and Ballads of Cumberland and the Lake Country* (London: John Russell Smith, 1874), p. 122.
67. M. Crowe, *The Extraterrestrial Life Debate, 1750–1900* (Mineola: Dover, 1999), p. 232.

to helping move copy, they influenced the generation of writers following Bailey towards sensuality.[68] D. G. Rossetti – long an admirer of Bailey – and his Pre-Raphaelite associates, with A. C. Swinburne and perhaps the Tennyson of *Maud*, were severally derided as 'fleshly' poets for assuming the same amorous postures Bailey strikes in *Festus*, a similarity of style that Theodore Watts notes, claiming, 'even the warm love-making . . . of our contemporary singers, may be traced . . . to the scenes between Festus and Lucifer, and their respective loves'.[69] Which is to say, if *Festus* is technically an epic, many readers experienced it, and appreciated it, as a collection of love-lyrics.

One of Bailey's alterations to the Faust legend that makes such an emphasis on sensuality plausible is his conversion of the titular character from an aged scholar to a youth. Whereas, for Goethe, Faust is exhausted at the end of a life-long quest for meaning, for Bailey, Festus is robust and eager after experience. This aspect of *Festus* – the amorous adventures of a young traveller out to experience the world – gives the poem a Byronic flair. A reviewer from *Blackwood's Magazine* even dubbed Bailey's hero 'a sort of poetical or sentimental Don Juan'.[70] Another reviewer uses terms that could well apply to any of the Byronic heroes – 'a compound of love, debauchery, pride, philosophy, and poetry' – to describe the title character.[71]

For some, the conflation of moving religious verse with bald eros was incongruous. The *New York Evangelist* warns, '[Bailey] mingles voluptuous conversation and the wildest, most passionate rhapsodies of love with his pretended serious and religious aspirings [*sic*] and impressions, as if one were as sacred as the other.'[72] But for most, the poem's air of charged sexuality and playful courtship recalled the best of Byron's epics without the attendant mockery of religious belief. In fact, Bailey sought consciously to distance himself from Byronic indecency. Of *Festus*, the poet once wrote to his father: 'There is nothing offensive in it; nothing Cainish.'[73] Rather, *Festus* offered readers what might be termed a sanctified Byronism, preserving Byron's episodic and sensualist tendencies in service to a more pious paradigm. This intense passion, combined with a grounding in Christian devotion, allowed the poet to go to places

68. See F. Boos, 'Class and Victorian Poetics', *Blackwell's Literary Compass*, Winter 2005.
69. Theodore R. Watts, 'Festus and Recent Poetry', *The Athenaeum*, 1 April 1876, p. 465.
70. *Blackwood's Magazine*, p. 422.
71. *New York Evangelist*, p. 186.
72. *New York Evangelist*, p. 186.
73. To Thomas Bailey, 26 April 1836. From a letter to Thomas Bailey, 26 April 1836. Qtd in Alan D. McKillop, 'A Victorian Faust', *PMLA*, 40:3, September 1925, p. 753.

where angels fear to tread, while still keeping safe in their holy company, and piling up readers – from churchmen to rakes – all the while.

Echoes of Byron ring beyond even the poem's amorous tangents. Also a native of Nottinghamshire – site of Byron's ancestral home – Bailey was well acquainted with the nineteenth century's other bestselling poet by the time he penned *Festus*, having even attended his lying-in-state and having apparently memorised *Childe Harold's Pilgrimage*.[74] No doubt by virtue of Bailey's familiarity, a Byronic presence looms throughout *Festus*. McKillop notes the tie, contending that 'passionate, disillusioned youth is the very core of Byronism and *Festus*'.[75] Despite the author's insistence to the contrary, *Festus* has especially close ties to Byron's *Cain*, whose hero journeys with another Lucifer to both 'Hades' and the 'Abyss of Space', settings mirrored in *Festus*.[76] Bailey's poem also pays homage to the quintessence of Byronic apocalypticism as the poem's hero dreams 'of general doom', similar to the dream visioned in Byron's 'Darkness'.[77]

Marketing

In addition to sharing penchants for episodic, sensualist, philosophically speculative epics, Bailey also followed Byron in leveraging his publishing practices to maximise readership. Byron's serialisation and manipulation of the news cycle are well known, but Bailey likewise used extra-textual methods to build his poem's audience. Still, perhaps it is unfair to ascribe, as some have, mercenary motives to Bailey's practice of expanding *Festus* in successive editions.[78] Rather than imagine the author stuffing his baggy book with poetic chaff he could not hawk elsewhere, we should consider him an artist who disbelieved in stable texts. In so doing, he resembled Goethe, for whom, as David Luke describes, the Faustian text is mutable, or he is like the Wordsworth of *The Prelude*, or the Whitman of the ever-changing *Leaves of Grass*.[79] Frederick Burwick's introduction to Coleridge's translation of *Faust* suggests that the mutability in which

---

74. John C. Francis, 'Philip James Bailey', *Notes and Queries*, 10, September 1902, pp. 242–3.
75. McKillop, p. 754.
76. For more on Byronic elements in *Festus*, see James Creighton Work, *A Study of the Hero in Spasmodic Dramas* (University of New Mexico, Doctoral Dissertation, 1973).
77. G. G. Byron, 'Darkness', *The Norton Anthology of English Literature*, 8th edn, ed. Stephen Greenblatt (New York and London: Norton, 2006), pp. 614–16.
78. See Tucker, p. 347: 'the elephantiasis of *Festus* imaged the enormity . . . of the author's egotism'.
79. D. Luke, introduction to J. W. von Goethe, *Faust* (Oxford: Oxford World Classics, 2008), pp. xliv–xlvii.

Bailey's text participates is of a piece with his subject, explaining that 'the Faust texts constitute . . . a site at the edge of chaos, where order and disorder, stasis and dynamism meet and interact'.[80] Bailey's later additions to *Festus* were not idiosyncratic; nor were they a function of hitching the apple-wagon to his racing stallion. In building the book in successive editions from the centre outward, he was participating in a tradition of dynamic texts, treating poems as organic and thus given to growth.

Finally, we should resist thinking of *Festus*' expansions as a marketing ploy because the book's actual marketing was so novel and successful, including its use of blurbs, gift editions and musical adaptations. Each edition of *Festus* beyond the first included what we now call 'blurbs' praising the work. It is possible that this is the first use of blurbs in English publishing, but however much this marketing technique may have been in effect for other authors or works, early readers found the trait remarkable; *Blackwood's* comments, for instance, that 'there is appended a series of laudatory extracts from reviews and magazines . . . their publication strikes us as a novelty, even in these advertising days'.[81] Moreover, early editors picked up on the dislocated force of Bailey's images and began offering special editions featuring bits of language removed from plot and context, for sheer enjoyment of the poetry. With these editions, it was possible to roam confidently with the cultured class, trading one's favourite lines from *Festus* without actually having read the whole poem. And, of course, each new, ever-expanding edition of the poem proper was met with fresh reviews, usually summarising the poem's popularity and influence and engaging the new material.

Three editions especially merit mention. First, *The Beauties of Festus* (1848) repackaged the best lines and passages for those who could not keep up with the book's prodigious growth.[82] Organised by topics and discussion points, it recast what some consider an egotistical or an idiosyncratic vision as a sociable work or a party game, even a devotional aid. Some headings in *The Beauties* are simple, such as 'Love', and others are strangely specific, such as 'Confusion of man on the appearance of Lucifer'. Few other narrative poems have borne such strange fruit, capable of being effective – and lucrative – even without context or narrative thrust. Rehashed like a biblical concordance, *The Beauties* relies entirely on force of imagery. Interestingly, the collection itself was edited by a self-styled 'Festonian', and later by 'A Student'. Fans of Bailey's work

---

80. F. Burwick and James McKusick (eds), *Faustus: From the German of Goethe* (Oxford: Oxford University Press, 2007), p. 127.
81. *Blackwood's Magazine*, p. 420.
82. Published in London by Longmans, Green & Co., 1848.

grew to be so fervent that they gave themselves names and created a community based around *Festus*.

Second, trading on the popularity of *The Beauties*, editors printed yet another edition called the *Festus Birthday Book* (1882), featuring line-sized segments arranged according to each month in the calendar year, like a daily devotional. Each citation from *Festus* therein is accompanied by a blank, on which the owner could write the names of friends with birthdays on the corresponding dates, the idea apparently being that lines from *Festus* would circulate in birthday cards.

Third, on the fiftieth anniversary of *Festus*' initial publication, a 'Jubilee' edition was issued. As Herbert Tucker notes, this took place a few years after the jubilee of Queen Victoria's coronation. Equating the historical significance of a poem's publication with the reign of the popular monarch is a bold move. That there was a market for such a publishing project speaks to the cultural force *Festus* wielded, even fifty years beyond its inception.

Yet another way that the *Festus* marketing machine reached the masses was through song. Readers whose appetite for the poem was unsatisfied with blurbs, *Beauties* or birthday cards could sing their favourite lines from the poem in settings such as that arranged by Louis Lavater as 'Ev'ry Leaf a Flower', or another by H. A. Rudall, sold as sheet music. Numerous methods like these set *Festus* apart from other works, its massive popularity aided, at least in part, by clever marketing schemes.

Though readers by the thousands bought *Festus* for its striking original poetry, they were also often buying a fine object. More or less from the start, editions of *Festus* were produced in gilt-embossed and illustrated editions on fine papers, like a family bible. An 1853 edition, published by Benjamin B. Mussey and Company, featured engraved renderings of sketches by Hammatt Billings, a Bostonian artist and architect whose clients also included such notables as Louisa May Alcott, Harriet Beecher Stowe, Alfred Lord Tennyson and Charles Dickens.[83] Thirteen images, 'after the manner of the School of Raphael and Thomas Cole', are spread throughout and included in this volume. Billings's illustrations later adorned several editions in both America and the UK.

As elsewhere, the illustrations helped to promote *Festus* not as a stand-alone work of a genius, but as an entire culture industry. One of Billings's images, illuminating the scene 'A Mountain—Sunrise',

---

83. J. F. O'Gorman, *Accomplished in All Departments of Art: Hammatt Billings of Boston, 1818–1874* (Amherst: University of Massachusetts Press, 1998), pp. ix, 12.

depicts Lucifer and Festus atop a precipice that overlooks a mountain-scape, all backdropped by a dawning sun (see page before Scene 4). Lucifer, garbed in a cloak and feathered cap, stands gesturing towards the landscape, his back to the artist's vantage point. Festus, also hatted, lounges at the cliff's edge. One arm props him up; the other, like Lucifer's, is outstretched towards the 'beauteous Earth' that dominates the pair's dialogue. Another illustration captures the poem's final scene, set in 'The Heaven of Heavens' where God stands among clouds, encircled by angels aloft. The Recording Angel, with the Book of Life in hand, is seated on a cloud below, opposite two angels trumpeting jubilantly. Festus kneels among them, his gaze fixed upward. Still below, a winged and crowned Lucifer, having been 'redeemed to archangelic state', also kneels reverently, with arms upraised. Images like these, incarnating Bailey's abstruse musings, helped to ground the poetry's ethereal nature.

Perhaps Bailey's legacy ought to extend even beyond his place as a Victorian bestseller and founder of a school of spectacularly popular poets because Bailey was a reformer in so many other ways as well. At many levels, *Festus* challenged the era's tastes – for how theology should be considered, for how poetry should be written, for how love-relationships should be conducted – rather than espousing them. Its striking difference, its scandal and, well, beauties, combined with shrewd marketing, deserve at least some of the credit for the poem's magnificent success. We need not agree with its early readers, that 'in richness of imagery and aptness of illustration . . . [*Festus*] has no competitor in modern times', or number it, as did British and American worthies, among the greatest productions of the age, but surely, if we make Peckham's 'scholarly attempt to find out what is . . . in the poem', modern readers will see what poetic wealth drew our Victorian forebears to such a frenzy of appreciation in the first place.[84]

84. *Dublin University Magazine*, p. 99.

Further Reading

Gilfillan, George, *Sketches Literary and Theological* (David Douglas, 1881).

Gosse, Edmund, *Portraits and Sketches* (Charles Scribner, 1912).

Nicoll, W. Robertson, *Literary Anecdotes of the 19th Century* (Hodder and Stoughton, 1896).

Tucker, Herbert, *Epic: Britain's Historic Muse 1790–1910* (Oxford University Press, 2012).

Ward, J. Philip, *Personal Recollections* (Nottingham: privately printed, 1905).

Weinstein, Mark A., *William Edmondstoune Aytoun and the Spasmodic Controversy* (Yale University Press, 1968).

Wilde, Lady, *Notes on Men, Women, and Books* (Ward and Downey, 1891).

Winter, William, *Old Friends: Being Literary Recollections of Other Days* (Moffat, Yard, and Co., 1909).

A Note on the Text

Festus was first published anonymously in 1839 by William Pickering, and then expanded in a second edition in 1845. Later editions in England, many of them longer than the last, were published in 1848, 1854, 1864, 1865, 1877, 1889, 1890 and 1903 by Chapman, Bell, Worthington, and Routledge. In America, editions began to be issued in 1845 by Benjamin B. Mussey, continuing in 1849, 1850, 1851, 1852 and 1854; then by Sanborn, Carter and Bazin in 1857; by J. Miller in 1860, 1862, 1865, 1867 and 1872; by Bell and Daldy in 1872; by Knox in 1888; and by Worthington in 1890. In all, reprintings aside, there were seventeen official editions of *Festus* published in America that issued from the seven distinct versions, differing in length, as shown in Table 1.[1] In Great Britain, there were thirteen official editions.[2] Several pirated editions also existed in both countries, about which Bailey frequently complained.

Table 1

Version	First publication	No. of lines
1	1839	8,103
2	1845	12,795
3	1848	15,603
4	1852	19,588
5	1864	23,359
6	1877	32,147
7	1889	39,159

The present volume is based on the second British edition issued by Pickering (1845), which Benjamin B. Mussey published as the first

1. For the most complete consideration of *Festus*' publishing history, see Morse Peckham, 'American Editions of "Festus": A Preliminary Survey', *The Princeton University Library Chronicle*, 8:4, 1947, pp. 177–84.
2. Morse Peckham, 'English Editions of Philip James Bailey's "Festus"', *The Papers of the Bibliographical Society of America*, 44:1, 1950, pp. 55–8.

American edition in the same year. I use this for two reasons. First, while the very first anonymously published editions of *Festus* were critically lauded, the reviews by Coventry Patmore, William Rossetti et al., as well as most American responses, relate to editions beyond the first. As such, that volume had less influence than the later, substantially changed, versions. When readers in the nineteenth century refer to *Festus* as an era-defining text, they are thinking of those editions beyond the first but before what some considered its decline, after parts of future books were incorporated in the third edition. Second, all editions of the poem beyond the first British one contain the radical plot element for which the poem was famous: the restitution of Lucifer to heaven at the eschaton. Reading contemporary accounts of the poem as heretical will make less sense to students who have read only the earlier, more orthodox, text. As the versions beyond 1845 contain mostly material available elsewhere, in Bailey's *The Angel World* (1850) and *The Mystic* (1855), this edition elects to include only that material original to *Festus*, from the version that earned him such a host of followers.

Explanatory annotations to various words are included when the term is described by the *Oxford English Dictionary* as 'rare' or 'obscure,' or when they unduly hinder the experience of reading the poem. Short forms and archaisms are expanded in annotations and given as footnotes. Specifically, obscure terms are rendered as written in the text and the modern variation footnoted, with a factual explanation of the reference. For example, where Bailey has 'Houris', a footnote reads 'Nymphs of the Moslem paradise'. Where he has 'Boodh', the line will be left as original, but a footnote reads 'Buddha: fifth-/sixth-century mystic given here as founder of Buddhism'. Terms such as 'Valhalla' or 'Elysian' and biblical references are left unglossed (the latter being too numerous).

Silent emendations have been made of extra spaces often left by printers before an exclamation mark, for example, but not before a comma or full stop. These have been removed. Mid-sentence capitalisations have been retained as authoritative: words such as 'Thee', 'Father', 'Maker' and 'Evil', wherever they occur, are left as printed in the 1845 edition. Misspellings or printer errors have been corrected in the text.

A critical modification that this edition makes is the inclusion of line numbers. Although no edition of *Festus* published in the author's lifetime contained line numbers, their absence reflects not an authorial design decision so much as the intended market. *Festus* was a popular work, intended to be read by a broad swath of the population. It was not, in the first instance, a 'library poem'. For a scholarly edition to be useful for students and researchers, they are essential, particularly in a poem running to thousands of lines. The following method has been adopted. Lines are counted beginning at '1' in each scene and followed sequentially through until the next scene, where they reset. Orphan lines resulting from varying paper sizes have been returned in this edition wherever space permits. Where it does not, the line has not been given a new number, but a space, with numbering continuing on the next authorial register.

Scenes have been denoted by the author in every edition of *Festus*, usually together with brief stage directions. Beginning in the sixth British edition, the author numbered the scenes as well, but changed the order for the seventh. In the present edition, these headings have been retained and numbered.

Works by Philip James Bailey

Festus (1839 . . . 1889)
The Angel World, and Other Poems (1850)
The Mystic, and Other Poems (1855)
The Age (1858)
'The International Policy of the Great Powers' (1861)
The Universal Hymn (1867)
'Nottingham Castle, an Ode' (1878)
'Causa Britannica, a Poem in Latin Hexameters with English Paraphrase' (1883)

Festus

By Philip James Bailey

DEDICATION

1. My father! unto thee to whom I owe
2. All that I am, all that I have and can;
3. Who madest me in thyself the sum of man
4. In all his generous aims and powers to know,
5. These first-fruits bring I; nor do thou forego
6. Marking when I the boyish feat began,
7. Which numbers now near three years from its plan
8. Not twenty summers had imbrowned my brow.
9. Life is at blood-heat every page doth prove.
10. Bear with it Nature means Necessity.
11. If here be aught which thou canst love, it springs
12. Out of the hope that I may earn that love
13. More unto me than immortality;
14. Or to have strang my harp with golden strings.

PROEM

1. Without all fear, without presumption, he
2. Who wrote this work would speak respecting it
3. A few brief words, and face his friend the world;
4. Revising, not reversing, what hath been.
5. Poetry is itself a thing of God;
6. He made His prophets poets; and the more
7. We feel of poesie do we become
8. Like God in love and power, — under-makers.
9. All great lays, equals to the minds of men,
10. Deal more or less with the Divine, and have
11. For end some good of mind or soul of man.
12. The mind is this world's, but the soul is God's;
13. The wise man joins them here all in his power.
14. The high and holy works, amid lesser lays,
15. Stand up like churches among village cots;
16. And it is joy to think that in every age,
17. However much the world was wrong therein,
18. The greatest works of mind or hand have been
19. Done unto God. So may they ever be!
20. It shews the strength of wish we have to be great,
21. And the sublime humility of might.
22. True fiction hath in it a higher end
23. Than fact; it is the possible compared
24. With what is merely positive, and gives
25. To the conceptive soul an inner world,
26. A higher, ampler Heaven than that wherein
27. The nations sun themselves. In that bright state
28. Are met the mental creatures of the men
29. Whose names are writ highest on the rounded crown
30. Of Fame's triumphal arch; the shining shapes
31. Which star the skies of that invisible land,
32. Which, whoso'er would enter, let him learn; —
33. 'Tis not enough to draw forms fair and lively,
34. Their conduct likewise must be beautiful;

35.   A hearty holiness must crown the work.
36.   As a gold cross the minster-dome, and show,
37.   Like that instonement[1] of divinity,
38.   That the whole building doth belong to God.
39.   And for the book before us, though it were,
40.   What it is not, supremely little, like
41.   The needled angle of a high church spire,
42.   Its sole end points to God the Father's glory,
43.   From all eternity seen; making clear
44.   His might and love in saving sinful man.
45.   One bard shows God as He deals with states and kings;
46.   Another, as He dealt with the first man;
47.   Another, as with Heaven and earth and hell;
48.   Ours, as He loves to order a chance soul
49.   Chosen out of the world, from first to last.
50.   And all along it is the heart of man
51.   Emblemed, created and creative mind.
52.   It is a statued mind and naked heart
53.   Which is struck out. Other bards draw men dressed
54.   In manners, customs, forms, appearances.
55.   Laws, places, times, and countless accidents
56.   Of peace or polity: to him these are not;
57.   He makes no mention, takes no compt of them; —
58.   But shows, however great his doubts, sins, trials,
59.   Whatever earthborn pleasures soil man's soul,
60.   What power soever he may gain of evil,
61.   That still, till death, time is; that God's great Heaven
62.   Stands open day and night to man and spirit;
63.   For all are of the race of God, and have
64.   In themselves good. The life-writ of a heart,
65.   Whose firmest prop and highest meaning was
66.   The hope of serving God as poet-priest,
67.   And the belief that He would not put back
68.   Love-offerings, though brought to Him by hands
69.   Unclean and earthy, e'en as fallen man's
70.   Must be; and most of all, the thankful show
71.   Of His high power and goodness in redeeming
72.   And blessing souls that love Him, spite of sin
73.   And their old earthy strain, — these are the aims,

---

1. Instonement: The act of turning to stone; petrifying. *Rare* (*OED*). *Festus* is the first known use.

74. The doctrines, truths, and staple of the story.
75. What theme sublimer than soul being saved?
76. 'Tis the bard's aim to show the mind-made world
77. Without, within; how the soul stands with God,
78. And the unseen realities about us.
79. It is a view of life spiritual
80. And earthly. Let all look upon it, then,
81. In the same light it was drawn and colored in;
82. In faith, in that the writer too hath faith,
83. Albeit an effect, and not a cause.
84. Faith is a higher faculty than reason,
85. Though of the brightest power of revelation;
86. As the snow-headed mountain rises o'er
87. The lightning, and applies itself to Heaven.
88. We know in day-time there are stars about us,
89. Just as at night, and name them what and where
90. By sight of science; so by faith we know,
91. Although we may not see them till our night,
92. That spirits are about us, and believe,
93. That, to a spirit's eye, all Heaven may be
94. As full of angels as a beam of light
95. Of motes. As spiritual, it shows all
96. Classes of life, perhaps, above our kind,
97. Known to tradition, reason, or God's word,
98. Whose bright foundations are the heights of Heaven.
99. As earthly, it embodies most the life
100. Of youth, its powers, its aims, its deeds, its failings;
101. And, as a sketch of world-life, it begins
102. And ends, and rightly, in Heaven and with God;
103. While Heaven is also in the midst thereof.
104. God, or all good, the evil of the world,
105. And man, wherein are both, are each displayed.
106. The mortal is the model of all men.
107. The foibles, follies, trials, sufferings —
108. And manifest and manifold are they —
109. Of a young, hot, un-world-schooled heart that has
110. Had its own way in life, and wherein all
111. May see some likeness of their own, — 'tis these
112. Attract, unite, and, sunlike, concentrate
113. The ever-moving system of our feelings.
114. The hero is the world-man, in whose heart
115. One passion stands for all, the most indulged.

116. The scenes wherein he plays his part are life,
117. A sphere whose centre is co-heavenly
118. With its divine original and end.
119. Like life, too, as a whole, the story hath
120. A moral, and each scene one, as in life, —
121. One universal and peculiar truth —
122. Shining upon it like the quiet moon,
123. Illustrating the obscure unequal earth; —
124. And though these scenes may seem to careless eyes
125. Irregular and rough and unconnected,
126. Like to the stones at Stonehenge, — though convolved,
127. And in primeval mystery, — still an use,
128. A meaning, and a purpose may be marked
129. Among them of a temple reared to God: —
130. The meaning alway dwelling in the word,
131. In secret sanctity, like a golden toy
132. Mid Beauty's orbed bosom. Scenes of earth
133. And Heaven are mixed, as flesh and soul in man.
134. Now, the religion of the book is this,
135. Followed out from the book God writ of old.
136. All creatures being faulty by their nature,
137. And by God made all liable to sin,
138. God only could atone — and unto none
139. Except Himself — for universal sin.
140. It is thus that God did sacrifice to God,
141. Himself unto Himself, in the great way
142. Of Triune mystery. His death, as man,
143. Was real as our own; and as, except
144. In the destruction of all life, there could
145. Be no atonement for its sin, while life
146. Doth necessarily result from God,
147. As thought and outward action from ourselves,
148. So the atonement must be to and by Him;
149. Which makes it justice equally with love;
150. For all His powers and attributes are equal,
151. And must make one in any act of His;
152. And every act of God is infinite.
153. He acts through all in all: the truth we know,
154. He doth Himself inbreathe; the ill we do,
155. He hath atoned for; and the scriptures show
156. That God doth suffer for the sins of those
157. Whom He hath made, that are liable to sin.

158. In all of us He hath His agony;
159. We are the cross, and death of God, and grave.
160. Him love then all the more, and worship Him
161. Who lived and died, and rose from death for us,
162. And is and reigns forever God in all.
163. Let each man think himself an act of God,
164. His mind a thought, his life a breath of God;
165. And let each try, by great thoughts and good deeds,
166. To show the most of Heaven he hath in him.
167. Many who read the word of life, much doubt
168. Whether salvation be of grace or faith,
169. Election, or repentance, or good works.
170. Or God's high will: reconcile all of them.
171. Each of the persons of the Triune God
172. Hath had His dispensation, hath it now;
173. The Father by His prophets, and the Son
174. In His own days, by His own deeds; and now
175. The Spirit, by the ministry of Christ;
176. And thus, by law, by gospel, and by grace,
177. The scheme of God's salvation is complete.
178. Salvation, then, is God-like, threefold; so
179. That under one or other, all may come;
180. By will of God alone, by faith in Christ,
181. And by repentance, and good works, and grace.
182. So there is one salvation of the Father,
183. One of the Son, another of the Spirit;
184. Each, the salvation of the Three in One.
185. The mortal in this lay is saved of will,
186. In manner as this hymn unfolds, which hath
187. Just warranty for every word from God's.
188.   O God! Thou wondrous One in Three,
189.   As mortals must Thee deem;
190.   Thou only canst be said to be,
191.   We but at best to seem.
192.   For Thou dost save, and Thou may'st slay,
193.   Canst make a mortal soul
194.   In Thee eternal; in a day
195.   Wilt bring to nought the whole.
196.   Thou hardenest, and Thou openest hearts,
197.   As in Thy Word is shown;
198.   Thou savest and destroyest parts,
199.   By Thy right will alone.

200.	Let down Thy grace, then, Lord! on all
201.	Whom Thou wilt save to live;
202.	Oh! if they stumble, stop their fall!
203.	Oh! if they fall, forgive!
204.	They are forgiven from the first,
205.	They are predestined Thine;
206.	And though in sin they were the worst,
207.	In Thee they are divine.
208.	They are, and were, and will be, Lord!
209.	In one, in Heaven, in Thee,
210.	Yea with the Spirit, and the Word,
211.	One God in Trinity.

212. These principles and doctrines pending not
213. Upon the action of the poem here,
214. But over and above it, influencing
215. Nevertheless the story, as the course
216. Of stars enwoven with our system, earth,
217. Vary the view of this life's hemisphere.
218. And mingle it more palpably with Heaven,
219. And with its changeless, ceaseless, boundless God.
220. It is thus that by creating to and from
221. Eternity, and multiplying ever
222. His own one Being through the universe
223. He doth eternize happiness, and make
224. Good infinite by making all in Him.
225. There is but one great right and good; and ill
226. And wrong are shades thereof, not substances.
227. Nothing can be antagonist to God.
228. Necessity, like electricity,
229. Is in ourselves and all things, and no more
230. Without us than within us; and we live,
231. We of this mortal mixture, in the same law
232. As the pure colourless intelligence
233. Which dwells in Heaven, and the dead Hadëan shades.
234. We will and act and talk of liberty;
235. And all our wills and all our doings both
236. Are limited within this little life.
237. Free will is but necessity in play, —
238. The clattering of the golden reins which guide
239. The thunder-footed coursers of the sun.
240. The ship which goes to sea informed with fire, —
241. Obeying only its own iron force,

242. Reckless of adverse tide, breeze dead, or weak
243. As infant's parting breath, too faint to stir
244. The feather held before it, — is as much
245. The appointed thrall of all the elements,
246. As the white-bosomed bark which woos the wind,
247. And when it dies desists. And thus with man;
248. However contrary he set his heart
249. To God, he is but working out His will;
250. And, at an infinite angle, more or less
251. Obeying his own soul's necessity.
252. He only hath freewill whose will is fate.
253. Evil and good are God's right hand and left.
254. By ministry of evil good is clear.
255. And by temptation virtue; as of yore
256. Out of the grave rose God. Let this be deemed
257. Enough to justify the portion weighed
258. To the great spirit Evil, named herein.
259. If evil seem the most, yet good most is:
260. As water may be deep and pure below
261. Although the face be filmy for a time.
262. And if the spirit of evil seem more in
263. The work than God, it is but to work His will,
264. Who therefore is all that the other seems.
265. And evil is in almost every scene
266. Of life more or less forward. Above all
267. The mystery of the Trinity is held,
268. Whose mystery is its reasonableness.
269. All that is said of Deity is said
270. In love and reverence. Be it so conceived.
271. What comes before and after the great world, —
272. Deep in the secretest abyss of Light,
273. And Being's most reserved immensity —
274. God alone knows eternally, who rends
275. The mantling Heavens with his hands; but with
276. The present is communion creatural;[2]
277. He liveth in the sacrament of life.
278. And for the soul of man delineate here —
279. The outline half invisible — is shown
280. The self-sought grace, the self-aspiring truth
281. And natural religion of the heart

---

2. Creatural: Creaturely.

282. Contrasting Godhood with humanity
283. Ever; whereas the Spirit aye unites.
284. Temptation, and its workings in the heart
285. Whose faint and false resistance but assists, —
286. Ambition, thirst of secret lore, joy, love —
287. Riverlike, doubling sometimes on itself —
288. Adventure, pleasure, travel heavenly
289. And earthly, friendship, passion, poesie,
290. Viewed ever in their spiritual end —
291. And power, celestial happiness and earth's
292. Millennial foretaste, ill annihilate.
293. The restoration of the angels lost,
294. And one salvation universal given
295. To all create, — all these, related, form,
296. With much beside, the body of the work: —
297. The islands, seas, and mainland of its orb.
298. Thus much then for this book. It aims to mark
299. The various beliefs as well as doubts
300. Which hold or search by turns the mind of youth
301. Unresting anywhere. Its heresies,
302. If such they be, are charitable ones; —
303. For they who read not in the blest belief
304. That all souls may be saved, read to no end.
305. We were made to be saved. We are of God.
306. Nor bates the book one tittle of the truth,
307. To smoothe its way to favour with the fearful.
308. All rests with those who read. A work or thought
309. Is what each makes it to himself, and may
310. Be full of great dark meanings, like the sea.
311. With shoals of life rushing; or like the air,
312. Benighted with the wing of the wild dove,
313. Sweeping miles broad o'er the far western woods,
314. With mighty glimpses of the central light —
315. Or may be nothing — bodiless, spiritless.
316. Now therefore to his work and to the world
317. The writer bids, God speed! It matters not
318. If they agree or differ. Each perchance
319. May bear true witness to another end.
320. Let then what hath been, be. It boots not here
321. To palliate misdoings. 'Twere less toil
322. To build Colossus than to hew a hill
323. Into a statue. Hail and farewell, all!

LUCIFER ASKS LEAVE TO TEMPT FESTUS. All the plates in this book are Hammatt Billings etchings.

SCENE 1

[Heaven]

1.   GOD. Eternity hath snowed its years upon them;
2.   And the white winter of their age is come,
3.   The World and all its worlds; and all shall end.
4.   SERAPHIM. God! God! God!
5.   As flames in skies
6.   We burn and rise
7.   And lose ourselves in Thee!
8.   Years on years!
9.   And nought appears
10.   Save God to be.
11.   God! God! God!
12.   To us no thought
13.   Hath Being brought
14.   Toward Thee that doth not move!
15.   Years on years!
16.   And what appears
17.   Save God to love?
18.   God! God! God!
19.   All Thou dost make
20.   Lies like a lake
21.   Below Thine infinite eye;
22.   Years on years!
23.   And all appears
24.   Save God to die.
25.   CHERUBIM. As sun and star.
26.   How high or far,
27.   Shew but a boundless sky;
28.   So creature mind
29.   Is all confined,
30.   To shew Thee, God, most High!
31.   The sun still burns,
32.   The sun still turns
33.   Round, round himself and round;

34. So creature mind
35. To self's confined,
36. But Thou God hast no bound!
37. Systems arise.
38. Or a world dies,
39. Each constant hour in air;
40. But creature mind,
41. In Heaven confined,
42. Lives on like Thee, God! there.
43. SERAPHIM AND CHERUBIM. God! God! God!
44. Thou fill'st our eyes
45. As were the skies
46. One burning, boundless sun!
47. While creature mind.
48. In path confined,
49. Passeth a spot thereon.
50. God! God! God!
51. LUCIFER. Ye thrones of Heaven, how bright, how pure ye are!
52. How have ye brightened since I saw ye first!
53. How have I darkened since ye saw me last!
54. What is the dark abyss of fire, and what
55. The ravenous heights of air, o'er which I reign,
56. In agony of glory, to these seats?
57. The loathsome cavern of the oracle,
58. O'er which ye rise in templed majesty,
59. Filled with the incense of all worshippers,
60. And echoing with the eloquence of God,
61. Which rolls in sunny clouds around the heavens.
62. Yet must I work through world and life my fate;
63. And winding through the wards of human hearts,
64. Steal their incarnate strength. Death does his work
65. In secret and in joy intense, untold,
66. As though an earthquake smacked its mumbling lips
67. O'er some thick peopled city. But for me,
68. Exists nor peace nor pleasure, even here,
69. Where all beside, the very faintest thought,
70. Is rapture. I will speak to God as erst.[1]
71. Father of spirit, as the sun of air!
72. Beginning of all ends, and end of all

---

1. Erst: As in erstwhile; as before.

73. Beginnings, throughout whole Eternity;
74. From whom Eternity and every power
75. Perfect, and pure cause, is and emanates!
76. Originator without origin!
77. End without end! Creator of all ages,
78. And sabbath of all Being; who hast made
79. All numbers sacred, who art all and one!
80. At whose right hand the wisdom of all worlds
81. Combined, is only fearful foolishness
82. Or inarticulate madness, — and Thou, Lord!
83. Maker and Perfecter of all, the one!
84. Being above all Being, God the Life!
85. Who art the way whereon the world proceeds
86. From God, all-making, and whereby returns
87. The ever generated universe! —
88. Who rulest all worlds in the law of light,
89. Thy nature and their own; who art before
90. All ages, angels, blessed, times and worlds!
91. Word that in every world art safe to save
92. All souls, impregned² with spirit, God-begot!
93. And Thou eternal spirit-Deity!
94. The sanctifier of the universe!
95. Being, and Life, and spirit, who dost make,
96. Destroyest, recreatest, makest God!
97. God one and Trine!³ Thou seest me here again;
98. Still, sunlike, though eclipsed, of blinding power
99. And fiery cause, and everness of ill;
100. Behold I bow before Thee; hear Thou me!
101. GOD. What wouldst thou, Lucifer?
102. LUCIFER. There is a youth
103. Among the sons of men I fain would have
104. Given up wholly to me.
105. GOD. He is thine,
106. To tempt.
107. LUCIFER. I thank Thee, Lord!
108. GOD. Upon his soul
109. Thou hast no power. All souls are mine for aye.
110. And I do give thee leave to this that he
111. May know my love is more than all his sin.

---

2. Impregned: Impregnated.
3. Trine: Another term for 'triune', or three.

112. And prove unto himself that nought but God
113. Can satisfy the soul He maketh great.
114. LUCIFER. Thou God art all in one! Thy infinite
115. Bounds Being. Thou hast said the world shall end.
116. The world is perfect, as concerns itself,
117. And all its parts and ends; not as towards Thee.
118. So man is likest and unlikest God,
119. Of all existence; therefore doth as much
120. Resemble Thee as any act a mind.
121. In him of whom I ask, I seek once more
122. To tempt the living world, and then depart.
123. THE HOLY GHOST. And I will hallow him to the ends of
      Heaven,
124. That though he plunge his soul in sin like a sword
125. In water, it shall nowise cling to him.
126. He is of Heaven. All things are known in Heaven,
127. Ere aimed at upon earth. The child is chosen.
128. SAINTS. Another soul
129. The Holy one
130. Hath chosen out of earth;
131. And there is none
132. Throughout the whole
133. like worthy of his birth.
134. GUARDIAN ANGEL. Oh! who hath joy like mine? Was
      I not here
135. When from Thy boundless bosom, as a star
136. Out of the air, that soul was kindled, Lord!
137. And given to me to guard and guide — while both,
138. Mid starry strains out of the depths of Heaven,
139. Fell at Thy feet in worship? — joy of joys!
140. To you, ye saints and angels, let me speak;
141. For ye I see rejoice with me. Ye know
142. What 'tis to triumph o'er temptation, what
143. To fall before it; how the young spirit faints —
144. The virgin tremor, the heart's ebb and flow.
145. When first some vast temptation calmly comes
146. And states itself before it, like the sun
147. Low looming in the west, above the wave
148. Of wimpling[4] streamlet, ere its waters grow

---

4. Wimpling: Winding or meandering.

149. To size aortal. Than the Fiend himself
150. There is no greater evil. Less the shame
151. Of yielding, more the glory of conquering,
152. In him, to whom he goes, this soul elect.
153. From infancy through childhood, up to youth,
154. Have I this soul attended; marked him blest
155. With all the sweet and sacred ties of life; —
156. The prayerful love of parents, pride of friends,
157. Prosperity, and health and ease, the aids
158. Of learning, social converse with the good
159. And gifted, and his heart all-lit with love,
160. Like to the rolling sea with living light; —
161. Hopeful and generous and earnest; rich
162. In commune with high spirits, loving truth
163. And wisdom for their own divinest selves;
164. Tracking the deeds of the world's glory, or
165. Conning the words of wisdom, Heaven-inspired,
166. As on the soul, in pure effectual ray,
167. The bright, transparent atoms, thought by thought,
168. Fall fixed for evermore. And thus his days,
169. Through sunny noon, or mooned eve, or night
170. Star-armied, shining through the deathless air,
171. All radiantly elapsed, in good or joy.
172. All this, for long, I marked. There grew, at length,
173. A change within his spirit; and I feared
174. A fatal and a final fall from good.
175. God's love seemed lost upon him. He became
176. Heart-deadened. Watching, warning, vain, I fled
177. Hither to intercede with God our Lord,
178. To bless him with salvation. We may plead
179. Alway for those we love, by leave divine.
180. Nor knew I till this moment, with all Heaven,
181. That, in the righteous providence of God,
182. That soul was saved. Thou knowest, Lord! the mould
183. Of mortals, and the infinite end whereto
184. The souls Thou savest are predestinate;
185. Oh! be Thy mercy mighty to this soul,
186. Fiend-threatened; nor permit him who presides
187. O'er Hell's eternal holocaust, too far
188. To tempt or tamper with the heart of man!
189. GOD. My mercy doth outstretch the universe;
190. Shall it not be sufficient for one soul?

191. LUCIFER. I am the wrath of God unto myself,
192. And made by Him to do my part. Do thou
193. Thine! they are far enough apart I ween.[5]
194. GUARDIAN ANGEL. The heaven-strung chords of man's
        immortal soul
195. Are not for thee to wither at thy will.
196. Bear witness, all ye blessed, to the word; —
197. Angels, intelligences, sons of God!
198. Ye who know nought but truth, feel nought but love,
199. Will nought but bliss, do nought but righteousness!
200. Whose life was ere the Heavens were conceived,
201. The stars begotten, or the ages born;
202. Ye many ordered hierarchies, which are
203. The love, truth, justice, majesty and might,
204. Dominion, glory, wisdom, bliss of God;
205. Ye through whose ministry of mercy — His
206. Immediate, ever instant, active, all
207. Spirits and worlds are governed — age by age
208. Gazing and gaining glory; ye who stand,
209. Stirless, before the throne, entranced in joy;
210. Or ye, whose life is to present all souls
211. Reborn to their Creator; or to search
212. The golden globed skies for deeds of grace;
213. And ye who move all Heavens, in whose names
214. The name of God is, as in angels' all;
215. The crown, the wisdom, the intelligence,
216. Kindness, and strength and beauty, splendour, worth,
217. Original and rule; and ye who move
218. Restless around the throne, the burning seven.
219. The virtue, power, salvation, fire and rest,
220. Blessing and praise of God; and ye who rule
221. Regions or kingdoms, states, tribes, families,
222. Ages and times, and seasons, and events;
223. Systems and elements, material powers,
224. Mental and spiritual; or ye who bear
225. Souls from the heaven to earth, from earth to heaven;
226. Ye tenants of the archetypal worlds
227. And spiritual spheres; and you, ye saints!
228. Freed once on earth into the liberty

5. Ween: To think, surmise. *Obsolete* (*OED*).

229. Of the necessity which is of God;
230. Yours are the many multitudes of stars.
231. And bliss and power for ever, ye are gods!
232. And live an endless life, bespoken here;
233. Bear witness, all, that happiness succeeds
234. To godliness; and that, despite of sin,
235. The world may recognise in all time's scenes,
236. Though belts of clouds bar half its burning disk,
237. The overruling, overthrowing power,
238. Which by our creature purposes works out
239. Its deeds, and by our deeds its purposes.
240. LUCIFER. God! for thy glory only can I act.
241. And for thy creatures' good. When creatures stray
242. Farthest from Thee, then warmest towards them burns
243. Thy love, even as yon sun beams hotliest on
244. The earth when distant most.
245. GOD. The earth whereon
246. He dwells, this grain selected from the sands
247. Of life, dies with him.
248. LUCIFER. God! I go to do
249. Thy will.
250. GOD. Thou, too, who watchest o'er the world
251. Whose end I fix, prepare to have it judged.
252. ANGEL OF EARTH. Let me not then have watched o'er
it in vain.
253. From age to age, from hour to hour I still
254. Have hoped it would grow better — hope so now;
255. 'Tis better than it once was, and hath more
256. Of mind and freedom than it ever had.
257. I love it more than ever. Thou didst give
258. It to me as a child. To me earth is
259. Even as the boundless universe to Thee;
260. Nay, more! for Thou couldst make another. It is
261. My world. Take it not from me Lord! Thou, Christ!
262. Mad'st it the altar where thou offeredst up
263. Thyself for the creation. Let it be
264. Immortal as Thy love. And altars are
265. Holy; and sister angels, sister orbs
266. Hail it afar as such. Oh! I have heard
267. World question world and answer; seen them weep
268. Each other if eclipsed for one red hour,
269. And of all worlds most generous was mine,

270. The tenderest and the fairest.
271. LUCIFER. Knowest thou not
272. God's son to be the brother and the friend
273. Of spirit everywhere? Or hath thy soul
274. Been bound for ever to thy foolish world?
275. ANGEL. Star unto star speaks light, and world to world
276. Repeats the password of the universe
277. To God; the name of Christ — the one great word
278. Well worth all languages in earth or Heaven.
279. SON OF GOD. Think not I lived and died for thine alone.
280. And that no other sphere hath hailed me Christ.
281. My life is ever suffering for love.
282. In judging and redeeming worlds is spent
283. Mine everlasting being.
284. LUCIFER. Earth he next
285. Will judge; for so saith God.
286. ANGEL OF EARTH. Be it not, Lord!
287. Thou art a God of goodness and of love;
288. He is the evil of the universe,
289. And loveth not the earth, Thy Son, nor Thee.
290. Thou knowest best.
291. LUCIFER. Behold now all yon worlds!
292. The space each fills shall be its successor.
293. Accept the consolation!
294. ANGEL OF EARTH. Earth! oh, Earth!
295. LUCIFER. 'Tis earth shall lead destruction; she shall end.
296. The stars shall wonder why she comes no more
297. On her accustomed orbit, and the sun
298. Miss one of his eleven of light; the moon,
299. An orphan orb, shall seek for earth for aye,
300. Through time's untrodden depths and find her not;
301. No more shall morn, out of the holy east,
302. Stream o'er the amber air her level light;
303. Nor evening, with the spectral fingers, draw
304. Her star-sprent[6] curtain round the head of earth;
305. Her footsteps never thence again shall grace
306. The blue sublime of heaven. Her grave is dug.
307. I see the stars, night-clad, all gathering
308. In long and dark procession. Death's at work.

6. Sprent: Sprinkled or spattered.

309. And, one by one, shall all yon wandering worlds,
310. Whether in orbed path they roll, or trail,
311. In an inestimable length of light,
312. Their golden train of tresses after them,
313. Cease; and the sun, centre and sire of light,
314. The keystone of the world-built arch of heaven
315. Be left in burning solitude. The stars,
316. Which stand as thick as dewdrops on the fields
317. Of heaven, and all they comprehend, shall pass.
318. The spirits of all worlds shall all depart
319. To their great destinies; and thou and I,
320. Greater in grief than worlds, shall live as now.
321. In hell's dark annals there is something writ,
322. Which shall amaze man yet. There! to thy earth!
323. ANGEL OF EARTH. There is a blind world, yet unlit by God,
324. Rolling around the extremest edge of light;
325. Where all things are disaster and decay,
326. The outcast of all being; no one thing
327. Fitting another; that is fit for thee.
328. Be that thy world! but not the living earth.
329. Stretch forth Thy shining shield, oh God! the heavens,
330. Over the prostrate earth, an armed friend.
331. And save her from the swift and violent hell
332. Her beauty hath enchanted! from the wrath
333. Of love like his, oh save her, though by death!
334. GOD. Destruction and salvation are the hands
335. Upon the face of time. When both unite,
336. The day of death dawns. Every orb exists
337. Unto its preappointed end: and earth,
338. My creature, the elect of worlds, ere all
339. Is saved. The world shall perish as a worm
340. Upon destruction's path; the universe
341. Evanish like a ghost before the sun,
342. Yea like a doubt before the truth of God,
343. Yet nothing more than death shall perish. Then,
344. Rejoice ye souls of God, regenerate,
345. Ye indwellers divine of Deity;
346. In Him ye are immortal as Himself!
347. SON OF GOD. O'er all things are eternity and change,
348. And special predilection of our God.
349. Thou who createst souls, as the sun clouds,
350. Out of the sea of spirit, sire of both

351. The first and second natures of Thy Son,
352. In whom the maker and the made make one,
353. Deific spirit! who in every world
354. Payeth creation's penalties; in all,
355. Is heir of God and nature, and in Thee,
356. And in self-worship, Deifies himself!
357. And you blest spirits for whom I died, for whom,
358. Forefated, fore-atoned for from the first,
359. All heaven reserves the fullness of its bliss;
360. Creator and created! witness, both,
361. How I have loved ye, as God-natured life
362. Alone can love and suffer! Let the earth
363. And every orb, the offspring of all air,
364. Perish; but all I die for, live for me.
365. GOD. The earth shall not be when her sabbath ends,
366. In the high close of order.
367. LUCIFER. Heaven, farewell!
368. Hell is more bearable than nothingness.
369. THRONES. Thou, God, art Lord of mercy! and Thy thoughts
370. Are high above the star-dust of the world!
371. DOMINATIONS. Yet o'er the meanest atom reignest Thou
372. Omnipotent, as o'er the universe!
373. POWERS. Thy might is self-creative, and Thy works
374. Immortal, temporal, destructible,
375. Are ever in Thy sight and blessed there!
376. The heavens are Thy bosom, and Thine eye
377. Is high o'er all existence; yea the worlds
378. Are but Thy shining foot-prints upon space!
379. PRINCEDOMS. Eternal Lord! Thy strength compels the
       worlds,
380. And bows the heads of ages; at Thy voice
381. Their unsubstantial essence wears away.
382. VIRTUES. All-favouring God! we glory but in Thee.
383. Ye Heavens exalt, expand yourselves! they come,
384. The infinite generations, all Divine,
385. Of Deity, our brethren and our friends!
386. ARCHANGELS. Thou who hast thousand names, as night
       hath stars,
387. Which light Thee up to eye create, yet not
388. One thousandth part illumine Thy boundlessness,
389. Nor that abyss of Being 'midst of which
390. Thy countless wonders constellate themselves;
391. Thy light, the light we dwell in shall at last

392. Fulfil the universe, and all be bliss;
393. The consummation of all ages come.
394. We praise Thee for Thy mercies, and for this,
395. The first, and last, and greatest of all boons.
396. ANGELS. Thee God! we praise
397. Through our ne'er sunsetting days,
398. And Thy just ways.
399. Divine:
400. In Thy hand is every spirit,
401. And the meed[7] the same may merit;
402. All which all the worlds inherit
403. Are Thine!
404. It is not unto creatures given
405. To scale the purposes of Heaven,
406. Alway just and kind;
407. But before Thy mighty breath,
408. Life and spirit, dust and death,
409. The boundless All is driven.
410. Like clouds by wind.
411. ANGEL OF EARTH. Woe! woe at last in Heaven!
412. Earth to death is given;
413. The ends of things hang still
414. Over them as a sky;
415. Do what we will,
416. All's for eternity!

SCENE 2

[*Wood and Water — Sunset*]
[*FESTUS alone*]

1. FESTUS. This is to be a mortal and immortal!
2. To live within a circle, — and to be
3. That dark point where the shades of all things around

---

7. Meed: The return for labour, wages.

4.   Meet, mix and deepen. All things unto me
5.   Shew their dark sides! somewhere there must be light.
6.   Oh! I feel like a seed in the cold earth;
7.   Quickening at heart, and pining for the air!
8.   Passion is destiny. The heart is its own
9.   Fate. It is well youth's gold rubs off so soon.
10. The heart gets dizzy with its drunken dance,
11. And the voluptuous vanities of life
12. Enchain, enchant, and cheat my soul no more.
13. My spirit is on edge. I can enjoy
14. Nought which has not the honied sting of sin;
15. That soothing fret which makes the young untried,
16. Longing to be beforehand with their nature,
17. In dreams and loneness cry, they die to live;
18. That wanton whetting of the soul, which while
19. It gives a finer, keener edge for pleasure,
20. Wastes more and dulls the sooner. Rouse thee, heart;
21. Bow of my life thou yet art full of spring!
22. My quiver still hath many purposes.
23. Yet what is worth a thought of all things here?
24. How mean, how miserable every care!
25. How doubtful, too, the system of the mind!
26. And then the ceaseless, changeless, hopeless round
27. Of weariness and heartlessness and woe
28. And vice and vanity! Yet these make life;
29. The life at least I witness if not feel.
30. No matter! we are immortal. How I wish
31. I could love men! for amid all life's quests
32. There seems but worthy one — to do men good.
33. It matters not how long we live but how.
34. For as the parts of one manhood while here
35. We live in every age; we think and feel
36. And feed upon the coming and the gone
37. As much as on the now time. Man is one:
38. And he hath one great heart. It is thus we feel,
39. With a gigantic throb athwart the sea,
40. Each others' rights and wrongs; thus are we men.
41. Let us think less of men and more of God!
42. Sometimes the thought comes swiftening over us,
43. Like a small bird winging the still blue air;
44. And then again, at other times, it rises
45. Slow, like a cloud which scales the skies all breathless,

46.   And just over head lets itself down on us.

47.   Sometimes we feel the wish across the mind

48.   Rush, like a rocket tearing up the sky,

49.   That we should join with God and give the world

50.   The slip; but while we wish, the world turns round,

51.   And peeps us in the face — the wanton world;

52.   We feel it gently pressing down our arm —

53.   The arm we had raised to do for truth such wonders;

54.   We feel it softly bearing on our side —

55.   We feel it touch and thrill us through the body —

56.   And we are fools and there's an end of us.

57.   'Tis a fine thought that sometime end we must.

58.   There sets the sun of suns! dies in all fire,

59.   Like Asher's[1] death-great monarch. God of might!

60.   We love and live on power. It is spirit's end.

61.   Mind must subdue. To conquer is its life.

62.   Why mad'st Thou not one spirit, like the sun,

63.   To king the world? And oh! might I have been

64.   That sun-mind, how I would have warmed the world

65.   To love and worship and bright life!

66.   LUCIFER. [*suddenly appearing*] Not thou!

67.   Hadst thou more power the more wouldst thou misuse.

68.   FESTUS. Who art thou, pray? I saw thee not before.

69.   It seems as thou hadst grown out of the air.

70.   LUCIFER. Thou knowest me well. Though stranger to thine eye,

71.   I am not to thy heart.

72.   FESTUS. I know thee not.

73.   LUCIFER. Come nearer! Look on me! I am above thee;

74.   Beneath thee, and around thee, and before thee.

75.   FESTUS. Why, art thou all things, or dost go through all?

76.   A spirit, or embodied blast of air?

77.   I feel thou art a spirit.

78.   LUCIFER. Yea I am.

79.   FESTUS. I knew it! I am glad, yet tremble so.

80.   What hours upon hours have I longed for this,

81.   And hoped that thought or prayer might produce!

82.   I have besought the stars, with tears, to send

83.   A power unto me; and have set the clouds

---

1. Asher: in this instance, Ashur, head of the Assyrian pantheon, who is associated with solar imagery.

84. Until I thought I saw one coming; but
85. The shadowy giant alway thinned away.
86. And I was fated unimmortalized.
87. What shall I do? Oh! let me kneel to thee!
88. LUCIFER. Nay, rise! and I'll not say, for thine own sake,
89. That thou dost pray in private to the Devil.
90. FESTUS. Father of lies thou liest!
91. LUCIFER. I am he!
92. It is enough to make the Devil merry,
93. To think that men call on me momently,
94. Deeming me ever dungeoned fast in Hell;
95. Swearers and swaggerers jeer at my name;
96. And oft indeed it is a special jest
97. With witling gallants. Let me once appear!
98. Woe's me! they faint and shudder — pale and pray;
99. The burning oath which quivered on the lip,
100. Starts back and sears and blisters up the tongue;
101. Confusion ransacks the abandoned heart,
102. Quells the bold blood, and o'er the vaulted brow
103. Slips the white woman-hand. To judgment, ho!
104. The very pivot of the earth seems snapped;
105. And down they drop like ruins to repent.
106. Such be the bravery of mighty man!
107. FESTUS. I must be mad; or mine eye cheats my brain;
108. And this strange phantom comes from overthought,
109. Like the white lightning from a day too hot.
110. It must be so. But I will pass it.
111. LUCIFER. Stay!
112. FESTUS. Oh save me God! He is reality!
113. LUCIFER. And now thou kneel'st to Heaven. Fye, graceless boy!
114. Mocking thy Maker with a cast-off prayer;
115. For had not I the first fruits of thy faith?
116. FESTUS. Tempter, away! From all the crowds of life
117. Why single me? Why score the young green bole[2]
118. For fellage? Go! Am I the youngest, worst?
119. No! Light the fires of hell with other souls;
120. Mine shall not burn with thee!
121. LUCIFER. Thou judge'st harshly.
122. Can I not touch thee without slaying thee?

---

2. Bole: The trunk of a tree.

123. FESTUS. Why art thou here? What wouldst thou have
   with me?
124. LUCIFER. 'Fore all I would have gentle words and looks.
125. FESTUS. I pray thee, go!
126. LUCIFER. I cannot quit thee yet.
127. But why so sad? Wilt kneel to me again?
128. This leafy closet is most apt for prayer.
129. FESTUS. Yes; I will pray for thee and for myself.
130. LUCIFER. Waste not thy prayers! I scatter them: they reach
131. No further than thy breath — a yard or so.
132. And as for me, I heed them, need them not.
133. My nature God knows and hath fixed; and He
134. Recks little of the manners of the world;
135. Wicked He holdeth it and unrepentant.
136. FESTUS. Therefore the more some ought to pray.
137. LUCIFER. To blow
138. A kiss, a bubble and a prayer hath like
139. Effect and satisfaction.
140. FESTUS. Let me hence!
141. Go tell thy blasphemies and lies elsewhere.
142. Thou scatter prayer! Make me Thy minister
143. One moment God! that I may rid the world
144. For ever of its evil. Oh! Thine arm!
145. LUCIFER. Canst rid thyself?
146. FESTUS. Alas no. Get thee gone!
147. Can nought insult thee nor provoke thy flight?
148. LUCIFER. I laugh alike at ruin and redemption.
149. I am the one which knows nor hope nor fear;
150. Which ne'er knew good nor e'er can know the worst.
151. What thinkest thou can anger me, or harm?
152. FESTUS. Wherefore didst thou quit Hell? To
153. drag me there?
154. LUCIFER. Thou wilt not guess mine errand. Deem'st thou
   aught
155. Which God hath made all evil? Me He made.
156. Oft I do good; and thee to serve I come.
157. FESTUS. Did I not hear thee boast with thy last breath
158. Not to have known what good was?
159. LUCIFER. From myself
160. I know it not; yet God's will I must work.
161. I come I say to serve thee.
162. FESTUS. Well! I would
163. Thou never hadst; but speak thy purpose straight.

164. LUCIFER. I heard thy prayer at sunset. I was here.
165. I saw thy secret longings, unsaid thoughts,
166. Which prey upon the breast like night-fires on
167. A heath. I know thy heart by heart. I read
168. The tongue when still as well as when it moves.
169. And thou didst pray to God. Did He attend?
170. Or turn His eye from the great glass of things,
171. Wherein He worshippeth eternally
172. Himself, to thee one moment? He did not.
173. I tell thee nought He cares for men. I came
174. And come to proffer thee the earth; to set
175. Thee on a throne — the throne of will unbound —
176. To crown thy life with liberty and joy.
177. And make thee free and mighty even as I am!
178. FESTUS. I would not be as thou art for Hell's throne;
179. Add Earth's — add Heaven's!
180. LUCIFER. I knew thy proud high heart.
181. To test its worth and mark I held it brave,
182. In shape and being thus myself I came;
183. Not in disguise of opportunity —
184. Not as some silly toy which serves for most —
185. Not in the mask of lucre, lust nor power —
186. Not in a goblin size nor cherub form —
187. But as the soul of Hell and evil came I
188. With leave to give the kingdom of the world —
189. The freedom of thyself.
190. FESTUS. Good; prove thy powers.
191. LUCIFER. Do I not prove them? Who but I, that have
192. Immortal might o'er mine own mind, and o'er
193. All hearts and spirits of the living world,
194. Would share it with another, or forgo,
195. One hour, the great enjoyment of the whole?
196. And who but I give men what each loves best?
197. FESTUS. Open the Heavens and let me look on God!
198. Open my heart and let me see myself!
199. Then I'll believe thee.
200. LUCIFER. Thou shalt not believe
201. For that I give thee, but for that I am.
202. Believe me first; then I will prove myself.
203. Though sick I know thee of the joys of sense,
204. Yet those thou lovest most I will make pure,
205. And render worthy of thy love; unfilm them,
206. That so thou mayst not dally with the blind.

207. Thou shalt possess them to their very souls.
208. Pleasure and love and unimagined beauty;
209. All, all that be delicious, brilliant, great,
210. Of worldly things are mine, and mine to give.
211. FESTUS. What can be counted pleasure after love?
212. Like the young lion which hath once lapped blood,
213. The heart can ne'er be coaxed back to aught else.
214. LUCIFER. I will sublime it for thee all to bliss;
215. As yet it hath but made thee wretched.
216. FESTUS. Spirit,
217. It is not bliss I seek; I care not for it.
218. I am above the low delights of life.
219. The life I live is in a dark cold cavern.
220. Where I wander up and down, feeling for something
221. Which is to be — and must be — what, I know not;
222. But the incarnation of my destiny
223. Is nigh.
224. LUCIFER. It is thy fate which weighs upon thee.
225. Necessity sits on humanity,
226. Like to the world on Atlas' neck. 'T is this,
227. And the sultry sense of overdrawn life.
228. FESTUS.   True;
229. The worm of the world hath eaten out my heart.
230. LUCIFER. I will renew it in thee. It shall be
231. The bosom favourite of every beauty,
232. Even like a rosebud. Thou shalt render happy,
233. By naming who may love thee. Come with me.
234. FESTUS. I have a love on earth, and one in Heaven.
235. LUCIFER. Thou shalt love ten as others love but one!
236. FESTUS. Oh! I was glad when something in me said
237. Come, let us worship beauty! and I bowed;
238. And went about to find a shrine; but found
239. None that my soul, when seeing, said enough, to.
240. Many I met with where I put up prayers,
241. And had them more than answered; and at such
242. I worshipped, partly because others did;
243. Partly because I could not help myself.
244. But none of these were for me; and away
245. I went champing and choking in proud pain;
246. In a burning wrath that not a sea could slake.
247. So I betook me to the sounding sea;
248. And overheard its slumberous mutterings
249. Of a revenge on man; whereat almost

250. I gladdened, for I felt savage as the sea.
251. I had only one thing to behold, the sea.
252. I had only one thing to believe, I loved;
253. Until that lonesome sameness grew sublime
254. And darkly beautiful as death, when some
255. Bright soul regains its star-home, or as Heaven
256. Just when the stars falter forth, one by one,
257. Like the first words of love from a maiden's lips.
258. There are points from which we can command our life;
259. When the soul sweeps the future like a glass;
260. And coming things, full freighted with our fate,
261. Jut out, dark, on the offing of the mind.
262. Let them come! Many will go down in sight;
263. In the billow's joyous dash of death go down.
264. At last came love; not whence I sought nor thought it;
265. As on a ruined and bewildered wight[3]
266. Rises the roof he meant to have lost for ever.
267. On came the living vessel of all love;
268. Terrible in its beauty as a serpent,
269. Rode down upon me like a ship full sail
270. And bearing me before it, kept me up
271. Spite of the drowning speed at which we drave
272. On, on, until we sank both. Was not this love?
273. LUCIFER. Why, how can I tell? I am not in love;
274. But I have oft times heard mine angels call
275. Most piteously on their lost loves in Heaven;
276. And, as I suffer, I have seen them come;
277. Seen starlike faces peep between the clouds,
278. And Hell become a tolerable torment.
279. Some souls lose all things but the love of beauty;
280. And by that love they are redeemable;
281. For in love and beauty they acknowledge good;
282. And good is God — the great Necessity.
283. I have not told thee half I will do for thee.
284. All secrets thou shalt ken — all mysteries construe;
285. At nothing marvel. All the veins which stretch,
286. Unsearchable by human eyes, of lore
287. Most precious, most profound, to thine shall bare
288. And vulgar lie like dust. The world within,
289. The world above thee, and the dark domain,

3. Wight: A living creature in general.

290. Mine own thou shalt o'er rule; and he alone
291. Who rightly can esteem such high delights.
292. He only merits — he alone shall have.
293. FESTUS. And if I have shall I be happier?
294. What is pleasure? What, happiness?
295. LUCIFER. It is that
296. I vouchsafe to thee.
297. FESTUS. Am I tempted thus
298. Unto my fall?
299. LUCIFER. God wills or lets it be.
300. How thinkest thou?
301. FESTUS. That I will go with thee.
302. LUCIFER. From God I come.
303. FESTUS. I do believe thee, spirit.
304. He will not let thee harm me. Him I love,
305. And thee I fear not. I obey Him.
306. LUCIFER. Good.
307. Both time and case are urgent. Come away!
308. FESTUS. Give me a breathing-time to fortify,
309. Within myself, the promise I have made.
310. LUCIFER. Expect me, then, at midnight, here. Remember
311. That thou canst any time repent.
312. FESTUS. Ay, true.
     [*Goes*]
313. LUCIFER. Repentance never yet did aught on earth;
314. It undoes many good things. Of all men,
315. Heaven shield me from the wretch who can repent!

SCENE 3

[*Water and Wood — Midnight*]
[*FESTUS, alone*]

1. All things are calm, and fair, and passive. Earth
2. Looks as if lulled upon an angel's lap
3. Into a breathless dewy sleep: so still,

4.   That we can only say of things, they be!
5.   The lakelet now, no longer vexed with gusts,
6.   Replaces on her breast the pictured moon
7.   Pearled round with stars. Sweet imaged scene of time
8.   To come, perchance, when this vain life o'erspent,
9.   Earth may some purer beings' presence bear;
10. Mayhap even God may walk among His saints,
11. In eminence and brightness like yon moon,
12. Mildly outbeaming all the beads of light
13. Strung o'er night's proud dark brow. How strangely fair
14. Yon round still star, which looks half suffering from,
15. And half rejoicing in its own strong fire;
16. Making itself a lonelihood of light,
17. Like Deity, where'er in Heaven it dwells.
18. How can the beauty of material things
19. So win the heart and work upon the mind,
20. Unless like-natured with them? Are great things
21. And thoughts of the same blood? They have like effect.
22. LUCIFER. Why doubt on mind? What matter how we call
23. That which all feel to be their noblest part?
24. Even spirits have a better and a worse:
25. For every thing created must have form.
26. Passions they have, somewhat like thine; but less
27. Of grossness and that downwardness of soul
28. Which men have. It is true they have no earth;
29. For what they live on is above themselves.
30. FESTUS. There seems a sameness among things; for mind
31. And matter speak, in causes, of one God.
32. The inward and the outward worlds are like;
33. The pure and gross but differ in degree.
34. Tears, feeling's bright embodied form, are not
35. More pure than dewdrops, Nature's tears, which she
36. Sheds in her own breast for the fair which die.
37. The sun insists on gladness; but at night,
38. When he is gone, poor Nature loves to weep.
39. LUCIFER. There is less real difference among things
40. Than men imagine. They overlook the mass,
41. But fasten each on some particular crumb,
42. Because they feel that they can equal that,
43. Of doctrine, or belief, or party cause.
44. FESTUS. That is the madness of the world — and that
45. Would I remove.

46.   LUCIFER. It is imbecility,
47.   Not madness.
48.   FESTUS. Oh! the brave and good who serve
49.   A worthy cause can only one way fail;
50.   By perishing therein. Is it to fail?
51.   No; every great or good man's death is a step
52.   Firm set towards their end — the end of being;
53.   Which is the good of all and love of God.
54.   The world must have great minds, even as great spheres
55.   Or suns, to govern lesser restless minds,
56.   While they stand still and burn with life; to keep
57.   Them in their places, and to light and heat them.
58.   If I desire immortal life for aught,
59.   It is to learn the mystery of mind
60.   And somewhat more of God. Let others rule
61.   Systems or succour saints, if such things please;
62.   To live like light or die in light like dew,
63.   Either! I should be blest.
64.   LUCIFER.   It may not be.
65.   For as we do not see the sun himself,
66.   It is but the light about him, like a ring
67.   Of glory round the forehead of a saint, so
68.   God thou wilt never see. His unveiled love
69.   Were terrible, too much for man to meet.
70.   FESTUS. Men have a claim on God; and none who hath
71.   A heart of kindness, reverence and love,
72.   But dare look God in the face and ask His smile.
73.   He dwells in no fierce light — no cloud of flame;
74.   And if it were, Faith's eye can look through Hell,
75.   And through the solid world. We must all think
76.   On God. Yon water must reflect the sky.
77.   Midnight! Day hath too much light for us,
78.   To see things spiritually. Mind and Night
79.   Will meet, though in silence, like forbidden lovers,
80.   With whom to see each other's sacred form
81.   Must satisfy. The stillness of deep bliss,
82.   Sound as the silence of the high hill-top
83.   Where thunder finds no echo — like God's voice
84.   Upon the worlding's proud, cold, rocky heart —
85.   Fills full the sky; and the eye shares with Heaven
86.   That look, so like to feeling, which the bright
87.   And glorious things of Nature ever wear.

88. There is much to think and feel of things beyond
89. This earth; which lie, as we deem, upwards — far
90. From the day's glare and riot — they are Night's!
91. Oh! could we lift the future's sable shroud!
92. LUCIFER. Behind a shroud what shouldst thou see but death?
93. FESTUS. Spirit is like the thread whereon are strung
94. The beads or worlds of life. It may be here,
95. It may be there that I shall live again;
96. In yon strange world whose long nights know no star,
97. But seven fair maidlike moons attending him
98. Perfect his sky — perchance in one of those —
99. But live again I shall wherever it be.
100. We long to learn the future — love to guess.
101. LUCIFER. The science of the future is to man,
102. But what the shadow of the wind might be.
103. Such thoughts are vain and useless.
104. FESTUS.   Forced on us.
105. LUCIFER. All things are of necessity.
106. FESTUS.   Then best.
107. But the good are never fatalists. The bad
108. Alone act by necessity, they say.
109. LUCIFER. It matters not what men assume to be;
110. Or good, or bad, they are but what they are.
111. FESTUS. What is necessity? Are we, and thou,
112. And all the worlds, and the whole infinite
113. We cannot see, but working out God's thoughts?
114. And have we no self-action? Are all God?
115. LUCIFER. Then hath He sin and all absurdity.
116. FESTUS. Yet, if created Being have free-will,
117. Is it not wrong to judge it may traverse
118. God's own high will, and yet impossible
119. To think on't otherwise?
120. LUCIFER.   It may be so.
121. All creature wills, and all their ends and powers
122. Must come within the boundless scope of God's.
123. FESTUS. And all our powers are but weaknesses
124. To what we shall have, and to that God hath.
125. Doth not the wish, too, point the likelihood
126. Of life to come?
127. LUCIFER. Boys wish that they were kings
128. And so with thee. A deathless spirit's state,
129. Freed from gross form and bodily weightiness,

130. Seems kingly by the side of souls like thine.
131. And boys and men will likely both be balked.
132. What if it be, that spirit, after death,
133. Is loosed like flesh into its elements?
134. The worlds which man hath constellated, hold
135. No fellowship in nature; nor perchance
136. As he hath systematised life, mind and soul.
137. But sooth to say, I know not aught of this.
138. I have no kind. No nature like to me
139. Exists. And human spirits must at least
140. Sleep till the day of doom, if it ever be.
141. FESTUS. Hast never known one free from body?
142. LUCIFER. None.
143. FESTUS. Why seek then to destroy them?
144. LUCIFER. It is my part.
145. Let ruin bury ruin. Let it be
146. Woe here, woe there, woe, woe, be everywhere!
147. It is not for me to know, nor thee, the end
148. Of evil. I inflict and thou must bear.
149. The arrow knoweth not its end and aim.
150. And I keep rushing, ruining along
151. Like a great river rich with dead men's souls.
152. For if I knew, I might rejoice; and that
153. To me by Nature is forbidden. I know
154. Nor joy nor sorrow; but a changeless tone
155. Of sadness like the nightwind's is the strain
156. Of what I have of feeling. I am not
157. As other spirits, — but a solitude
158. Even to myself; I the sole spirit sole.
159. FESTUS. Can none of thine immortals answer me?
160. LUCIFER. None, mortal!
161. FESTUS. Where then is thy vaunted power?
162. LUCIFER. It is better seen as thus I stand apart
163. From all. Mortality is mine — the green
164. Unripened universe. But as the fruit
165. Matures, and world by world drops mellowed off
166. The wrinkling stalk of Time, as thine own race
167. Hath seen of stars now vanished — all is hid
168. From me. My part is done. What after comes
169. I know not more than thou.
170. FESTUS. Raise me a spirit!
171. Awake ye dead! out with the secret, death!

172. The grave hath no pride nor the rise-again.
173. Let each one bring the bane whereof he died.
174. Bring the man his, the maiden hers! Oh! half
175. Mankind are murderers of themselves or souls.
176. Yea, what is life but lingering suicide?
177. Wake, dead! Ye know the truth; yet there ye lie
178. All mingling, mouldering, perishing together
179. Like run sand in the hour-glass of old Time.
180. Death is the mad world's asylum. There is peace;
181. Destruction's quiet and equality.
182. Night brings out stars as sorrow shews us truths:
183. Though many, yet they help not; bright, they light not.
184. They are too late to serve us: and sad things
185. Are aye too true. We never see the stars
186. Till we can see nought but them. So with truth.
187. And yet if one would look down a deep well,
188. Even at noon, we might see those same stars
189. Far fairer than the blinding blue — the truth;
190. Probe the profound of thine own nature, man!
191. And thou may'st see reflected, e'en in life,
192. The worlds, the Heavens, the ages; by and by,
193. The coming come. Then welcome, world-eyed Truth!
194. But there are other eyes men better love
195. Than Truth's: for when we have her she is so cold,
196. And proud, we know not what to do with her.
197. We cannot understand her, cannot teach;
198. She makes us love her, but she loves not us;
199. And quits us as she came and looks back never.
200. Wherefore we fly to Fiction's warm embrace,
201. With her to relax and bask ourselves at ease;
202. And, in her loving and unhindering lap
203. Voluptuously lulled, we dream at most
204. On death and truth: she knows them, loves them not;
205. Therefore we hate them and deny them both.
206. Call up the dead!
207. LUCIFER. Let rest while rest they may!
208. For free from pain and from this world's wear and tear
209. It may be a relief to them to rot;
210. And it must be that at the day of doom,
211. If mortals should take up immortal life,
212. They will curse me with a thunder which shall shake
213. The sun from out the socket of his sphere.

214. The curse of all created. Think on it!
215. FESTUS. Those souls thou mean'st whom thou
216. Hast ruined, damned.
217. LUCIFER. Nor only those; when once the virgin bloom
218. Of soul is soiled — and rudely hath my hand
219. Swept o'er the swelling clusters of all life —
220. Little it matters whether crushed or touched
221. Scarcely: each speaks the spoiler hath been there.
222. The saved, the lost, shall curse me both alike:
223. God too shall curse me, and I, I, myself.
224. That curse is ever greatening — quick with hell;
225. The coming consummation of all woe.
226. FESTUS. O man, be happy! Die and cease for ever!
227. Why wear we not the shroud alway, that robe
228. Which speaks our rank on earth, our privilege?
229. To know I have a deathless soul I would lose it.
230. LUCIFER. Believest thou all I tell thee?
231. FESTUS.   All, I do.
232. Stringing the stars at random round her head,
233. Like a pearl network, there she sits — bright night!
234. I love night more than day — she is so lovely.
235. But I love night the most because she brings
236. My love to me in dreams which scarcely lie;
237. Oh! all but truth and lovelier oft than truth!
238. Let me have dreams like these, sweet Night, for ever,
239. When I shall wake no more; an endless dream
240. Of love and holy beauty 'mid the stars.
241. LUCIFER. I see thy heart and I will grant thy wish.
242. I have lied to thee. I have command over spirits.
243. Whom wilt thou that I call?
244. FESTUS.   Mine Angela!
245. LUCIFER. There is an Angel ever by thine hand.
246. What seest thou?
247. FESTUS. It is my love! It is she!
248. My glory! spirit! beauty, let me touch thee.
249. Nay, do not shrink back: well then I am wrong:
250. Thou didst not use to shrink from me, my love.
251. Angela! dost thou hear me? Speak to me.
252. And thou art there — looking alive and dead.
253. Thy beauty is then incorruptible.
254. I thought so, oft as I have looked on thee.
255. Thou art too much even now for me as once.

256. I cannot gather what I raved to say;
257. Nor why I had thee hither. Stay, sweet sprite!
258. Dear art thou to me now, as in that hour
259. When first Love's wave of feeling, spray-like broke
260. Into bright utterance, and we said we loved.
261. Yea, but I must come to thee. Move no more!
262. Art thou in death or Heaven or from the stars?
263. Have I done wrong in calling for thee thus?
264. What art thou? Speak, love; whisper me as wont
265. In the dear times gone bye; or durst thou not
266. Unfold the mystery of thine and mine
267. Own being? Was it Death who hushed thy lips?
268. Is his cold finger there still? Let me come!
269. She is not!
270. LUCIFER. And thou canst not bring her back.
271. FESTUS. I will not, cannot be without her. Call her!
272. LUCIFER. I call on spirits and I make them come:
273. But they depart according to their own will.
274. Another time and she shall speak with thee —
275. Ere long — and she shall shew thee where she dwells.
276. And how doth pass her immortality; —
277. If lengthening decay can so be called.
278. Can lines finite one way be infinite
279. Another? And yet such is deathlessness.
280. FESTUS. It is hard to deem that spirits cease, that thought
281. And feeling flesh-like perish in the dust.
282. Shall we know those again in a future state
283. Whom we have known and loved on earth? Say yes!
284. LUCIFER. The mind hath features as the body hath.
285. FESTUS. But is it mind which shall rerise?
286. LUCIFER. Man were
287. Not man without the mind he had in life.
288. FESTUS. Shall all defects of mind and fallacies
289. Of feeling be immortalized? all needs,
290. All joys, all sorrows, be again gone through,
291. Before the final crisis be imposed?
292. Shall Heaven but be old earth created new?
293. Or earth, treelike, transplanted into Heaven,
294. To flourish by the waters of all life,
295. And we within its shade, as heretofore.
296. Cropping its fruit, with life-seeds cored at heart?
297. LUCIFER. Man's nature, physical and psychical,

298. Will be together raised, changed, glorified;
299. And all shall be alike, like God; and all
300. Unlike each other, and themselves. The earth
301. Shall vanish from the thoughts of those she bore,
302. As have the idols of the olden time
303. From men's hearts of the present. All delight
304. And all desire, shall be with Heavenly things.
305. And the new nature God bestowed on man.
306. FESTUS. Then man shall be no more man, but an Angel.
307. LUCIFER. When he is dead and buried. What remains, —
308. That such an obscure, contradictory, thing
309. Should be perpetuated anywhere?
310. FESTUS. Oh! if God hates the flesh, why made He it
311. So beautiful that e'en its semblance maddens?
312. Am I to credit what I think I have seen?
313. Or am I suffering some deceit of thine?
314. LUCIFER. I am explaining, not deluding.
315. FESTUS. True.
316. Defining night by darkness, death by dust
317. I run the gauntlet of a file of doubts,
318. Each one of which down hurls me to the ground.
319. I ask a hundred reasons what they mean,
320. And every one points gravely to the ground,
321. With one hand, and to Heaven with the other.
322. In vain I shut mine eyes. Truth's burning beam
323. Forces them open, and when open, blinds them.
324. LUCIFER. Doubly unhappy!
325. FESTUS. I am too unhappy
326. To die; as some too way-worn cannot sleep.
327. Planets and suns, that set themselves on fire
328. By their own rapid self-revolvements, are
329. But like some hearts. Existence I despise.
330. The shape of man is wearisome; a bird's,
331. A worm's — a whirlwind's, I would change with aught.
332. Time! dash thine hour-glass down. Have done with this!
333. The course of Nature seems a course of Death,
334. And nothingness the sole substantial thing.
335. LUCIFER. Corruption springs from Light: 'tis the same power
336. Creates, preserves, destroys: the matter which
337. It works on, being one ever-changing form, —
338. The living and the dying and the dead.

339. FESTUS. I'll not believe a thing which I have known
340. Hell was made hell for me, and I am mad.
341. LUCIFER. True venom churns the froth out of the lips;
342. It works, and works like any waterwheel.
343. And she then was the maiden of thy heart.
344. Well, I have promised. Ye shall meet again.
345. FESTUS. I loved her for that she was beautiful;
346. And that to me she seemed to be all nature
347. And all varieties of things in one:
348. Would set at night in clouds of tears, and rise
349. All light and laughter in the morning: yea,
350. And that she never schooled within her breast
351. One thought or feeling, but gave holiday
352. To all; and that she made all even mine
353. In the communion of love: and we
354. Grew like each other for we loved each other —
355. She, mild and generous as the sun in spring;
356. And I, like earth all budding out with love.
357. LUCIFER. And then, love's old end, falsehood: nothing worse
      worse
358. I hope?
359. FESTUS. What's worse than falsehood? to deny
360. The god which is within us, and in all
361. Is love? Love hath as many vanities
362. As charms; and this, perchance, the chief of both:
363. To make our young heart's track upon the first,
364. And snowlike fall of feeling which overspreads
365. The bosom of the youthful maiden's mind,
366. More pure and fair than even its outward type.
367. If one did thus, was it from vanity?
368. Or thoughtlessness, or worse? Nay, let it pass.
369. The beautiful are never desolate;
370. But some one alway loves them — God or man.
371. If man abandons, God himself takes them.
372. And thus it was. She whom I once loved died.
373. The lightning loathes its cloud — the soul its clay.
374. Can I forget that hand I took in mine,
375. Pale as pale violets; that eye, where mind
376. And matter met alike divine? ah, no!
377. May God that moment judge me when I do!
378. Oh! she was fair: her nature once all spring.
379. And deadly beauty like a maiden sword;

380. Startlingly beautiful. I see her now!
381. Whatever thou art thy soul is in my mind;
382. Thy shadow hourly lengthens o'er my brain.
383. And peoples all its pictures with thyself.
384. Gone, not forgot — passed, not lost — thou shalt shine
385. In Heaven like a bright spot in the sun!
386. She said she wished to die, and so she died;
387. For, cloudlike, she poured out her love, which was
388. Her life, to freshen this parched heart. It was thus:
389. I said we were to part, but she said nothing.
390. There was no discord — it was music ceased —
391. Life's thrilling, bounding, bursting joy. She sate
392. Like a house-god, her hands fixed on her knee;
393. And her dark hair lay loose and long around her,
394. Through which her wild bright eye flashed like flint.
395. She spake not, moved not, but she looked the more,
396. As if her eye were action, speech and feeling.
397. I felt it all; and came and knelt beside her.
398. The electric touch solved both our souls together.
399. Then comes the feeling which unmakes, undoes;
400. Which tears the sealike soul up by the roots
401. And lashes it in scorn against the skies.
402. Twice did I madly swear to God, hand clenched,
403. That not even He nor death should tear her from me.
404. It is the saddest and the sorest sight
405. One's own love weeping; — but why call on God,
406. But that the feeling of the boundless bounds
407. All feeling, as the welkin doth the world?
408. It is this which ones us with the whole and God.
409. Then first we wept; then closed and clung together;
410. And my heart shook this building of my breast,
411. Like a live engine booming up and down.
412. She fell upon me like a snow-wreath thawing.
413. Never were bliss and beauty, love and woe,
414. Ravelled and twined together into madness,
415. As in that one wild hour; to which all else,
416. The past, is but a picture — that alone
417. Is real, and for ever there in front;
418. Making a black blank on one side of life
419. Like a blind eye. But after that I left her:
420. And only saw her once again alive.
421. LUCIFER. Well, shall we go?

422. FESTUS. This moment. I am ready.
423. Farewell ye dear old walks and trees! farewell
424. Ye waters! I have loved ye well. In youth
425. And childhood it hath been my life to drift
426. Across ye lightly as a leaf; or skim
427. Your waves in yon skiff, swallowlike; or lie
428. Like a loved locket on your sunny bosom.
429. Could I, like you, by looking in myself
430. Find mine own Heaven — farewell! Immortal, come!
431. The morning peeps her blue eye on the east.
432. LUCIFER. Think not so fondly as thy foolish race,
433. Imagining a Heaven from things without;
434. The picture on the passing wave call Heaven —
435. The wavelet, life — the sands beneath it, death;
436. Daily more seen till, lo! the bed is bare.
437. This fancy fools the world.
438. FESTUS. Let us away!

FESTUS AND LUCIFER ON THE MOUNTAIN AT SUNRISE

SCENE 4

[*A Mountain — Sunrise*]
[*FESTUS and LUCIFER*]

1.   FESTUS. Hail beauteous Earth! Gazing o'er thee, I all —
2.   Forget the bounds of being; and I long
3.   To fill thee, as a lover pines to blend
4.   Soul, passion, yea existence, with the fair
5.   Creature he calls his own. I ask for nought
6.   Before or after death but this, — to lie.
7.   And look, and live, and bask, and bless myself
8.   Upon thy broad bright bosom. From thee I
9.   Sprang, and to thee I turn, heart, arm and brain.
10.   Yes, I am all thine own. Thou art the sole
11.   Parent. To rock and river, plain and wood
12.   I cry, ye are my kin. While I, O Earth!
13.   Am but an atom of thee, and a breath,
14.   Passing unseen and unrecorded like
15.   The tiny throb here in my temple's pulse.
16.   Thou art for ever and the sacred bride
17.   Of heaven, — worthy the passion of our God.
18.   O! full of light, love, grace! — the grace of all
19.   Who owe to thee their life; thy Maker's love;
20.   His face's light. All thine rejoice in thee;
21.   Thou in thyself for aye; rolling through air
22.   As seraphs' song out of their trumpet lips
23.   Rolls round the skies of Heaven. See the sun!
24.   God's crest upon His azure shield the Heavens.
25.   Canst thou, a spirit, look upon him?
26.   LUCIFER. Ay.
27.   I led him from the void, where he was wrought.
28.   By this right hand, up to the glorious seat
29.   His brightness overshadows; built his throne
30.   On piles of gold; and laid his chambers on
31.   Beams of gold: wrapped a veil of fire around
32.   His face; and bade him reign and burn like me.

33.   There, ever since, sat warming into life
34.   These worlds as in a nest, he has and is.
35.   But fall he must. I have done, do, nought else
36.   From my first thought to this and to my last.
37.   No matter; it is beneath this mind of mine
38.   To reck of aught. I bear, have borne the ill
39.   Of ages, of eternities — and must.
40.   I care not. I shall sway the world as now,
41.   Which worse and worse sinks with me as I sink.
42.   Till finite souls evanish as a vapour;
43.   Till immortality, the proud thing, perish;
44.   And God alone be and eternity.
45.   Then will I clap my hands and cry to Him,
46.   I have done! Have Thy will now! There is none but Thee.
47.   I am the first created being. I
48.   Will be the last to perish and to die.
49.   FESTUS. Thou art a fit monitor, methinks, of pleasure.
50.   LUCIFER. To the high air sunshine and cloud are one;
51.   Pleasure and pain to me. Thou and the earth
52.   Alone feel these as different — for Ye
53.   Are under them — the Heavens and I above.
54.   FESTUS. But tell me, have ye scenes like this in Hell?
55.   LUCIFER. Nay, not in Heaven.
56.   FESTUS. What is Heaven? not the toys
57.   Of singing, love and music? such a place
58.   Were fit for women only.
59.   LUCIFER. Heaven is no place;
60.   Unless it be a place with God, allwhere.
61.   It is the being good — the knowing God —
62.   The consciousness of happiness and power;
63.   With knowledge which no spirit e'er can lose
64.   But doth increase in every state; and aught
65.   It most delights in the full leave to do.
66.   But why consume me with such questions? Why
67.   Add earth to Hell, in the great chain of worlds
68.   Which God in wrath hath bound about me?
69.   FESTUS. Why!
70.   'Twas therefore that I closed with thee, great Fiend!
71.   That thou mightst answer all things I proposed,
72.   Or bring me those who would do.
73.   LUCIFER. All these things
74.   Thou wilt know sometime, when to see and know

75. Are one; to see a thing and comprehend
76. The nature of it essentially; perceive
77. The reason and the science of its being,
78. And the relations with the universe
79. Of all things actual or possible,
80. Mortal, immortal, spiritual, gross.
81. This, when the spirit is made free of Heaven,
82. Is the divine result; proportioned still
83. To the intelligence as human; for
84. There are degrees in Heaven as everything,
85. By God's will. Unimaginable space
86. As full of suns as is earth's sun of atoms,
87. Faileth to match His boundless variousness;
88. And ever must do, though a thousand worlds,
89. As diverse from each other as is thine
90. From any of thy system's, were elanced[1]
91. Each minute into life unendingly.
92. All of yon worlds, and all who dwell in them.
93. Stand in diverse degrees of bliss and being.
94. Through the ten thousand times ten thousandth grade
95. Of blessedness, above this world's and man's
96. Ability to feel or to conceive,
97. The soul may pass and yet know nought of Heaven,
98. More than a dim and miniature reflection
99. Of its most bright infinity; — for God
100. Makes to each spirit its peculiar Heaven; —
101. And yet is Heaven a bright reality,
102. As this or any of yon worlds; a state
103. Where all is loveliness and power and love;
104. Where all sublimest qualities of mind,
105. Not infinite, are limited alone
106. By the surrounding Godhood, and where nought
107. But what produceth glory and delight,
108. To creature and Creator is; where all
109. Enjoy entire dominion o'er themselves,
110. Acts, feelings, thoughts, conditions, qualities.
111. Spirit and soul and mind; all under God,
112. For spirit is soul Deified; — while earth,
113. To the immortal vast, God-natured Spirit,

---

1. Elanced: Cast or thrown. *Obsolete* (*OED*).

114. Is but a spell, which having served to light,
115. A lamp, is cast into consuming fire.
116. FESTUS. And Hell? Is it nought but pits and chains and
      flames?
117. LUCIFER. An ever greatening sense of ill and woe.
118. Aye crushing down the soul, but filling never
119. Its infinite capacity of pain.
120. FESTUS. But human nature is not infinite,
121. And therefore cannot suffer endlessly.
122. LUCIFER. God may create in time what shall endure
123. Unto Eternity. With Him is no
124. Distinction, nor in that which is of Him.
125. FESTUS. Then is not soul of God, but man and earth.
126. Soul when made spirit is of earth no more.
127. Nor time, but of Eternity and Heaven.
128. 'Tis but when in the body, and bent down
129. To worldly ends, that human souls become
130. Objects of time, as most are, till the hour
131. Comes when the soul of man shall be made one
132. With God's spirit; and where shall woe be then?
133. Where, sin? where, suffering? when the mortal soul
134. Shall be Divinised and eternised by
135. God's very spirit put upon it?
136. LUCIFER.   How
137. Can souls begotten to predestined doom,
138. From and before all worlds, be deemed of earth?
139. FESTUS. Things spiritual, as belonging God,
140. Are known unto Him, and predestined from
141. Eternity, nor these alone; but Flesh
142. Forms not nor does it need the care of Fate.
143. LUCIFER. The object of eternal knowledge must
144. Have like existence.
145. FESTUS.   Then it cannot be
146. Bound unto torment; that would be to bring
147. Torture on godlike essence.
148. LUCIFER. Hast not heard,
149. How thine existence here, on earth, is but
150. The dark and narrow section of a life
151. Which was with God, long ere the sun was lit,
152. And shall be yet, when all the bold bright stars
153. Are dark as death-dust — Immortality
154. And Wisdom tending thee on either hand,

155. Thy divine sisters? But do thou believe
156. E'en what thou wilt. It matters not to me.
157. FESTUS. Is it the nature or the deed of God
158. To render finite follies infinite,
159. Or to eternise sin and death in fire?
160. For so long as the punishment endures,
161. The crime lasts. Were it not for thy presence
162. Spirit! I would not deem Hell were.
163. LUCIFER.   Let not
164. My presence pass for more than it is worth,
165. I pray, nor yet my absence. Trust me, I
166. Could wish, with thee, that Hell were blotted out
167. Of utmost space. 'Tis man himself aye makes
168. His own God and his hell. But this is truth.
169. FESTUS. The truth is perilous never to the true
170. Nor knowledge to the wise; and to the fool,
171. And to the false, error and truth alike.
172. Error is worse than ignorance. But say: —
173. How can eternal punishment be due
174. To temporal offences, to a pulse
175. Of momentary madness?
176. LUCIFER.   Pardon me.
177. Sin is not temporary. Nothing is,
178. Of spiritual nature, but hath cause
179. Immortal and immortal end in all,
180. As spirits. Therefore till the soul shall be
181. By grace redeified, as is the soul,
182. So is the sin, for ever before God.
183. FESTUS. Sin is not of the spirit, but of that
184. Which blindeth spirit, heart and brain.
185. LUCIFER. Believe so.
186. The law of all the worlds is retribution.
187. FESTUS. But is it so of God?
188. LUCIFER. The laws of Heaven
189. Are not of earth; there law is liberty.
190. FESTUS. Thou thundercloud of spirits, darkening
191. The skies and wrecking earth! Could I hate men
192. How I should joy with thee, even as an eagle,
193. Nigh famished, in the fellowship of storms;
194. But I still love them. What will come of men?
195. LUCIFER. Whatever may, perdition is their meed.
196. Were Heaven dispeopled for a ministry

197. To warn them of their ways; were thou and I
198. To monish[2] them; were Heaven, and Earth, and Hell
199. To preach at once, they still would mock and jeer
200. As now; but never repent until too late;
201. Until the everlasting hour had struck.
202. FESTUS. Men might be better if we better deemed
203. Of them. The worst way to improve the world
204. Is to condemn it. Men may overget
205. Delusion — not despair.
206. LUCIFER. Why love mankind?
207. The affections are thy system's weaknesses;
208. The wasteful outlets of self-maintenance.
209. FESTUS. The wild flower's tendril, proof of feebleness,
210. Proves strength; and so we fling our feelings out,
211. The tendrils of the heart, to bear us up.
212. O Earth! how drear to think to tear oneself,
213. Even for an hour, from looks like this of thine;
214. From features, oh! so fair; to quit for aye
215. The luxury of thy side. Why, why art thou
216. Thus glorious, and 'twere not to sate the soul,
217. And chide us for the senseless dream of Heaven?
218. The still strong stream sweeps onward to its end,
219. Like one of the great purposes of God;
220. Or like, may be, a soul like mine to Him.
221. Along yon deep blue vein upon thy bosom,
222. Earth! I could float for ever. See it there —
223. Winding among its green and smiling isles,
224. Like Charity amidst her children dear;
225. Or Peace, rejoicing in her olive wreaths,
226. And gladdening as she glides along the lands,
227. LUCIFER. And yet all this must end — must pass; drop down
228. Oblivion like a pebble in a pit:
229. For God shall lay His hand upon the earth,
230. And crush it up like a red leaf.
231. FESTUS. Not be?
232. I cannot root the thought, nor hold it firm.
233. LUCIFER. This same sweet world which thou wouldst fondly deem
234. Eternal, may be; which I soon shall see

2. Monish: To admonish.

235. Destruction suck back as the tide a shell.
236. FESTUS. It will not be yet. I'll woo thee, world, again,
237. And revel in thy loveliness and love.
238. I have a heart with room for every joy:
239. And since we must part sometime, while I may,
240. I'll quaff the nectar in thy flowers, and press
241. The richest clusters of thy luscious fruit
242. Into the cup of my desires. I know
243. My years are numbered not in units yet.
244. But I cannot live unless I love and am loved;
245. Unless I have the young and beautiful
246. Bound up like pictures in my book of life.
247. It is the intensest vanity alone
248. Which makes us bear with life. Some seem to live,
249. Whose hearts are like those unenlightened stars
250. Of the first darkness — lifeless, timeless, useless —
251. With nothing but a cold night air about them;
252. Not suns — not planets — darkness organized:
253. Orbs of a desert darkness: with not one soul
254. To light its watchfire in the wilderness,
255. And civilize the solitude one moment.
256. There are such seemingly; but how or why
257. They live I know not. This to me is life;
258. That if life be a burden, I will join
259. To make it but the burden of a song:
260. I hate the world's coarse thought. And this is life;
261. To watch young beauty's budlike feelings burst
262. And load the soul with love; — as that pale flower,
263. Which opes at eve, spreads sudden on the dark
264. Its yellow bloom, and sinks the air down with sweets.
265. Let Heaven take all that's good — Hell all that's foul;
266. Leave us the lovely! and we will ask no more.
267. LUCIFER. To me it seems time all should end. The sky
268. Grows grey. It is not so bright nor blue as once.
269. Well I remember, as it were yesterday,
270. When earth and Heaven went happy, hand in hand,
271. With all the morning dew of youth about them;
272. With the bright unworldly hearts of youth and truth
273. And the maiden bosoms of the beautiful: —
274. Ere earth sinned, or the pure indignant Heavens
275. Retreated high, nigh God; when earth was all
276. A creeping mass alive with shapeless things:

277. And when there were but three things in the world —
278. Monsters, mountains and water: before age
279. Had thickened the eyes of stars; and while the sea,
280. Rejoicing like a ring of saints round God,
281. Or Heaven on Heaven about some newborn sun.
282. In its sublime samesoundingness, laughed out
283. And cried not I! Like God I never rest.
284. FESTUS. God hath his rest; earth hers. Let me have mine.
285. Yet must I look on thee, fair scene, again,
286. Ere I depart. The glory of the world
287. Is on all hands. In one encircling ken,
288. I gaze on river, sea, isle, continent,
289. Mountain, and wood, and wild, and fire-lipped hill,
290. And lake, and golden plain, and sun, and Heaven,
291. Where the stars brightly die, whose death is day;
292. City and port and palace, ships and tents,
293. Lie massed and mapped before me. All is here.
294. The elements of the world are at my feet.
295. Above me and about me. Now would I
296. Be and do somewhat beside that I am.
297. Canst thou not give me some ethereal slave,
298. Of the pure essence of an element —
299. Such as my bondless brain hath oft times drawn
300. In the divine insanity of dreams —
301. To stand before me and obey me, spirit?
302. LUCIFER. Call out, and see if aught arise to thee.
303. FESTUS. Green dewy Earth, who standest at my feet,
304. Singing and pouring sunshine on thy head,
305. As näiad native water, speak to me!
306. I am thy son. Canst thou not now, as once,
307. Bring forth some being dearer, liker to thee
308. Than is my race, — Titan or tiny fay,
309. Stream-nymph or wood-nymph? She hath ceased to speak,
310. Like God, except in thunder, or to look
311. Unless in lightning. Miracles, with earth,
312. Are out of fashion as with Heaven.
313. LUCIFER. More's
314. The pity. Call elsewhere! Old Earth is hard
315. Of hearing, maybe.
316. FESTUS. I beseech thee, Sea!
317. Tossing thy wavy locks in sparkling play,
318. Like to a child awakening with the light

319. To laughter. Canst not thou disgulph[3] for me,
320. From thy deep bosom, deep as Heaven is high,
321. Of all thy sea-gods one, or sea-maids?
322. LUCIFER. None!
323. FESTUS. I half despair. Fire! that art slumbering there,
324. Like some stern warrior in his rocky fort,
325. After the vast invasion of the world,
326. Hast not some flaming imp, or messenger
327. Of empyrean element, to whom,
328. In virtue of his nature, are both known
329. The secrets of the burning, central, void below,
330. And yon bright Heaven, out of whose aëry fire
331. Are wrought the forms of angels and the thrones?
332. Hast none at hand to do my bidding? Come!
333. Breathe out a spirit for me! One I ask
334. That shall be with me always, as a friend,
335. And not like thee, who despotisest o'er
336. The heart thou seek'st to serve. I must be free.
337. LUCIFER. All finite souls must serve; their widest sway
338. Is but the rule of service. This fair earth
339. Which thou dost boast so much of, why, thou see'st
340. 'T is but the particoloured, scummy dross
341. Of the original element wherefrom
342. The fiery worlds were framed.
343. FESTUS. Air! and thou, Wind!
344. Which art the unseen similitude of God
345. The Spirit, His most meet and mightiest sign;
346. The earth with all her steadfastness and strength,
347. Sustaining all, and bound about with chains
348. Of mountains, as is life with mercies, ranging round
349. With all her sister orbs the whole of Heaven,
350. Is not so like the unlikenable One
351. As thou. Ocean is less divine than thee;
352. For although all but limitless, it is yet
353. Visible, many a land not visiting.
354. But thou art, Lovelike, everywhere; o'er earth,
355. O'er ocean triumphing, and aye with clouds,
356. That like the ghost of ocean's billows roll,
357. Decking or darkening Heaven. The sun's light

---

3. Disgulph: To send forth (as from a gulf).

358. Floweth and ebbeth daily like the tides;
359. The moon's doth grow or lessen, night by night;
360. The stirless stars shine forth by fits and hide,
361. And our companion planets come and go; —
362. And all are known, their laws and liberties.
363. But no man can foreset[4] thy coming, none
364. Reason against thy going; thou art free,
365. The type impalpable of Spirit, thou.
366. Thunder is but a momentary thing,
367. Like a world's deathrattle, and is like death;
368. And lightning, like the blaze of sin, can blind
369. Only and slay. But what are these to thee,
370. In thine all-present variousness? Now,
371. So light as not to wake the snowiest down
372. Upon the dove's breast, winning her bright way
373. Calm and sublime as Grace unto the soul,
374. Towards her far native grove; now, stern and strong
375. As ordnance, overturning tree and tower;
376. Cooling the white brows of the peaks of fire —
377. Turning the sea's broad furrows like a plough, —
378. Fanning the fruitening plains, breathing the sweets
379. Of meadows, wandering o'er blinding snows,
380. And sands like sea-beds and the streets of cities,
381. Where men as garnered grain lie heaped together;
382. Freshening the cheeks, and mingling oft the locks
383. Of youth and beauty 'neath star-speaking eve;
384. Swelling the pride of canvas, or, in wrath,
385. Scattering the fleets of nations like dead leaves:
386. In all, the same o'ermastering sightless force,
387. Bowing the highest things of earth to earth,
388. And lifting up the dust unto the stars;
389. Fatelike, confounding reason, and like God's
390. Spirit, conferring life upon the world, —
391. Midst all corruption incorruptible;
392. Monarch of all the elements! hast thou
393. No soft Eolian sylph, with sightless wing,
394. To spare a mortal for an hour?
395. LUCIFER. Peace, peace!
396. All nature knows that I am with thee here,

---

4. Foreset: To set in front, put to the front. *Obsolete (OED)*.

397. And that thou need'st no minor minister.
398. To thee I personate the world — its powers.
399. Beliefs, and doubts and practices.
400. FESTUS. Are all
401. Mine invocations fruitless, then?
402. LUCIFER. They are.
403. Let us enjoy the world!
404. FESTUS. If 'twas God's will
405. That thou shouldst visit me He shall not send
406. Temptation to my heart in vain. Sweet world!
407. We all still cling to thee. Though thou thyself
408. Passest away, yet men will hanker about thee,
409. Like mad ones by their moping haunts. Men pass,
410. Cleaving to things themselves which pass away,
411. Like leaves on waves. Thus all things pass for ever,
412. Save mind and the mind's meed.
413. LUCIFER. Let us too pass!

FESTUS AND CLARA IN THE GARDEN

SCENE 5

[Alcove and Garden]
[FESTUS and CLARA]

1. FESTUS. What happy things are youth and love and sunshine!
2. How sweet to feel the sun upon the heart!
3. To know it is lighting up the rosy blood,
4. And with all joyous feelings, prism-hued,
5. Making the dark breast shine like a spar grot.[1]
6. We walk among the sunbeams as with angels.
7. CLARA. Yes, there are feelings so serene and sweet,
8. Coming and going with a musical lightness,
9. That they can make amends for their passingness,
10. And balance God's condition to decay;
11. As yon light fleecy cloudlet floating along,
12. Like golden down from some high angel's wing,
13. Breaks but relieves and beautifies the blue.
14. I wonder if ever I could love another.
15. How I should start to see upon the sward
16. A shadow not thine own armlinked with mine!
17. See, here is a garland I have bound for thee.
18. FESTUS. Nay, crown thyself; it will suit thee better, love.
19. Place wreaths of everlasting flowers on tombs,
20. And deck with fading beauties forms that fade.
21. Put it away, — I will no crown save this:
22. And could the line of dust which here I trace
23. Upon my brow but warrant dust beneath —
24. And nothing more — or could this bubble frame,
25. Informed with soul, lashed from the stream of life
26. By its own impetus, but burst at once,
27. And vanish part on high and part below,
28. I would be happy, nor would envy death.

---

1. Grot: A fragment or particle. *Obsolete* (*OED*).

29.   Could I, like Heaven's bolt, earthing quench myself,
30.   This moment would I burn me out a grave.
31.   Might I but be as many years in dying
32.   As I have lived — that might be some relief.
33.   CLARA. What canst thou mean?
34.   FESTUS. Mean? Is there not a future?
35.   The past, the present and the coming, curse each!
36.   The future, curse it!
37.   CLARA. Shall we not ever live
38.   And love as now?
39.   FESTUS. Ay, live I fear we must.
40.   CLARA. And love: because we then are happiest
41.   We shall lack nothing having love: and we,
42.   We must be happy everywhere — we two!
43.   For spiritual life is great and clear,
44.   And self-continuous as the changeless sea,
45.   Rolling the same in every age as now;
46.   Whether o'er mountain tops, where only snow
47.   Dwells, and the sunbeam hurries coldly by;
48.   Or o'er the vales, as now, of some old world
49.   Older than ancient man's. As is the sea's,
50.   So is the life of spirit, and the kind.
51.   And then with natures raised, refined and freed
52.   From these poor forms, our days shall pass in peace
53.   And love; no thought of human littleness
54.   Shall cross our high calm souls, shining and pure
55.   As the gold gates of Heaven. Like some deep lake
56.   Upon a mountain summit they shall rest,
57.   High above cloud and storm of life like this,
58.   All peace and power, and passionless purity;
59.   Or if a thought of other troubled times
60.   Ruffle it for a moment, it shall pass
61.   Like a chance raindrop on its heavenward face.
62.   I love to meditate on bliss to come.
63.   Not that I am unhappy here; but that
64.   The hope of higher bliss may rectify
65.   The lower feeling which we now enjoy.
66.   This life, this world is not enough for us;
67.   They are nothing to the measure of our mind.
68.   For place we must have space; for time we must have
69.   Eternity; and for a spirit godhood.
70.   FESTUS. Mind means not happiness: power is not good.

71. CLARA. True bliss is to be found in holy life;
72. In charity to man — in love to God:
73. Why should such duties cease, such powers decay?
74. Are they not worthy of a deathless state —
75. A boundless scope — a high uplifted life?
76. Man, like the air-born eagle who remains
77. On earth only to feed and sleep and die;
78. But whose delight is on his lonely wing,
79. Wide sweeping as a mind, to force the skies
80. High as the lightfall ere, begirt with clouds,
81. It dash this nether world — immortal man
82. Rushes aloft, right upwards, into Heaven.
83. O faith of Christ, sole honour of the world!
84. FESTUS. What know men of religion, save its forms?
85. CLARA. True faith nor biddeth nor abideth form.
86. The bended knee, the eye uplift is all
87. Which man need render; all which God can bear.
88. What to the faith are forms? A passing speck,
89. A crow upon the sky. God's worship is
90. That only He inspires; and His bright words,
91. Writ in the red-leaved volume of the heart,
92. Return to him in prayer, as dew to Heaven.
93. Our proper good we rarely seek or make;
94. Mindless of our immortal powers and their
95. Immortal end, as is the pearl of its worth,
96. The rose its scent, the wave its purity.
97. FESTUS. Come, we will quit these saddening themes. Wilt sing
98. To me? for I am gloomy; and I love
99. Thy singing, sacred as the sound of hymns,
100. On some bright Sabbath morning, on the moor,
101. Where all is still save praise; and where hard by
102. The ripe grain shakes its bright beard in the sun;
103. The wild bee hums more solemnly; the deep sky,
104. The fresh green grass, the sun, and sunny brook,
105. All look as if they knew the day, the hour;
106. And felt with man the need and joy of thanks.
107. CLARA. I cannot sing the lightsome lays of love.
108. Many thou know'st who can; but none that can
109. Love thee as I do — for I love thy soul;
110. And I would save it, Festus! Listen then:
111.   Is Heaven a place where pearly streams

112.	Glide over silver sand?
113.	Like childhood's rosy dazzling dreams
114.	Of some far faery land?
115.	Is Heaven a clime where diamond dews
116.	Glitter on fadeless flowers?
117.	And mirth and music ring aloud
118.	From amaranthine bowers?
119.	Ah no; not such, not such is Heaven!
120.	Surpassing far all these;
121.	Such cannot be the guerdon[2] given
122.	Man's wearied soul to please.
123.	For saint and sinner here below
124.	Such vain to be have proved:
125.	And the pure spirit will despise
126.	Whatever the sense hath loved.
127.	There we shall dwell with Sire and Son,
128.	And with the mother-maid,
129.	And with the Holy Spirit, one:
130.	In glory like arrayed:
131.	And not to one created thing
132.	Shall our embrace be given;
133.	But all our joy shall be in God;
134.	For only God is Heaven.
135.	FESTUS. I know that thou dost love me. I in vain
136.	Strive to love aught of earth or Heaven but thee.
137.	Thou art my first, last, only love; nor shall
138.	Another even tempt my heart. Like stars,
139.	A thousand sweet and bright and wondrous fair,
140.	A thousand deathless miracles of beauty,
141.	They shall ever pass at all but eyeless distance,
142.	And never mix with thy love; but be lost
143.	All, meanly in its moonlike lustrousness.
144.	CLARA. How still the air is! the tree tops stir not:
145.	But stand and peer on Heaven's bright face as though
146.	It slept and they were loving it: they would not
147.	Have the skies see them move for summers; would they?
148.	See that sweet cloud! It is watching us, I am certain.
149.	What have we here to make thee stay one second?
150.	Away! thy sisters wait thee in the west,

2. Guerdon: A reward.

151. The blushing bridesmaids of the sun and sea.
152. I would I were like thee, thou little cloud,
153. Ever to live in Heaven: or seeking earth
154. To let my spirit down in drops of love:
155. To sleep with night upon her dewy lap;
156. And, the next dawn, back with the sun to Heaven;
157. And so on through eternity, sweet cloud!
158. I cannot but think that some senseless things
159. Are happy. Often and often have I watched
160. A gossamer line sighing itself along
161. The air, as it seemed; and so thin, thin and bright,
162. Looking as woven in a loom of light,
163. That I have envied it, I have, and followed; —
164. Oft watched the seabird's down blown o'er the wave,
165. Now touching it, now spirited aloft,
166. Now out of sight, now seen, — till in some bright fringe
167. Of streamy foam, as in a cage, at last
168. A playful death it dies, and mourned its death.
169. FESTUS. But thinkest thou the future is a state
170. More positive than this; or that it can be
171. Aught but another present, full of cares,
172. And toils, perhaps, and duties; that the soul
173. Will ever be more nigh to God than now,
174. Save as may seem from mind's debility:
175. Just as the sun, from weakness of the eye,
176. And the illusions made by matter's forms,
177. Seems hot and wearied resting on the hill?
178. It would be well, I think, to live as though
179. No more were to be looked for; to be good
180. Because it is best, here; and leave hope and fear
181. For lives below ourselves. If earth persuades not
182. That I owe prayer and praise and love to God,
183. While all I have He gives, will Heaven? will Hell?
184. No; neither, never!
185. CLARA. I think not all with thee.
186. Have I not heard thee hint of spirit-friends?
187. Where are they now?
188. FESTUS. Ah! close at hand, mayhap.
189. I have a might immortal; and can ken
190. With angels. Neither sky nor night nor earth
191. Hinder me. Through the forms of things I see
192. Their essences; and thus, even now, behold —

193. But where I cannot show to thee — far round,
194. Nature herself — the whole effect of God.
195. Mind, matter, motion, heat, time, love, and life,
196. And death and immortality; those chief
197. And first-born giants all are there; all parts,
198. All limbs of her their mother; she is all.
199. CLARA. And what does she?
200. FESTUS. Produce: it is her life.
201. The three named last, life, death, deathlessness,
202. Glide in elliptic path round all things made —
203. For none save God can fill the perfect whole:
204. And are but to eternity as is
205. The horizon to the world. At certain points
206. Each seems the other; now, the three are one;
207. Now, all invisible; and now, as first,
208. Moving in measured round.
209. CLARA. How look these beings?
210. FESTUS. Ah! Life looks gaily and gloomily in turns;
211. With a brow chequered like the sward, by leaves
212. Between which the light glints; and she, careless, wears
213. A wreath of flowers — part faded and part fresh.
214. And Death is beautiful and sad and still:
215. She seems too happy; happier far than life —
216. In but one feeling, apathy: and on
217. Her chill white brow frosts bright, a braid of snow.
218. CLARA. And Immortality?
219. FESTUS. She looks alone;
220. As though she would not know her sisterhood.
221. And on her brow a diadem of fire,
222. Matched by the conflagration of her eye,
223. Outflaming even that eye which in my sleep
224. Beams close upon me till it bursts from sheer
225. O'erstrainedness of sight, burns.
226. CLARA. What do they?
227. FESTUS. Each strives to win me to herself.
228. CLARA. How?
229. FESTUS.   Death
230. Opens her sweet white arms and whispers, peace!
231. Come say thy sorrows in this bosom! This
232. Will never close against thee; and my heart,
233. Though cold, cannot be colder much than man's.
234. Come! All this soon must end; and soon the world

235. Shall perish leaf by leaf, and land by land;
236. Flower by flower — flood by flood — and hill
237. By hill, away; Oh! come, come! Let us die.
238. CLARA. Say that thou wilt not die!
239. FESTUS. Nay, I love Death.
240. But Immortality, with finger spired,
241. Points to a distant, giant world — and says
242. There, there is my home! Live along with me!
243. CLARA. Canst see that world?
244. FESTUS. Just — a huge shadowy shape;
245. It looks a disembodied orb — the ghost
246. Of some great sphere which God hath stricken dead:
247. Or like a world which God hath thought — not made.
248. CLARA. Follow her Festus! Does she speak again?
249. FESTUS. She never speaks but once; and now, in scorn,
250. Points to this dim, dwarfed, misbegotten sphere.
251. CLARA. Why let her pass?
252. FESTUS. That is the great world-question.
253. Life would not part with me; and from her brow
254. Tearing her wreath of passion-flowers, she flung
255. It round my neck and dared me struggle then.
256. I never could destroy a flower: and none
257. But fairest hands like thine can grace with me
258. The plucking of a rose. And Life, sweet Life!
259. Vowed she would crop the world for me and lay it
260. Herself before my feet even as a flower.
261. And when I felt that flower contained thyself —
262. One drop within its nectary kept for me,
263. I lost all count of those strange sisters three;
264. And where they be I know not. But I see
265. One who is more to me.
266. CLARA.   I know not how
267. Thou hast this power and knowledge. I but hope
268. It comes from good hands; if it be not thine
269. Own force of mind. It is much less what we do
270. Than what we think, which fits us for the future.
271. I wish we had a little world to ourselves;
272. With none but we two on it.
273. FESTUS.   And if God
274. Gave us a star, what could we do with it
275. But that we could without it? Wish it not!
276. CLARA. I'll not wish then for stars; but I could love

277.   Some peaceful spot where we might dwell unknown,
278.   Where home-born joys might nestle round our hearts
279.   As swallows round our roofs — and blend their sweets
280.   Like dewy-tangled flowerets in one bed.
281.   FESTUS. The sweetest joy, the wildest woe is love;
282.   The taint of earth, the odour of the skies,
283.   Is in it. Would that I were aught but man!
284.   The death of brutes, the immortality
285.   Of fiend or angel, better seems than all
286.   The doubtful prospects of our painted dust.
287.   And all Morality can teach is — Bear!
288.   And all Religion can inspire is — Hope!
289.   CLARA. It is enough. Fruition of the fruit
290.   Of the great Tree of Life, is not for earth.
291.   Stars are its fruit, its lightest leaf is life.
292.   The heart hath many sorrows beside love,
293.   Yea many as the veins which visit it.
294.   The love of aught on earth is not its chief
295.   Nor ought to be. Inclusive of them all
296.   There is the one main sorrow, life; — for what
297.   Can spirit, severed from the great one, God,
298.   Feel but a grievous longing to rejoin
299.   Its infinite — its author — and its end?
300.   And yet is life a thing to be beloved,
301.   And honored holily, and bravely borne.
302.   A man's life may be all ease, and his death
303.   By some dark chance, unthought of agony: —
304.   Or life may be all suffering, and decease
305.   A flower-like sleep; — or both be full of woe,
306.   Or each comparatively painless. Blame
307.   Not God for inequalities like these!
308.   They may be justified. How canst thou know?
309.   They may be only seeming. Canst thou judge?
310.   They may be done away with utterly
311.   By loving, fearing, knowing God the Truth.
312.   In all distress of spirit, grief of heart,
313.   Bodily agony, or mental woe,
314.   Rebuffs and vain assumptions of the world,
315.   Or the poor spite of weak and wicked souls,
316.   Think thou on God! Think what he underwent
317.   And did for us as man. Weigh thou thy cross
318.   With Christ's, and judge which were the heavier.

319.   Joy even in thine anguish! — such was His,
320.   But measurelessly more. Thy suffering
321.   Assimilateth thee to Him. Rejoice!
322.   Think upon what thou shalt be! Think on God!
323.   Then ask thyself, what is the world, and all
324.   Its mountainous inequalities? Ah, what!
325.   Are not all equal as dust-atomies?
326.   FESTUS. My soul's orb darkens as a sudden star,
327.   Which having for a time exhausted earth
328.   And half the Heavens of wonder, mortally
329.   Passes for ever, not eclipsed, consumed; —
330.   All but a cloudy vapour darkening there,
331.   The very spot in space it once illumed.
332.   Once to myself I seemed a mount of light;
333.   But now, a pit of night. — No more of this!
334.   Here have I lain all day in this green nook,
335.   Shaded by larch and hornbeam, ash and yew;
336.   A living well and runnel at my feet,
337.   And wild flowers, dancing to some delicate air;
338.   An urn-topped column and its ivy wreath
339.   Skirting my sight as thus I lie and look
340.   Upon the blue, unchanging, sacred skies:
341.   And thou, too, gentle Clara, by my side,
342.   With lightsome brow and beaming eye, and bright
343.   Long glorious locks, which drop upon thy cheek
344.   Like goldhued cloudflakes on the rosy morn.
345.   Oh! when the heart is full of sweets to overflowing,
346.   And ringing to the music of its love,
347.   Who but an angel or an hypocrite
348.   Could speak or think of happier states?
349.   CLARA.   Farewell!
350.   Remember what thou saidst about the stars. [*goes*]
351.   FESTUS. Oh! why was woman made so fair? or man
352.   So weak as to see that more than one had beauty?
353.   It is impossible to love but one.
354.   And yet I dare not love thee as I could;
355.   For all that the heart most longs for and deserves,
356.   Passes the soonest and most utterly.
357.   The moral of the world's great fable, life.
358.   All we enjoy seems given to deceive,
359.   Or may be, undeceive us; who cares which?
360.   And when the sum is done, and we have proved it,

361. Why work it over and over still again?
362. I am not what I would be. Hear me, God!
363. And speak to me in thine invisible likeness
364. The wind, as once of yore. Let me be pure!
365. Oh! I wish I was a pure child again.
366. As ere the clear could trouble me: when life
367. Was sweet and calm as is a sister's kiss;
368. And not the wild and whirlwind touch of passion,
369. Which though it hardly light upon the lip,
370. With breathless swiftness sucks the soul out of sight
371. So that we lose it, and all thought of it.
372. What is this life wherein Thou hast founded me,
373. But a bright wheel which burns itself away,
374. Benighting even night with its grim limbs,
375. When it hath done and fainted into darkness?
376. Flesh is but fiction, and it flies away;
377. The gaunt and ghastly thing we bear about us
378. And which we hate and fear to look upon
379. Is truth; in death's dark likeness limned[3] — no more.

SCENE 6

[*Anywhere*]
[*FESTUS and LUCIFER meeting*]

1. FESTUS. God hath refused me: wilt thou do it for me?
2. Or shall I end with both? remake myself?
3. LUCIFER. Now that is the one thing which I cannot do.
4. Am I not open with thee? why choose that?
5. FESTUS. Because I will it. Thou art bound to obey.
6. LUCIFER. The world bears marks of my obedience.
7. FESTUS. Off! I am torn to pieces. Let me try
8. And gather up myself into a man,

---

3. Limned: Illuminated. *Obsolete* (*OED*).

9.   As once I was. I have done with thee! Dost hear?

10.   LUCIFER. Thou canst not mean this.

11.   FESTUS. Once for all — I do.

12.   LUCIFER. It is men who are deceivers — not the Devil.

13.   The first and worst of all frauds is to cheat

14.   Oneself. All sin is easy after that.

15.   FESTUS. I feel that we must part: part now or never;

16.   And I had rather of the two it were now.

17.   LUCIFER. This is my last walk through my favourite world:

18.   And I had hoped to have enjoyed it with thee.

19.   For thee I quitted Hell; for thee I warped

20.   And shrivelled up my soul into a man:

21.   For thee I shed my shining wings; for thee

22.   Put on this mask of flesh, this mockery

23.   Of motion, and this seeming shape like thine.

24.   And by my woe, I swear that were I now,

25.   For thy false heart, to give my spirit spring,

26.   I would scatter soul and body both to Hell,

27.   And let one burn the other.

28.   FESTUS.   If thou darest!

29.   Lift but the finger of a thought of ill

30.   Against me, and — thou durst not. Mark, we part.

31.   LUCIFER. Well; as thou wilt. Remember that thy heart

32.   Will shed its pleasures as thine eye its tears;

33.   And both leave loathsome furrows.

34.   FESTUS.   Thinkest thou

35.   That I will have no pleasures without thee,

36.   Who marrest all thou makest and even more?

37.   LUCIFER. Thou canst not; save indeed some poor trite thing

38.   Called moderation, every one can have;

39.   And modesty, God knows, is suffering.

40.   FESTUS. Now will I prove thee liar for that word,

41.   And that the very vastest out of Hell.

42.   With perfect condemnation I abjure

43.   My soul; my nature doth abhor itself;

44.   I have a soul to spare!   [*goes*]

45.   LUCIFER.   A hundred, I.

46.   I have him yet: for he is mine to tempt.

47.   Gold hath the hue of hell flames: but for him

48.   I will lay some brilliant and delicious lure

49.   Which shall be worth perdition to a seraph.

50.   Most men glide quietly and deeply down:

51.   Some seek the bottom like a cataract.
52.   Now he shall find it, seek it how he will.
53.   None ever went without once taking breath.
54.   It is passion plunges men into mine arms;
55.   But it matters not; Hell burns before them all.
56.   It is by Hell-light they do their chiefest deeds;
57.   And by Hell-light they shine unto each other;
58.   And Hell through life's thick fog glares red and round;
59.   And but for Hell they would grope in utter dark.

SCENE 7

[*A Country Town — Market-place — Noon*]
[*LUCIFER and FESTUS*]

1.   LUCIFER. These be the toils and cares of mighty men!
2.   Earth's vermin are as fit to fill her thrones
3.   As these high Heaven's bright seats.
4.   FESTUS. Men's callings all
5.   Are mean and vain; their wishes more so: oft
6.   The man is bettered by his part or place.
7.   How slight a chance may raise or sink a soul!
8.   LUCIFER. What men call accident is God's own part.
9.   He lets ye work your will — it is His own:
10.   But that ye mean not, know not, do not. He doth.
11.   FESTUS. What is life worth without a heart to feel
12.   The great and lovely, and the poetry
13.   And sacredness of things? for all things are
14.   Sacred, — the eye of God is on them all,
15.   And hallows all unto it. It is fine
16.   To stand upon some lofty mountain-thought
17.   And feel the spirit stretch into a view;
18.   To joy in what might be if will and power
19.   For good would work together but one hour.
20.   Yet millions never think a noble thought:

21. But with brute hate of brightness bay a mind
22. Which drives the darkness out of them, like hounds.
23. Throw but a false glare round them, and in shoals
24. They rush upon perdition: that's the race.
25. What charm is in this world-scene to such minds
26. Blinded by dust? What can they do in Heaven,
27. A state of spiritual means and ends?
28. Thus must I doubt — perpetually doubt.
29. LUCIFER. Who never doubted never half believed.
30. Where doubt there truth is — 'tis her shadow. I
31. Declare unto thee that the past is not.
32. I have looked over all life, yet never seen
33. The age that had been. Why then fear or dream
34. About the future? Nothing but what is, is;
35. Else God were not the Maker that He seems,
36. As constant in creating as in being.
37. Embrace the present! Let the future pass.
38. Plague not thyself about a future. That
39. Only which comes direct from God, His spirit,
40. Is deathless. Nature gravitates without
41. Effort; and so all mortal natures fall
42. Deathwards. All aspiration is a toil;
43. But inspiration cometh from above,
44. And is no labour. The earth's inborn strength
45. Could never lift her up to yon stars, whence
46. She fell; nor human soul, by native worth,
47. Claim Heaven as birthright, more than man may call
48. Cloudland his home. The soul's inheritance,
49. Its birth-place, and its death-place, is of earth,
50. Until God maketh earth and soul anew;
51. The one like Heaven, the other like Himself.
52. So shall the new Creation come at once;
53. Sin, the dead branch upon the tree of Life,
54. Shall be cut off for ever; and all souls
55. Concluded in God's boundless amnesty.
56. FESTUS. Thou windest and unwindest faith at will.
57. What am I to believe?
58. LUCIFER. Thou mayst believe
59. But that which thou art forced to.
60. FESTUS.   Then I feel
61. That instinct of immortal life in me,
62. Which prompts me to provide for it.

 63. LUCIFER.   Perhaps.
 64. FESTUS. Man hath a knowledge of a time to come —
 65. His most important knowledge: the weight lies
 66. Nearest the short end; and the world depends
 67. Upon what is to be. I would deny
 68. The present, if the future. Oh! there is
 69. A life to come, or all's a dream.
 70. LUCIFER. And all
 71. May be a dream. Thou seest in thine, men, deeds.
 72. Clear, moving, full of speech and order; then
 73. Why may not all this world be but a dream
 74. Of God's? Fear not! Some morning God may waken.
 75. FESTUS. I would it were. This life's a mystery.
 76. The value of a thought cannot be told;
 77. But it is clearly worth a thousand lives
 78. Like many men's. And yet men love to live
 79. As if mere life were worth their living for.
 80. What but perdition will it be to most?
 81. Life's more than breath and the quick round of blood
 82. It is a great spirit and a busy heart.
 83. The coward and the small in soul scarce do live.
 84. One generous feeling — one great thought — one deed
 85. Of good, ere night, would make life longer seem
 86. Than if each year might number a thousand days, —
 87. Spent as is this by nations of mankind.
 88. We live in deeds, not years; in thoughts, not breaths;
 89. In feelings, not in figures on a dial.
 90. We should count time by heart-throbs. He most lives
 91. Who thinks most — feels the noblest — acts the best.
 92. Life's but a means unto an end — that end,
 93. Beginning, mean and end to all things — God.
 94. The dead have all the glory of the world.
 95. Why will we live and not be glorious?
 96. We never can be deathless till we die.
 97. It is the dead win battles. And the breath
 98. Of those who through the world drive like a wedge,
 99. Tearing earth's empires up, nears death so close
100. It dims his well-worn scythe. But no? the brave
101. Die never. Being deathless, they but change
102. Their country's arms for more — their country's heart.
103. Give then the dead their due; it is they who saved us.
104. The rapid and the deep — the fall, the gulph

105. Have likenesses in feeling and in life.
106. And life, so varied, hath more loveliness
107. In one day than a creeping century
108. Of sameness. But youth loves and lives on change
109. Till the soul sighs for sameness; which at last
110. Becomes variety, and takes its place.
111. Yet some will last to die out thought by thought,
112. And power by power, and limb of mind by limb.
113. Like lambs upon a gay device of glass,
114. Till all of soul that's left be dry and dark;
115. Till even the burden of some ninety years
116. Hath crashed into them like a rock; shattered
117. Their system as if ninety suns had rushed
118. To ruin earth — or Heaven had rained its stars;
119. Till they become, like scrolls, unreadable
120. Through[1] dust and mould. Can they be cleaned and read?
121. Do human spirits wax and wane like moons?
122. LUCIFER. The eye dims and the heart gets old and slow;
123. The lithe limb stiffens, and the sun-hued locks
124. Thin themselves off, or whitely wither; — still
125. Ages not spirit, even in one point,
126. Immeasurably small; from orb to orb,
127. In ever rising radiance, shining like
128. The sun upon the thousand lands of earth.
129. Look at the medley, motley throng we meet!
130. Some smiling — frowning some; their cares and joys
131. Alike not worth a thought — some sauntering slowly
132. As if destruction never could o'ertake them;
133. Some hurrying on as fearing judgment swift
134. Should trip the heels of Death and seize them living.
135. FESTUS. Grief hallows hearts even while it ages heads;
136. And much hot grief, in youth, forces up life
137. With power which too soon ripens and which drops.
138. [*A funeral passes.*]
139. Whose funeral is this ye follow, friends?
140. LUCIFER. Would ye have grief, let me come! I am woe.
141. MOURNER. We want no grief: Festus! she died of grief.
142. FESTUS. Did ye say she died? oh! I knew her then.
143. Set down the body; let me look upon her!

---

1. Through: Here, a silent emendation of 'Throught' as printed in the original. *OED* has 'Origin uncertain; perhaps the same word as 'through'.

144. Now, Son of God! what dost Thou now in heaven
145. While one so beautiful lies earthening here?
146. I will give up the future for the past;
147. The winged spirit and the starry home
148. If Thou wilt let her live, and make me love.
149. MOURNER. She was a lock of Heaven which Heaven
         gave earth.
150. And took again, because unworthy of her.
151. FESTUS. Her air was an immortal's; I have seen
152. Stars look on it with feeling; and her eye.
153. Wherever she went, it won her way like wine.
154. Men bowed to it as to the lifted Host.
155. How could I be so cruel? Who but I?
156. And now, corruption, come; sit; feast thyself!
157. This is the choicest banquet thou hast been at.
158. Thou art my happier, only rival: thou
159. Who takest love from the living — life from beauty —
160. Beauty from death — whole robber of the world!
161. MOURNER. The moment after thou desertedst her
162. A cloud came over the prospect of her life;
163. And I foresaw how evening would set in,
164. Early and dark and deadly. She was true.
165. FESTUS. Did I not love thee too? pure! perfect thing!
166. This is a soul I see and not a body.
167. Go, beauty, rest for aye; go, starry eyes,
168. And lips like rosebuds peeping out of snow;
169. Go, breast love-filled as a boat's sail with wind,
170. Leaping from wave to wave as leaps a child
171. Thoughtless o'er grassy graves; go, locks, which have
172. The golden embrowmnent of a lion's eye!
173. Yet one more look; farewell, thou well and fair!
174. All who but loved thee shall be deathless. Nought
175. Named but with thee can perish. Thou and Death
176. Have made each other purer, lovelier, seem,
177. Like snow and moonlight. Never more for thee
178. Let eyes be swollen like streams with latter rains!
179. To die were rapture having lived with thee.
180. Thy soul hath passed out of a bodily Heaven
181. Into a spiritual. Rest for aye! —
182. Pure as the dead, in life; the dead are holy.
183. I would I were among them. Let us pass!
184. Living is but a habit; and I mean
185. To break myself of it soon.

186. LUCIFER. Too soon thou canst not.
187. Men heed not of the day, how nigh none knows,
188. Which brings the consummation of the world.
189. But in my ear the old machine already
190. Begins to grate. They would not credit warning,
191. Or I would up and cry, Repent! I will.
192. Here is a fair gathering and I feel moved.
193. Mortals, Repent! the world is nigh to its end;
194. On its last legs and desperately sick.
195. See ye not how it reels round all day long?
196. BOYS. Oh! here's a ranter. Come, here's fun.
197. I know the church service by heart.
198. BYSTANDER. Be off! Amen!
199. You'll serve the church by keeping out of it.
200. LUCIFER. I am a preacher come to tell ye truth.
201. I tell ye too there is no time to be lost;
202. So fold your souls up neatly, while ye may;
203. Direct to God in Heaven; or some one else
204. May seize them, seal them, send them — you know where.
205. The world must end. I weep to think of it.
206. But you, you laugh! I knew ye would. I know
207. Men never will be wise till they are fools
208. For ever. Laugh away! The time will come.
209. When tears of fire are trickling from your eyes,
210. Ye will blame yourselves for having laughed at me.
211. I warn ye, men: prepare! repent! be saved!
212. I warn ye, not because I love, but know ye.
213. God will dissolve the world, as she of old
214. Her pearl, within His cup and swallow ye
215. In wrath: although to taste ye would be poison,
216. And death and suicide to aught but God.
217. Again I warn ye. Save himself who can!
218. Do ye not oft begin to seek salvation?
219. You? you? and fail, as oft, to find? Sink? Cease?
220. And shall I tell ye, brethren, why ye fail
221. Once and for ever? why, there is no past;
222. And the future is the fiction of a fiction;
223. The present moment is eternity;
224. It is that ye have sucked corruption from the world
225. Like milk from your own mothers: it is in
226. Your soul-blood and your soul-bones. Earth does not
227. Wean one out of a thousand sons to Heaven.

228. Beginnings are alike: it is ends which differ.
229. One drop falls, lasts, and dries up — but a drop;
230. Another begins a river: and one thought
231. Settles a life, an immortality:
232. And that one thought ye will not take to good.
233. Now I will tell ye just one other truth:
234. Ye hate the truth as snails salt — it dissolves ye,
235. Body and soul — but I don't mind. So, now:
236. Up to this moment ye are all, each, damned.
237. What are ye now? still damned! It will be the same
238. To-morrow — and the next day — and the next:
239. Till some fine morning ye will wake in fire.
240. Ye see I do not mince the truth for ye.
241. Belike ye think your lives will dribble out
242. As brooks in summer dry up. Let us see!
243. Try: dike them up: they stagnate — thicken — scum.
244. That would make life worse than death. Well, let go!
245. Where are ye then? for life, like water, will
246. Find its last level: what level? The grave.
247. It is but a fall of five feet after all;
248. That cannot hurt ye; it is but just enough
249. To work the wheel of life; so work away!
250. Ye may think that I do not know the terms
251. And treasures whereupon ye live so high.
252. But I know more than most men, modestly
253. Speaking. I know I am lost, and ye too. God
254. Could only save me by destroying me;
255. So that I have no advantage over you.
256. And therefore think ye will the rather bear
257. One of your own state to advise for ye
258. Now don't you envy me, good folks, I pray, —
259. Envy's a coal comes hissing hot from hell.
260. Twill be such coals will burn ye by the way.
261. Your other preachers first think they are safe.
262. Now I say, broadly, I am the worst among ye;
263. And God knows I have no need to wrong myself,
264. Nor you. I boast not of it, but as truth:
265. It is little to be proud of, credit me.
266. What is salvation? What is safety? Think!
267. Who wants to know? Does any?
268. THE CROWD. All of us.
269. LUCIFER. Then I will not tell ye. You shall wait until

270. Some angel come and stir your stagnant souls:
271. Then plunge into yourselves and rise redeemed.
272. Come, I'll unroll your hearts and read them to ye.
273. To say ye live is but to say ye have souls,
274. That ye have paid for them and mean to play them,
275. Till some brave pleasure wins the golden stake,
276. And rakes it up to death as to a bank.
277. Ye live and die on what your souls will fetch;
278. And all are of different prices: therefore Hell
279. Cannot well bargain for mankind in gross;
280. But each soul must be purchased, one by one.
281. This it is makes men rate themselves so high:
282. While truly ye are worth little; but to God
283. Ye are worth more than to yourselves. By sin
284. Ye wreak your spite against God — that ye know:
285. And knowing, will it. But I pray, I beg,
286. Act with some smack of justice to your Maker,
287. If not unto yourselves. Do! It is enough
288. To make the very Devil chide mankind —
289. Such baseness, such unthankfulness! Why he
290. Thanks God he is no worse. You don't do that.
291. I say be just to God. Leave off these airs.
292. Know your place — speak to God — and say, for once,
293. Go first, Lord! Take your finger off your eye!
294. It blocks the universe and God from sight.
295. Think ye your souls are worth nothing to God?
296. Are they so small? What can be great with God?
297. What will ye weigh against the Lord? Yourselves?
298. Bring out your balance: get in, man by man:
299. Add earth, heaven, hell, the universe; that's all
300. God puts his finger in the other scale,
301. And up we bounce, a bubble. Nought is great
302. Nor small with God — for none but He can make
303. The atom indivisible, and none
304. But He can make a world: He counts the orbs,
305. He counts the atoms of the universe.
306. And makes both equal — both are infinite.
307. Giving God honor, never underrate
308. Yourselves: after Him ye are everything.
309. But mind! God's more than everything; He is God.
310. And what of me? No, us? no! I mean the Devil?
311. Why see ye not he goes before both you
312. And God? Men say — as proud as Lucifer —

313. Pray who would not be proud with such a train?
314. Hath he not all the honor of the earth?
315. Why Mammon sits before a million hearths
316. Where God is bolted out from every house.
317. Well might He say He cometh as a thief;
318. For He will break your bars and burst your doors
319. Which slammed against Him once, and turn ye out,
320. Roofless and shivering, 'neath the doom-storm; Heaven
321. Shall crack above ye like a bell in fire,
322. And bury all beneath its shining shards.
323. He calls: ye hear not. Lo! he comes — ye see not.
324. No; ye are deaf as a dead adder's ear:
325. No; ye are blind as never bat was blind,
326. With a burning bloodshot blindness of the heart;
327. A swimming, swollen senselessness of soul.
328. Listen! Whom love ye most? Why him to whom
329. Ye in your turn are dearest. Need I name?
330. Oh no! But all are devils to themselves;
331. And every man his own great foe. Hell gets
332. Only the gleanings; earth hath the full wain;²
333. And hell is merry at its harvest home.
334. But ye are generous to sin and grudge
335. The gleaners nothing; ask them, push them in.
336. Let not an ear, a grain of sin be lost;
337. Gather it, grind it up; it is our bread:
338. We should be ashamed to waste the gifts of God.
339. Why is the world so mad? Why runs it thus
340. Raving and howling round the universe?
341. Because the Devil bit it from the birth!
342. The fault is all with him. Fear nothing, friends!
343. It is fear which beds the far to-come with fire
344. As the sun does the west: but the sun sets;
345. Well; still ye tremble — tremble, first at light,
346. Then darkness. Tremble! ye dare not believe.
347. No, cowards! sooner than believe ye would die;
348. Die with the black lie flapping on your lips
349. Like the soot-flake upon a burning bar.
350. Be merry, happy if ye can: think never
351. Of him who slays your souls, nor Him who saves.
352. There is time enough for that when ye are a-dying.

2. Wain: Profit, advantage. *Obsolete* (*OED*).

353. Keep your old ways! It matters not this once.
354. Be brave! Ye are not men whom meat and wine
355. Serve to remind but of the sacrament;
356. To whom sweet shapes and tantalizing smiles
357. Bring up the Devil and the ten commandments —
358. And so on — but I said the world must end.
359. I am sorry; it is such a pleasant world:
360. With all its faults it is perfect — to a fault:
361. And you, of course, end with it. Now how long
362. Will the world take to die? I know ye place
363. Great faith upon death-bed repentances;
364. The suddener the better. I know ye often
365. Begin to think of praying and repenting;
366. But second thoughts come and ye are worse than ever;
367. As over new white snow a filthy thaw.
368. Ye do amaze me verily. How long
369. Will ye take heart on your own wickedness,
370. And God's forbearance? Have ye cast it up?
371. Come now; the year and month, day, hour and minute,
372. Sin's golden cycle. Do ye know how long
373. Exactly Heaven will grant ye? how long God, —
374. Who when he had slain the world and wasted it,
375. Hung up His bow in Heaven, as in his hall
376. A warrior after battle — will yet bear
377. Your contumely and scorn of His best gifts, —
378. Man's mockery of man? But never mind!
379. Some of us are magnificently good,
380. And hold the head up high like a giraffe;
381. You, in particular, and you — and you.
382. Good men are here and there, I know; but then, —
383. You must excuse me if I mention this —
384. My duty is to tell it you — the world,
385. Like a black block of marble, jagged with white,
386. As with a vein of lightning petrified,
387. Looks blacker than without such; looks in truth,
388. So gross the heathen, gross the Christian too —
389. Like the original darkness of void space,
390. Hardened. Instead of justice, love and grace,
391. Each worth to man the mission of a God,
392. Injustice, hate, uncharitableness,
393. Triequal reign round earth, a Trinity of Hell.
394. Ye think ye never can be bad enough:

395. And as ye sink in sin, ye rise in hope.
396. And let the worst come to the worsts you say,
397. There always will be time to turn ourselves,
398. And cry for half an hour or so to God:
399. Salvation, sure, is not so very hard —
400. It need not take one long; and half an hour
401. Is quite as much as we can spare for it.
402. We have no time for pleasures. Business! business!
403. No! ye shall perish sudden and unsaved.
404. The priest shall, dipping, die. Can man save man?
405. Is water God? The counsellor, wise fool!
406. Drop down amid his quirks and sacred lies —
407. The judge, while dooming unto death some wretch,
408. Shall meet at once his own death, doom, and judge.
409. The doctor, watch in hand, and patient's pulse,
410. Shall feel his own heart cease its beats — and fall:
411. Professors shall spin out, and students strain
412. Their brains no more; art, science, toil shall cease.
413. The world shall stand still with a rending jar,
414. As though it struck at sea. The halls where sit
415. The heads of nations shall be dumb with death.
416. The ship shall after her own plummet sink,
417. And sound the sea herself and depths of death.
418. At the first turn Death shall cut off the thief,
419. And dash the gold bag in his yellow brain.
420. The gambler, reckoning gains, shall drop a piece;
421. Stoop down and there see death; — look up, there God.
422. The wanton, temporizing with decay,
423. And qualifying every line which vice
424. Writes bluntly on the brow, inviting scorn,
425. Shall pale through plastered red: and the loose, low sot
426. See clear, for once, through his misty, o'erbrimmed eye.
427. The just, if there be any, die in prayer.
428. Death shall be every where among your marts,
429. And giving bills which no man may decline —
430. Drafts upon Hell one moment after date.
431. Then shall your outcries tremble amid the stars:
432. Terrors shall be about ye like a wind:
433. And fears come down upon ye like a house.
434. FESTUS. Yon man looks frightened.
435. LUCIFER. Then it is time to stop.
436. I hope I have done no good. He will soon forget

437. His soul. Flesh soaks it up as sponge does water.
438. Now wait! I will rub them backwards like a cat;
439. And you shall see them spit and sparkle up.
440. Let us suppose a case, friends! You are men;
441. And there is God! and I will be the Devil.
442. Very well. I am the Devil.
443. ONE [*says*].   I think you are.
444. You look as if you lived on buttered thunder.
445. LUCIFER. Nay, be not wroth. Ye would crucify the Devil,
446. I do believe, if he a moment vexed you.
447. I know well which ye choose: but choose again!
448. Time or eternity? Speak, Hell or Heaven?
449. THE CROWD. He's a mad ranter: down with him! —
450. FESTUS. Let him be!
451. LUCIFER. Stand by me, Festus, and I will by thee.
452. Why, God and man! this is the second time
453. That I have run for my life.
454. FESTUS.   Nay, nay, come back!
455. They will not harm thee: they would chair thee round
456. The market-place, knew they but whom thou art.
457. Peace, there my friends! one minute; let us pray!
458. Grant us, oh God! that in thy holy love
459. The universal people of the world
460. May grow more great and happy every day;
461. Mightier, wiser, humbler, too, towards Thee.
462. And that all ranks, all classes, callings, states
463. Of life, so far as such seem right to Thee,
464. May mingle into one, like sister trees,
465. And so in one stem flourish: — that all laws
466. And powers of government be based and used
467. In good and for the people's sake; — that each
468. May feel himself of consequence to all,
469. And act as though all saw him; — that the whole,
470. The mass of every nation may so do
471. As is most worthy of the next to God;
472. For a whole people's souls, each one worth more
473. Than a mere world of matter, make combined,
474. A something godlike — something like to Thee.
475. We pray thee for the welfare of all men.
476. Let monarchs who love truth and freedom feel
477. The happiness of safety and respect
478. From those they rule, and guardianship from Thee.
479. Let them remember they are set on thrones

480. As representatives, not substitutes
481. Of nations, to implead with God and man.
482. Let tyrants who hate truth, or fear the free,
483. Know that to rule in slavery and error,
484. For the mere ends of personal pomp and power,
485. Is such a sin as doth deserve a hell
486. To itself sole. Let both remember, Lord!
487. They are but things like-natured with all nations;
488. That mountains issue out of plains, and not
489. Plains out of mountains, and so likewise kings
490. Are of the people, not the people of kings.
491. And let all feel, the rulers and the ruled,
492. All classes and all countries, that the world
493. Is Thy great halidom;[3] that Thou art King,
494. Lord! only owner and possessor. Grant
495. That nations may now see, it is not kings.
496. Nor priests they need fear so much as themselves;
497. That if they keep but true to themselves, and free,
498. Sober, enlightened, godly — mortal men
499. Become impassible as air, one great
500. And indestructible substance as the sea.
501. Let all on thrones and judgment-seats reflect
502. How dreadful Thy revenge through nations is
503. On those who wrong them; but do Thou grant, Lord!
504. That when wrongs are to be redressed, such may
505. Be done with mildness, speed, and firmness, not
506. With violence or hate, whereby one wrong
507. Translates another — both to Thee abhorrent.
508. The bells of time are ringing changes fast.
509. Grant, Lord! that each fresh peal may usher in
510. An era of advancement, that each change
511. Prove an effectual, lasting, happy gain.
512. And we beseech Thee, overrule, oh God!
513. All civil contests to the good of all;
514. All party and religious difference
515. To honourable ends, whether secured
516. Or lost; and let all strife, political
517. Or social, spring from conscientious aims,
518. And have a generous self-ennobling end,
519. Man's good and Thine own glory in view always!

3. Halidom: Holiness, sanctity. *Obsolete* (*OED*).

520. The best may then fail and the worst succeed
521. Alike with honour. We beseech Thee, Lord!
522. For bodily strength, but more especially
523. For the soul's health and safety. We entreat thee
524. In thy great mercy to decrease our wants,
525. And add autumnal increase to the comforts
526. Which tend to keep men innocent, and load
527. Their hearts with thanks to Thee as trees in bearing: —
528. The blessings of friends, families, and homes,
529. And kindnesses of kindred. And we pray
530. That men may rule themselves in faith in God,
531. In charity to each other, and in hope
532. Of their own souls' salvation: — that the mass,
533. The millions in all nations may be trained,
534. From their youth upwards, in a nobler mode,
535. To loftier and more liberal ends. We pray
536. Above all things, Lord! that all men be free
537. From bondage, whether of the mind or body; —
538. The bondage of religious bigotry,
539. And bald antiquity, servility
540. Of thought or speech to rank and power; be all
541. Free as they ought to be in mind and soul
542. As well as by state-birthright; — and that Mind,
543. Time's giant pupil, may right soon attain
544. Majority, and speak and act for himself!
545. Incline Thou to our prayers, and grant, oh Lord!
546. That all may have enough, and some safe mean
547. Of worldly goods and honours, by degrees,
548. Take place, if practicable, in the fitness
549. And fulness of Thy time. And we beseech Thee,
550. That Truth no more be gagged, nor conscience dungeoned,
551. Nor science be impeached of godlessness,
552. Nor faith be circumscribed, which as to Thee,
553. And the soul's self affairs is infinite;
554. But that all men may have due liberty
555. To speak an honest mind, in every land,
556. Encouragement to study, leave to act
557. As conscience orders. We entreat Thee, Lord!
558. For Thy Son's sake to take away reproach
559. Of all kinds from Thy church, and all temptation
560. Of pomp or power political, that none
561. May err in the end for which they were appointed
562. To any of its orders, low or high;

563. And no ambition, of a worldly cast,
564. Leaven the love of souls unto whose care
565. They feel propelled by Thy most holy spirit.
566. Be every church established, Lord! in truth.
567. Let all who preach the word, live by the word,
568. In moderate estate; and in Thy church, —
569. One, universal, and invisible
570. World-wards, yet manifest unto itself,
571. May it seem good, dear Saviour, in Thy sight,
572. That orders be distinguished, not by wealth,
573. But piety and power of teaching souls.
574. Equalise labour, Lord! and recompense.
575. Let not a hundred humble pastors starve,
576. In this or any land of Christendom,
577. While one or two, impalaced, mitred, throned
578. And banqueted, burlesque if not blaspheme
579. The holy penury of the Son of God;
580. The fastings, the foot-wanderings, and the preachings
581. Of Christ and His first followers. Oh that the Son
582. Might come again! There should be no more war,
583. No more want, no more sickness; with a touch,
584. He should cure all disease, and with a word,
585. All sin; and with a look to Heaven, a prayer,
586. Provide bread for a million at a time.
587. But till that perfect advent grant us, Lord!
588. That all good institutions, orders, claims,
589. Charitably proposed, or in the aid
590. Of Thy divine foundation, may much prosper,
591. And more of them be raised and nobly filled; —
592. That Thy word may be taught throughout all lands,
593. And save souls daily to the thrones of Heaven! —
594. And we entreat Thee, that all men whom Thou
595. Hast gifted with great minds may love Thee well,
596. And praise Thee for their powers, and use them most
597. Humbly and holily, and, lever-like,
598. Act but in lifting up the mass of mind
599. About them; knowing well that they shall be
600. Questioned by Thee of deeds the pen hath done,
601. Or caused, or glozed;[4] inspire them with delight
602. And power to treat of noble themes and things,

---

4. Glozed: Made glozes or glosses upon; discoursed upon, expounded, interpreted. *Obsolete* (*OED*).

603. Worthily, and to leave the low and mean —
604. Things born of vice or day-lived fashion, in
605. Their naked native folly: — make them know
606. Fine thoughts are wealth, for the right use of which
607. Men are and ought to be accountable, —
608. If not to Thee, to those they influence:
609. Grant this we pray Thee, and that all who read,
610. Or utter noble thoughts, may make them theirs,
611. And thank God for them, to the betterment
612. Of their succeeding life; — that all who lead
613. The general sense and taste, too apt, perchance,
614. To be led, keep in mind the mighty good
615. They may achieve, and are in conscience, bound,
616. And duty, to attempt unceasingly
617. To compass. Grant us, All-maintaining Sire!
618. That all the great mechanic aids to toil
619. Man's skill hath formed, found, rendered, — whether used
620. In multiplying works of mind, or aught
621. To obviate the thousand wants of life,
622. May much avail to human welfare now
623. And in all ages, henceforth and for ever!
624. Let their effect be, Lord! to lighten labour,
625. And give more room to mind, and leave the poor
626. Some time for self-improvement. Let them not
627. Be forced to grind the bones out of their arms
628. For bread, but have some space to think and feel
629. Like moral and immortal creatures. God!
630. Have mercy on them till such time shall come;
631. Look Thou with pity on all lesser crimes,
632. Thrust on men almost when devoured by want,
633. Wretchedness, ignorance and outcast life!
634. Have mercy on the rich, too, who pass by
635. The means they have at hand to fill their minds
636. With serviceable knowledge for themselves,
637. And fellows, and support not the good cause
638. Of the world's better future! Oh, reward
639. All such who do, with peace of heart and power
640. For greater good. Have mercy, Lord! on each
641. And all, for all men need it equally.
642. May peace and industry and commerce weld
643. Into one land all nations of the world,
644. Rewedding those the Deluge once divorced.

645. Oh! may all help each other in good things,
646. Mentally, morally, and bodily!
647. Vouchsafe, kind God! Thy blessing to this isle,
648. Specially! May our country ever lead
649. The world, for she is worthiest; and may all
650. Profit by her example, and adopt
651. Her course, wherever great, or free, or just.
652. May all her subject colonies and powers
653. Have of her freedom freely, as a child
654. Receiveth of its parents. Let not rights
655. Be wrested from us to our own reproach,
656. But granted. We may make the whole world free,
657. And be as free ourselves as ever, more!
658. If policy or self-defence call forth
659. Our forces to the field, let us in Thee
660. Place, first, our trust, and in Thy name we shall
661. O'ercome, for we will only wage the right.
662. Let us not conquer nations for ourselves,
663. But for Thee, Lord! who hast predestined us
664. To fight the battles of the future now,
665. And so have done with war before Thou comest.
666. Till then, Lord God of armies, let our foes
667. Have their swords broken and their cannon burst,
668. And their strong cities levelled; and while we
669. War faithfully and righteously, improve,
670. Civilize, christianize the lands we win
671. From savage or from nature, Thou, oh God!
672. Wilt aid and hallow conquest, as of old,
673. Thine own immediate nation's. But we pray
674. That all mankind may make one brotherhood,
675. And love and serve each other; that all wars
676. And feuds die out of nations, whether those
677. Whom the sun's hot light darkens, or ourselves
678. Whom he treats fairly, or the northern tribes
679. Whom ceaseless snows and starry winters blench,
680. Savage or civilized, — let every race,
681. Red, black or white, olive, or tawny-skinned,
682. Settle in peace and swell the gathering hosts
683. Of the great Prince of Peace! Oh! may the hour
684. Soon come when all false gods, false creeds, false prophets, —
685. Allowed in Thy good purpose for a time, —
686. Demolished, the great world shall be at last,

687. The mercy-seat of God, the heritage
688. Of Christ, and the possession of the Spirit,
689. The comforter, the wisdom! shall all be
690. One land, one home, one friend, one faith, one law,
691. Its ruler God, its practice righteousness,
692. Its life peace! For the one true faith we pray
693. There is but one in Heaven and there shall be
694. But one on earth, the same which is in Heaven.
695. Prophecy is more true than history.
696. Grant us our prayers, we pray, Lord! in the name
697. And for the sake of Thy Son Jesus Christ,
698. Our Saviour and Redeemer, who with Thee,
699. And with the Holy Spirit, reigneth God
700. Over all worlds, one blessed Trinity! —
701. THE CROWD. Amen!
702. LUCIFER. Well, friends, we'll sing a hymn; then part.
703. I give it out, and you sing — all of you.
704.   Oh! Earth is cheating Earth
705.   From age to age for ever;
706.   She laughs at faith and worth,
707.   And dreams she shall die never;
708.   Never, never, never!
709.   And dreams she shall die never.
710.   And Hell is cursing Hell
711.   From age to age for ever;
712.   Its groans ring out the knell
713.   Of souls that may die never;
714.   Never, never, never!
715.   Of souls that may die never.
716.   But Heaven is blessing Heaven
717.   From age to age for ever;
718.   And its thanks to God are given
719.   For bliss that can die never;
720.   Never, never, never!
721.   For bliss that can die never.
722. My blessing be upon ye all; now go!
723. FESTUS. I wonder what these people make of thee.
724. LUCIFER. Ay, manner's a great matter.
725. FESTUS. They deserve
726. All the rebuke thou gavest them and more.
727. What mountains of delusion men have reared!
728. How every age hath bustled on to build

729. Its shadowy mole — its monumental dream!
730. How faith and fancy, in the mind of man,
731. Have spuriously mingled, and how much
732. Shall pass away for aye, as pass before
733. Yon sun, the Lord of steadfastness and change,
734. The visionary landscapes of the skies; —
735. The golden capes far stretching into Heaven,
736. The snow-piled cloud-crags, the bright winged isles
737. Which dot the deep, impassive, ocean air;
738. Like a disbanded rainbow, of all hues,
739. Fit for translated fairy's Paradise; —
740. Or as before the eye of musing child,
741. The faces Fancy forms in clouds and fire
742. Of glowing angel or of darkening fiend.
743. Arts, superstition, arms, philosophy,
744. Have each in turn possessed, betrayed, and mocked us.
745. Yes, vain philosophy, thine hour is come!
746. Thy lips were lined with the immortal lie,
747. And dyed with all the look of truth. Men saw,
748. Believed, embraced, detested, cast thee off.
749. Those lights, the morn of Truth's immortal day,
750. As thou didst falsely swear them, have they not
751. Vanished, the mere auroras of the mind?
752. And thou didst vow to gather clear again
753. The fallen waters of humanity;
754. To smooth the flaw from out an eye; to piece
755. A pounded pearl. Thank God! I am a man;
756. Not a philosopher! Rivers may rot,
757. Never revive the root of oak fire-bolted.
758. Come, let us to the hills! where none but God
759. Can overlook us; for I hate to breathe
760. The breaths and think the thoughts of other men.
761. In close and clouded cities, where the sky
762. Frowns like an angry Father mournfully.
763. I love the hills and I love loneliness.
764. And oh! I love the woods, those natural fanes[5]
765. Whose very air is holy; and we breathe
766. Of God; for He doth come in special place.
767. And, while we worship, He is there for us!

---

5. Fanes: Temples.

768. LUCIFER. It is time that something should be done for the
     poor.
769. The sole equality on earth is death;
770. Now, rich and poor are both dissatisfied.
771. I am for judgment: that will settle both.
772. Nothing is to be done without destruction.
773. Death is the universal salt of states!
774. Blood is the base of all things — law and war,
775. I could tame this lion age to follow me.
776. I should like to macadamize⁶ the world;
777. The road to Hell wants mending.
778. FESTUS. Come away!

---

6. Macademize: To make or repair (a road) according to McAdam's method. *Rare; perhaps obsolete* (*OED*).

THE RIDE. FESTUS AND LUCIFER

SCENE 8

[*The Surface*]
[*LUCIFER and FESTUS*]

1.   LUCIFER. Wilt ride?
2.   FESTUS. I'll have an hour's ride.
3.   LUCIFER. Be mine the steeds! be me the guide!
4.   Come hither, come hither,
5.   My brave black steed!
6.   And thou, too, his fellow,
7.   Hither with speed!
8.   Though not so fleet
9.   As the steeds of Death,
10. Your feet are as sure,
11. Ye have longer breath.
12. Ye have drawn the world
13. Without wind or bait.
14. Six thousand years.
15. And it waxeth late;
16. So take me this once,
17. And again to my home,
18. And rest ye and feast ye.
19. They come, they come.
20. FESTUS. Tossing their manes like
21. Pitchy surge; and lashing
22. Their tails into a
23. Tempest; their eyes flashing,
24. Like shooting thunderbolts.
25. LUCIFER. Come, know your masters, colts!
26. Up, and away!
27. FESTUS. Hurrah! Hurrah!
28. The noblest pace the world e'er saw.
29. I swear by Heaven we'll beat the sun.
30. In the longest heat that ever was run;
31. If we keep it up as we have begun.
32. LUCIFER. I told thee my steeds

33.   Were a gallant pair.
34.   FESTUS. And they were not thine,
35.   They might be divine.
36.   LUCIFER. Thine is named Ruin;
37.   And Darkness mine.
38.   FESTUS.   Like all of thy deeds.
39.   Now that's unfair.
40.   LUCIFER.   A civiller and gentler beast
41.   Thou hast never crossed at least.
42.   Now, look around!
43.   FESTUS.   Why, this is France.
44.   Nature is here like a living romance.
45.   Look at its vines and streams and skies,
46.   Its glancing feet and dancing eyes!
47.   LUCIFER. 'Tis a strange nation, light yet strong,
48.   Fierce of heart and blithe of tongue;
49.   Prone to change; so fond of blood
50.   She wounds herself to quaff her own.
51.   FESTUS. Oh! it's a brave and lovely land;
52.   And well deserving every good
53.   Which others wish themselves alone,
54.   Could she but herself command.
55.   LUCIFER. On! On! no more delay!
56.   Or we'll not ride round
57.   The world all day.
58.   FESTUS. Good horse, get off the ground!
59.   LUCIFER. Sit firm! and if our horses please,
60.   We will take at once the Pyrenees.
61.   'T was bravely leapt!
62.   FESTUS. Ay, this is Spain:
63.   Europe's last land
64.   'Twill e'er remain;
65.   Last in the progress of the earth;
66.   The last in liberty;
67.   The last in wealth and worth;
68.   The last in bigotry.
69.   LUCIFER. Turn thy steed, and slacken rein;
70.   Quick! we must be back again:
71.   O'er the vale hid in the mountain,
72.   O'er the merry forest fountain;
73.   Ruin and Darkness! we must fly
74.   O'er crag and rift,

75. Swift — swift — swift
76. As the glance of an eye.
77. FESTUS. That is Italy — the grave
78. And resurrection of the slave.
79. LUCIFER. And there lies Greece, whose soul
80. Men say hath fled.
81. FESTUS. Perhaps some God may come
82. And raise the dead.
83. LUCIFER. Norward now we'll hold our course.
84. Thine I think is the bolder horse;
85. But bear him up with a harder hand!
86. Rough riding this o'er Swisserland.
87. FESTUS. So all have found it who have tried;
88. High as their Alps the people's pride,
89. Never to have bowed before
90. The tyrant or the conqueror.
91. LUCIFER. Away, away! before thee lie
92. The fields and floods of Germany.
93. FESTUS. Well I love thee, Father-land!
94. Sire of Europe, as thou art!
95. Be free! and crouch no more, but stand!
96. Thy noblest son will take thy part.
97. Oh! sooner let the mountains bend
98. Beneath the clouds, when tempests lour,
99. Than nations stoop their sky compeering heads
100. In homage to some petty despot's power!
101. The worm which suffers mincing into parts,
102. May sprout forth heads and tails, but grows no hearts.
103. LUCIFER. There lies Austria! Famous land
104. For fiddlesticks and sword-in-hand.
105. FESTUS. And Poland, whom truly unhappy we call.
106. Unworthy to rise — unwilling to fall.
107. Forge into swords thy feudal chain!
108. Smite e'en the souls of foes in twain!
109. The fetters have been bound in vain
110. Round England's arms: and we are free
111. As the souls of our sires in Heaven which be.
112. That earth should have so few
113. Men, Fathers, like to you!
114. LUCIFER. What matter who be free or slaves;
115. For all there is one tyranny, the grave's;
116. Or freedom, may be. On! on! haste!
117. FESTUS. What land is yonder wide, white waste?

118. LUCIFER. Ha! 'tis Russia's gentle realm:
119. Whose sceptre is the sword — whose crown, the helm.
120. FESTUS. I swear by every atom which exists,
121. I better love this reckless ride
122. O'er hill and forest, lake and river wide;
123. O'er sunlit plain and through the mountain mists,
124. Than aught which thou hast given beside.
125. LUCIFER. See what a long long track
126. Of dust and fire behind,
127. For miles and miles aback!
128. And shrill and strong,
129. As we shoot along,
130. Whistles and whirrs,
131. Like a forest of firs
132. Falling, the cold north wind.
133. FESTUS. Look! my way I can only read
134. By the sparks from the hoof of my giant steed.
135. LUCIFER. Where art thou now?
136. FESTUS.   In Tartar land;
137. I know by the deserts of salt and sand.
138. Nor aim nor end hath a wandering life:
139. Best reaps but rest, and strife but strife.
140. With the nations round
141. They ne'er have mixed;
142. For good or ill
143. They stand all still;
144. Their bodies but rove,
145. Their minds are fixed.
146. And yonder lies old China's wall,
147. Where gods of gold do men enthral;
148. Gods whose gold's their only worth.
149. LUCIFER. Well, is not gold the god of earth?
150. Now southward, hey! for Hindostan!
151. The sun beats down both beast and man.
152. Insect and herb for life do gasp;
153. The river reeks and faints the asp.
154. FESTUS. But blithe are we,
155. And our steeds, I trow;[1]
156. And the mane of mine

---

1. Trow: To believe, have faith in, trust. *Obsolete* (*OED*).

157. Yet bears the snow
158. Which fell on us
159. By Caucasus.
160. By the four beasts! but this is warm.
161. LUCIFER. Away! Away!
162. Nor stint nor stay;
163. We'll reach the sea before yon storm.
164. FESTUS. Wilt take the sea?
165. LUCIFER. Ay, that will we!
166. And swim as we ride.
167. Our steeds astride;
168. Come leap, leap off with me!
169. FESTUS. What? shall we leap
170. Sheer off this steep,
171. A mile the sea above?
172. LUCIFER. Leap as to save
173. From worse than a grave
174. The maid thou most dost love!
175. FESTUS. There is a rapture in the headlong leap.
176. The wedgelike cleaving of the closing deep!
177. A feeling full of hardihood and power
178. With which we court the waters that devour.
179. Oh! 'tis a feeling great, sublime, supreme,
180. Like the ecstatic[2] influence of a dream.
181. To speed one's way thus o'er the sliding plain;
182. And make a kindred being with the main.
183. LUCIFER. By Chaos! this is gallant sport;
184. A league at every breath;
185. Methinks if I ever have to die,
186. I'll ride this rate to death.
187. FESTUS. Away, away upon the whitening tide,
188. Like lover hastening to embrace his bride,
189. We hurry faster than the foam we ride.
190. Dashing aside the waves which round us cling,
191. With strength like that which lifts an eagle's wing
192. Where the stars dazzle and the angels sing.
193. LUCIFER. We scatter the spray.
194. And break through the billows,
195. As the wind makes way
196. Through the leaves of willows!

---

2. Ecstatic: 'Extatic' in the original. *OED* therefore contains no reference.

197. FESTUS. In vain they urge their armies to the fight:
198. Their surge-crests crumble 'neath our stroke of might.
199. We meet and fear not; mount — now rise, now fall —
200. And dare, with full-nerved arm, the rage of all.
201. Through anger-swollen wave or sparkling spray,
202. Nothing it recks; we hold our perilous way
203. Right onward! till we feel the whirling brain
204. Ring with the maddening music of the main;
205. Till the fixed eyeball strives and strains to ken.
206. Yet loathes to see the shore and haunts of men;
207. And the blood, half starting through each ridgy vein,
208. In the unwieldy hand sets black with pain.
209. Then let the tempest cloud on cloud come spread,
210. And tear the stormy terrors of his head;
211. Let the wild sea-bird wheel around my brow,
212. And shriek — and swoop — and flap her wing as now!
213. It gladdens! on! ye boisterous billows, roll!
214. And keep my body; ye have ta'en my soul.
215. Thou element! the type which God hath given,
216. For eyes and hearts too earthy, of His Heaven!
217. Were Heaven a mockery, I would never mourn
218. While o'er thy bosom I might still be borne;
219. While yet to me the power and joy was given
220. To fling my breast on thine, and mingle earth with Heaven.
221. LUCIFER. See yonder! now we quit the main;
222. For here's the Cape, here's land again, —
223. And scour we must o'er Afric's plain.
224. FESTUS. Away, away! on either hand
225. Nor town nor tower,
226. Nor shade nor shower —
227. Nothing but sun and sand.
228. LUCIFER. See, there they are! I knew, right soon,
229. We would light on the mountains of the moon.
230. Over them! over, nought forbids!
231. FESTUS. Yonder the Nile and the Pyramids?
232. Hurrah! by my soul!
233. At every bound
234. I see, I feel
235. The earth rush round.
236. I see the mountains slide away —
237. That side night and this side day.
238. LUCIFER. Shall we go to America?
239. FESTUS. Why, have we time?

240. LUCIFER. Oh, plenty;
241. Be there, too, ere we reckon twenty.
242. Another run, another bound!
243. And we shall leave this lion ground.
244. FESTUS. The sea again! the swift bright sea!
245. LUCIFER. Hold hard, and follow me!
246. Well, now we have travelled upon the waves.
247. Wilt travel a time beneath?
248. And visit the sea-born in their caves;
249. And look on the rainbow-tinted wreath
250. Of weeds, beset with pearls, wherewith
251. The mermaid binds her long green hair.
252. Or rouse the sea-snake from his lair?
253. FESTUS. Ay, ay! down let us dive!
254. LUCIFER. Look up! we lack not stars;
255. And every star thou seest's alive:
256. A little globe of life — light — love.
257. Whose every atom is a living being;
258. Each the other's bosom seeing,
259. Each enlightening the other.
260. FESTUS. Oh! how unlike the world above.
261. Where each doth mainly, vainly strive
262. To dim or to outshine his brother!
263. LUCIFER. Come on! come on!
264. FESTUS.   Are those bright spars,
265. Or eyes of things which ne'er forgive.
266. That seem to play on us, and glare
267. With rage that we so far should dare
268. To search the hidden deeps.
269. Where tide, the moonslave, sleeps?
270. Where the wind breathes not, and the wave
271. Walks softly as above a grave; —
272. Where coral worms, in countless nations,
273. Build rocks up from the sea's foundations; —
274. Where the islands strike their roots
275. Far from the old mainland;
276. And spring like desert-fruits.
277. Shook off by God's strong hand,
278. Up from their bed of sand.
279. Look, listen! there is music in the cave,
280. Where ocean sleeps, and brightness in the wave
281. The sea-bird makes its pillow, and the star,

282. Last born of Heaven, its azure mirror; — far
283. And wide, the pale, fine, fire of ocean flows,
284. Softly sublime like lightnings in repose —
285. Till roused, anon, afar its flaming spray it throws.
286. LUCIFER. There! now we stand
287. On the world's-end-land!
288. Over the hills
289. Away we go!
290. Through fire, and snow,
291. And rivers, whereto
292. All others are rills.
293. FESTUS. Through the lands of silver,
294. The lands of gold;
295. Through lands untrodden,
296. And lands untold.
297. LUCIFER. By strait and bay
298. We must away;
299. Through swamp, and plain,
300. And hurricane.
301. FESTUS. And that dark cloud of slaves
302. Which yet may rise; —
303. Though nought shall blot the bannered stars
304. From Freedom's skies.
305. America! half-brother of the world!
306. With something good and bad of every land;
307. Greater than thee have lost their seat —
308. Greater scarce none can stand.
309. Thy flag now flouts the skies,
310. The highest under Heaven;
311. Save the red cross, whereto are given
312. All victories.
313. LUCIFER. Our horses snort and snuff the sea.
314. And pant for where we ought to be.
315. FESTUS. Well, here we are! and as we flew in,
316. I said, let Darkness follow Ruin!
317. LUCIFER. 'Twas right. Spur on! Come, Darkness, come!
318. Think of thy well-strown[3] stall!
319. FESTUS. For me, I care not what's to come.
320. Nor for the fate by which I fall;

---

3. Strown: Scattered with rushes or straw. *Archaic* (*OED*).

321. But I would that I were Ocean's son,
322. The solitary brave,
323. Like yon sea-snake, to climb upon
324. The crest of the bounding wave.
325. Oh! happy, if at last I lie
326. Within some pearled and coral cave;
327. While over head the booming surge
328. And moaning billow shall chaunt my dirge;
329. And the storm-blast, as it sweepeth by,
330. Shall, answering, howl to the mermaid's sigh,
331. And the nightwind's mournful minstrelsy,
332. Their requiem over my grave.
333. LUCIFER. Through morn and midnight, sunset and high noon,
334. One hour hath ta'en us; — o'er all land and sea,
335. O'er opening earthquake and iceberg, have we
336. Swept in swift safety. 'T will be over, soon.
337. Behold the common, narrow sea,
338. Which, like a strong man's arm,
339. Keeps back two foes whose lips are white,
340. Whose hearts with rage are warm.
341. FESTUS. England! my country, great and free!
342. Heart of the world, I leap to thee!
343. How shall my country fight
344. When her foes rise against her,
345. But with thine arm, O Sea!
346. The arm which thou lent'st her?
347. Where shall my country be buried
348. When she shall die?
349. Earth is too scant for her grave:
350. Where shall she lie?
351. She hath brethren more than a hundred,
352. And they all want room;
353. They may die and may lie where they live —
354. They shall not mix with her doom.
355. Where but within thine arms,
356. O sea, O sea?
357. Wherein she hath lived and gloried,
358. Let her rest be!
359. We will rise and will say to the sea,
360. Flow over her!
361. We will cry to the depths of the deep,

362. Cover her!
363. The world hath drawn his sword,
364. And his red shield drips before him: —
365. But, my country, rise!
366. Thou canst never die
367. While a foe hath life to fly;
368. Rise land, and gore him!
369. LUCIFER. Now get on land, and hie along
370. O'er forest, copse, and glade;
371. We have but a league or two more to go
372. Before our journey's made;
373. With speed that flings the sun into the shade!
374. FESTUS. See the gold sunshine patching,
375. And streaming and streaking across
376. The gray-green oaks; and catching,
377. By its soft brown beard, the moss.
378. LUCIFER. Ah! here we get an open plain:
379. Here we'll get down.
380. Away, good steeds! be off again!
381. FESTUS. We must be near to Town.
382. I am bound to thee for ever
383. By the pleasure of this day;
384. Henceforth we will never sever,
385. Come what come may.

SCENE 9

[A Village Feast — Evening]
[FESTUS, LUCIFER and OTHERS]

1. FESTUS. It is getting dark. One has to walk quite close,
2. To see the pretty faces that we meet.
3. LUCIFER.   A disagreeable necessity,
4. Truly.
5. FESTUS.   We'll rest upon this bridge. I am tired.

6. Yon tall slim tree! does it not seem as made
7. For its place there, a kind of natural maypole? —
8. Beyond, the lighted stalls stored with the good
9. Things of our childhood's world, and behind them,
10. The shouting showman and the clashing cymbal;
11. The open doored cottages and blazing hearth, —
12. The little ones running up with naked feet,
13. And cake in either hand, to their mother's lap, —
14. Old and young laughing, schoolboys with their play-things,
15. Clowns cracking jokes, and lasses with sly eyes,
16. And the smile settling in their sunflecked cheeks,
17. Like noon upon the mellow apricot; —
18. Make up a scene I can for once give in to.
19. It must please all, the social and the selfish.
20. Are they not happy?
21. LUCIFER.   Why, it matters not.
22. They seem so: that's enough.
23. FESTUS. But not the same.
24. LUCIFER. Yet truth and falsehood meet in seeming, like
25. The falling leaf and shadow on the pool's face.
26. And these are joys, like beauty, but skin deep.
27. FESTUS. Remove all such and what's the joy of earth?
28. 'Tis they create the appetite of life —
29. Give zest and relish to the lot of millions.
30. And take the taste for them away — what's left?
31. A dry ungainly skeleton of soul.
32. LUCIFER. Power is aye above the soul and joy
33. Below it. Pleasure men prefer to power.
34. [*Children at play*]
35. FESTUS. Play away, good ones!
36. AN OLD MAN. Pity the poor blind man!
37. FESTUS. Here is substantial pity.
38. OLD MAN. Heaven reward you!
39. FESTUS. Blind as the blue skies after sunset. Blind!
40. And I am tired of looking on what is.
41. One might as well see beauty never more,
42. As look upon it with an empty eye.
43. I would this world were over. I am tired.
44. Nought happens but what happens to one's self,
45. And all hath happened I have wished, and more.
46. Our pleasures all pass from us, one by one,
47. With that relief which sighing gives the heart,

48.   Though each sigh leaves it lower. It is sad
49.   To think how few our pleasures really are:
50.   And for the which we risk eternal good.
51.   There's nothing that can satisfy one's self,
52.   Except one's self. Well, it is very sad,
53.   And by the time we come of age we have felt
54.   In one degree or other, all that age
55.   Can offer. We have reaped our field ere noon
56.   The rest is reproduction; sowing — reaping —
57.   Losing again. Toil and gain tire alike.
58.   We cannot live too slowly to be good
59.   And happy, nor too much by line and square.
60.   But youth is burning to forestall its nature,
61.   And will not wait for time to ferry it
62.   Over the stream, but flings itself into
63.   The flood, and perishes. And yet, why not?
64.   There is no charm in time as time, nor good.
65.   The long days are no happier than the short ones.
66.   'Tis sometime now since I was here. We leave
67.   Our home in youth — no matter to what end; —
68.   Study — or strife — or pleasure, or what not:
69.   And coming back in few short years, we find
70.   All as we left it, outside; the old elms,
71.   The house, grass, gates, and latchet's selfsame click:
72.   But lift that latchet, — all is changed as doom:
73.   The servants have forgotten our step, and more
74.   Than half of those who knew us know us not.
75.   Adversity, prosperity, the grave,
76.   Play a round game with friends. On some the world
77.   Hath shot its evil eye, and they are passed
78.   From honor and remembrance, and a stare
79.   Is all the mention of their names receives;
80.   And people know no more of them than of
81.   The shapes of clouds at midnight, a year back.
82.   LUCIFER. Let us move on to where the dancing is;
83.   We soon shall see how happy they all are.
84.   Here is a loving couple quarrelling.
85.   And there, another. It is quite distressing.
86.   See yonder. Two men fighting!
87.   FESTUS.   What avail
88.   These vile exceptions to the rule of joy?
89.   LUCIFER. Behold the happiness of which thou spakest!

90. The highest hills are miles below the sky,
91. And so far is the lightest heart below
92. True happiness.
93. FESTUS.   This is a snakelike world.
94. And always hath its tail within its mouth,
95. As if it ate itself, and moralled[1] time.
96. The world is like yon children's merry-go-round;
97. What men admire are carriages and hobbies,
98. Which the exalted manikins[2] enjoy.
99. There is a noisy ragged crowd below
100. Of urchins drives it round, who only get
101. The excitement for their pains — best gain perhaps:
102. For it is not they who labour that grow dizzy
103. Nor sick — that's for the idle, proud above,
104. Who soon dismount, more weary of enjoying
105. Than those below of working; and but fair.
106. It is wretchedness or recklessness alone
107. Keeps us alive. Were we happy we should die.
108. Yet what is death? I like to think on death:
109. It is but the appearance of an apparition.
110. One ought to tremble; but oughts stand for nothing.
111. I hate the thought of wrinkling up to rest;
112. The toothlike aching ruin of the body,
113. With the heart all out, and nothing left but edge.
114. Give me the long high bounding feel of life,
115. Which cries, let me but leap unto my grave,
116. And I'll not mind the when nor where. We never
117. Care less for life than when enjoying it.
118. Oh! I should love to die. What is to die?
119. I cannot hold the meaning more than can
120. An oak's arms clasp the blast that blows on it.
121. There is an air-like something which must be.
122. And yet not to be seen, nor to be touched.
123. I am made up to die; for having been
124. Every thing, there is nothing left but nothing
125. To be again.
126. LUCIFER. Hark! here is a ballad-singer.
127. BALLAD-SINGER. All of my own composing!

---

1. Moralled: Symbolized. *Obsolete (OED)*. *Festus* is the reference.
2. Manikins: People who are undersized or puny. *Obsolete (OED)*. The idea here is that, from their height, mankind is diminutive, as also in the scale of their pleasures.

128. FESTUS. Yes, Yes — we know.
129. SINGER.
130.   My gipsy maid! my gipsy maid!
131.   I bless and curse the day
132.   I lost the light of life, and caught
133.   The grief which maketh grey.
134.   Would that the light which blinded me
135.   Had saved me on my way!
136.   My night-haired love! so sweet she was,
137.   So fair and blithe was she;
138.   Her smile was brighter than the moon's,
139.   Her eyes the stars might see.
140.   I met her by her lane-spread tent,
141.   Beside a moss-green stone,
142.   And bade her make, not mock, my fate,
143.   My fortune was her own.
144.   Thou art but yet a boy, she said.
145.   And I a woman grown.
146.   I am a man in love, I cried;
147.   My heart was early manned:
148.   She smiled, and only drooped her eyes,
149.   And then let go my hand.
150.   We stood a minute: neither spake
151.   What each must understand.
152.   I told her, so she would be mine
153.   And follow where I went,
154.   She straight should have a bridal bower
155.   Instead of gipsy tent.
156.   Or would she have me wend with her,
157.   The world between should fall;
158.   For her I would fling up faith and friends,
159.   And name, and fame, and all.
160.   Her smile so bright froze while I spake,
161.   And ice was in her eye;
162.   So near, it seemed ere touch her heart
163.   I might have kissed the sky.
164.   I said that if she loved to rule,
165.   Or if she longed to reign,
166.   I would make her Queen of every race
167.   Which tearlike trode the world's sad face,
168.   Or bleed at every vein.
169.   She laid her finger on her lip,

170.	And pointed to the sky;
171.	There is no God to come, she said:
172.	Dost thou not fear to die?
173.	And what is God, I said, to thee?
174.	Thy people worship not.
175.	The good, the happy, and the free,
176.	She said, they need no God.
177.	I looked until I lost mine eyes;
178.	I felt as though I were
179.	In a dark cave, with one weak light
180.	The light of life — with her;
181.	And that was wasting fast away;
182.	I watched but would not stir.
183.	Again she took my hand in hers,
184.	And read it o'er and o'er;
185.	Ah! eyes so young, so sweet, I said.
186.	Make as they read love's lore.
187.	She held my hand — I trembled whilst —
188.	For sorely soon I felt
189.	She made the love-cross she foretold,
190.	And all the woe she dealt.
191.	Unhappy I should be, she said,
192.	And young to death be given;
193.	I told her I believed in her,
194.	Not in the stars of Heaven.
195.	Hush! we breathe Heaven, she said, and bowed;
196.	And the stars speak through me.
197.	Let Heaven, I cried, take care of Heaven!
198.	I only care for thee.
199.	She shrank: I looked, and begged a kiss:
200.	I knew she had one for me;
201.	She would deny me none, she said,
202.	But give me none would she.
203.	My gipsy maid! my gipsy maid!
204.	'Tis three long years like this,
205.	Since there I gave and got from thee
206.	That meeting, parting kiss.
207.	I saw the tears start in her eye,
208.	And trickle down her cheek,
209.	Like falling stars across the sky,
210.	Escaping from their Maker's eye:
211.	I saw, but spared to speak.

212.	Go, and forget! she said, and slid
213.	Below her lowly tent.
214.	I will not, cannot — hear me, girl!
215.	She heard not, and I went.
216.	At eve, by sunset, I was there,
217.	The tent was there no more;
218.	The fire which warmed her flickered still —
219.	The fire she sat before.
220.	I stood by it, till through the dark
221.	I saw not where it lay;
222.	And then like that my heart went out
223.	In ashy grief and gray.
224.	My gipsy maid! my gipsy maid!
225.	Oh! let me bless this day;
226.	This day it was I met thee first,
227.	And yet it shall be and is cursed,
228.	For thou hast gone away.
229.	LUCIFER. Another, please — not quite so gloomy, friend.
230.	GIRL. I wonder if the tale it tells be true.
231.	SINGER. I dare say — but you want a merrier.
232.	Every man's life has its apocrypha;
233.	Mine has, at least. I have said more than need be.
234.	It happened, too, when I was very young.
235.	We never meet such gipsies when we are old;
236.	And yet we more complain of youth than age.
237.	Now, make a ring, good people. Let me breathe!
238.	[*sings*]
239.	Oh! the wee green neuk, the sly green neuk,
240.	The wee sly neuk for me!
241.	Whare the wheat is wavin' bright and brown,
242.	And the wind is fresh and free.
243.	Whare I weave wild weeds, and out o' reeds
244.	Kerve whissles as I lay;
245.	And a douce low voice is murmurin by
246.	Through the lee-lang simmer day.
247.	Oh! the wee green neuk, &c.
248.	And whare a' things luik as though they lo'ed
249.	To languish in the sun;
250.	And that if they feed the fire they dree,
251.	They wadna ae pang were gone.
252.	Whare the lift aboon is still as death,
253.	And bright as life can be;

254.   While the douce low voice says, na, na, na!
255.   But ye mauna luik sae at me.
256.   Oh! the wee green neuk, &c.
257.   Whare the lang rank bent is saft and cule.
258.   And freshenin' till the feet;
259.   And the spot is sly, and the spinnie high,
260.   Whare my luve and I mak seat:
261.   And I teaze her till she rins, and then
262.   I catch her roun' the tree;
263.   While the poppies shak' their heids and blush:
264.   Let 'em blush till they drap, for me!
265.   Oh! the wee green neuk, &c.
266. FESTUS. And all who know such feelings and such scenes
267. Will, I am sure, reward you. Here — take this.
268. OTHERS. And this, and this — too!
269. SINGER. Thank ye all, good friends!
270. FESTUS. There's much that hath no merit but its truth,
271. And no excuse but nature. Nature does
272. Never wrong: 't is society which sins.
273. Look on the bee upon the wing among flowers;
274. How brave, how bright his life! Then mark him hived.
275. Cramped, cringing in his self-built, social cell.
276. Thus is it in the world-hive: most where men
277. Lie deep in cities as in drifts — death drifts,
278. Nosing each other like a flock of sheep;
279. Not knowing and not caring whence nor whither
280. They come or go, so that they fool together.
281. LUCIFER. It is quite fair to halve these lives and say
282. This side is nature's, that society's.
283. When both are side-views only of one thing.
284. FARMER. I am glad to see you come among us, sir.
285. PARSON. Why, I have but little comfort in these pastimes;
286. And any heart, turned Godwards, feels more joy
287. In one short hour of prayer, than e'er was raised
288. By all the feasts on earth since their foundation.
289. But no one will believe us; as if we
290. Had never known the vain things of the world.
291. Nor lain and slept in sin's seducing shade,
292. Listless, until God woke us; made us feel
293. We should be up and stirring in the sun;
294. For everything had to be done ere night.
295. What is all this joy and jollity about?

296. Grant there may be no sin. What good is it?
297. FARMER. I can't defend these feasts, Sir, and can't blame.
298. PARSON. Good evening, friends! Why, Festus! I rejoice
299. We meet again. I have a young friend here,
300. A student — who hath staid with us of late.
301. You would be glad, I know, to know each other.
302. Therefore be known so.
303. FESTUS.   You are a student, Sir.
304. STUDENT. I profess little; but it is a title
305. A man may claim perhaps with modesty.
306. FESTUS. True. All mankind are students. How to live
307. And how to die forms the great lesson still.
308. I know what study is: it is to toil
309. Hard, through the hours of the sad midnight watch,
310. At tasks which seem a systematic curse,
311. And course of bootless penance. Night by night,
312. To trace one's thought as if on iron leaves;
313. And sorrowful as though it were the mode
314. And date of death we wrote on our own tombs:
315. Wring a slight sleep out of the couch, and see
316. The self-same moon, which lit us to our rest.
317. Her place scarce changed perceptibly in Heaven.
318. Now light us to renewal of our toils. —
319. This, to the young mind, wild and all in leaf,
320. Which knowledge, grafting, paineth. Fruit soon comes,
321. And more than all our troubles pays us powers;
322. So that we joy to have endured so much:
323. That not for nothing have we slaved and slain
324. Ourselves almost. And more; it is to strive
325. To bring the mind up to one's own esteem:
326. Who but the generous fail? It is to think,
327. While thought is standing thick upon the brain
328. As dew upon the brow — for thought is brain-sweat;
329. And gathering quick and dark, like storms in summer,
330. Until convulsed, condensed, in lightning sport,
331. It plays upon the heavens of the mind, —
332. Opens the hemisphered abysses here,
333. And we become revealers to ourselves.
334. STUDENT. When night hath set her silver lamp on high,
335. Then is the tune for study; when Heaven's light
336. Pours itself on the page, like prophecy
337. On time, unglooming all its mighty meanings;

338. It is then we feel the sweet strength of the stars,
339. And magic of the moon.
340. LUCIFER.   It's a bad habit.
341. STUDENT. And wisdom dwells in secret and on high,
342. As do the stars. The sun's diurnal glare
343. Is for the daily herd; but for the wise,
344. The cold pure radiance of the night-born light,
345. Wherewith is inspiration of the truth.
346. There was a time when I would never go
347. To rest before the sun rose; and for that,
348. Through a like length of time as that now gone,
349. The world shall speak of me six thousand years hence.
350. LUCIFER. How know you that the world won't end
      to-morrow?
351. PARSON. I now, an early riser, love to hail
352. The dreamy struggles of the stars with light,
353. And the recovering breath of earth, sleep-drowned,
354. Awakening to the wisdom of the sun,
355. And life of light within the tent of Heaven; —
356. To kiss the feet of Morning as she walks
357. In dewy light along the hills, while they,
358. All odorous as an angel's fresh-culled crown,
359. Unveil to her their bounteous loveliness.
360. STUDENT. I am devote to study. Worthy books
361. Are not companions — they are solitudes:
362. We lose ourselves in them and all our cares.
363. The further back we search the human mind, —
364. Mean in the mass, but in the instance great —
365. Which starting first with Deities and stars
366. And broods of beings earth-born, Heaven-begot,
367. And all the bright side of the broad world, now
368. Dotes[3] upon dreams and dim atomic truths,
369. Is all for comfort and no more for glory —
370. The nobler and more marvellous it shews.
371. Trifles like these make up the present time;
372. The Iliad and the Pyramids the past.
373. FESTUS. The future will have glory not the less.
374. I can conceive a time when the world shall be
375. Much better visibly and when, as far
376. As social life and its relations tend,

---

3. 'Doats' in original. It appears to be a coinage. *OED* has no reference for the term.

377. Men, morals, manners shall be lifted up
378. To a pure height we know not of nor dream; —
379. When all men's rights and duties shall be clear,
380. And charitably exercised and borne;
381. When education, conscience, and good deeds
382. Shall have just equal sway, and civil claims;
383. Great crimes shall be cast out, as were of old
384. Devils possessing madmen: — Truth shall reign.
385. Nature shall be rethroned, and man sublimed.
386. STUDENT. Oh! then may Heaven come down again to earth;
387. And dwell with her, as once, like to a friend.
388. Lucifer. As like each other as a sword and scythe.
389. Oh! then shall lions mew and lambkins roar!
390. FESTUS. And having studied — what next?
391. STUDENT.   Much I long
392. To view the capital city of the world.
393. The mountains, the great cities, and the sea,
394. Are each an era in the life of youth.
395. FESTUS. There to get worldly ways, and thoughts and
      schemes;
396. To learn to detect, distrust, despise mankind —
397. To ken a false factitious glare amid much
398. That shines with seeming saintlike purity —
399. To gloss misdeeds — to trifle with great truths —
400. To pit the brain against the heart, and plead
401. Wit before wisdom, — these are the world's ways:
402. It learns us to lose that in crowds which we
403. Must after seek alone — our innocence;
404. And when the crowd is gone.
405. STUDENT.   Not only that:
406. There all great things are round one. Interests,
407. Mighty and mountainous of estimate,
408. Are daily heaped or scattered 'neath the eye.
409. Great deeds, great thoughts, great schemes, and crimes, and all
410. Which is in purpose, or in practice, great
411. Of human nature — there are common things.
412. Men make themselves be deathless as in spite;
413. As if they waged some lineal feud with time;
414. As though their fathers were immortal, too.
415. And immortality an every-day
416. Accomplishment.
417. FESTUS.   Fie! fie! 'tis more for this:
418. Amid gayer people and more wanton ways,

419. To give a loose to all the lists of youth —
420. To train your passion flowers high ahead,
421. And bind them on your brow as others do.
422. The mornlit revel and the shameless mate —
423. The tabled hues of darkness and of blood —
424. The published bosom and the crowning smile —
425. The cup excessive; and if aught there be
426. More vain than these or wanton — that to have —
427. Have all but always in intent, effect,
428. Or fact. Nay, nay, deny it not: I know.
429. Youth hath a strange and strong desire to try
430. All feelings on the heart: it is very wrong,
431. And dangerous, and deadly: strive against it!
432. STUDENT. It might be some old sage was warning us.
433. FESTUS. Youth might be wise. We suffer less from pains
434. Than pleasures.
435. STUDENT.   I should like to see the world,
436. And gain that knowledge which is —
437. FESTUS.   Barrener
438. Than ice; possessing and producing nought
439. But means and forms of death or vanity.
440. The world is just as hollow as an eggshell.
441. It is a surface not a solid, mind:
442. And all this boasted knowledge of the world
443. To me seems but to mean acquaintance with
444. Low things, or evil, or indifferent.
445. FARMER. Much more is said of knowledge than it's worth.
446. A man may gain all knowledge here, and yet
447. Be, after death, as much in the dark as I.
448. LUCIFER. What makes you know of living after death?
449. FARMER. Why, nothing that I know; and there it is, —
450. But something I am told has told me so.
451. No angel ever came to me to prove it;
452. And all my friends have died, and left no ghosts.
453. FESTUS. All that is good a man may learn from himself
454. And much, too, that is bad.
455. PARSON.   Nay, let me speak!
456. Aught that is good the soul receives of God
457. When He hath made it His; and until then
458. Man cannot know, nor do, nor be, aught good.
459. Oh! there is nought on earth worth being known
460. But God and our own souls — the God we have

461. Within our hearts; for it is not the hope,
462. Nor faith, nor fear, nor notions others have
463. Of God can serve us, but the sense and soul
464. We have of Him within us; and, for men,
465. God loves us men each individually,
466. And deals with us in order, soul by soul.
467. LUCIFER. What are your politics?
468. FARMER.   I have none.
469. LUCIFER.   Good.
470. FARMER. I have my thoughts. I am no party man.
471. I care for measures more than men, but think
472. Some little may depend upon the men;
473. Something in fires depends upon the grate.
474. FIRST BOY. What are your colours?
475. SECOND.   Blue as Heaven.
476. THIRD.   And mine
477. Are yellow as the sun.
478. FIRST.   Mine, green as grass.
479. SECOND. Green's forsaken, and yellow's forsworn,
480. And blue's the colour that shall be worn.
481. STUDENT. As to religion, politics, law, and war,
482. But little need be said. All are required,
483. And all are well enough. Of liberty,
484. And slavery, and tyranny we hear
485. Much; but the human mind affects extremes.
486. The heart is in the middle of the system;
487. And all affections gather round the truth,
488. The moderated joys and woes of life.
489. I love my God, my country, kind and kin,
490. Nor would I see a dog wronged of his bone.
491. My country! if a wretch should e'er arise,
492. Out of thy countless sons, who would curtail
493. Thy freedom, dim thy glory, — while he lives
494. May all earth's peoples curse him — for of all
495. Hast thou secured the blessing; — and if one
496. Exist who would not arm for liberty,
497. Be he too cursed living, and when dead,
498. Let him be buried downwards, with his face
499. Looking to Hell, and o'er his coward grave
500. The hare skulk in her form.
501. LUCIFER.   Nay, gently, friend.
502. Curse nothing, not the Devil. He's beside you —

503. For aught you know.
504. STUDENT. I neither know nor care.
505.   [*They pass some card-players*]
506. FESTUS. Kings, queens, knaves, tens would trick the
      world away.
507. And it were not, now and then, for some brave ace.
508. STUDENT. You see yon wretched starved old man; his brow
509. Grooved out with wrinkles, like the brown dry sand
510. The tide of life is leaving?
511. LUCIFER.   Yes, I see him.
512. STUDENT. Last week he thought he was about to die;
513. So he bade gold be strewn beneath his pillow.
514. Gold on a chest that he might lie and see.
515. And gold put in a basin on his bed,
516. That he might dabble with his fingers in.
517. He's going now to grope for pence or pins.
518. He never gave a pin's worth in his life.
519. What would you do to him?
520. LUCIFER.   I would have him wrought
521. Into a living wire, which, beaten out,
522. Might make a golden network for the world;
523. Then melt him inch by inch and hell by hell,
524. Where is the law of wrath.
525. STUDENT.   Oh, charity!
526. It is a thought the Devil might be proud of —
527. Once and away. Misers and spendthrifts may
528. Torment each other in the world to come.
529. FESTUS. Men look on death as lightning, always far
530. Off, or in Heaven. They know not it is in
531. Themselves, a strong and inward tendency,
532. The soul of every atom, every hair:
533. That nature's infinite electric life,
534. Escaping from each isolated frame,
535. Up out of earth, or down from Heaven, becomes
536. To each its proper death, and adds itself
537. Thus to the great reunion of the whole.
538. There is a man in mourning! What does he here?
539. STUDENT. He has just buried the only friend he had,
540. And now comes hither to enjoy himself.
541. FESTUS. Why will we dedicate the dead to God,
542. And not ourselves, the living? Oft we speak,
543. With tears of joy and trust, of some dear friend

544. As surely up in Heaven; while that same soul,
545. For aught we know, may be shuddering even in Hell
546. To hear his name named; or there may be no
547. Soul in the case — and the fat icy worm,
548. Give him a tongue, can tell us all about him.
549. STUDENT. Here is music. Stay. That simple melody
550. Comes on the heart like infant innocence —
551. Pure feeling pure; while yet the new-bodied soul
552. Is swinging to the motion of the heavens,
553. And scarce hath caught, as yet, earth's backening[4] course.
554. FESTUS. The heart is formed as earth was — its first age
555. Formless and void, and fit but for itself;
556. Then feelings half alive, just organized,
557. Come next, — then creeping sports and purposes, —
558. Then animal desires, delights, and loves —
559. For love is the first and granite-like effect
560. Of things — the longest and the highest: next
561. The wild and winged desires, youth's saurian[5] schemes
562. Which creep and fly by turns; which kill, and eat,
563. And do disgorge each other: comes at length
564. The mould of perfect matchless manhood — then
565. Woman divides the heart, and multiplies it.
566. The insipidity of innocence
567. Palls: it is guilty, happy, and undone.
568. A death is laid upon it, and it goes —
569. Quits its green Eden for the sandy world,
570. Where it works out its nature, as it may,
571. In sweat, smiles, blood, tears, cursings, and what not.
572. And giant sins possess it; and it worships
573. Works of the hand, head, heart — its own or others —
574. A creature worship, which excludeth God's:
575. The less thrusts out the greater. Warning comes,
576. But the heart fears not — feels not; till at last
577. Down comes the flood from Heaven; and that heart,
578. Broken inwards, earthlike, to its central hell;
579. Or like the bright and burning eye we see
580. Inly, when pressed hard backwards on the brain,
581. Ends and begins again — destroyed, is saved.

4. Backening: Keeping back, retarding (*OED*).
5. Saurian: Pertaining to the reptile order Sauria (*OED*); 'reptilian' is probably the intention.

582. Every man is the first man to himself,
583. And Eves are just as plentiful as apples;
584. Nor do we fall, nor are we saved by proxy.
585. The Eden we live in is our own heart;
586. And the first thing we do, of our free choice,
587. Is sure and necessary to be sin.
588. LUCIFER. The only right men have is to be damned.
589. What is the good of music, or the beauty?
590. Music tells no truths.
591. FESTUS.   Oh! there is nought so sweet
592. As lying and listening music from the hands,
593. And singing from the lips, of one we love —
594. Lips that all others should be turned to. Then
595. The world would all be love and song; Heaven's harps
596. And orbs join in: the whole be harmony —
597. Distinct, yet blended — blending all in one
598. Long and delicious tremble like a chord.
599. But to Thee, God! all being is a harp,
600. Whereon Thou makest mightiest melody.
601. Hast ever been in love?
602. STUDENT.   I never was.
603. FESTUS. 'Tis love which mostly destinates our life.
604. What makes the world in after life I know not,
605. For our horizon alters as we age:
606. Power only can make up for the lack of love —
607. Power of some sort. The mind at one time grows
608. So fast, it fails; and then its stretch is more
609. Than its strength; but, as it opes, love fills it up,
610. Like to the stamen in the flower of life,
611. Till for the time we well-nigh grow all love;
612. And soon we feel the want of one kind heart
613. To love what's well, and to forgive what's ill,
614. In us, — that heart we play for at all risks.
615. STUDENT. How can the heart which lies embodied deep,
616. In blood and bone, set like a ruby eye
617. Into the breast, be made a toy for beauty,
618. And, vane-like, blown about by every wanton sigh?
619. How can the soul, the rich star-travelled stranger,
620. Who here sojourneth only for a purchase,
621. Risk all the riches of his years of toil,
622. And his God-vouched inheritance of Heaven,
623. For one light momentary taste of love?

624. FESTUS. It is so; and when once you know the sport —
625. The crowded pack of passions in full cry —
626. The sweet deceits, the tempting obstacles —
627. The smile, the sigh, the tear, and the embrace —
628. All the delights of love at last in one,
629. With kisses close as stars in the milky way,
630. In at the death you cry, though 'twere your own!
631. STUDENT. Upon my soul, most sound morality!
632. Nothing is thought of virtue, then, nor judgment?
633. FESTUS. Oh! everything is thought of — but not then,
634. And — judgment — no! it is nowhere in the field.
635. STUDENT. Slow-paced and late arriving, still it comes.
636. I cannot understand this love; I hear
637. Of its idolatry, not its respect
638. FESTUS. Respect is what we owe; love what we give.
639. And men would mostly rather give than pay.
640. Morality's the right rule for the world,
641. Nor could society cohere without
642. Virtue; and there are those whose spirits walk
643. Abreast of angels and the future, here.
644. Respect and love thou such.
645. LUCIFER.   Of course you wish
646. Women to love you rather than love them.
647. It is better. Now, you say you are a student.
648. All things take study; what more than the face —
649. Whether your own, or hers you look and long at?
650. There are many ways to one end: here is one: —
651. You are good-looking; but that matters little:
652. It only pleases them. To please yourself
653. Your face may be as ugly as the —— Well, well;
654. But you must cultivate yourself: it will pay you.
655. Study a dimple; work hard at a smile:
656. The things most delicate require most pains.
657. Practice the upward — now the sidelong glance—
658. Now the long passionful unwinking gaze,
659. Which beats itself at last, and sees air only.
660. Be restless, and distress yourself for her.
661. Take up her hand — press it, and pore on it —
662. Let it drop — snatch it again as though you had
663. Let slip so much of honor or of Heaven.
664. Swear — vow by all means — never miss an oath:
665. If broken, why it only spoils itself;

666. It is a broken oath and not an whole one.
667. Frown — toss about — let her lips be for a time:
668. But steal a kiss at last like fire from Heaven.
669. Weep if you can, and call the tears heat-drops.
670. Droop your head — sigh deep — play the fool, in short,
671. One hour, and she will play the fool for ever.
672. Mind! it is folly to tell women truth;
673. They would rather live on lies so they be sweet.
674. Never be long in one mind to one love.
675. You change your practice with your subject. All
676. Differ. But yet, who knows one woman well
677. By heart, knows all. It is my experience;
678. And I advise on good authority.
679. So thank me for my lecture on delusion.
680. FESTUS. Time laughs at love. It is a hateful sight
681. That bald old grey-beard jeering the boy, Love.
682. But as to women: that game has two sides.
683. Passion is from affection; and there is nought
684. So maddening and so lowering as to have
685. The worse in passion. Think, when one by one,
686. Pride, love, and jealousy, and fifty more
687. Great feelings column up to force a heart.
688. And all are beaten back— all fail — all fall:
689. The tower intact: but risk it: we must learn.
690. To know the world, be wise and be a fool.
691. The heart will have its swing — the world its way:
692. Who seeks to stop them, only throws himself down.
693. We must take as we find: go as they go.
694. Or stand aside. Let the world have the wall.
695. How do you think, pray, to get through the world?
696. STUDENT. I mean not to get through the world
697. But over it.
698. FESTUS.   Aspiring! You will find at all,
699. The world is all up-hill when we would do;
700. All down-hill when we suffer. Nay, it will part
701. Like the Red Sea, so that the poor may pass.
702. We make our compliments to wretchedness,
703. And hope the poor want nothing, and are well.
704. But I mean, what profession will you choose?
705. Surely you will do something for a name.
706. STUDENT. Names are of much more consequence than
        things.

707. FESTUS. Well; here's our honest, all-exhorting friend
708. The parson — here the doctor. I am sure
709. The Devil might act as moderator there,
710. And do mankind some service.
711. LUCIFER.   In his way.
712. STUDENT. But I care neither for men's souls nor bodies.
713. FESTUS. What say you to the law? are you ambitious?
714. STUDENT. Nor do I mind for other people's business.
715. I have no heart for their predicaments:
716. I am for myself. I measure every thing
717. By, what is it to me? from which I find
718. I have but little in common with the mass,
719. Except my meals and so forth; dress and sleep.
720. I have that within me I can live upon:
721. Spider-like, spin my place out anywhere.
722. FESTUS. To none of all the arts and sciences, —
723. Astronomy nor entomology,
724. Nor gunnery, for instance, then you feel
725. Attracted heartily and mentally?
726. STUDENT. Why no; there are so many rise and fall,
727. One knows not which to choose. As for the stars,
728. I never look on them without dismay.
729. Earth has outrun them in our modern mind,
730. By worlds of odds. Enough for us, it seems,
731. And our cold calculators to jot down
732. Their revolutions, distances, and squares; —
733. And the bright laws which stars and spirits rule,
734. Are all laid out and buried grave on grave.
735. The fourfold worlds and elemental spheres,
736. Which in concentric circles, like the ring
737. That the magician stands in, from on high
738. Give spiritual calling to our earth,
739. And lord it over her, yet in such wise,
740. That still by them we may conjoin our souls
741. Unto the starry spirits of all worlds;
742. Beyond the changeful mansions of the moon,
743. Beyond the burning heart of heaven, where dwell
744. The governors of nature and the blest,
745. All knowing spirits and celestial,
746. And divine demons; are all gone — extinct.
747. There is no danger now of knowing aught
748. Which ought not to be known. No more of that! —

749. And you, ye planetary sons of light!
750. From him who hovereth, moth-like, round the sun
751. To six-mooned Uranus, Light's loftiest round.
752. Your aspects, dignities, ascendancies,
753. Your partile quartiles, and your plastic trines,
754. And all your Heavenly houses and effects,
755. Shall meet no more devout expounders here.
756. You too, ye juried signs, earth's sunny path
757. Upon her wheeling orbit, all farewell!
758. Your exaltations and triplicities,
759. Fiery, airy, and the rest; your falls,
760. And detriments, and governments, and gifts,
761. Are all abolished. Henceforth ye shall shine
762. In vain to man. Diurnal, cardinal,
763. Nocturnal, equinoctial, hot or dry,
764. Earthy, or moist, or feminine, or fixed,
765. Luxurious, violent, bicorporate,
766. Masculine, barren, and commanding, cold,
767. Fruitful or watery, or what not, now
768. It matters nothing. The joy of Jupiter,
769. The exaltation of the Dragon's head,
770. The sun's triplicity and glorious
771. Day house on high, the moon's dim detriment,
772. And all the starry inclusions of all signs —
773. Shall rise, and rule, and pass, and no one know
774. That there are spirit-rulers of all worlds,
775. Which fraternise with earth, and, though unknown,
776. Hold in the shining voices of the stars
777. Communion on high, ever and everywhere. —
778. The mystic charm of numbers and the sole
779. Oneness which is in all, of nature's great
780. Triadic principle, in all things seen;
781. In man thus, as composed of thrice three forms
782. Intrinsic; first, corporeally, blood,
783. Body, and bones; next, intellectively,
784. Imagination, judgment, memory;
785. And thirdly, spiritually, mind and soul,
786. And spirit, which unites with God the whole
787. Being, and comes from and returns to Him, —
788. Allures no more man's mind debased. Thus, too,
789. Of alchemy; the golden starry stone,
790. Invisible, the principle of life,

791. The quintessence of all the elements,
792. Is still unbought; — still flows the stream of pearl
793. Beneath the magic mountain; still the scent
794. As of a thousand amaranthine wreaths, which lures
795. All life unto its sweetness, floats around
796. Mistlike, the shining bath where Luna laves,
797. Or Sol, bright brother of that mooned maid,
798. Triumphs in light; — the spiritual sun,
799. The Heavenly Earth smaragdine,[6] and the fire-
800. Spirit of life, the live land still exist,
801. Immortally, internally unseen. —
802. Still breathes the Paradisal air around
803. The universal whole; the watery fire,
804. Destructive, yet impalpable to sense,
805. The initial and conclusion of the world,
806. Yea, the beginning and the end of Death,
807. The secret which is shared 'tween God and man,
808. And which is nature only, wholly, still
809. In Heavenly gloom incomprehensible
810. Wait the Deific will; yea, still the light
811. Whereto all elements contribute, burns
812. About us and within us, world and soul; —
813. The primal sperm and matter of the world,
814. Whose centre is the limit of all things, —
815. The snowy gold, the star and spirit seed
816. Which is to render rich and deathless all, —
817. The self-begot, self-wedded, and self-born,
818. Which the wind carries in its womb, all have,
819. And few receive; the spirit of the earth
820. The water of immortal life still lives: —
821. The universal solvent of disease
822. Still bounds through nature's veins; and still, in fine,
823. The secrets only to be told by fire
824. Starry or beamless, central and extreme,
825. Burn to be born. And other natures may
826. Use them, and do. In Demogorgon's hall
827. Still sits the universal mystery
828. Throned in itself and ministered unto
829. By its own members: — Man, alas! alone,

6. Smaragdine: Of an emerald green (*OED*).

830. The recreant spirit of the universe,
831. Contemns the operations of the light;
832. Loves surface-knowledge; calls the crimes of crowds
833. Virtue: adores the useful vices; licks
834. The gory dust from off the feet of war,
835. And swears it food for gods, though fit for fiends
836. Only; — reversing just the Devil's state
837. When first he entered on this orb of man's, —
838. A fallen angel's form, a reptile's soul.
839. LUCIFER. Oh! this is libelous to man and fiend
840. And brute together.
841. STUDENT.   All are art and part
842. Of the same mystic treason. But enough; —
843. The most material, immaterial
844. Departments of pure wisdom are despised.
845. For well we know that, properly prepared,
846. Souls self-adapted knowledge to receive
847. Are by the truth desired, illumined; man's
848. Spirit, extolled, dilated, clarified,
849. By holy meditation and divine
850. Lore, fits him to convene with purer powers
851. Which do unseen surround us aye and gladden
852. In human good and exaltation; thus
853. The face of Heaven is not more clear to one,
854. Than to another outwardly; but one
855. By strong intention of his soul perceives,
856. Attracts, unites himself to essences
857. And elemental spirits of wider range
858. And more beneficent nature, by whose aid
859. Occasion, circumstance, futurity
860. Impress on him their image, and impart
861. Their secrets to his soul; thus chance and lot
862. Are sacred things; thus dreams are verities.
863. But oh! alas for all earth's loftier lore,
864. And spiritual sympathy of worlds! —
865. There shall be no more magic nor cabala,
866. Nor Rosicrucian nor Alchymic lore,
867. Nor fairy fantasies; no more hobgoblins,
868. Nor ghosts, nor imps, nor demons. Conjurors,
869. Enchanters, witches, wizards, shall all die
870. Hopeless and heirless; their divining arts
871. Supernal or infernal — dead with them.

872. And so 'twill doubtless be with other things
873. In time; therefore I will commit my brain
874. To none of them.
875. FESTUS.   Perchance 'twere wiser not.
876. Man's heart hath not half uttered itself yet,
877. And much remains to do as well as say.
878. The heart is some time ere it finds its focus.
879. And when it does, with the whole light of nature
880. Strained through it to a hair 's breadth, it but burns
881. The things beneath it, which it lights to death.
882. Well, farewell, Mr. Student. May you never
883. Regret those hours which make the mind, if they
884. Unmake the body; for the sooner we
885. Are fit to be all mind, the better. Blest
886. Is he whose heart is the home of the great dead,
887. And their great thoughts. Who can mistake great thoughts?
888. They seize upon the mind — arrest, and search,
889. And shake it — bow the tall soul as by wind —
890. Rush over it like rivers over reeds,
891. Which quaver in the current— turn us cold,
892. And pale, and voiceless; leaving in the brain
893. A rocking and a ringing, — glorious,
894. But momentary, madness might it last,
895. And close the soul with Heaven as with a seal!
896. In lieu of all these things whose loss thou mournest,
897. If earnestly or not I know not, use
898. The great and good and true which ever live,
899. And are all common to pure eyes and true.
900. Upon the summit of each mountain-thought
901. Worship thou God; for Deity is seen
902. From every elevation of the soul.
903. Study the Light; attempt the high; seek out
904. The soul's bright path; and since the soul is fire
905. Of heat intelligential, turn it aye
906. To the all-Fatherly source of light and life;
907. Piety purifies the soul to see
908. Perpetual apparitions of all grace
909. And power, which to the sight of those who dwell
910. In ignorant sin are never known. Obey
911. Thy genius, for a minister it is
912. Unto the throne of Fate. Draw to thy soul,
913. And centralise the rays which are around

914. Of the Divinity. Keep thy spirit pure
915. From worldly taint by the repellant strength
916. Of virtue. Think on noble thoughts and deeds,
917. Ever. Count o'er the rosary of truth;
918. And practice precepts which are proven wise.
919. It matters not then what thou fearest. Walk
920. Boldly and wisely in that light thou hast; —
921. There is a hand above will help thee on.
922. I am an omnist, and believe in all
923. Religions, — fragments of one golden world
924. Yet to be relit in its place in Heaven —
925. For all are relatively true and false,
926. As evidence and earnest of the heart
927. To those who practice, or have faith in them.
928. The absolutely true religion is
929. In Heaven only, yea in Deity.
930. But foremost of all studies, let me not
931. Forget to bid thee learn Christ's faith by heart.
932. Study its truths, and practice its behests:
933. They are the purest, sweetest, peacefullest,
934. Of all immortal reasons or records:
935. They will be with thee when all else have gone.
936. Mind, body, passion, all wear out — not faith,
937. Nor truth. Keep thy heart cool, or rule its heat
938. To fixed ends: waste it not upon itself.
939. Not all the agony of all the damned,
940. Fused in one pang, vies with that earthquake throb
941. Which wakens it from waste to let us see
942. The world rolled by for aye; and that we must
943. Wait an eternity for our next chance,
944. Whether it be in Heaven or elsewhere.
945. STUDENT.   Sir,
946. I will remember this most grave advice,
947. And think of you with all respect.
948. FESTUS.   Well, mind!
949. The worst men often give the best advice.
950. Our deeds are sometimes better than our thoughts.
951. Commend me, friend, to every one you meet:
952. I am an universal favourite.
953. Old men admire me deeply for my beauty,
954. Young women for my genius and strict virtue,
955. And young men for my modesty and wisdom.

956. All turn to me, whenever I speak, full-faced,
957. As planets to the sun, or owls to a rushlight.
958. Farewell!
959. STUDENT. I hope to meet again.
960. FESTUS.   And I. —
961. Yonder's a woman singing. Let us hear her.
962. SINGER. In the gray church tower
963.   Were the clear bells ringing
964.   When a maiden sat in her lonely bower
965.   Sadly and lowly singing,
966.   And thus she sang, that maiden fair,
967.   Of the soft blue eyes and the long light hair:
968.   This hand hath oft been held by one
969.   Who now is far away;
970.   And here I sit and sigh alone
971.   Through all the weary day.
972.   Oh, when will he I love return!
973.   Oh, when shall I forget to mourn!
974.   Along the dark and dizzy path
975.   Ambition madly runs,
976.   'Tis there they say his course he hath,
977.   And therefore love he shuns.
978.   Oh, fame and honour bind his brow,
979.   For so he would be with me now!
980.   In the gray church tower
981.   Were the clear bells ringing,
982.   When a bounding step in that lonely bower
983.   Broke on the maiden singing;
984.   She turned, she saw; oh, happy fair!
985.   For her love who loved her so well was there!
986. LUCIFER. And we might trust these youths and maidens fair,
987. The world was made for nothing but love, love!
988. Now I think it was made but to be burned.
989. FESTUS. And if I love not now, while woman is
990. All bosom to the young, when shall I love?
991. Who ever paused on passion's fiery wheel?
992. Or trembling by the side of her he loved
993. Whose lightest touch brings all but madness, ever
994. Stopped coldly short to reckon up his pulse?
995. The car comes — and we lie — and let it come;
996. It crushes — kills — what then! It is joy to die.
997. Enough shall not fool me. I fling the foil

998. Away. Let me but look on aught which casts
999. The shadow of a pleasure, and here I bare
1000. A breast which would embrace a bride of fire.
1001. Pleasure — we part not! No! It were easier
1002. To wring God's lightnings from the grasp of God.
1003. I must be mad; but so is all the world.
1004. Folly. It matters not. What is the world
1005. To me? Nought. I am all things to myself.
1006. If my heart thundered, would the world rock? Well —
1007. Then let the mad world fight its shadow down;
1008. There soon will be nor sun, nor world, nor shadow.
1009. And thou, my blood, my bright red running soul —
1010. Rejoice thou, like a river in thy rapids!
1011. Rejoice — thou wilt never pale with age, nor thin;
1012. But in thy full dark beauty, vein by vein,
1013. Fold by fold, serpent-like, encircling me
1014. Like a stag, sunstruck, top thy bounds and die.
1015. Throb, bubble, sparkle, laugh and leap along!
1016. Make merry while the holidays shall last.
1017. Heart! I could tear thee out, thou fool! thou fool!
1018. And strip thee into shreds upon the wind:
1019. What have I done that thou shouldst serve me thus?
1020. LUCIFER. Let us away. We have had enough of this.
1021. FESTUS. The night is glooming on us. It is the hour
1022. When lovers will speak lowly, for the sake
1023. Of being nigh each other; and when love
1024. Shoots up the eye like morning on the east,
1025. Making amends for the long northern night
1026. They passed ere either knew the other loved.
1027. It is the hour of hearts, when all hearts feel
1028. As they could love to mad death, finding aught
1029. To give back fire; for love, like nature, is
1030. War — sweet war! Arms! To arms! so they be thine
1031. Woman! Old people may say what they please —
1032. The heart of age is like an emptied wine-cup,
1033. Its life lies in a heel-tap — how can they judge?
1034. 'Twere a waste of time to ask how they wasted theirs.
1035. But while the blood is bright, breath sweet, skin smooth,
1036. And limbs all made to minister delight —
1037. Ere yet we have shed our locks like trees their leaves,
1038. And we stand staring bare into the air —
1039. He is a fool who is not for love and beauty.

1040. I speak unto the young, for I am of them,
1041. And alway shall be. What are years to me?
1042. Traitors! that vice-like fang the hand ye lick;
1043. Ye fall like small birds beaten by a storm
1044. Against a dead wall, dead. I pity ye.
1045. Oh! that such mean things should raise hope or fear;
1046. Those Titans of the heart, that fight at Heaven
1047. And sleep by fits on fire; whose slightest stir's
1048. An earthquake. I am bound and blest to youth!
1049. Oh! give me to the young — the fair — the free —
1050. The brave, who would breast a rushing burning world
1051. Which came between them and their hearts' delight.
1052. None but the brave and beautiful can love.
1053. Oh, for the young heart like a fountain playing!
1054. Flinging its bright fresh feelings up to the skies
1055. It loves and strives to reach — strives, loves in vain:
1056. It is of earth, and never meant for Heaven.
1057. Let us love both, and die. The sphinx-like heart,
1058. Consistent in its inconsistency,
1059. Loathes life the moment that life's riddle is read:
1060. The knot of our existence is untied,
1061. And we lie loose and useless. Life is had;
1062. And then we sigh, and say, can this be all?
1063. It is not what we thought — it is very well —
1064. But we want something more — there is but death.
1065. And when we have said, and seen, and done, and had,
1066. Enjoyed and suffered, all we have wished and feared —
1067. From fame to ruin, and from love to loathing —
1068. There can come but one more change — try it — death.
1069. Oh! it is great to feel we care for nothing —
1070. That hope, nor love, nor fear, nor aught of earth
1071. Can check the royal lavishment of life;
1072. But like a streamer strown upon the wind,
1073. We fling our souls to fate and to the future.
1074. And to die young is youth's divinest gift, —
1075. To pass from one world fresh into another,
1076. Ere change hath lost the charm of soft regret,
1077. And feel the immortal impulse from within
1078. Which makes the coming, life — cry, alway, on!
1079. And follow it while strong — is Heaven's last mercy.
1080. There is a fire-fly in the southern clime
1081. Which shineth only when upon the wing;

1082. So is it with the mind: when once we rest,
1083. We darken. On! said God unto the soul
1084. As to the earth, for ever. On it goes,
1085. A rejoicing native of the infinite —
1086. As a bird of air — an orb of heaven.

SCENE 10

[*The centre*]
[*FESTUS and LUCIFER*]

1. LUCIFER. Behold us in the fire-crypts of the world!
2. Through seas and buried mountains tomblike tract,
3. Fit to receive the skeleton of Death
4. When he is dead — through earthquakes, and the bones
5. Of earthquake-swallowed cities, have we wormed
6. Down to the ever burning forge of fire,
7. Whereon in awful and omnipotent ease
8. Nature, the delegate of God, brings forth
9. Her everlasting elements, and breathes
10. Around that fluent heat of life which clothes
11. Itself in lightnings wandering through the air,
12. And pierces to the last and loftiest pore
13. Of Earth's snow-mantled mountains. In these vaults
14. Are hid the archives of the universe
15. And here the ashes of all ages gone,
16. Each finally inurned. These pillars stand,
17. Earth's testimony to eternity.
18. FESTUS. All that is solid now was fluid once
19. Water, or air, or fire, or some one
20. Permanent, permeating, element;
21. As in this focal, world-evolving fire
22. Like what I see around — the vacuous power
23. Whereon the world is based, e'en as wherein
24. It rolls, I must believe.

25. LUCIFER.   The original
26. Of all things is one thing. Creation is
27. One whole. The differences a mortal sees
28. Are diverse only to the finite mind.
29. FESTUS. This marble-walled immensity o'erroofed
30. With pendant mountains glittering, awes my soul.
31. God's hand hath scooped the hollow of this world;
32. Yea, none but His could; and I stand in it,
33. Like a forgotten atom of the light,
34. Some star hath lost upon its lightning flight.
35. LUCIFER. Here mayst thou lay thy hand on nature's heart,
36. And feel its thousand yeared throbbings cease.
37. High overhead, and deep beneath our feet,
38. The sea's broad thunder booms, scarce heard; around,
39. The arches, like uplifted continents
40. Of starry matter, burning inwardly,
41. Stand; and, hard by, earth's gleaming axle sleeps.
42. All moving, all unmoved.
43. FESTUS.   Age here on age
44. Lie heaped like withered leaves. And must it end?
45. LUCIFER. God worketh slowly: and a thousand years
46. He takes to lift His hand off. Layer on layer
47. He made earth, fashioned it and hardened it
48. Into the great, bright, useful thing it is;
49. Its seas, life-crowded, and soul-hallowed lands
50. He girded with the girdle of the sun,
51. That sets its bosom glowing like Love's own
52. Breathless embrace, close-clinging as for life; —
53. Veined it with gold, and dusted it with gems,
54. Lined it with fire, and round its heart-fire bowed
55. Rock-ribs unbreakable; until at last
56. Earth took her shining station as a star,
57. In Heaven's dark hall, high up the crowd of worlds.
58. All this and thus did God; and yet it ends.
59. The ball He rolled and rounded, melts away
60. E'en now to its constituent atomies.
61. FESTUS. It is enough. Though here were posited
62. All secrets of existence, natural
63. Or supernatural, dwell not here would I,
64. Though 'twere to drain profoundest fountains. No!
65. I love it not, the science nor the scene.
66. I long to know again the fresh green earth,

67. The breathing breeze, the sea and sacred stars.
68. These recollections crowd upon my soul,
69. As constellations on the evening skies,
70. And will not be forgotten. Let us leave!
71. LUCIFER. Aught that reminds the exile of his home
72. Is surely pleasant. I, friend, am content.
73. FESTUS. I cannot be content with less than Heaven.
74. O Heaven, I love thee ever! sole and whole,
75. Living and comprehensive of all life;
76. Thee, agy world, thee, universal Heaven,
77. And heavenly universe! thee, sacred seat
78. Of intellective Time, the throned stars
79. And old oracular night; — by night or day,
80. To me thou canst not but be beautiful,
81. Boundless, all-central, universal sphere!
82. Whether the sun all-light thee, or the moon,
83. Embayed in clouds, mid starry islands round,
84. With mighty beauty inundate the air; —
85. Or when one star, like a great drop of light,
86. From her full flowing urn hangs tremulous, —
87. Yea, like a tear from her the eye of night,
88. Let fall o'er nature's volume as she reads: —
89. Or, when in radiant thousands, each star reigns
90. In imparticipable royalty,
91. Leaderless, uncontrasted with the light
92. Wherein their light is lost, the sons of fire,
93. Arch element of the Heavens; — when storm and cloud
94. Debar the mortal vision of the eye
95. From wandering o'er thy threshold, — more and more
96. I love thee, thinking on the splendid calm
97. Which bounds the deadly fever of these days —
98. The higher, holier, spiritual Heaven.
99. And when this world, within whose heartstrings now
100. I feel myself encoiled, shall be resolved,
101. Thee I shall be permitted still, perchance,
102. To love and live in endlessly.
103. LUCIFER.   All here
104. Thou seest hath holden fellowship with gods;
105. With eldest Time and primal matter, space,
106. And stars, and air, and all-inherent fire,
107. The watery deep and chaos, night, the all,
108. And the interior immortality,

109. And first-begotten Love. These rocks retain
110. Their caverned footsteps printed in pure fire.
111. Those were the times, the ancient youth of earth,
112. The elemental years, when earth and Heaven
113. Made one in holy bridals, — royal gods
114. Their bright immortal issue: when men's minds
115. Were vast as continents, and not as now
116. Minute and indistinguishable plots,
117. With here and there acres of untilled brains; when lived
118. The great original, broad-eyed, sunken race,
119. Whose wisdom, like these sea-sustaining rocks,
120. Hath formed the base of the world's fluctuous lore: —
121. When too, by mountainous travail, human might
122. Sought to possess the everlasting Heavens,
123. And incommunicable, by the right
124. Of self-acquirement and high kindred with
125. Celestial virtues; — when the mortal powers —
126. Forecounsel, wisdom, and experience,
127. Teachers of all arts, founders of all good,
128. With Godhood strove, and gloriously failed —
129. In failure half successful; as these scenes,
130. Fire-fountains, and volcano-utterances,
131. Earth-heavings, island vomitings, evince.
132. FESTUS. The world hath made such comet-like advance
133. Lately on science, we may almost hope,
134. Before we die of sheer decay, to learn
135. Something about our infancy. But me
136. This troubles not. Were all earth's mountain chains
137. To utter fire at once, what a grand show
138. Of pyrotechny for our neighbor moon!
139. Let us ascend; but not through the charred throat
140. Of an extinct volcano.
141. LUCIFER.   This way — down.
142. So shalt thou thread the world at once.
143. FESTUS.   Haste, haste.

FESTUS WORSHIPPING

SCENE 11

[*A ruined Temple*]
[*FESTUS and LUCIFER*]

1.   FESTUS. Here will I worship solely.
2.   LUCIFER.   Tis a fane
3.   Once sacred to the Sun.
4.   FESTUS.   It matters not
5.   What false god here hath falsely been adored,
6.   Or what life-hating rites these walls have viewed:
7.   The truly holy soul, which hath received
8.   The unattainable, can hallow hell.
9.   Now to the only true and Triune God
10.   These walls shall echo praise, if never yet
11.   Bring me a morsel of the fire without;
12.   For I will make a sacred offering
13.   To God, as though the High Priest of the world.
14.   He lacks not consecration at best hands
15.   Whom Thou hast hallowed, Lord, by choice; and these,
16.   The elements I offer, Thou hast made
17.   Holy, by making them.
18.   LUCIFER.   Lo! here is fire.
19.   I will await thee in the air.
20.   FESTUS.   Withdraw!
21.   Thine, Lord! are all the elements and worlds; —
22.   The sun is Thy bright servant, and the moon
23.   Thy servant's servant; — the round rushing earth,
24.   The lifeful air, the thousand winged winds,
25.   The Heaven-kinned fire, the continental clouds,
26.   The sea broad breasted, and the tranced lake,
27.   The rich arterial rivers, and the hills
28.   Which wave their woody tresses in the breeze,
29.   In grateful undulation, all are Thine; —
30.   Thine are the snow-robed mountains circling earth

31. As the white spirits God the Saviour's throne; —
32. Thine the bright secrets, central in all orbs,
33. And rudimental mysteries of life.
34. The sun-starred night, the ever-maiden morn,
35. The all-prevailing day, consummate eve,
36. Confess them Thine through the perpetual world: —
37. All art hath wrought from earth, or science lured
38. From truth, like flame out of the fire cloud, are
39. Thine; — Thine the glory, all belongs to Thee,
40. Finite, indefinite and infinite,
41. As mountains to a world, as worlds to Heaven.
42. The high doomed city and the toilful town
43. And early hamlet, — all that live or die,
44. That flourish or decay, that change, or stand
45. Before Thy face, unchanged, exist for Thee,
46. Or are not at Thy bidding; Thine, all souls;
47. Atom and world, the universe is Thine! —
48. Thou canst as easily turn Thy kindest eye
49. From comprehending the bright Infinite,
50. To this crushed temple, where the wild flower decks
51. Its earthquake-rifted walls, and the birds build
52. In corners of its columned capitals, —
53. And to this crumbling heart I offer here,
54. As trust Thine own Eternity. Behold!
55. Accept, I pray Thee, Lord! this sacrifice;
56. These elemental offerings simple, pure,
57. Which in the name of man I make to Thee,
58. Formless, save prostrate soul and kneeling heart —
59. In token of Thy perfect monarchy
60. And all comprising mercy. These are they!
61. A flowery turf, a branch, a burning coal,
62. A cup of water and an empty bowl;
63. This air-filled bowl is typic of the world
64. Thou fillest with Thy spirit, and the soul,
65. Receptive of Thy life-conferring truth; —
66. This the symbolic element wherefrom
67. We are to be reborn, wherein made pure;
68. Those whom Thou choosest are to be redeemed
69. Out of the mighty multitudes of men;
70. Yet all as of one nature be redeemed.

71. This coal, torn flaming from the earth, proclaims
72. Thy sin-consuming mercy as of earth;
73. And may our souls ever aspire to Thee,
74. As these pale flames unto the stars; this turf
75. Is as the earthy nature and abode
76. We would subject to Thee; and lieth here,
77. The representative of every star
78. And world-extended matter! Lord! this branch,
79. Which waveth high o'er all, oh, let it sign
80. Thine own Eternal Son's humanity,
81. Which was on earth yet ever lives in Heaven,
82. Redemptive of all Being. Golden Branch!
83. Which, in the eld-time, seer's and sybil's words,
84. Full of dark central thought and mystic truth,
85. Foretold should overspread the spirit world,
86. And with its fruit heal every wound of Death, —
87. Tree of eternal life, Thee all adore.
88. Accept this prayer, O Saviour! that if men
89. Can nothing do but sin, Thou mayst forgive
90. The creature crime, and bring back all to Thee.
91. Thou art the one who made the universe;
92. Yet didst Thou walk on earth; Thou brakest bread
93. And drankest wine with men, betokening so
94. Thine own complete, Divine Humanity.
95. May all obey Thy words and do Thy will!
96. We praise Thee God, our father; whoso would
97. Be saved, let him believe in Thee Triune.
98. Thou doest all things rightly; all are best,
99. Sorrow, or joy, or power, or suffering.
100. Providing, therefore, all things that must be
101. And ought to be, as Thou dost and hast done,
102. From the beginning even to the end,
103. This heart let cease from prayer, these lips from praise,
104. Save that which life shall offer pauselessly.
105. Now go I forth again, refreshed, consoled,
106. Upon my time-enduring pilgrimage.
107. Ho! Lucifer!
108. LUCIFER. I wait thee.
109. FESTUS.   Whither next?
110. LUCIFER. As thou wilt, apposite or opposite.

111. 'Tis light translateth night; 'tis inspiration
112. Expounds experience; 'tis the west explains
113. The east: 'tis time unfolds Eternity.

SCENE 12

[*A Metropolis — Public Place*]
[*FESTUS and LUCIFER*]

1. FESTUS. What can be done here?
2. LUCIFER.   Oh! a thousand things,
3. As well as elsewhere.
4. FESTUS.   True; it is a place
5. Where passion, occupation, or reflection,
6. May find fit food or field; but suits not me.
7. My burden is the spirit, and my life
8. Is henceforth solely spiritual.
9. LUCIFER.   Well; —
10. At the occurrent season, too, it shall
11. Be satisfied. It might be even now.
12. From things about us. But look, here comes a man
13. Thou knowest well.
14. FESTUS.   I do. Stop friend! of late
15. I have not seen thee. Whither goest thou now?
16. FRIEND. I am upon my business, and in haste.
17. FESTUS. Business! I thought thou wast a simple schemer.
18. FRIEND. Mayhap I am.
19. FESTUS.   There is a visionary
20. Business, as well as visionary faith.
21. FRIEND. I have been, all life, living in a mine,
22. Lancing the world for gold. I have not yet
23. Fingered the right vein. Oh! I often wish
24. The time would come again, which science prates of,
25. When earth's bright veins ran ruddy, virgin gold.
26. FESTUS. When the world's gold melts, all the poorer metals,
27. All things less pure, less precious, all beside,

28. Will vanish; nought be left but gems and gold.
29. If all were rich, gold would be penniless.
30. LUCIFER. I have a secret I would fain impart
31. To one who would make right use of it. Now, mark!
32. Chemists say there are fifty elements.
33. And more; — wouldst know a ready recipe
34. For riches? —
35. FRIEND.   That indeed I would, good sir.
36. LUCIFER. Get then these fifty earths, or elements.
37. Or what not. Mix them up together. Put
38. All to the question. Tease them well with fire.
39. Vapour and trituration — every way;
40. Add the right quantity of lunar rays;
41. Boil them, and let them cool, and watch what comes.
42. FRIEND. Thrice greatest Hermes! but it must be; yes!
43. I'll go and get them; good day, — instantly. [*goes*]
44. LUCIFER. He'll be astonished, probably.
45. FESTUS.   He will,
46. In any issue of the experiment.
47. Perhaps the nostrum may explode and blow him
48. Body and soul to atoms and to —
49. LUCIFER.   Nonsense!
50. FESTUS. There needs no satire on men's rage for gold;
51. Their nature is the best one, and excuse.
52. And now what next?
53. LUCIFER. Why let us take our ease
54. Beside this feathery fountain. It is cool
55. And pleasant, and the people passing by,
56. Fit subjects for two moralists like us.
57. Here we can speculate on policy,
58. On social manners, fashions, and the news.
59. Now the political aspect of the world,
60. At present, is most cheerful. To begin,
61. Like charity, at home. Out of all wrongs
62. The most atrocious, the most righteous ends
63. Are happiest wrought.
64. FESTUS.   It ofttimes chances so.
65. LUCIFER. Take of the blood of martyrs, tears of slaves,
66. The groans of prisoned patriots, and the sweat
67. Wrung from the bones of Famine, like parts. Add
68. Vapour of orphan's sigh, and wail of all

69. Whom war hath spoiled, or law first fanged, then gorged; —
70. The stifled breath of man's free natural thought, —
71. The tyrant's lies; the curses of the proud;
72. The usurpations of the lawful heir,
73. The treasonous rebellions of the wise,
74. The poor man's patient prayers; and let all these
75. Simmer, some centuries, o'er the slow red fire
76. Of human wrath; and there results, at last,
77. A glorious constitution and a grand
78. Totality of nothings; — as we see. —
79. [*Soldiers pass; music, etc.*]
80. Man is a military animal,
81. Glories in gunpowder, and loves parade;
82. Prefers them to all things.
83. FESTUS.   Of recipes,
84. Enough! Life's but a sword's length, at the best.
85. LUCIFER. War, war, still war! from age to age, old Time
86. Hath washed his hands in the heart's blood of Earth.
87. FESTUS. Ye fields of death! ye are earth's purest pride;
88. For what is life to freedom? War must be
89. While men are what they are; while they have bad
90. Passions to be roused up; while ruled by men;
91. While all the powers and treasures of a land
92. Are at the beck of the ambitious crowd;
93. While injuries can be inflicted, or
94. Insults be offered; yea, while rights are worth
95. Maintaining, freedom keeping, or life having,
96. So long the sword shall shine; so long shall war
97. Continue, and the need for war remain.
98. LUCIFER. And yet all war shall cease.
99. FESTUS.   It must and shall.
100. Some news seems stirring; what I know not yet.
101. LUCIFER, Nor I. I heard that one of Saturn's moons
102. Had flown upon his face and blinded him.
103. 'T was also said, in circles I frequent
104. At times, his outer ring was falling off.
105. If I should find, I'll keep it. It might fit
106. A little finger such as mine, I think.
107. Poor Saturn! much I doubt he is breaking up.
108. But for these news, I know not what they be.
109. Someone perhaps has lit on a new vein
110. Of stars in Heaven: or cracked one with his teeth,

111. To look inside it, or made out at last
112. The circulation of the light; or what
113. Think'st thou?
114. FESTUS.   I know not. Ask!
115. LUCIFER.   Sir, what's the news?
116. PASSER-BY. The news are good news, being none at all.
117. LUCIFER. Your goodness, Sir, I deem of like extent.
118. We heard the great Bear was confined of twins.
119. STRANGER. 'Tis not unlikely stars do propagate.
120. FESTUS. And so much for civility and news.
121. This city is one of the world's social poles,
122. Round which events revolve: here, dial-like,
123. Time makes no movement but is registered.
124. LUCIFER. Yon gaudy equipage! hast ever seen
125. A drowning dragon-fly floating down a brook,
126. Topping the sunny ripples as they rise,
127. Till in some ambushed eddy it is sucked down
128. By something underneath? Thus with the rich; —
129. Their gilding makes their death conspicuous.
130. FESTUS. Some men are nobly rich, some nobly poor,
131. Some the reverse. Rank makes no difference.
132. LUCIFER. The poor may die in swarms unheeded. They
133. But swell the mass of columned ciphers. Oh,
134. Ye poor, ye wretched, ye bowed down by woe!
135. Thank God for something, though it were but this,
136. Ye fire, ye ashes!
137. FESTUS.   Thou art surely mad.
138. LUCIFER. I meant to moralize. I cannot see
139. A crowd, and not think on the fate of man —
140. Clinging to error as a dormant bat
141. To a dead bough. Well, 'tis his own affair.
142. FESTUS. All homilies on the sorts and lot of men
143. Are vain and wearisome. I want to know
144. No more of human nature. As it is,
145. I honour it and hate it. Let that do.
146. LUCIFER. Here is a statue to some mighty man
147. Who bent his name on the drum of the world's ear
148. Till it was stupefied, and, I suppose,
149. Not knowing what it was about, reared up
150. This marble mockery of mortality,
151. Which shall outlive the memory of the man
152. And all like him who water earth with blood,

153. And sow with bones, or any good he did,
154. As eagles outlive gnats. But never mind!
155. Why carp at insect sins, or crumblike crimes?
156. The world, the great imposture still succeeds;
157. Still, in Titanic immortality,
158. Writhes 'neath the burning mountain of its sins.
159. FESTUS. There's an old adage about sin and some one.
160. The world is not exactly what I thought it,
161. But pretty nearly so; and after all,
162. 'Tis not so bad as good men make it out,
163. Nor such a hopeless wretch.
164. LUCIFER.　　For all the world
165. Not I would slander it. Dear world, thou art
166. Of all things under Heaven by me most loved,
167. The most consistent, the least fallible.
168. Believe me ever thine affectionate
169. LUCIFER. P.S. Sweet, remember me!
170. FESTUS. Wilt go to the Cathedral?
171. LUCIFER.　　No, indeed;
172. I have just confessed.
173. FESTUS.　　Well, to the concert, then?
174. LUCIFER. Some fifteen hundred thousand million years
175. Have passed since last I heard a chorus.
176. FESTUS.　　Good!
177. LUCIFER. In sooth, I cannot calculate the time.
178. There are no eras in Eternity,
179. No ages. Time is as the body, and
180. Eternity the spirit of existence.
181. FESTUS. That would I learn and prove.
182. LUCIFER.　　The finite soul
183. Can never learn the Infinite, nor be
184. Informed by it, unaided.
185. FESTUS.　　Be it so.
186. What shall we do?
187. LUCIFER. I put myself in your hands.
188. FESTUS. Wilt go on 'Change?[1]
189. LUCIFER. I rarely speculate.
190. Steady receipts are mostly to my taste.
191. Besides, I spurn the system. Take my arm.

---

1. 'Change: The stock-exchange.

192. FESTUS. But something must be done to pass the time.
193. LUCIFER. True; let us pass, then, all time.
194. FESTUS.   I shall be
195. Most happy; only shew me how.
196. LUCIFER.   Why, thus.
197. I have the power to make thy spirit free
198. Of its poor frame of flesh, yet not by death, —
199. And reunite them afterwards! Wilt thou
200. Entrust thyself to me?
201. FESTUS.   In God I trust.
202. And in His word of safety. Have thy will.
203. Where shall it be effected?
204. LUCIFER.   Here and now.
205. Recline thou calmly on yon marble slab,
206. As though asleep. The world will miss thee not;
207. Its complement is perfect. I will mind
208. That no impertinent meddler troubles there
209. Thy tranced frame. The brain shall cease its life-
210. Engrossing business, and the living blood,
211. The wine of life which maketh drunk the soul,
212. Sleep in the sacred vessels of the heart.
213. Three steps the sun hath taken from his throne.
214. Already, downwards, and ere he hath gone,
215. Who calmeth tempests with his mighty light,
216. We will return; and till then the bright rain
217. Of yonder fountain fails not.
218. FESTUS.   Thus be it!
219. Come! we are wasting moments here that now
220. Belong, of right, to immortality,
221. And to another world.
222. LUCIFER.   Prepare! —
223. FESTUS.   And thou?
224. LUCIFER. I vanish altogether.
225. FESTUS.   Excellent!
226. LUCIFER. Body and spirit part! —

THE SPIRIT OF FESTUS DISEMBODIED

SCENE 13

[*Air*]
[*LUCIFER* and *FESTUS*]

1.   FESTUS. Where, where am I?
2.   LUCIFER. We are in space and time, just as we were
3.   Some half a second since; where would'st thou be?
4.   FESTUS. I would be in Eternity and Heaven;
5.   The spirit and the blessed spirit, of Existence.
6.   LUCIFER. And thou shalt be, and shalt pass
7.   All secondary nature; all the rules
8.   And the results of time: upon thy spirit
9.   These things shall act no more; their hands shall be
10.   Withered upon thee, as the ray of life
11.   Returns to that it came from: they shall cease
12.   In thee, like lightning in the deadening sea.
13.   But not now; we have worlds to go through, first.
14.   When spirit hath deposited its earth,
15.   And brightly, freely flows, self-purified
16.   In its own action, acted on by God,
17.   It holds the starry transcript of the skies
18.   Booklike within its bosom, evermore.
19.   But thine even now, exhausted, not exhaled,
20.   Bears the design of earthly discontent,
21.   Not sacred satisfaction. Unto him
22.   Whose soul is saved, all things are clear as stars,
23.   And, to the chosen, safety: — to none else.
24.   Nor cold insurgent heart, nor menial mind
25.   Can compass this: it is the way of God:
26.   The starry path of Heaven which none can tread
27.   But spirits high as Heaven, which He hath raised;
28.   Who were of Him before all worlds, and are
29.   Beloved and saved for ever while they live.
30.   Thou of the world art yet, with motives, means,
31.   And ends as others.
32.   FESTUS. I will no more of it.

33.   LUCIFER. Oh, dream it not! Thou knowest not the depth
34.   Of nature's dark abyss, thyself, nor God.
35.   Light over strong and darkness over long
36.   Blind equally the eye. Thou mayst yet rise
37.   And fall as often as the sea.
38.   FESTUS.   How comes it,
39.   Being a spirit, that I see not all
40.   As spirit should?
41.   LUCIFER.   Thou lackest life and death.
42.   The life of Heaven and the death of earth.
43.   Then wouldst thou see in harmony with God,
44.   Creation's strife.
45.   FESTUS.   Death alters not the spirit!
46.   LUCIFER. Death must be undergone ere understood.
47.   One world is as another. Rest we here! —

SCENE 14

[Another and a better World]
[FESTUS and LUCIFER]

1.   FESTUS. What a sweet world! Which is this, Lucifer?
2.   LUCIFER. This is the star of evening and of beauty.
3.   FESTUS. Otherwise Venus. I will stay here.
4.   LUCIFER.   Nay:
5.   It is but a visit.
6.   FESTUS.   Let us look about us.
7.   It is Heaven, it must be; aught so beautiful
8.   Must, I am sure, have feeling. Cannot worlds live?
9.   Least things have life. Why not the greatest, too?
10.   An atom is a world, a world an atom
11.   Seen relatively: Death an act of Life.
12.   LUCIFER. This is a world where every loveliest thing
13.   Lasts longest; where decay lifts never head
14.   Above the grossest forms, and matter here

15.   Is all transparent substance; the flower fades not,
16.   The beautiful die never here: Death lies
17.   Adreaming — he has nought to do — the babe
18.   Plays with his darts. Nought dies but what should die.
19.   Here are no earthquakes, storms, nor plagues; no Hell
20.   At heart; no floating flood on high. The soil
21.   Is ever fresh and fragrant as a rose —
22.   The skies, like one wide rainbow, stand on gold —
23.   The clouds are light as rose leaves — and the dew,
24.   'Tis of the tears which stars weep, sweet with joy —
25.   The air is softer than a loved one's sigh —
26.   The ground is glowing with all priceless ore,
27.   And glistening with gems like a bride's bosom —
28.   The trees have silver stems and emerald leaves —
29.   The fountains bubble nectar — and the hills
30.   Are half alive with light. Yet it is not Heaven.
31.   FESTUS. Oh, how this world should pity man's! I love
32.   To walk earth's woods when the storm bends his bow,
33.   And volleys all his arrows off at once;
34.   And when the dead brown branch comes crashing close
35.   To my feet, to tread it down, because I feel
36.   Decay my foe: and not to triumph's worse
37.   Than not to win. It is wrong to think on earth;
38.   But terror hath a beauty even as mildness;
39.   And I have felt more pleasure far on earth;
40.   When, like a lion or a day of battle,
41.   The storm rose, roared, shook out his shaggy mane,
42.   And leaped abroad on the world, and lay down red,
43.   Licking himself to sleep as it got light;
44.   And in the cataract-like tread of a crowd,
45.   And its irresistible rush, flooding the green
46.   As though it came to doom, than e'er I can
47.   Feel in this faery orb of shade and shine.
48.   I love earth!
49.   LUCIFER.   Thou art mad to dote on earth
50.   When with this sphere of beauty.
51.   FESTUS.   It is the blush
52.   Of being; surely, too, a maiden world,
53.   Unmarred by thee. Touch it not, Lucifer!
54.   LUCIFER. It is too bright to tarnish.
55.   FESTUS.   Didst thou fail?
56.   LUCIFER. I cannot fail. With me success is nature.

57. I am the cause, means, consequence of ill.

58. Thou canst not yet enjoy a sensuous world —

59. Refined though ne'er so little o'er thine own,

60. And yet wouldst enter Heaven. Valhalla's halls,

61. And sculls o'erbrimmed with mead, Elysian plains —

62. Eden, where life was toilless, and gave man

63. All things to live with, nothing to live for; —

64. The Moslem's bowers of love, and streams of wine

65. And palaces of purest adamant,

66. Where dark-eyed houris,[1] with their young white arms,

67. The ever virgin, woo and welcome ye,

68. The Chaldee's[2] orbs of gold, where dwells the primal Light

69. Were all too pure for thee; yet shalt thou be

70. Surely in Heaven, ere Death unlock the heart.

71. I said that I would show thee marvels here;

72. For here dwell many angels — many souls

73. Who have run pure through earth, or been made pure

74. By their salvation since. It is a mart

75. Where all the holy spirits of the world

76. Perform sweet interchange, and purchase truth

77. With truth, and love with love. Hither came He,

78. The Son — the Saviour of the universe;

79. Not in the stable-state He went to earth —

80. A servant unto slaves; but as a God,

81. Carrying His kingdom with Him, and His Heaven.

82. FESTUS. Lo, here are spirits! and all seem to love

83. Each other.

84. LUCIFER.   He hath only half a heart

85. Who loves not all.

86. FESTUS.   Speak for me to some angel.

87. See, here is one, a very soul of beauty:

88. It is the muse. I know her by the lyre

89. Hung on her arm, and eye like fount of fire.

90. MUSE. Mortal, approach! I am the holy Muse,

91. Whom all the great and bright of spirit choose —

92. 'Tis I who breathe my soul into the lips

93. Of those great lights whom death nor time eclipse:

---

1. Houris: Nymphs of the Moslem paradise.
2. Chaldee: The ancient Chaldeans (9th–6th century BC) were eventually assimilated into Babylon and were known for their gold wealth.

94. 'Tis I who wing the loving heart with song
95. And set its sighs to music on the tongue:
96. It is I who watch, and, with sweet dreams, reward
97. The starry slumbers of the youthful bard;
98. For I love every thing that is sweet and bright.
99. And but this morn, with the first wink of light
100. A sunbeam left the sun, and, as it sped,
101. I followed, watched, and listened what it said:
102. Wherefore, with all this brightness am I given
103. From sun to earth? Am I not fit for Heaven?
104. From God I came once; and, though worlds have passed,
105. Ages, and dooms, yet I am light to the last.
106. Whatever God hath once bent to His will
107. Is sacred; so the world's to be loved still.
108. What of this swift, this bright, but downward being,
109. Too burning to be borne — too brief for seeing?
110. What is mine aim — mine end? I would not die
111. In dust, or water, or an idiot's eye:
112. I would not cease in blood, nor end in fire,
113. Nor light the loveless to their low desire:
114. No; let me perish on the poet's page,
115. Where he kisses from his beauty's brow all age;
116. Spelling it fair for aye, and wrinkle scorning,
117. As when first that brow brake on him like a morning.
118. But yet I cannot quit this line I tread,
119. Though it lead and leave me to the eyeless dead:
120. It is mine errand: 'tis for this I come,
121. And live, and die, and go down to my doom.
122. This is my fate — right and bright to speed on.
123. God is His own God: fate and fall are one.
124. Straight from the sun I go, like life from God,
125. But, spite of all, the world's air warps our way,
126. And crops the roses off the cheek of day;
127. As some false friend, who holds our fall in trust,
128. Oils our decline, and hands us to the dust.
129. Where are the sunbeams gone of the young green earth?
130. Search dust and night: our death makes clear our birth —
131. It said — and saw earth; and one moment more
132. Fell bright beside a vine-shadowed cottage door:
133. In it came — glanced upon a glowing page,
134. Where, youth forestalling and foreshortening age —
135. Weak with the work of thought, a boyish bard,

136. Sate suing night and stars for his reward.
137. The sunbeam swerved and grew, a breathing, dim,
138. For the first time, as it lit and looked on him:
139. His forehead faded — pale his lip and dry —
140. Hollow his cheek — and fever fed his eye.
141. Clouds lay about his brain, as on a hill,
142. Quick with the thunder thought, and lightning will.
143. His clenched hand shook from its more than midnight clasp,
144. Till his pen fluttered like a winged asp,
145. Save that no deadly poison blacked its lips:
146. 'Twas his to life-enlighten, not eclipse;
147. Nor would he shade one atom of another,
148. To have a sun his slave, a god his brother.
149. The young moon laid her down as one who dies,
150. Knowing that death can be no sacrifice,
151. For that the sun, her god, through nature's night
152. Shall make her bosom to grow great with light.
153. Still he sate, though his lamp sunk; and he strained
154. His eyes to work the nightness which remained.
155. Vain pain! he could not make the light he wanted.
156. And soon thought's wizard ring gets disenchanted.
157. When earth was dayed — was morrowed — the first ray
158. Perched on his pen, and diamonded its way; —
159. The sunray that I watched; which, proud to mark
160. The line it loved as deathless, there died dark —
161. Died in the only path it would have trod,
162. Were there as many ways as worlds to God, —
163. There, in the eye of God again to burn,
164. As all man's glory unto God's must turn.
165. And so may sunbeams ever guide his pen,
166. And God his heart, who lights the morn of men;
167. For this life is but Being's first faint ray;
168. And sun on sun, and heaven on heaven, make up God's day.
169. And were there suns in day as stars in night,
170. They would shew but like one ray from out His full-sphered
     light;
171. As but one momentary gleam would fly;
172. Or, as years, the arrows of eternity.
173. FESTUS. Poets are all who love — who feel great truths —
174. And tell them; and the truth of truths is love.
175. There was a time — oh, I remember well!
176. When, like a sea-shell with its seaborn strain,

177. My soul aye rang with music of the lyre;
178. And my heart shed its lore as leaves their dew —
179. A honey dew, and throve on what it shed.
180. All things I loved; but song I loved in chief.
181. Imagination is the air of mind;
182. Judgment its earth, and memory its main;
183. Passion its fire. I was at home in Heaven:
184. Swiftlike I lived above: once touching earth,
185. The meanest thing might master me: long wings
186. But baffled. Still and still I harped on song.
187. Oh! to create within the mind is bliss;
188. And, shaping forth the lofty thought, or lovely,
189. We seek not, need not Heaven: and when the thought —
190. Cloudy and shapeless, first forms on the mind,
191. Slow darkening into some gigantic make,
192. How the heart shakes with pride and fear, as heaven
193. Quakes under its own thunder: or as might,
194. Of old, the mortal mother of a god,
195. When first she saw him lessening up the skies.
196. And I began the toil divine of verse,
197. Which like a burning-bush, doth guest a god.
198. But this was only wing-flapping — not flight;
199. The pawing of the courser ere he win;
200. Till, by degrees, from wrestling with my soul,
201. I gathered strength to keep the fleet thoughts fast,
202. And made them bless me. Yes, there was a time
203. When tomes of ancient song held eye and heart —
204. Were the sole lore I recked of: the great bards
205. Of Greece, of Rome, and mine own master land,
206. And they who in the holy book are deathless, —
207. Men who have vulgarized sublimity,
208. And bought up truth for the nations; parted it,
209. As soldiers lotted once the garb of God, —
210. Men who have forged gods — uttered — made them pass:
211. In whose words, to be read with many a heaving
212. Of the heart, is a power, like wind in rain —
213. Sons of the sons of God, who, in olden days,
214. Did leave their passionless Heaven for earth and woman,
215. Brought an immortal to a mortal breast;
216. And, like a rainbow clasping the sweet earth,
217. And melting in the covenant of love,
218. Left here a bright precipitate of soul,

219. Which lives for ever through the lines of men,
220. Flashing, by fits, like fire from an enemy's front —
221. Whose thoughts, like bars of sunshine in shut rooms,
222. Mid gloom, all glory, win the world to light —
223. Who make their very follies like their souls;
224. And, like the young moon with a ragged edge,
225. Still, in their imperfection, beautiful —
226. Whose weaknesses are lovely as their strengths,
227. Like the white nebulous matter between stars,
228. Which, if not light, at least is likest light, —
229. Men whom we build our love round like an arch
230. Of triumph, as they pass us on their way
231. To glory and to immortality;
232. Men whose great thoughts possess us like a passion
233. Through every limb and the whole heart; whose words
234. Haunt us as eagles haunt the mountain air;
235. Thoughts which command all coming times and minds,
236. As from a tower a warden, — fix themselves
237. Deep in the heart as meteor stones in earth,
238. Dropped from some higher sphere; the words of gods,
239. And fragments of the undeemed tongues of Heaven.
240. Men who walk up to fame as to a friend
241. Or their own house, which from the wrongful heir
242. They have wrested, from the world's hard hand and gripe, —
243. Men who, like Death, all bone, but all unarmed,
244. Have ta'en the giant world by the throat, and thrown him;
245. And made him swear to maintain their name and fame
246. At peril of his life — who shed great thoughts
247. As easily as an oak looseneth its golden leaves
248. In a kindly largess to the soil it grew on —
249. Whose rich dark ivy thoughts, sunned o'er with love,
250. Flourish around the deathless stems of their names —
251. Whose names are ever on the world's broad tongue,
252. Like sound upon the falling of a force —
253. And make our eyes bright as we speak of them —
254. Whose hearts have a look southwards, and are open
255. To the whole noon of nature, — these I have waked
256. And wept o'er, night by night; oft pondering thus:
257. Homer is gone; and where is Jove? and where
258. The rival cities seven? His song outlives
259. Time, tower, and god — all that then was save Heaven.
260. MUSE. Yea, but the poor perfections of thine earth

261. Shall be as little as nothing to thee here.
262. FESTUS. God must be happy, who aye makes; and since
263. Mind's first of things, who makes from mind is blest
264. O'er men. Thus saith the bard to his work: — I am
265. Thy god and bid thee live as my God me:
266. I live or die with thee, soul of my soul!
267. Thou camest and went'st, sunlike, from morn to eve:
268. And smiledst fire upon my heaving heart,
269. Like the sun in the sea, till it arose
270. And dashed about its house all might and mirth,
271. Like ocean's tongue in Staffa's³ stormy cave.
272. Thou art a weakly reed to lean upon;
273. But, like that reed the false one filched from Heaven,
274. Full of immortal fire — immortal as
275. The breath of God's lips — every breath a soul.
276. MUSE. Mortal! the muse is with thee: leave her not.
277. FESTUS.   Once my ambition to another end
278. Stirred, stretched itself, but slept again. I rose
279. And dashed on earth the harp, mine other heart,
280. Which, ringing, brake; its discord ruinous
281. Harmony still; and coldly I rejoiced
282. No other joy I had, wormlike, to feed
283. Upon my ripe resolve. It might not be:
284. The more I strove against, the more I loved it.
285. LUCIFER. Come, let us walk along. So say farewell.
286. FESTUS. I will not.
287. MUSE. No; my greeting is forever.
288. LUCIFER. Well, well, come on!
289. FESTUS. Oh! shew me that sweet soul
290. Thou brought'st to me the first night that we met.
291. She must be here, where all are good and fair:
292. And thou didst promise me.
293. LUCIFER. Is that not she
294. Walking alone, up-looking to thine earth?
295. For, lo! it shineth through the mid-day air.
296. FESTUS. It is! it is!
297. LUCIFER. Well, I will come again. [*Goes*].
298. FESTUS. Knowest thou me, mine own immortal love?

3. Staffa: The island of Staffa, Scotland, is known for its deep, threatening caves and
    basalt columns.

299. How shall I call thee? Say, what mayest thou be!
300. ANGELA. I am a spirit, Festus; and I love
301. Thy spirit, and shall love, when once like mine,
302. More than we ever did or can even now.
303. Pure spirits are of Heaven all heavenly.
304. Yet marvel not to meet me in this guise,
305. All radiant like a diamond as it is.
306. We wander in what way we will through all
307. Or any of these worlds, and wheresoe'er
308. We are, there Heaven is, here, and there too, God.
309. FESTUS. Thou dost remember me.
310. ANGELA. Ay, every thought
311. And look of love which thou hast lent to me,
312. Comes daily through my memory as stars
313. Wear through the dark.
314. FESTUS. And thou art happy, love?
315. ANGELA. Yes: I am happy when I can do good.
316. FESTUS. To be good is to do good. Who dwell here?
317. Are they all deathless — happy?
318. ANGELA.   All are not:
319. Some err, though rarely — slightly. Spirits sin
320. Only in thought; and they are of a race
321. Higher than thine — have fewer wants and less
322. Temptations — many more joys — greater powers.
323. They need no civil sway: each rules himself —
324. Obeys himself: all live, too, as they choose,
325. And they choose nought but good. They who have come
326. From earth, or other orb, use the same powers,
327. Passions, and purposes, they had ere death;
328. Although enlarged and freed, to nobler ends,
329. With better means. Here the hard warrior whets
330. The sword of truth, and steels his soul against sin.
331. The fierce and lawless wills which trooped it over
332. His breast — the speared desires that overran
333. The fairest fields of virtue, sleep and lie
334. Like a slain host 'neath snow; he dyes his hands
335. Deep in the blood of evil passions. Mind!
336. There is no passion evil in itself;
337. In Heaven we shall enjoy all to right ends.
338. There sit the perfect women, perfect men; —
339. Minds which control themselves, hearts which indulge
340. Designs of wondrous goodness, but so far

341. Only, as soul extolled to bliss and power
342. Most high, sees fit for each, divinely. Here,
343. The statesman makes new laws for growing worlds,
344. Through their forefated ages. Here, the sage
345. Masters all mysteries, more and more, from day
346. To day, watching the thoughts of men and angels
347. Through moral microscopes; or hails afar,
348. By some vast intellectual instrument,
349. The mighty spirits, good or bad, which range
350. The space of mind; some spreading death and woe
351. On far off worlds — some great with good and life.
352. And here the poet, like that wall of fire
353. In ancient song, surrounds the universe;
354. Lighting himself, where'er he soars or dives,
355. With his own bright brain— this is the poet's heaven.
356. Here he may realize each form or scene
357. He e'er on earth imagined; or bid dreams
358. Stand fast, and faery palaces appear.
359. Here he has Heaven to hear him; to the which
360. He sings, with manlike voice and song, the love
361. Which lent him his whole strength, as is the wont
362. Of all great spirits and good throughout the world.
363. Oh! happiest of the happy is the bard!
364. Here, too, some pluck the branch of peace wherewith
365. To greet a suffering saint, and shew his flood
366. Of woe hath sunken: this I love to do.
367. My love, we shall be happy here.
368. FESTUS.   Shall I
369. Ever come here?
370. ANGELA.   Thou mayest. I will pray for thee,
371. And watch thee.
372. FESTUS.   Thou wilt have, then, need to weep.
373. This heart must run its orbit. Pardon thou
374. Its many sad deflections. It will return
375. To thee and to the primal goal of Heaven.
376. ANGELA. Practice thy spirit to great thoughts and things,
377. That thou mayst start, when here, from vantage ground.
378. We can foretell the future of ourselves,
379. And fateful only to himself is each.
380. FESTUS. I do not fear to die; for, though I change
381. The mode of being, I shall ever be.
382. World after world will fall at my right hand;

383. The glorious future be the past despised:
384. All now that seemeth bright will soon seem dim,
385. And darker grow, like earth, as we approach it;
386. While I still stand upon yon heaven which now
387. Hangs over me. If aught can make me seek
388. Other to be than that lost soul I fear me,
389. It is, that thou lovest me. Heaven were not Heaven
390. Without thee.
391. LUCIFER. I am here now. Art thou ready?
392. Let us go.
393. ANGELA.   Well — farewell. It makes me grieve
394. To bid a loved one back to yon false world —
395. To give up even a mortal unto death.
396. Thou wilt forget me soon, or seek to do.
397. FESTUS. When I forget that the stars shine in air—
398. When I forget that beauty is in stars —
399. When I forget that love with beauty is —
400. Will I forget thee: till then, all things else.
401. Thy love to me was perfect from the first,
402. Even as the rainbow in its native skies:
403. It did not grow: let meaner things mature.
404. ANGELA. The rainbow dies in heaven, and not on earth;
405. But love can never die; from world to world,
406. Up the high wheel of heaven, it lives for aye.
407. Remember that I wait thee, hoping, here.
408. Life is the brief disunion of that nature
409. Which hath been one and same in Heaven ere now,
410. And shall be yet again, renewed by Death.
411. Come to me when thou diest!
412. FESTUS. I will, I will.
413. ANGELA. Then, in each other's arms, we will waft through
     space,
414. Spirit in spirit, one! or we will dwell
415. Among these immortal groves; or watch new worlds,
416. As, like the great thoughts of a Maker-mind,
417. They are rounded out of chaos: and we will
418. Be oft on earth with those we love, and help them;
419. For God hath made it lawful for good souls
420. To make souls good; and saints to help the saintly.
421. That thou right soon mayst fold unto thy heart
422. The blissful consciousness of separate
423. Oneness with God, in Him in whom alone

424. The saved are deathless, shall become, for thee,
425. My earliest, earnest, and most constant prayer.
426. Oh! what is dear to creatures of the earth?
427. Life, love, light, liberty! But dearer far
428. Than all — and oh! an universe more divine —
429. The gift, which God endows his chosen with,
430. Of His own uncreated glory, — His
431. Before all worlds, all ages, and reserved
432. Till after all for those He loves and saves.
433. As when the eye first views some Andean chain
434. Of shadowy rolling mountains, based on air,
435. Height upon height, aspiring to the last,
436. Even to Heaven, in sunny snow sheen, up
437. Stretching like angel's pinions, nor can tell
438. Which be the loftiest nor the loveliest;
439. As when an army, wakening with the sun,
440. Starts to its feet all hope, spear after spear
441. And line on line reundulating light,
442. While night's dull watchfires reek themselves away,
443. So feels the spirit when it first receives
444. The bright and mountainous mysteries of God,
445. Containing Heaven, moving themselves towards us,
446. In their free greatness, as by ships at sea
447. Come icebergs, pure and pointed as a star
448. Afar off glittering, of invisible
449. Depth, and dissolving in the light above.
450. FESTUS. My prayer shall be that thy prayer be fulfilled.
451. I must to earth again. Farewell, sweet soul!
452. ANGELA. Farewell! I love thee, and will oft be with thee.
453. LUCIFER. I like earth more than this: I rather love
454. A splendid failing than a petty good;
455. Even as the thunderbolt, whose course is downwards,
456. Is nobler far than way fire which soars.
457. FESTUS. I am determined to be good again —
458. Again? When was I otherwise than ill?
459. Does not sin pour from my soul like dew from earth,
460. And, vapouring up before the face of God,
461. Congregate there in clouds between Heaven and me?
462. What wonder that I lack delight of life?
463. For it is thus — when amid the world's delights,
464. How warm so'er we feel a moment among them —
465. We find ourselves, when the hot blast hath blown,

466. Prostrate, and weak, and wretched, even as I am.
467. I wish that I could leap from off this star,
468. And dash my soul to atoms like a glass.
469. LUCIFER. I have done nothing for thee yet. Thou shalt
470. See Heaven, and Hell, and all the sights of space,
471. When'er thou choosest.
472. FESTUS.   Not then now.
473. LUCIFER. Up! rise!
474. FESTUS. No; I'll be good: and will see none of them.
475. Earth draws us like a loadstone. We are coming.

SCENE 15

[A large Party and Entertainment]
[FESTUS, Ladies, and Others]

1. FESTUS. My Helen! let us rest awhile,
2. For most I love thy calmer smile;
3. We'll not be missed from this gay throng,
4. They dance so eagerly and long;
5. And were one half to go away,
6. I'll bet the rest would scarce perceive it.
7. HELEN. With thee I either go or stay,
8. Prepared, the same, to like or leave it.
9. These two, perhaps, will take our places.
10. They seem to stand with longing faces.
11. FESTUS. Then sit we, love, and sip with me
12. And I will teach thyself to thee.
13. Thy nature is so pure and fine,
14. 'Tis most like wine;
15. Thy blood, which blushes through each vein,
16. Rosy champagne;
17. And the fair skin which o'er it grows,
18. Bright as its snows.
19. Thy wit, which thou dost work so well,

20.   Is like cool moselle;
21.   Like madeira, bright and warm;
22.   Is thy smile's charm;
23.   Claret's glory hath thine eye,
24.   Or mine must lie;
25.   But nought can like thy lips possess
26.   Deliciousness;
27.   And now that thou'rt divinely merry,
28.   I'll kiss and call thee sparkling sherry.
29.   HELEN. I sometimes dream that thou wilt leave me
30.   Without thy love, even me, lonely;
31.   And oft I think, though oft it grieve me,
32.   That I am not thy one love only:
33.   But I shall always love thee till
34.   This heart, like earth in death, stand still.
35.   FESTUS. I love thee, and will leave thee never,
36.   Until my soul leave life for ever.
37.   If earth can from her children run,
38.   And leave the seasons — leave the sun, —
39.   If yonder stars can leave the sky,
40.   Bright truants from their home in heaven —
41.   Immortals who deserve to die,
42.   Were death not too good to be given, —
43.   If Heaven can leave and live from God,
44.   And man tread off his cradle clod —
45.   If God can leave the world He sowed,
46.   Right in the heart of space to fade —
47.   Soul, earth, star, Heaven, man, world, and God
48.   May part — not I from thee, sweet maid.
49.   Ah! see again my favourite dance,
50.   See the wavelike line advance;
51.   And now in circles break,
52.   Like raindrops on a lake:
53.   Now it opens, now it closes
54.   Like a wreath dropping into roses.
55.   HELEN. It is a lovely scene,
56.   Fair as aught on earth;
57.   And we feel, when it hath been,
58.   At heart a dearth;
59.   As from the breaking up of some bright dream —
60.   The failing of a fountain's spray-topt stream.
61.   WILL. Ladies — your leave — we'll choose a Queen

62. To rule this fair and festive scene.
63. CHARLES. And it were best to choose by lot,
64. So none can hold herself forgot.
65. [*They draw lots: it falls to Helen.*]
66. FESTUS. I knew, my love, how this would be;
67. I knew that Fate must favour thee.
68. ALL. Lady fair! we throne thee Queen!
69. Be thy sway as thou hast been —
70. Light, and lovely, and serene.
71. FESTUS. Here — wear this wreath! No ruder crown
72. Should deck that dazzling brow;
73. Or ask yon halo from the moon —
74. 'T would well beseem thee now.
75. I crown thee, love; I crown thee, love;
76. I crown thee Queen of me!
77. And oh! but I am a happy land,
78. And a loyal land to thee.
79. I crown thee, love; I crown thee, love;
80. Thou art Queen in thine own right!
81. Feel! my heart is as full as a town of joy:
82. Look! I've crowded mine eyes with light.
83. I crown thee, love; I crown thee, love;
84. Thou art Queen by right divine!
85. And thy love shall set neither night nor day
86. O'er this subject heart of mine.
87. I crown thee, love; I crown thee, love;
88. Thou art Queen by the right of the strong!
89. And thou didst but win where thou mightst have slain,
90. Or have bounden in thraldom long.
91. I crown thee, love; I crown thee, love;
92. Thou art my Queen for aye!
93. As the moon doth Queen the night, my love;
94. As the night doth crown the day;
95. I crown thee, love; I crown thee, love;
96. Queen of the brave and free!
97. For I'm brave to all beauty but thine, my love;
98. And free to all beauty by thee.
99. HELEN. Here in this court of pleasure, blest to reign,
100. If not the loveliest, where all are fair,
101. We still, one hour, our royalty retain,
102. To out-queen all in kindness and in care.
103. Love, beauty, honour, bravery, and wit —

104. Was ever Queen served by such noble slaves?
105. The peerage of the heart — for Heaven's court fit:
106. We'll dream no more that earth hath ills or graves.
107. With mirth, and melody, and love we reign:
108. Begin we, then, our sweet and pleasurous sway:
109. And here, though light, so strong is beauty's chain,
110. That none shall know how blindly they obey.
111. We have but to lay on one light command —
112. That all shall do the most what best they love;
113. And Pleasure hath her punishments at hand,
114. For all who will not pleasure's rule approve.
115. But no! there's none of us can disobey,
116. Since, by our one command, we free ye thus;
117. And, as our powers must on your pleasures stay —
118. Support — and you will reign along with us.
119. FESTUS. Ha! Lucifer! How now?
120. LUCIFER. I come in sooth to keep my vow.
121. FESTUS. Thy vow?
122. LUCIFER. To revel in earth's pleasures.
123. And tire down mirth in her own measures.
124. FESTUS. Go thy ways: I shrink and tremble
125. To think how deep thou canst dissemble;
126. For who would dream that in yon breast
127. The heart of Hell was burning?
128. Or deem that strange and listless guest
129. Some priceless spirit earning?
130. I hear, from every footstep, rise
131. A trampled spirit's smothered cries.
132. CHARLES. Fest, engage fair Marian's hand.
133. FESTUS. Pass me; she is free no less
134. Than I, who by my queen will stand —
135. May it please her loveliness!
136. HELEN. Festus, we know the love, and see,
137. Which was with Marian and thee.
138. FESTUS. I will not dance to-night again,
139. Though bid by all the Queens that reign.
140. HELEN. What, Festus! treason and disloyalty
141. Already to our gentle royalty?
142. FESTUS. No — I was wrong — but to forgive
143. Be thy sublime prerogative!
144. HELEN. Most amply, then, I pardon thee;
145. In proof whereof, come, dance with me.

146. [*A dance*]
147. LAURENCE. How sweetly Marian sweeps along;
148. Her step is music, and her voice is song.
149. Silver sandalled foot! how blest
150. To bear the breathing heaven above,
151. Which on thee, Atlas-like, doth rest,
152. And round thee move.
153. Ah! that sweet little foot; I swear
154. I could kneel down and kiss it there.
155. I should not mind if she were Pope;
156. I would change my faith.
157. CHARLES. Works, too, we hope.
158. LAURENCE. Ah! smile on me again with that sweet smile,
159. Which could from Heaven my soul to thee beguile;
160. As I mine eye would turn from awful skies
161. To hail the child of sun and storm arise;
162. Or, from eve's holy azure, to the star
163. Which beams and becks the spirit from afar;
164. For fair as yon star-wreath which high doth shine,
165. And worthy but to deck a brow like thine;
166. Pure as the light from orbs which ne'er
167. Hath blessed us yet in this far sphere;
168. As eyes of seraphs lift alone
169. Through ages on the holy throne;
170. So bright, so fair, so free from guile,
171. And freshening to my heart thy smile;
172. Ay, passing all things here, and all above,
173. To me, thy look of beauty, truth and love.
174. HARRY. Thy friend hath led his lady out.
175. FESTUS. He looks most wickedly devout.
176. FANNY. When introduced, he said he knew her,
177. And had been long devoted to her.
178. EMMA. Indeed — but he is too gallant,
179. And serves me far more than I want.
180. He vows that he could worship me —
181. Why — look! he is now upon his knee!
182. LUCIFER. I quaff to thee this cup of wine,
183. And would, though men had nought but brine —
184. E'en the brine of their own tears,
185. To cool those lying lips of theirs;
186. And were it all one molten pearl,
187. I would drain it to thee, girl;

188. Ay, though each drop were worth of gold
189. Too many pieces to be sold;
190. And though, for each I drank to thee,
191. Fate add an age of misery:
192. For thou canst conjure up my spirit
193. To aught immortals may inherit;
194. To good or evil, woe or weal —
195. To all that fiends or angels feel;
196. And wert thou to perdition given,
197. I'd join thee in the scorn of Heaven!
198. EMMA. Oh fy! to only think of such a fate!
199. LUCIFER. Better than not to think on't till too late.
200. They'd not believe me, Festus, if I told them.
201. That Hell, and all its hosts, this hour behold them.
202. FESTUS. Scarcely — that Devil here again!
203. But though my heart burst in the strain,
204. I will be happy, might and main!
205. So wreathe my brow with flowers.
206. And pour me purple wine,
207. And make the merry hours
208. Dance, dance, with glee like thine.
209. While thus enraptured, I and thou,
210. Love crowns the heart, as flowers the brow.
211. The rosy garland twine
212. Around the noble bowl,
213. Like laughing loves that shine
214. Upon the generous soul;
215. Be mine, dear maid, the loves, and thou
216. Shalt ever bosom them as now.
217. Then plunge the blushing wreath
218. Deep in the ruddy wine;
219. As the love of thee till death
220. Is deep in heart of mine.
221. While both are blooming on my brow,
222. I cannot be more blest than now.
223. LUCIFER. Thou talk'st of hearts, in style to me, quite fresh:
224. The human heart's about a pound of flesh.
225. FESTUS. Forgive him, love, and aught he says.
226. HELEN. What is that trickling down thy face?
227. FESTUS. Oh, love, that is only wine
228. From the wreath which thou didst twine;
229. And, casting in the bowl, I bound,

230. For coolness' sake, my temples round.
231. HELEN. I thought 'twas a thorn which was tearing thy brow;
232. And if it were only a rose-thorn was tearing,
233. Why, whether of gold or of roses, as now,
234. A crown, if it hurt us, is hardly worth wearing.
235. LUCY. From what fair maid hadst thou that flower?
236. It came not from my wreath nor me.
237. CHARLES. Love lives in thee as in a flower,
238. And sure this must have dropped from thee —
239. From thy lip, or from thy cheek:
240. See, its sister blushes speak.
241. Nay, never harm the harmless rose,
242. Though given by a stranger maid:
243. 'Tis sad enough to feel that flower
244. Feels it must fade.
245. And trouble not the transient love,
246. Though by another's side I sigh;
247. It is enough to feel the flame
248. Flicker and die.
249. And thou to me art flame and flower
250. Of rosier body, brighter breath:
251. But softer, warmer than the truth —
252. As sleep than death.
253. FESTUS. The dead of night: earth seems but seeming —
254. The soul seems but a something dreaming.
255. The bird is dreaming in its nest,
256. Of song, and sky, and loved one's breast;
257. The lap-dog dreams, as round he lies,
258. In moonshine of his mistress' eyes:
259. The steed is dreaming, in his stall,
260. Of one long breathless leap and fall:
261. The hawk hath dreamt him thrice of wings
262. Wide as the skies he may not cleave;
263. But waking, feels them clipt, and clings
264. Mad to the perch 'twere mad to leave:
265. The child is dreaming of its toys —
266. The murderer of calm home joys;
267. The weak are dreaming endless fears —
268. The proud of how their pride appears:
269. The poor enthusiast who dies,
270. Of his life dreams the sacrifice —
271. Sees, as enthusiast only can,

272. The truth that made him more than man;
273. And hears once more, in visioned trance,
274. That voice commanding to advance,
275. Where wealth is gained — love, wisdom won,
276. Or deeds of danger dared and done.
277. The mother dreameth of her child —
278. The maid of him who hath beguiled —
279. The youth of her he loves too well;
280. The good of God— the ill of Hell, —
281. Who live of death — of life who die —
282. The dead of immortality.
283. The earth is dreaming back her youth;
284. Hell never dreams, for woe is truth;
285. And Heaven is dreaming o'er her prime,
286. Long ere the morning stars of time;
287. And dream of Heaven alone can I,
288. My lovely one, when thou art nigh.
289. HELEN. Let some one sing. Love, mirth and song,
290. The graces of this life of ours,
291. Go ever hand in hand along,
292. And ask alike each other's powers.
293. LUCY. [*sings*]
294.   For every leaf the loveliest flower[1]
295.   Which Beauty sighs for from her bower —
296.   For every star a drop of dew —
297.   For every sun a sky of blue —
298.   For every heart a heart as true.
299.   For every tear by pity shed
300.   Upon a fellow-sufferer's head,
301.   Oh! be a crown of glory given;
302.   Such crowns as saints to gain have striven —
303.   Such crowns as seraphs wear in Heaven.
304.   For all who toil at honest fame,
305.   A proud, a pure, a deathless name;
306.   For all who love, who loving bless,
307.   Be life one long, kind, close caress —
308.   Be life all love, all happiness.

---

1. This lyric was turned into a stand-alone poem entitled 'Song' and reprinted in magazines and anthologies such as *Heart Music for Working People*, ed. Erskine J. Clarke (Partridge: London, 1857), and many others throughout the ensuing decades. It was set to music by Louis Lavater as 'For Ev'ry Leaf' in 1933.

309. LUCIFER. Tell me what's the chiefest pleasure
310. In this world's high heaped measure?
311. ALL. Power — beauty — love — wealth — wine!
312. LUCIFER. All different votes!
313. FANNY. Come, Frederic — thine?
314. What may thy joy-judgment be?
315. FREDERIC. I scarce know how to answer thee;
316. Each, apart, too soon will tire;
317. All together slake desire.
318. So ask not of me the one chief joy of earth,
319. For that I'm unable to say;
320. But here is a wreath which will loose its chief worth,
321. If ye pluck but one flower away.
322. Then these are the joys that should never dispart —
323. The joys which are dearest to me:
324. As the song, and the dance, and the laugh of the heart,
325. Thou, girl, and the goblet be.
326. LUCIFER. Oh, excellent! the truth is clear —
327. The one opinion, too, I love to hear.
328. HELEN. Is this a Queen's fate — to be left alone?
329. I wish another had the throne.
330. Festus! why art thou not here,
331. Beside thy liege and lady dear?
332. FESTUS. My thoughts are happier oft than I,
333. For they are ever, love, with thee;
334. And thine, I know, as frequent fly
335. O'er all that severs us, to me;
336. Like rays of stars that meet in space,
337. And mingle in a bright embrace.
338. Never load thy locks with flowers,
339. For thy cheek hath a richer flush;
340. And than wine, or the sunset hour,
341. Or the ripe yew-berry's blush.
342. Never braid thy brow with lights,
343. Like the sun, on its golden way
344. To the neck and the locks of night,
345. From the forehead fair of day.
346. Never star thy hand with stones,
347. For, for every dead light there,
348. Is a living glory gone,
349. Than the brilliant far more fair.
350. Nay, nay; wear thy buds, braids, gems!

351. Let the lovely never part;
352. Thou alone canst rival them,
353. Or in nature, or in art.
354. Be not sad; — thou shalt not be:
355. Why wilt mourn, love, when with me?
356. One tear that in thine eye doth start
357. Could wash all purpose from my heart,
358. But that of loving thee;
359. If I could ever think to wrong
360. A love so riverlike, deep, pure, and long.
361. HELEN. I cast mine eyes around, and feel
362. There is a blessing waiting;
363. Too soon our hearts the truth reveal.
364. That joy is disenchanting.
365. FESTUS. I am a wizard, love; and I
366. A new enchantment will supply;
367. And the charm of thine own smile
368. Shall thine own heart of grief beguile.
369. Smile — I do command thee rise
370. From the bright depths of those eyes!
371. By the bloom wherein thou dwellest,
372. As in a rose-leaved nest;
373. By the pleasure which thou tellest,
374. And the bosom which thou swellest,
375. I bid thee rise from rest;
376. By the rapture which thou causest,
377. And the bliss while e'er thou pausest,
378. Obey my high behest!
379. HELEN. Dread magician! Cease thy spell;
380. It hath wrought both quick and well.
381. FESTUS. Ah! thou hast dissolved the charm!
382. Ah! thou hast outstepped the ring!
383. Who shall answer for the harm
384. Beauty on herself will bring?
385. Come, I will conjure up again that smile —
386. The scarce departed spirit. There it is!
387. Settling and hovering round thy lips the while,
388. Like some bright angel o'er the gates of bliss.
389. And I could sit and set that rose-bright smile,
390. Until it seem to grow immortal there —
391. A something abstract even of all beauty,
392. As though 'twere in the eye or in the air.

393. Ah! never may a heavier shadow rest
394. Than thine own ringlets' on that brow so fair;
395. Nor sob, nor sorrow, shake the perfect breast
396. Which looks for love, as doth for death despair.
397. And now the smile, the sigh, the blush, the tear —
398. Lo! all the elements of love are here.
399. Oh, weep not — wither not the soul
400. Made saturate with bliss;
401. I would not have one briny tear
402. Embitter Beauty's kiss.
403. Nay, weep not, fear not! woe nor wrath
404. Can touch a soul like thine,
405. More than the lightning's blinding path
406. May strike the stars divine.
407. Sing, then, while thy lover sips,
408. And hear the truth that wine discloses;
409. Music lives within thy lips
410. Like a nightingale in roses.
411. HELEN. [*sings*]
412.   Oh! love is like the rose,
413.   And a month it may not see,
414.   Ere it withers where it grows —
415.   Rosalie!
416.   I loved thee from afar;
417.   Oh! my heart was lift to thee
418.   Like a glass up to a star —
419.   Rosalie!
420.   Thine eye was glassed in mine
421.   As the moon is in the sea,
422.   And its shine was on the brine —
423.   Rosalie!
424.   The rose hath lost its red,
425.   And the star is in the sea,
426.   And the briny tear is shed —
427.   Rosalie!
428. FESTUS. What the stars are to the night, my love,
429. What its pearls are to the sea, —
430. What the dew is to the day, my love,
431. Thy beauty is to me.
432. HELEN. I am but here the under-queen of beauty
433. For yonder hangs the likeness of the goddess;
434. And so to worship her is our first duty.

435. The heavenly minds of old first taught the heavenly bodies
436. Were to be worshipped; and the idolatry
437. Holds to this hour; though, Beauty! but of thine.
438. I am thy priestess, and will worship thee,
439. With all this brave and lovely train of mine;
440. Lo! we all kneel to thee before thy pictured shrine.
441. Yes — there, thou goddess of the heart,
442. Immortal beauty, there!
443. Thou glory of Jove's free-love skies,
444. E'en like thyself too fair,
445. Too bright, too sweet for mortal eyes,
446. For earthly hearts too strong;
447. Thy golden girdle lift'st and drawest
448. The heavens and earth along.
449. Oh! thou art as the cloudless moon,
450. Undimmed and unarrayed;
451. No robe hast thou, no crown save yon —
452. Goddess! thy long locks' soft and sunbright braid.
453. And there's thy son, Love — beauty's child —
454. World-known for strangest powers —
455. Boy-god thy place is blest o'er all!
456. Smil'st thou at thoughts of ours?
457. And there, by thy luxurious side,
458. The Queen of Heaven and Jove
459. Stands; and the deep delirious draught
460. Drinks, from thy looks, of love,
461. And lips, which oft have kissed away
462. The thunders from his brow
463. Who ruled, men say, the world of worlds,
464. As God our God rules now.
465. And thou art yet as great o'er this
466. As erst o'er olden sky;
467. Of all Heaven's darkened deities
468. The last live light on high.
469. God after God hath left thee lone,
470. Which lived on human breath;
471. When prayers were breathed to them no more,
472. The false ones pined to death.
473. But in the service of young hearts
474. To loveliness and love;
475. Live thou shalt while yon wandering world
476. Named unto thee shall move.

477. No fabled dream art thou: all god,
478. Our souls acknowledge thee;
479. For what would life from love be worth,
480. Or love from beauty be?
481. Come, universal beauty, then,
482. Thou apple of God's eye,
483. To and through which all things were made —
484. Things deathless — things that die.
485. Oh! lighten — live before us there —
486. Leap in yon lovely form,
487. And give a soul. She comes! it breathes —
488. So bright — so sweet — so warm.
489. Our sacrifice is over: let us rise!
490. For we have worshipped acceptably here;
491. And let our glowing hearts and glimmering eyes,
492. O'erstrained with gazing on thy light too near,
493. Prove that our worship, Goddess was sincere!
494. FESTUS. I read that we are answered. The soft air
495. Doubles its sweetness; and the fainting flowers,
496. Down hanging on the walls in wreaths so fair,
497. Bud forth afresh, as in their birth-day bowers,
498. Dew-laden, as oppressed with love and shame,
499. The rose-bud drops upon the lily's breast;
500. Brighter the wine, the lamps have softer flame,
501. Thy kiss flows freer than the grape first pressed.
502. WILL. A dance, a dance!
503. HELEN. Let us remain!
504. FESTUS. We will not tempt your sport again.
505. HELEN. Behold where Marian sits alone,
506. The dance all sweeping round,
507. Like to some goddess hewn in stone,
508. With blooming garlands bound.
509. FESTUS. Tell me, Marian, what those eyes
510. Can discover in the skies? —
511. Those eyes, that look, so bright, so sweet their hue,
512. As they had gained from gazing on that view
513. The high and starry beauty of their blue.
514. MARIAN. For earth my soul hath lost all love,
515. But Heaven still loves and watches o'er me;
516. Why should I not, then, look above,
517. And pass, and pity all before me?
518. FESTUS. Oh! if yon worlds that shine o'er this,

519. Have more of joy — of passion less —
520. I would not change earth's chequered bliss
521. For thrice the joys those orbs possess;
522. Which seem so strange their nature is,
523. Faint with excess of happiness.
524. MARIAN. Thy heart with others hath its rest,
525. And it shall wake with me;
526. And if within another breast
527. Thy heart hath made itself a nest,
528. Mine is no more for thee.
529. Heart-breaker, go! I cannot choose
530. But love thee, and thy love refuse;
531. And if my brow grow lined while young,
532. And youth fly cheated from my cheek,
533. 'T is, that there lies below my tongue
534. A word I will not speak;
535. For I would rather die than deem
536. Thou art not the glory thou didst seem.
537. But if engirt by flood or fire,
538. Who would live that could expire?
539. Who would not dream, and dreaming die,
540. If to wake were misery?
541. FESTUS. Whose woes are like to my woes?
542. What is madness?
543. The mind, exalted to a sense of ill,
544. Soon sinks beyond it into utter sadness,
545. And sees its grief before it like a hill.
546. Oh! I have suffered till my brain became
547. Distinct with woe, as is the skeleton leaf
548. Whose green hath fretted off its fibrous frame,
549. And bare to our immortality of grief.
550. MARIAN. Like the light line that laughter leaves
551. One moment on a bright young brow;
552. So truth is lost ere love believes
553. There can be aught save truth below.
554. FESTUS. But as the eye aye brightlier beams
555. For every fall the lid lets on it,
556. So oft the fond heart happier dreams
557. For the soft cheats love puts upon it.
558. MARIAN. I never dreamed of wretchedness;
559. I thought to love meant but to bless.
560. FESTUS. It once was bliss to me to watch

561. Thy passing smile, and sit and catch
562. The sweet contagion of thy breath —
563. For love is catching — from such teeth;
564. Delicate little pearl-white wedges,
565. All transparent at the edges.
566. MARIAN. False flatterer cease!
567. FESTUS. It is my fate
568. To love, and make who love me hate.
569. MARIAN. No! 'tis to sue — to gain — deceive —
570. To tire of — to neglect — and leave:
571. The desolation of the soul
572. Is what I feel —
573. A sense of lostness that leaves death
574. But little to reveal;
575. For death is nothing but the thought
576. Of something being again nought.
577. HELEN. Cease, lady, cease those aching sighs,
578. Which shake the tear-drops from thine eyes,
579. As morning wind, with wing fresh wet,
580. Shakes dew out of the violet.
581. Forgive me, if the love once thine
582. Hath changed itself unsought to me;
583. I did not tempt it from thy heart,
584. I nothing knew of thee;
585. And soon, perchance, 't will be my part
586. As thou now art, to be.
587. MARIAN. I blame no heart, no love, no fate,
588. And I have nothing to forgive;
589. I wish for nought, repent of nought,
590. Dislike nought but to live.
591. HELEN. Nay, sing; it will relieve thy heart.
592. MARIAN. I cannot sing a mirthful strain;
593. And feel too much to act my part
594. E'en of an ebbing vein.
595. FESTUS. Our hearts are not in our own hands:
596. Why wilt thou make me say
597. I cannot love as once I loved?
598. MARIAN. Hear! — 't is for this I stay —
599. To say we part — for ever part:
600. But oh! how wide the line
601. Between thy Marian's bursting heart
602. And that proud heart of thine.

603. And thou wilt wander here and there,
604. Ever the gay and free;
605. To other maids wilt fondly swear,
606. As thou hast sworn to me;
607. And I — oh! I shall but retire
608. Into my grief alone;
609. And kindle there the hidden fire,
610. That burns, that wastes unknown.
611. And love and life shall find their tomb
612. In that sepulchral flame: —
613. Be happy — none shall know for whom —
614. I will not dream thy name.
615. FESTUS. As sings the swan with parting breath,
616. So I to thee;
617. While love is leaving — worse than life —
618. Forewarningly.
619.   Speak not, nor think thou, any ill of me,
620.   If thou wouldst not die soon and wretchedly.
621.   I cannot waver on my path
622.   To shun fair lady's love or wrath.
623.   Nor condescend the world to undeceive
624.   Which doth delight in error and believe.
625.   Thus then farewell, dear lady, ere I go:
626.   And dearly have I earned my lightest woe.
627.   Oh! if we e'er have loved, lady,
628.   We must forego it now;
629.   Though sore the heart be moved, lady,
630.   When bound to break its vow.
631.   I'll always think on thee,
632.   And thou sometimes — on whom, lady?
633.   And yet those thoughts must be
634.   Like flowers flung on the tomb, lady,
635.   Then think that I am blest, lady,
636.   Though aye for thee I sigh;
637.   In peace and beauty rest, lady,
638.   Nor mourn and mourn as I.
639.   From one we love to part, lady,
640.   Is harder than to die;
641.   I see it by thy heart, lady,
642.   I feel it by thine eye.
643.   Thy lightest look can tell
644.   Thy heaviest thought to me, lady;

645.	Oh! I have loved thee well,

645.   Oh! I have loved thee well,
646.   But well seems ill with thee, lady;
647.   Though sore the heart be moved, lady,
648.   When bound to break its vow —
649.   Yet if we ever loved, lady,
650.   We must forego it now. —
651. LUCIFER. Come, I must separate you two:
652. Such wretchedness will never do.
653. The little cloud of grief which just appears,
654. If left to spread, will drown us all in tears.
655. EMMA. Oblige us, pray, then, with a song.
656. CHARLES. I am sure he has a singing face.
657. WILL. At church I heard him loud and long.
658. LUCIFER. Pardon — but you are doubly wrong.
659. HELEN. Obey, I beg. Here — give him place.
660. LUCIFER. I have not sung for ages, mind;
661.   So you must take me as you find.
662.   This is a song supposed of one —
663.   A fallen spirit — name unknown —
664.   Fettered upon his fiery throne —
665.   Calling on his once angel-love.
666.   Who still remaineth true above. [*sings*]
667.   Thou hast more music in thy voice
668.   Than to the spheres is given,
669.   And more temptations on thy lips
670.   Than lost the angels Heaven.
671.   Thou hast more brightness in thine eyes
672.   Than all the stars which burn,
673.   More dazzling art thou than the throne
674.   We fallen dared to spurn.
675.   Go search through Heaven — the sweetest smile
676.   That lightens there is thine;
677.   And through Hell's burning darkness breaks
678.   No frown so fell as mine.
679.   One smile — 't will light, one tear — 't will cool;
680.   These will be more to me
681.   Than all the wealth of all the worlds,
682.   Or boundless power could be.
683. HELEN. Entreat him, pray, to sing again.
684. LUCIFER. Any thing any one desires.
685. FESTUS. Your loveliness hath but to deign
686. To will, and he'll do all that will requires.

687. LUCIFER. [*sings.*] Oh! many a cloud
688.   Hath lift its wing.
689.   And many a leaf
690.   Hath clad the spring;
691.   But there shall be thrice
692.   The leaf and cloud,
693.   And thrice shall the world
694.   Have worn her shroud,
695.   Ere there's any like thee,
696.   But where thou wilt be.
697.   Oh! many a storm
698.   Hath drenched the sun,
699.   And many a stream
700.   To sea hath run;
701.   But there shall be thrice
702.   The storm and stream.
703.   Ere there's any like thee.
704.   But in angel's dream;
705.   Or in look, or in love.
706.   But in Heaven above.
707. LUCY. What is love? Oh! I wonder so,
708. Do tell me — who pretends to know?
709. FRANK. Ask not of me, love, what is love?
710. Ask what is good of God above —
711. Ask of the great sun what is light —
712. Ask what is darkness of the night —
713. Ask sin of what may be forgiven —
714. Ask what is happiness of Heaven —
715. Ask what is folly of the crowd —
716. Ask what is fashion of the shroud —
717. Ask what is sweetness of thy kiss —
718. Ask of thyself what beauty is;
719. And, if they each should answer, I!
720. Let me, too, join them with a sigh.
721. Oh! let me pray my life may prove,
722. When thus, with thee, that I am love.
723. FESTUS. I cannot love as I have loved.
724. And yet I know not why;
725. It is the one great woe of life
726. To feel all feeling die;
727. And one by one the heartstrings snap,
728. As age comes on so chill;

729. And hope seems left that hope may cease,
730. And all will soon be still.
731. And the strong passions, like to storms,
732. Soon rage themselves to rest,
733. Or leave a desolated calm —
734. A worn and wasted breast;
735. A heart that like the Geyser spring,
736. Amidst its bosomed snows,
737. May shrink, not rest — but with its blood
738. Boils even in repose.
739. And yet the things one might have loved
740. Remain as they have been, —
741. Truth ever lovely, and one heart
742. Still sacred and serene;
743. But lower, less, and grosser things
744. Eclipse the world-like mind,
745. And leave their cold dark shadow where
746. Most to the light inclined.
747. And then it ends as it began,
748. The orbit of our race,
749. In pains and tears, and fears of life,
750. And the new dwelling place.
751. From life to death — from death to life
752. We hurry round to God,
753. And leave behind us nothing but
754. The path that we have trod.
755. HELEN. In vain I try to lure thy heart
756. From grief to mirth.
757. It were as easy to ward off
758. Night from the earth.
759. FESTUS. Fill! I'll drink it till I die —
760. Helen's lip and Helen's eye!
761. An eye which outsparkles
762. The beads of the wine,
763. With a hue which outdarkles
764. The deeps where they shine.
765. Come! with that lightly flushing brow,
766. And darkly splendid eye,
767. And white and wavy arms which now,
768. Like snow-wreaths on the dark brown bough,
769. So softly on me lie.
770. Come! let us love, while love we may,

771. Ere youth's bright sands be run;
772. The hour is nigh when every soul
773. Which 'scapeth evil's dread control,
774. Nor drains the furies' fiery bowl,
775. Shall into Heaven for aye,
776. And love its God alone.
777. HELEN. Now let me leave my throne; and if the hours
778. Have measured every moment by a kiss,
779. As I do think, since first ye gave these flowers,
780. It was to teach us how to dial bliss.
781. Farewell, dear crown, thy mistress will not wear.
782. Save when she sitteth royally alone.
783. Farewell, too, throne! not quickly wilt thou bear
784. A happier form, if fairer than mine own.
785. WILL. The ladies leave us!
786. LUCIFER. Oh! by all means let them;
787. But say, for Heaven itself, we'll not forget them;
788. Say we will pledge them to the top of breath,
789. As loud as thunder, and as deep as death.
790. FESTUS. [apart]. Where is thy grave, my love?
791. I want to weep.
792. High as thou art this earth above,
793. My woe is deep;
794. And my heart is cold as is thy grave,
795. Where I can neither soothe nor save.
796. Whatever I say, or do, or see,
797. I think and feel alone to thee.
798. Oh! can it — can it be forgiven,
799. That I forget thou art in Heaven?
800. Thou wilt forgive me this, and more:
801. Love spends his all, and still hath store.
802. Thou wilt forgive, if beauty's wile
803. Should win, perforce, one glance from me;
804. When they, whose art it is to smile,
805. Can never smile my heart from thee;
806. And if with them I chance to be,
807. And give mine ear up to their singing,
808. It wind-like, only wakes the sea,
809. In all its mad monotony,
810. Of memory forth thy music ringing.
811. Thou wilt forgive, if now and then
812. I link with hands less loved than thine;

813. Whose gold-like touch makes kings of men,
814. But wakes no will in blood of mine;
815. And if with them I toss the wine,
816. And set my soul in love's ripe riot,
817. It echoes not — this desert shrine,
818. Where still thy love from Heaven doth shine,
819. Moon-like, across some ruin's quiet.
820. Thou wilt forgive me, if my feet
821. Should move to music with the fair;
822. When, at each turn, I burn to meet
823. Thy stream-like step and aery air;
824. And if, before some beauty there,
825. Mine eye may forge one glance of gladness,
826. It is but the ripple of despair,
827. That shows the bed is all but bare,
828. And nought scarce left but stony sadness.
829. Thou wilt forgive, if e'er my heart
830. Err from the orbit of its love;
831. When even the bliss-bright stars will start
832. Earthwards, some lower sphere to prove.
833. Thou wilt forgive, if soft white arms
834. Embrace, by fits, this breast of mine;
835. When, while amid their pillowy charms,
836. My heart can kiss no heart but thine;
837. And if these lips but rarely pine
838. In the pale abstinence of sorrow,
839. It is, that nightly I divine,
840. As I this world-sick soul recline,
841. I shall be with thee ere the morrow.
842. Thou wilt forgive, if once with thee
843. I limned the outline of a Heaven;
844. But go and tell our God, from me,
845. He must forgive what He hath given;
846. And, if we be by passion driven
847. To love, and all its natural madness,
848. Tell Him, that man by love hath thriven,
849. And that by love he shall be shriven;
850. For God is love where love is gladness.
851. Thou wilt forgive, if clay-bound mind
852. Can scarce discover that thou art;
853. But wait! I feel the outward wind
854. Rush fresh into my fluttering heart.

855. Perchance thy spirit stays in yon mild star
856. In peace, and flame-like purity, and prayer;
857. And, oh! when mine shall fly from earth afar,
858. I will pray God that it may join thine there:
859. 'Twere doubling Heaven, that Heaven with thee to share.
860. And, while thou leadest music and her lyre,
861. Like a sunbeam holden by its golden hair,
862. May I, too, mingling with the immortal choir,
863. Love thee, and worship God! what more may soul desire?
864. Enough for me! but, if there be
865. More, it shall be left for thee.
866. WALTER. If any thing I love in chief,
867. It is that flowery rich relief
868. That wine doth chase on mortal metal
869. Before good wine begins to settle;
870. But all seem smilingly serenely dull,
871. And melancholy as the moon at full.
872. Quenched by their company they seem,
873. Like sparks of fire in clouds of steam.
874. CHARLES. They who mourn the lack of wit,
875. Shew, at least, no more of it.
876. FESTUS. I cannot bear to be alone,
877. I hate to mix with men;
878. To me there's torture in the tone
879. Which bids me talk again.
880. Like silly nestlings, warned in vain,
881. My heart's young joys have flown;
882. While singing to them, even then,
883. They left me one by one.
884. I envy every soul that dies
885. Out of this world of care:
886. I envy e'en the lifeless skies,
887. That they enshrine thee there.
888. And would I were the bright blue air
889. Which doth insphere thine eyes,
890. That thou mightst meet me everywhere,
891. And feel these faithful sighs.
892. E'en as the bubble that is mixed
893. Of air and wine right red,
894. So my heart's love is shared betwixt
895. The living and the dead.
896. If on her breast I lay my head,

897. My heart on thine is fixed: —
898. Wilt thou I loose, as I have said,
899. Or keep the soul thou seek'st?
900. From me thou canst not pass away
901. While I have soul or sight; —
902. I see thee on my waking way,
903. And in my dreams thee bright;
904. I see thee in the dead of night,
905. And the full life of day;
906. I know thee by a sudden light;
907. It is thy soul, I say.
908. If yonder stars be filled with forms
909. Of breathing clay like ours,
910. Perchance the space that spreads between
911. Is for a spirit's powers;
912. And loving as we two have loved
913. In spirit and in heart,
914. Whether to space or star removed,
915. God will not bid us part.
916. FRANK. As to this seat — its late and fair possessor
917. Should, ere she went, have chosen her successor.
918. FESTUS. In right of her who sat thereon
919. I think I might demand the throne;
920. I rather choose to let it be.
921. ALL. George shall be King of the company!
922. GEORGE. My loving subjects! I shall first promulge
923. A few good rules by which to indulge;
924. They are good, according to my thinking,
925. And shall be held the laws of drinking.
926. First — each man shall do what he chooses,
927. Provided that he ne'er refuses,
928. But shall be sworn, by stand and stopper,
929. To drink as much as I think proper.
930. WILL. Stay! — all of you who think, with me,
931. This law should pass,
932. Will please to signify the same
933. By emptying their glass.
934. WALTER. Filling again and emptying, and so on,
935. At each law — pari passu,[2] as we go on.

---

2. Pari passu: A Latin phrase meaning 'equal footing'.

936. GEORGE. Secondly — no man shall be held as mellow
937. Who can distinguish blue from yellow.
938. Thirdly — no man shall miss his turn nor toast,
939. Nor yet give more than two at once, at most.
940. Fourthly — if one at table should fall under.
941. There let him lie — so much extinguished thunder.
942. Fifthly — let all, in such case, who still stay,
943. Like living lightnings, but the brighter play.
944. Sixthly, and last but one — mind this, there shan't
945. Be aught said that is not irrelevant.
946. Seventhly — if any of these edicts should not
947. Be kept, it shall be good to plead, I would not.
948. CHARLES. Oh, let the royal law
949. Be writ in rosy wine!
950. And read and kept
951. At every feast
952. Where wit and mirth combine.
953. FESTUS. How sweetly shine the steadfast stars,
954. Each eyeing, sister-like, the earth;
955. And softly chiding scenes like this,
956. Of senseless and profaning mirth.
957. LUCIFER. Thou art ever prating of the stars
958. Like an old soldier of his scars;
959. Thou shouldst have been a starling, friend,
960. And not an earthling: end!
961. FESTUS. And could I speak as many times
962. Of each as there are stars in Heaven,
963. I could not utter half the thoughts —
964. The sweet thoughts one to me hath given.
965. The holy quiet of the skies
966. May waken well the blush of shame,
967. Whene'er we think that thither lies
968. The Heaven we heed not — ought not name.
969. Oh, Heaven! let down thy cloudy lids,
970. And close thy thousand eyes;
971. For each, in burning glances, bids
972. The wicked fool be wise.
973. LUCIFER. I can interpret well the stars.
974. CHARLES. Indeed! they need interpreters.
975. LUCIFER. Then thus, in their eternal tongue
976. And musical thunders, all have sung
977. To every ear which ear hath given,

978. From birth to death, this note of Heaven: —
979. Deathlings! on earth drink, laugh, and love!
980.   Ye mayn't hereafter — under or above.
981.   Yes, this the tale they all have told,
982.   Since first they made old Chaos shrink —
983.   Since first they flocked creation's fold,
984.   And filled all air like flakes of gold
985.   Which drop yon royal drink:
986.   For as the moon doth madmen rule,
987.   It is, that near and few they are;
988.   And so in Heaven each single star
989.   Doth sway some reasonable fool,
990.   Whether on earth or other sphere;
991.   For what's above is what is here.
992.   Moons and madmen only change;
993.   What can truth or stars derange?
994.   EDWARD. Brave stars, bright monitors of joy!
995.   Right well ye time your hours of warning;
996.   For, sooth to say, the eve's employ
997.   Doth wax less lovely towards the morning.
998.   So push the goblet gaily round —
999.   Drink deep of its wealth — drink on!
1000.   Our earthly joy too soon doth cloy,
1001.   Our life is all but gone;
1002.   And, not enjoy yon glorious cup,
1003.   And all the sweets which lie,
1004.   Like pearls, within its purple well —
1005.   Who would not hate to die?
1006.   WILL. And who, without the cheering glance
1007.   Of woman's witching eye,
1008.   Could stand against the storms of fate,
1009.   Or cankering care defy?
1010.   It adds fresh brightness to the bowl;
1011.   Then why will men repine?
1012.   Content we'll live with Heaven's best gifts —
1013.   With woman, and with wine.
1014.   HARRY. Cups while they sparkle —
1015.   Maids while they sigh;
1016.   Bright eyes will darkle —
1017.   Lips grow dry.

1018. Cheek while the dew-drops
1019. Water its rose;
1020. Life's fount hath few drops
1021. Dear as those.
1022. Arms while they tighten —
1023. Hearts as they heave:
1024. Love cannot brighten
1025. Life's dark eve.
1026. GEORGE. Oh! the wine is like life;
1027. And the sparkles that play
1028. By the lips of the bowl
1029. Are the loves of the day.
1030. Then kiss the bright bubble
1031. That breaks in its rise;
1032. Oh! love is a trouble,
1033. As light when it dies.
1034. CHARLES. Let the young be glad! though cares in crowds
1035. Leave scarce a break of blue,
1036. Yet hope gives wings to morning clouds;
1037. And while their shade the sky enshrouds —
1038. By love and wine, which through them shine —
1039. They are turned to a golden hue.
1040. Then give us wine, for we ought to shine
1041. In the hour of dark and dew.
1042. FESTUS. Well might the thoughtful race of old
1043. With ivy twine the head
1044. Of him they hailed their god of wine, —
1045. Thank God! the lie is dead;
1046. For ivy climbs the crumbling hall
1047. To decorate decay;
1048. And spreads its dark deceitful pall
1049. To hide what wastes away.
1050. And wine will circle round the brain
1051. As ivy o'er the brow,
1052. Till what could once see far as stars
1053. Is dark as Death's eye now.
1054. Then dash the cup down! 'tis not worth
1055. A soul's great sacrifice:
1056. The wine will sink into the earth,
1057. The soul, the soul — must rise.

1058. CHARLES. A toast!
1059. FREDERIC. Here's beauty's fairest flower —
1060. The maiden of our own birth-land!
1061. HARRY. Pale face! — oh for one happy hour
1062. To hold my splendid Spaniard's hand!
1063. FESTUS. Why differ on which is the fairest form,
1064. When all are the same the heart to warm?
1065. Although by different charms they strike,
1066. Their power is equal and alike.
1067. Ye bigots of beauty! behold I stand forth,
1068. And drink to the lovely all over the earth.
1069. Come, fill to the girl by the Tagus'³ waves!
1070. Wherever she lives there's a land of slaves.
1071. And here's to the Scot! with her deep blue eye,
1072. Like the far off lochs 'neath her hill-propt sky.
1073. To her of the green Isle! whose tyrants deform
1074. The land, where she beams like the bow in the storm.
1075. To the Norman! so noble, and stately and tall;
1076. Whose charms, ever changing, can please as they pall:
1077. Two bowls in a breath! here's to each and to all!
1078. Come fill to the English! whose eloquent brow
1079. Says, pleasure is passing, but coming, and now;
1080. Oh! her eyes o'er the wine are like stars o'er the sea,
1081. And her face is the face of all Heaven to me.
1082. And here's to the Spaniard! that warm blooming maid,
1083. With her step superb, and her black locks' braid.
1084. To her of dear Paris! with soul-spending glance,
1085. Whose feet, as she's sleeping, look dreaming a dance.
1086. To the maiden whose lip like a rose-leaf is curled,
1087. And her eye like the star-flag above it unfurled!
1088. Here's to beauty, young beauty, all over the world!
1089. WILL. Hurrah! a glorious toast;
1090. 'T would warm a ghost.
1091. FESTUS. It moves not me. I cannot drink
1092. The toast I have given.
1093. There! — Earth may pledge it, and she will —
1094. Herself and her beauty to Heaven.
1095. Drink to the dead — youth's feelings vain!
1096. Drink to the heart — the battered wreck,
1097. Hurled from all passion's stormy main!

---

3. Tagus: The longest river on the Iberian peninsula.

1098. Though aye the billows o'er it break,
1099. The ruin rots, nor rides again.
1100. CHARLES. Friend of my heart! away with care,
1101. And sing, and dance, and laugh;
1102. To love, and to the favourite fair,
1103. The wine-cup ever quaff.
1104. Oh, drink to the lovely! whatever they are.
1105. Though fair as snow — as light;
1106. For whether or falling, or fixed the star,
1107. They both are heavenly bright.
1108. Out upon Care! he shall not stay
1109. Within a heart like thine;
1110. There's nought in Heaven or earth can weigh
1111. Down youth, and love, and wine.
1112. Then drink with the merry! though we must die,
1113. Like beauty's tear we'll fall;
1114. We have lived in the light of a loved one's eye,
1115. And to live, love, and die is all.
1116. FESTUS. Vain is the world and all it boasts:
1117. How brief Love's pleasure's date!
1118. We turn the bowl and all forget
1119. The bias of our fate.
1120. GEORGE. How goes the enemy?
1121. LUCIFER. What can he mean?
1122. FESTUS. He asks the hour.
1123. LUCIFER. Aha! Then I
1124. Advise, if Time thy foe hath been,
1125. Be quick! shake hands, man, with Eternity.

SCENE 16

[*A Churchyard*]
[*FESTUS and LUCIFER beside a Grave*]

1. FESTUS. Let years crowd on, and age bow down
2. My body to the earth which gave,

3.   As yon grey, worn out, crumbling stone
4.   Dips o'er the grave!
5.   What, though for me no music thrill,
6.   Nor mirth delight, nor beauty move;
7.   Though the heart stiffen and wax still,
8.   And make no love;
9.   Still, deep and bright, like river gold,
10.   Imbedded here thy love shall lie —
11.   Sun-grains, that with the sands are rolled,
12.   Of memory.
13.   Shall that soul never burst the tomb,
14.   Draped in long robes of living light?
15.   Or, worm-like, alway eat the gloom
16.   And dust of night?
17.   LUCIFER. Oh! life in sporting on earth lies,
18.   Till death share up the rich green sod;
19.   But if the spirit lives or dies,
20.   Why try ye God?
21.   What should it never smile nor sigh
22.   From cheeks or lips but those beneath?
23.   Doth love not weigh the world's vast lie?
24.   Doth life not death?
25.   FESTUS. I ask why man should suffer death?
26.   LUCIFER. Answer — what right to life hath he?
27.   God gives and takes away your breath:
28.   What more have ye?
29.   Breath is your life, and life your soul;
30.   Ye have it warm from His kind hands:
31.   Then yield it back to the great Whole
32.   When He demands.
33.   Why, deathling, wilt thou long for Heaven?
34.   Why seek a bright but blinding way?
35.   Go, thank thy God that He hath given
36.   Night upon day:
37.   Go, thank thy God that thou hast lived,
38.   And ask no more: 't is all He gave:
39.   'T is all there needs to be believed —
40.   God and the grave.
41.   FESTUS. For Thee, God, will I save my heart;
42.   For Thee my nature's honour keep;

43.　Then, soul and body, all or part —
44.　Rest, wake, or sleep!

SCENE 17

[Space]
[FESTUS and LUCIFER]

1.　FESTUS. Listen! I hear the harmonies of Heaven,
2.　From sphere to sphere and from the boundless round
3.　Re-echoing bliss to those serenest heights
4.　Where angels sit and strike their emulous harps,
5.　Wreathed round with flowers and diamonded with dew;
6.　Such dew as gemmed the everduring blooms
7.　Of Eden winterless, or as all night
8.　The tree of Life wept from its every leaf
9.　Unwithering. And now methinks I hear
10.　The music of the murmur of the stream
11.　Which through the Bridal City of the Lord
12.　Floweth all life for ever; and the breath
13.　Through the star-shading branches of that Tree
14.　Transplanted now to Heaven, but once on earth,
15.　Whose fruit is for all Beings — breathed of God.
16.　Oh! breathe on me, inspiring spirit-breath!
17.　Oh! flow to me, ye heart-reviving waves;
18.　Freshen the faded soul that droops and dies.
19.　LUCIFER. The universe is but the gate of Heaven.
20.　Lo! from this highest orb, the crown of space
21.　And footstool unto Heaven, we can look up
22.　And gain a glimpse of glory unconceived.
23.　FESTUS. See how yon angels stretch their shining arms,
24.　Wave their star-haunting wings which gleam like glass,
25.　And locks that look like Morning's when she comes

26.   Triumphant in the East. Is this their joy
27.   O'er some world penitent?
28.   LUCIFER. Lo! there it rides;
29.   Blest to discharge on Heaven's all peaceful shores
30.   Its long accumulated load of life,
31.   Its deathless freight, — pilgrims of time and space.
32.   Yon guilty orb of hesitating light
33.   Slow looming, there, on its dark path, goes up
34.   At the forewritten hour, as do all worlds
35.   To God, to judgment; and the earthquake groans
36.   Which rend its adamantine breast forebode
37.   Its agonizing doom.
38.   FESTUS. And doth not Heaven
39.   Grieve with the lost as gladden with the saved?
40.   LUCIFER. How many immortals mourn at the decree
41.   Of righteous wisdom, which alone to them
42.   Is bliss sufficient, being infinite?
43.   FESTUS. If God hath made all He alone it is
44.   Who hath to answer for all.   .
45.   LUCIFER. He hath made.
46.   To secondary natures it seems just
47.   That justice should be realised, and there
48.   Is one example extant in the skies.
49.   FESTUS. But wherefore did it not repent in Time?
50.   LUCIFER. What unto us is Time, stands before God
51.   Eternity. Repentance is the grief
52.   For and effectual abstinence from sin,
53.   Which secondary natures without God
54.   Cannot attain to.
55.   FESTUS. Cloudy and clear by turns
56.   Thy words as Heaven. I know not what to think
57.   Nor how to act.
58.   LUCIFER. It is natural; and none
59.   Can aim or hit but as appointed them.
60.   There is but one great sinner, Human nature,
61.   Predict of every world and predicate:
62.   The wicked one, the Enemy of God,
63.   To be destroyed in the eternal fire
64.   Of His wrath, even thus in Deity —
65.   In whom as they begin must all things end.
66.   God loveth only His own spirit, so
67.   All that is base shall perish. From the first

68.   These things were fixed, and are and aye shall be
69.   Consummating, and are revealed as writ
70.   In words always fulfilled and burning truth
71.   Under the buried basements of the skies,
72.   Which after overthrown shall reäppear.
73.   The unenlightened mind sees Deity
74.   In all things, but the spiritual soul
75.   All things in God. Now, ere we higher rise,
76.   Look downwards from this coping of the world;
77.   And know that down to the profoundest depth
78.   Of utter space, where not an atom mars
79.   The void invisible, it were easier far
80.   To cast a line and calculate its rate,
81.   Or pierce all space, nor cross the path of light,
82.   Than fathom man's dark heart or sound his soul.

SCENE 18

[*Heaven*]
[*LUCIFER and FESTUS, entering*]

1.   THE ARCHANGELS. Infinite God! Thy will is done:
2.   The world's last sand is all but run:
3.   The night is feeding on the sun.
4.   LUCIFER. All-being God! I come to Thee again,
5.   Nor come alone. Mortality is here.
6.   Thou bad'st me do my will, and I have dared
7.   To do it. I have brought him up to Heaven.
8.   GOD.
9.   Thou canst not do what is not willed to be.
10. Suns are made up of atoms, Heaven of souls;
11. And souls and suns are but the atoms of
12. The body I, God, dwell in. What wilt thou
13. With him who is here with thee?
14. LUCIFER. Shew him God.

15. GOD.
16. No being, upon part of whom the curse
17. Of death rests — were it only on his shadow,
18. Can look on God and live.
19. LUCIFER. Look, Festus, look!
20. FESTUS. Eternal fountain of the Infinite,
21. On whose life-tide the stars seem strown like bubbles,
22. Forgive me that an atomie of being
23. Hath sought to see its Maker face to face.
24. I have seen all Thy works and wonders, passed
25. From star to star, from space to space, and feel
26. That to see all which can be seen is nothing,
27. And not to look on Thee the Invisible.
28. The spirits that I met all seemed to say,
29. As on they sped upon their starward course,
30. And slackened their lightning wings one moment o'er me,
31. I could not look on God whatever I was.
32. And Thou didst give this spirit at my side
33. Power to make me more than them immortal.
34. So when we had winged through Thy wide world of things,
35. And seen stars made and saved, destroyed and judged,
36. I said — and trembled lest Thou shouldst not hear me,
37. And make Thyself right ready to forgive,
38. I will see God, before I die, in Heaven.
39. Forgive me, Lord!
40. GOD.
41. Rise, mortal! look on me.
42. FESTUS. Oh! I see nothing but like dazzling darkness.
43. LUCIFER. I knew how it would be. I am away.
44. FESTUS. I am Thy creature, God! oh, slay me not,
45. But let some angel take me, or I die.
46. GENIUS. Come hither, Festus.
47. FESTUS. Who art thou?
48. GENIUS.   I am
49. One who hath aye been by thee from thy birth,
50. Thy guardian angel, thy good genius.
51. FESTUS. I knew thee not till now.
52. GENIUS. I am never seen
53. In the earth's low thick light, but here in Heaven,
54. And in the air which God breathes, I am clear.
55. I tell to God each night thy thoughts and deeds;
56. And watching o'er thee both on earth and here,

57. Pray unto Him for thee and intercede.
58. FESTUS. And this is Heaven. Lead on. Will God forgive
59. That I did long to see Him?
60. GENIUS. It is the strain
61. Of all high spirits towards Him. Thou couldst not
62. Even if thou wouldst, behold God; masked in dust,
63. Thine eye did light on darkness; but when dead,
64. And the dust shaken off the shining essence,
65. God shall glow through thee as through living glass,
66. And every thought and atom of thy being
67. Shall guest His glory, be overbright with God.
68. Hadst thou not been by faith immortalized
69. For the instant, then thine eye had been thy death.
70. Come, I will shew thee Heaven and all angels.
71. Lo! the recording angel.
72. FESTUS.   Him I see
73. High-seated, and the pen within his hand
74. Plumed like a storm-portending cloud which curves
75. Half over Heaven, and swift, in use divine,
76. As is a warrior's spear!
77. GENIUS. The book wherein
78. Are writ the records of the universe,
79. Lies like a world laid open at his feet.
80. And there, the Book of Life which holds the names,
81. Formed out in starry brilliants, of God's sons, —
82. The spirit-names which angels learn by heart,
83. Of worlds beforehand. Wilt thou see thine own?
84. FESTUS. My name is written in the Book of Life;
85. It is enough. That constellated word
86. Is more to me and clearer than all stars,
87. Henceforward and for aye.
88. GENIUS. Raise still thine eyes!
89. Thy gleaming throne! hewn from that mount of light
90. Which was before created light or night
91. Never created, Heaven's eternal base,
92. Whereon God's throne is 'stablished. Sit on it!
93. FESTUS. Nay, I will forestall nothing more than sight.
94. GENIUS. Turn then and view yon streams where spirits sport
95. Quaffing immortal life, preparing aye
96. For higher and intenser Being still.
97. These are the upper fountains of the Heavens,
98. The emanations of Eternity;

  99. By washing them in which they purify
100. Their eyes to penetrate the essential light
101. In all things hidden, seen alone by eyes
102. Fire-spirited, etherially clear,
103. Which like the fabled stone, conceived of fire,
104. Son of the sun, transmutes all seen to soul.
105. And such the bliss and power reserved for man;
106. Yet but the surface-shadow canst thou see.
107. The substance is to be. Behold yon group
108. Of spirits blest! in their divinest eyes
109. The spirit speaks, and shews that in their own
110. All doubt and want hath ceased, as death hath ceased.
111. Hither they come, rejoicing, marvelling.
112. FESTUS. How all with kindly wonder look on me!
113. Mayhap I tell of earth to their pure sense.
114. Some seem as if they knew me. I know none.
115. But how claim kinship with the glorified
116. Unless with them like-glorified! Yet, yes —
117. It is — it must be; — that angelic spirit! —
118. My heart outruns me — mother! see thy son.
119. ANGEL. Child, how art thou here?
120. FESTUS. God hath let me come.
121. ANGEL. Hast thou not come unbidden and unprepared?
122. FESTUS. Forgive me, if it be so. I am come.
123. And I have ever said there are two who will
124. Forgive me aught I do — my God and thou!
125. ANGEL. I do! may He!
126. FESTUS. Dear mother, thou art blessed;
127. And I am blessed, too, in knowing thee.
128. ANGEL. Son of my hopes on earth and prayers in Heaven!
129. The love of God! oh, it is infinite
130. Even as our imperfections. Promise, child,
131. That thou wilt love Him more and more for this,
132. And for His boundless kindness thus towards me.
133. Now, my son, hear me! for the hours of Heaven
134. Are not as those of earth; and all is all
135. But lost that is not given unto God.
136. Oft have I seen with joy thy thoughts of Heaven,
137. And holy hopes, which track the soul with light,
138. Rise from dead doubts within thy troubled breast,
139. As souls of drowned bodies from the sea,
140. Upwards to God, and marked them so received,

141. That oh! my soul hath overflowed with rapture
142. As now thine eye with tears. But oh! my son
143. Beloved! fear thou ever for thy soul;
144. It yet hath to be saved. Nought perfect stands
145. But that which is in Heaven. God is all-kind;
146. And long time hath he made thee think of Him;
147. Think on Him yet in time. Ere I left earth,
148. With the last breath which air would spare for me,
149. With the last look which light would bless me with,
150. I prayed thou mightst be happy and be wise —
151. And half the prayer I brought myself to God —
152. And lo! thou art unhappy and unwise.
153. FESTUS. Blessed one! I rejoice that thou art clear,
154. And all who have cared for me, of my misdeeds.
155. Thy spirit was on those who nurtured me.
156. All word and practice that could be of good,
157. Was given me; so that my sin is splendid.
158. Yes! if I have sinned, I have sinned sublimely;
159. And I am glad I suffer for my faults.
160. I would not if I might, be bad and happy,
161. ANGEL. God laughs at ill by man made and allows it.
162. The vaunt of mountainous evil and the power
163. To challenge Heaven from a molehill, child!
164. FESTUS. God hath made but few better hearts than mine,
165. However much it fail in the wise ways
166. Of the world, as living in the dull dark streets
167. Of forms and follies wherein men build themselves.
168. ANGEL. The goodness of the heart is shewn in deeds
169. Of peacefulness and kindness. Hand and heart
170. Are one thing with the good as thou shouldst be.
171. The splendour of corruption hath no power
172. Nor vital essence; and content in sin
173. Shews apathy, not satisfied control.
174. Do my words trouble thee? Then treasure them.
175. Pain overgot gives peace as death does Heaven.
176. All things that speak of Heaven speak of peace.
177. Peace hath more might than war. High brows are calm.
178. Great thoughts are still as stars; and truths, like suns,
179. Stir not; though many systems tend round them.
180. Mind's step is still as death's; and all great things
181. Which cannot be controlled, whose end is good.
182. Behold yon throne! there, Love, Faith, Hope are one!

183. There, judgment, righteousness, and mercy make
184. One and the same thing. God's salvation is
185. His vengeance, and his wrath glory, as on earth
186. Destruction restoration to the pure.
187. Humanity is perfected in Heaven.
188. FESTUS. I did not make myself, nor plan my soul.
189. I am no angel nursed in the lap of light,
190. Nor fed on milk immortal of the stars,
191. Nor golden fruit grown in the summery suns.
192. How am I answerable for my heart?
193. It is my master, and is free with me,
194. As fixed with fate, even as a star which moves,
195. Yet moveth only on a certain course
196. In certain mode; — its liberties are laws.
197. Its laws tyrannic; I cannot hinder it,
198. It cannot hinder God. All that we do
199. Or bear is settled from eternity;
200. Whereof is no beginning, midst, nor end.
201. To act, is ours; quite sure, whatever we do,
202. Whether it be for our own good or ill,
203. Or others' ill or good, it is for God's
204. Glory — the same and always: it is ordered.
205. The soul is but an organ, and it hath
206. No power of good and evil in itself.
207. More than the eye hath power of light or dark.
208. God fitted it for good; and evil is
209. Good in another way we are not skilled in.
210. The good we do is of His own good will, —
211. The ill, of His own letting. Doth not nature —
212. All light in life, shine, marsh-like, too, in death?
213. Yea, wandering fires wait even on rottenness
214. Like a stray gleam of thought in an idiot's brain.
215. And thus I look on souls that seem decaying
216. In sin, and flying off by elements.
217. All may not live again; but all which do
218. Must change perpetually e'en in Heaven;
219. And not by death to death, but life to life.
220. ANGEL. No! step by step, and throne by throne, we rise
221. Continually towards the infinite,
222. And ever nearer — never near — to God.
223. FESTUS. Yet merit or demerit none I see
224. In nature, human or material,

225. In passions or affections good or bad.
226. We only know that God's best purposes
227. Are oftenest brought about by dreadest sins.
228. Is thunder evil or is dew divine?
229. Does virtue lie in sunshine, sin in storm?
230. Is not each natural, each needful, best?
231. How know we what is evil from what good?
232. Wrath and revenge God claimeth as His own.
233. And yet men speculate on right and wrong
234. As upon day and night, forgetting both
235. Have but one cause, and that the same — God's will,
236. Originally, ultimately Him.
237. All right is right divine. A worm hath rights
238. A king cannot despoil him of, nor sin;
239. Yet wrongs are things necessitate, like wants,
240. And oft are well permitted to best ends.
241. A double error sometimes sets us right.
242. In man there is no rule of right and wrong
243. Inherent as mere man. Why, conscience is
244. The basest thing of all. Its life is passed
245. In justifying and condemning sin;
246. Accomplice, traitor, judge and headsman, too,
247. But conscience knows its business and performs.
248. Nothing is lost in nature; and no soul,
249. Though buried in the centre of all sin,
250. Is lost to God; but there it works His will
251. And burns conformably. The weakest things
252. Are to be made the examples of His might;
253. The most defective, of His perfect grace,
254. Whene'er He thinketh well. Oh! everything
255. To me seems good and lovely and immortal;
256. The whole is beautiful; and I can see
257. Nought wrong in man nor nature, nought not meant;
258. As from His hands it comes who fashions all,
259. All holy as His word. The world is but
260. A revelation. He breathes Himself upon us
261. Before our birth, as o'er the formless void
262. He moveth at first, and we are all inspired
263. With His spirit. All things are God or of God.
264. For the whole world is in the mind of God
265. What a thought is in ours. Why boast we then
266. Of aught? All that is good belongs to God;

267. And good and God are all things, or shall be.
268. ANGEL. There lacks in souls like thine unsaved, unraised,
269. The light within — the light of perfectness —
270. Such as there is in Heaven. The soul hath sunk
271. And perished like a light-house in the sea;
272. It is for God to raise it and rebuild.
273. GENIUS. And his, thy son's, He will raise. Since with me
274. I have shewn him infinite wonders: we have oped
275. And scanned the golden scroll of Fate, wherein
276. Are writ, in God's own hand, all things which happen.
277. There we have seen the record of his being —
278. His long temptation, sin, and suffering.
279. FESTUS. And hear it, oh beloved and blessed one!
280. Mine own salvation!
281. ANGEL. God is great in love;
282. Infinite in His nature, power, and grace;
283. Creating, and redeeming, and destroying —
284. Infinite infinitely. But in love —
285. Oh! it is the truth transcendant over all —
286. When thus to one poor spirit He gives His hand,
287. He seems to impart His own unboundedness
288. Of bliss. We seem to be hardly worth destroying,
289. And much less saving; yet He loveth each
290. As though all were His equal.
291. FESTUS.   I know all
292. I have to go through henceforth, — all the doubts,
293. Passions of life, and woes; but knowing them
294. Hinders them not; I bear obeyingly;
295. And pine no more, as once when I looked back
296. And saw how life had balked, and foiled, and fooled me.
297. Fresh as a spouting spring upon the hills
298. My heart leapt out to life; it little thought
299. Of all the vile cares that would rill into it,
300. And the low places it would have to go through, —
301. The drains, the crossings, and the mill-work after.
302. God hath endowed me with a soul that scorns life —
303. An element over and above the world's:
304. But the price one pays for pride is mountain-high,
305. There is a curse beyond the rack of death —
306. A woe, wherein God hath put out His strength—
307. A pain past all the mad wretchedness we feel,
308. When the sacred secret hath flown out of us,

309. And the heart broken open by deep care, —
310. The curse of a high spirit famishing,
311. Because all earth but sickens it.
312. ANGEL. Go, child!
313. Fulfil thy fate! Be — do— bear— and thank God!
314. To me it seems as I had lived all ages
315. Since I left earth; and thou art yet scarce man.
316. FESTUS. It was not, mother, that I knew thy face;
317. The luminous eclipse that is on it now,
318. Though it was fair on earth, would have made it strange
319. Even to one who knew as well as he loved thee;
320. And if these time-tired eyes ever imaged thine,
321. It was but for a moment, and the sight
322. Passed; and my life was broken like a line
323. At the first word — but my heart cried out in me.
324. ANGEL. I knew thee well. And now to earth again!
325. Go, son! and say to all who once were mine —
326. I love them, and expect them.
327. FESTUS.   Blessed one!
328. I will!
329. ANGEL.   I charge thee, Genius, bear him safely.
330. GENIUS. Through light, and night, and all the powers of air,
331. I have a passport.
332. ANGEL.   God be with thee, child!
333. GENIUS. Come!
334. FESTUS. I feel happier, better, nobler now.
335. See where she sits, and smiles, and points me out
336. To those who sit along with her. Who are
337. The two?
338. GENIUS.   One is the mother of mankind,
339. And one the mother of the Man who saved
340. Mankind; and she, thine own, the mother of
341. The last man of mankind — for thou art he.[1]
342. FESTUS. Am I? It is enough: I have seen God.
343. GENIUS. God and His great idea, the universe,
344. Are over and above us. Be the one
345. Worshipped, the other reverently proved.
346. Wilt sojourn for a time among the worlds,

---

1. The three women are the biblical Eve; Mary, the mother of Jesus; and Festus' own
    mother.

347. And test their natures?
348. FESTUS.   Gladly.
349. GENIUS.   Seek we, then,
350. All rareness and variety these worlds
351. Can offer, ere we reach thine orb. Descend!
352. Now is the age of worlds.

FESTUS AND THE ANGEL

[A Visit]
[FESTUS and HELEN]

1.   HELEN. Come to the light, love! Let me look on thee!
2.   Let me make sure I have thee. Is it thou?
3.   Is this thy hand? Are these thy velvet lips, —
4.   Thy lips so lovable? Nay, speak not yet!
5.   For oft as I have dreamed of thee, it was
6.   Thy speaking woke me. I will dream no more.
7.   Am I alive? And do I really look
8.   Upon these soft and sea-blue eyes of thine,
9.   Wherein I half believe I can espy
10. The riches of the sea? These dark rolled locks!
11. Oh God! art Thou not glad, too, he is here! —
12. Where hast thou been so long? Never to hear,
13. Never to see, nor see one who had seen thee —
14. Come now, confess it was not kind to treat
15. Me in this manner.
16. FESTUS. I confess, my love,
17. But I have been where neither tongue, nor pen,
18. Nor hand could give thee token where I was;
19. And seen, but 'tis enough! I see thee now.
20. I would rather look upon thy shadow there,
21. Than Heaven's bright thrones for ever.
22. HELEN. Where hast been?
23. FESTUS. Say, am I altered?
24. HELEN. Nowise.
25. FESTUS. It is well.
26. Then in the resurrection we may know
27. Each other. I have been among the worlds,
28. Angels and spirits bodiless.
29. HELEN.   Great God!
30. Can it be so?
31. FESTUS. It is: — and that both here
32. And elsewhere. When the stars come, thou shalt see

33.   The track I travelled through the light of night;
34.   Where I have been, and whence my visitors.
35.   HELEN. And thou hast been with angels all the while,
36.   And still dost love me?
37.   FESTUS.   Constantly as now.
38.   But for the time I did devote my soul
39.   To their divine society, I knew
40.   Thou wouldst forgive, yet dared not trust myself
41.   To see thee, or to pen one word, for fear
42.   Thy love should overpower the plan conceived,
43.   And acting, in my mind, of visiting
44.   The spirits in their space-embosomed homes.
45.   HELEN. Forgive thee! 'tis a deed which merits love.
46.   And should I not be proud, too, who can say,
47.   For me he left all angels?
48.   FESTUS.   I forethought
49.   So thou wouldst say; but with an offering
50.   Came I provided, even with a trophy
51.   Of love angelic, given me for thee;
52.   For angel bosoms know no jealousy.
53.   HELEN. Shew me.
54.   FESTUS. It is of jewels I received
55.   From one who snatched them from the richest wreck
56.   Of matter ever made, the holiest
57.   And most resplendent.
58.   HELEN. Why, what could it be?
59.   Jewels are baubles only; whether pearls
60.   From the sea's lightless depths, or diamonds
61.   Culled from the mountain's crown, or chrysolith,[1]
62.   Cat's eye or moonstone, toys are they at best.
63.   Jewels are not of all things in my sight
64.   Most precious.
65.   FESTUS. Nor in mine. It is in the use
66.   Of which they may be made their value lies;
67.   In the pure thoughts of beauty they call up,
68.   And qualities they emblem. So in that
69.   Thou wearest there, thy cross; — to me it is
70.   Suggestive of bright thoughts and hopes in Him
71.   Whose one great sacrifice availeth all,

1. Chrysolith: Coinage unique to *Festus*, probably suggesting a huge block (a monolith) made of chrysolite, a gemstone that is variety of olivine.

72. Living and dead, through all Eternity.
73. Not to the wanderer over southern seas
74. Rises the constellation of the Cross
75. More lovelily o'er sky and calm blue wave,
76. Than does to me that bright one on thy breast.
77. As diamonds are purest of all things,
78. And but embodied light which fire consumes
79. And renders back to air, that nought remains, —
80. And as the cross is symbol of our creed,
81. So let that ornament signify to thee
82. The faith of Christ, all purity, all light,
83. Through fervency resolving into Heaven.
84. Each hath his cross, fair lady, on his heart.
85. Never may thine be heavier or darker
86. Than that now on thy breast, so light and bright,
87. Rising and falling with its bosom-swell.
88. HELEN. I thank thee for that wish, and for the love
89. Which prompts it — the immeasurable love
90. I know is mine, and I with none would share.
91. Forgive me; I have not yet felt my wings.
92. Now have I not been patient? Let me see
93. My promised present.
94. FESTUS. Look, then — they are here;
95. Bracelets of chrysoprase.[2]
96. HELEN. Most beautiful!
97. FESTUS. Come, let me clasp them, dearest, on thine arms;
98. For these of those are worthy, and are named
99. In the foundation stones of the bright city.
100. Which is to be for the immortal saved,
101. Their last and blest abode; and such their hue,
102. The golden green of Paradisal plains
103. Which lie about it boundlessly, and more
104. Intensely tinted with the burning beauty
105. Of God's eye, which alone doth light that land,
106. Than our earth's cold grass garment with the sun;
107. Though even in the bright, hot, blue-skied East,
108. Where he doth live the life of light and Heaven;
109. Where, o'er the mountains, at midday is seen

---

2. Chrysoprase: The ancient name of a golden-green precious stone, now generally believed to have been a variety of the beryl (*OED*).

110. The morning star, and the moon tans at night
111. The cheek of careless sleeper. Take them, love.
112. There are no nobler earthly ornaments
113. Than jewels of the city of the saved.
114. HELEN. But how are these of that bright city? I
115. Am eager for their history.
116. FESTUS.   They are
117. Thereof prophetically, and have been —
118. What I will shew thee presently, when I
119. Relate the story of the angel who
120. Gave them to me.
121. HELEN.   Well; I will wait till then,
122. Or any time thou choosest: 'tis enough
123. That I believe thee always; — but would know,
124. If not in me too curious to ask,
125. How came about these miracles? Hast thou raised
126. The fiend of fiends, and made a compact dark,
127. Sealed with thy blood, symbolic of the soul,
128. Whereby all power is given thee for a time,
129. All means, all knowledge, to make more secure
130. Thy spirit's dread perdition at the end?
131. I of such awful stories oft have heard,
132. And the unlawful lore which ruins souls.
133. Myself have charms, foresee events in dreams;
134. Can prophesy, prognosticate, know well
135. The secret ties between many magic herbs
136. And mortal feelings, nor condemn myself
137. For knowing what is innocent; but thou!
138. Thy helps are mightier far and more obscure.
139. Was it with wand and circle, book and skull,
140. With rites forbid and backward-jabbered prayers,
141. In cross-roads or in churchyard, at full moon,
142. And by instruction of the ghostly dead,
143. That thou hast wrought these wonders, and attained
144. Such high transcendent powers and secrets? Speak!
145. Or is man's mastery over spirits not
146. Of such a vile and vulgar consequence?
147. FESTUS. Were not my heart as guiltless of all mirth
148. As is the oracle of an extinct god
149. Of its priest-prompted answer, I might smile
150. To list such askings. Mind's command o'er mind,
151. Spirit's o'er spirit, is the clear effect

152. And natural action of an inward gift,
153. Given of God, whereby the incarnate soul
154. Hath power to pass free out of earth and death
155. To immortality and Heaven, and mate
156. With beings of a kind, condition, lot,
157. All diverse from his own. This mastery
158. Means but communion, the power to quit
159. Life's little globule here, and coalesce
160. With the great mass about us. For the rest,
161. To raise the Devil were an infant's task
162. To that of raising man. Why, every one
163. Conjures the Fiend from Hell into himself
164. When Passion chokes or blinds him. Sin is Hell.
165. HELEN. How dost thou bring a spirit to thee, Festus?
166. FESTUS. It is my will which makes it visible.
167. HELEN. What are those like whom thou hast seen?
168. FESTUS.   They come,
169. The denizens of other worlds, arrayed
170. In diverse form and feature, mostly lovely;
171. In limb and wing ethereal finer far
172. Than an ephemeris'[3] pinion; others, armed
173. With gleaming plumes, that might overcome an air
174. Of adamantine denseness, pranked with fire.
175. All are of different offices and strengths,
176. Powers, orders, tendencies, in like degrees
177. As men, with even more variety;
178. Of different glories, duties, and delights.
179. Even as the light of meteor, satellite,
180. Planet and comet, sun, star, nebula,
181. Differ, and nature also, so do theirs.
182. With them is neither need, nor sex, nor age,
183. Nor generation, growth, decay, nor death;
184. Or none whom I have known; there may be such.
185. Mature they are created and complete,
186. Or seem to be. Perfect from God they come.
187. Yet have they different degrees of beauty,
188. Even as strength and holy excellence.

---

3. Ephemeris: A system for tabulating celestial bodies that goes back at least to ancient
   Babylonian astrology, though it appears to have also been used to describe the ephemeral
   bodies themselves (that is, comets). The sense here is probably meant to be 'fine as a
   comet's tail'.

189. Some seem of milder and more feminine
190. Nature than others, Beauty's proper sex,
191. Shewn but by softer qualities of soul,
192. More lovable than awful, more devote
193. To deeds of individual piety,
194. And grace, than mighty missions fit to task
195. Sublimest spirits, or the toil intense
196. Of cultivating nations of their kind;
197. Or working out from the problem of the world
198. The great results of God, — result, sum, cause.
199. These ofttimes charged with delegated powers,
200. Formative or destructive; those, in chief,
201. Ordained to better and to beautify
202. Existence as it is; with careful love
203. To tend upon particular worlds or souls;
204. Warning and training whom they love, to tread
205. The soft and blossom-bordered, silvery paths,
206. Which lead and lure the soul to Paradise,
207. Making the feet shine which do walk on them;
208. While each doth God's great will alike, and both
209. With their whole nature's fullness love His works.
210. To love them lifts the soul to Heaven.
211. HELEN.   Let me, then!
212. Whence come, they?
213. FESTUS. Many of them come from orbs
214. Wherein the rudest matter is more worth
215. And fair than queenly gem; the dullest dust
216. Beneath their feet is rosy diamond: —
217. Others, direct from Heaven; but all in high
218. And serious love towards those to whom they come.
219. None but the blest are free to visit where
220. They choose. The lost are slaves for ever; here
221. Never but on their Master's merciless
222. Business, nor elsewhere. Still sometimes with these
223. Dark spirits have I held communion,
224. And in their soul's deep shadow, as within
225. A mountain cavern of the moon, conversed
226. With them, and wormed from them the gnawing truth
227. Of their extreme perdition; marking oft
228. Nature revealed by torture, as a leaf
229. Unfolds itself in fire and writhes the while,
230. Burning, yet unconsumed. Others there are

231. Come garlanded with flowers unwithering,
232. Or crowned with sunny jewels, clad in light,
233. And girded with the lightning, in their hands
234. Wands of pure rays arrowy starbeams; some
235. Bright as the sun self-lit, in stature tall,
236. Strong, straight and splendid as the golden reed
237. Whereby the height, and length, and breadth, and depth,
238. Of the descendant city of the skies,
239. In which God sometime shall make glad with man,
240. Were measured by the angel; (the same reed
241. Wherewith our Lord was mocked that angel found
242. Close by the Cross and took; God made it gold,
243. And now it makes the sceptre of His Son
244. Over all worlds; the sole bright rule of Heaven,
245. The measure of immortal life, the scale
246. Of power, love, bliss, and glory infinite): —
247. Some gorgeous and gigantic, who with wings
248. Wide as the wings of armies in the field
249. Drawn out for death, sweep over Heaven, and eyes
250. Deep, dark as sea-worn caverns, with a torch
251. At the end, far back, glaring. Some with wings
252. Like an unfainting rainbow, studded round
253. With stones of every hue and excellence,
254. Writ o'er with mystic words which none may read,
255. But those to whom their spiritual state
256. Gives correlative meaning, fit thereto.
257. Some of these visit me in dreams; with some
258. Have I made one in visions, in their own
259. Abodes of brightness, blessedness, and power:
260. And know moreover I shall joy with them,
261. Ere long their sacred guest, through ages yet
262. To come, in worlds not now perhaps create,
263. As they have been mine here: and some of them
264. In unimaginable splendours I
265. Have walked with through their winged worlds of light,
266. Double and triple particoloured suns,
267. And systems circling each the other, clad
268. In tints of light and air, whereto this earth
269. Hath nothing like, and man no knowledge of: —
270. Orbs heaped with mountains, to the which ours are
271. Mere grave-mounds, and their skies flowered with stars,
272. Violet, rose or pearl-hued, or soft blue,

273. Golden or green, the light now blended, now
274. Alternate; many moons and planets, full,
275. Crescent, or gibbous-faced, illumining
276. In periodic and intricate beauty,
277. At once those strange and most felicitous skies.
278. HELEN. How I should love to visit other worlds,
279. Or see an angel!
280. FESTUS.   Wilt thou now?
281. HELEN.   I dare not
282. Not now at least. I am not in the mood.
283. Ere I behold a spirit I would pray.
284. FESTUS. Light as a leaf thy step, or arrowy
285. Footing of breeze upon a waveless pool;
286. Sudden and soft, too, like a waft of light,
287. The beautiful immortals come to me;
288. Oh, ever lovely, ever welcome they!
289. HELEN. But why art thou, of all men, favoured thus?
290. To say there is a mystery in this
291. Or aught is only to confess God. Speak!
292. FESTUS. It is God's will that I possess this power,
293. Thus to attract great spirits to mine own,
294. As steel magnetically charged draws steel;
295. Himself the magnet of the universe,
296. Round whom all spirits tremble and towards whom
297. All tend.
298. HELEN. If as thou sayest, it is good: —
299. May it be an immortal good to thee.
300. FESTUS. There is no keeping back the power we have.
301. He hath no power who hath not power to use.
302. Some of these bodies whom I speak of are
303. Pure spirits, others bodies soulical:
304. For spirit is to soul as wind to air.
305. They give me all I seek, and at a wish
306. Would furnish treasures, thrones, or palaces;
307. But all these things have I eschewed, and chosen
308. Command of mind alone, and of the world
309. Unbodied and all-lovely.
310. HELEN.   Is not this
311. Pleasure too much for mortal to be good?
312. FESTUS. All pleasure is with Thee, God! elsewhere, none
313. Not silver-ceiled hall nor golden throne,
314. Set thick with priceless gems, as Heaven with stars,

315. Or the high heart of youth with its bright hopes; —
316. Nor marble gleaming like the white moonlight,
317. As 't were an apparition of a palace
318. Inlaid with light as is a waterfall; —
319. Not rainbow-pinions coloured like yon cloud,
320. The sun's broad banner o'er his western tent,
321. Can match the bright imaginings of a child
322. Upon the glories of his coming years;
323. How equal then, the full-assured faith
324. Of him to whom the Saviour hath vouchsafed
325. The Heaven of His bosom? What can tempt
326. In its performance equal to that promise?
327. My soul stands fast to Heaven as doth a star;
328. And only God can move it who moves all.
329. There are who might have soared to what I spurned;
330. And like to heavenly orders human souls;
331. Some fitted most for contemplation, some
332. For action, these for thrones, and those for wheels.
333. HELEN. Tell me what they discourse upon, these angels?
334. FESTUS. They speak of what is past or coming, less
335. Of present things or actions. Some say most
336. About the future, others of the gone,
337. The dim traditions of Eternity,
338. Or Time's first golden moments. One there was —
339. From whose sweet lips elapsed as from a well,
340. Continuously, truths which made my soul
341. As they sank in it, fertile with rich thoughts —
342. Spake to me oft of Heaven, and our talk
343. Was of divine things always — angels, Heaven,
344. Salvation, immortality, and God;
345. The different states of spirits and the kinds
346. Of Being in all orbs, or, physical,
347. Or intellectual. I never tired
348. Preferring questions, but at each response
349. My soul drew back, sea-like, into its depths
350. To urge another charge on him. This spirit
351. Came to me daily for a long, long time,
352. Whene'er I prayed his presence. Many a world
353. He knew right well which man's eye never yet
354. Hath marked, nor ever may mark while on earth;
355. Yet grew his knowledge every time he came.
356. His thoughts all great and solemn and serene,

357. Like the immensest features of an orb,
358. Whose eyes are blue seas, and whose clear broad brow,
359. Some cultured continent, came ever round
360. From truth to truth — day bringing as they came.
361. He was to me an all-explaining spirit,
362. Teaching divine things by analogy
363. With mortal and material. Thus of God,
364. He shewed, as the three primal rays make one
365. Sole beam of Light, so the three Persons make
366. One God; neither without the other is.
367. However bright or beautiful itself
368. The theme he touched, he made it more so by
369. His own light, like a fire-fly on a flower.
370. And one of all I knew the most of, yet
371. The least can say of him; for full oft
372. Our thoughts drown speech, like to a foaming force,
373. Which thunders down the echo it creates.
374. Yet must I somewhat tell of him. He was
375. The spirit evil of the universe,
376. Impersonate. Oh strange and wild to know!
377. Perdition and destruction dwelt in him,
378. Like to a pair of eagles in one nest.
379. Hollow and wasteful as a whirlwind was
380. His soul; his heart as earthquake, and engulphed
381. World upon world. In him they disappeared
382. As might a morsel in a lion's maw,
383. The world which met him rolled aside to let him
384. Pass on his piercing path. His eyeballs burned
385. Revolving lightnings like a world on fire;
386. Their very night was fatal as the shade
387. Of Death's dark valley. And his space-spread wings —
388. Wide as the wings of Darkness when she rose
389. Scowling, and backing upwards, as the sun,
390. Giant of Light, first donned his burning crown,
391. Gladdening all Heaven with his inaugural smile, —
392. Were stained with the blood of many a starry world:
393. Yea, I have seen him seize upon an orb,
394. And cast it careless into worldless space,
395. As I might cast a pebble in the sea.
396. His might upon this earth was wondrous most.
397. He stood a match for mountains. Ocean's depths
398. He clove unto their rock-bed, as a sword,

399. Through blood and muscle to the central bone,
400. With one swoop of his arm. His brow was pale —
401. Pale as the life-blood of the undying worm
402. Which writhes around its frame of vital fire.
403. His voice blew like the desolating gust
404. Which strips the trees, and strews the earth with death.
405. His words were ever like a wheel of fire,
406. Rolling and burning this way now, now that:
407. Now whirling forth a blinding beam, now soft
408. And deep as Heaven's own luminous blue — and now
409. Like to a conqueror's chariot wheel they came,
410. Sodden with blood and slow, revolving death:
411. And every tone fell on the ear and heart,
412. Heavy and harsh and startling, like the first
413. Handful of mould cast on the coffined dead,
414. As though he claimed them his.
415. LUCIFER. [*entering.*]   Dost recognize
416. The portrait, lady?
417. HELEN.   Festus! who is this?
418. What portrait? —
419. FESTUS. Wherefore comest thou? Did I not
420. Claim privacy one evening?
421. LUCIFER.   Why, indeed —
422. I simply called, as I was on my way
423. To Jupiter — and he's a mouthful, mind; —
424. To keep the proverbs, too, in countenance.
425. Any commands for our planetary friends?
426. I go. Make my excuses! [*Goes.*]
427. FESTUS. A mistake,
428. Dearest; but rectified. [*Apart.*] And he is gone!
429. Hell hath its own again. Some sorrow chills
430. Ever the spirit, like a cloudlet nursed
431. In the star-giant's bosom.
432. HELEN. Tell me, love,
433. More of these angels!
434. FESTUS. There was one I loved
435. Of those immortals, of a lofty air,
436. Dimly divine and sad, and side by side
437. Him whom I spake of first she oft would stand
438. With her fair form — shadow illuminate —
439. Like to the dark moon in the young one's arms.
440. She never murmured at the doom which made

441. The sorrow that contained her, as the air
442. Infolds the orb whereon we dwell, but spake
443. Of God's will alway as most good and wise.
444. She had but little pleasure; but her all,
445. Such as it was, was in devising plans
446. Of bliss to come, or in the tales of Time
447. And the sweet early earth. She was in truth
448. Our earth's own angel. Oftimes would she dwell
449. With long and luminous sweetness on her theme,
450. Unwearying, unpausing, as a world.
451. The sun would rise and set; the soul-like moon,
452. In passive beauty and receptive light, —
453. Absorbing inspiration from the sun,
454. As doth from God His prophet ceaselessly —
455. She too would rise and set; and the far stars,
456. The third estate of Light, complete the round
457. Of the divine day; — still our angel spake,
458. And still I listened to the eloquent tongue
459. Which e'en on earth retained the tone of Heaven.
460. The shadow of a cloud upon a lake,
461. O'er which the wind hath all day held his breath,
462. Is not more calm and fair than her dear face—
463. So sweetly sad and so consolingly,
464. When she spake even on the end of earth.
465. Save that her eye grew darker, and her brow
466. Brighter with thought, as with galactic light
467. Mid Heaven when clearest, at such times, not I
468. Had known that earth were dearer unto her
469. Than other of the visitants divine,
470. Which hallow oft mine hours; — save, too, that then,
471. As though to touch but on that topic had,
472. Torpedo-like, numbed thought, she would straight cease
473. All converse suddenly, and kneel and seem
474. Inwardly praying with much power, — rise,
475. And vanish into Heaven. My mind is full
476. Of stories she hath told me of our world.
477. No word an angel utters lose I ever.
478. One I will tell thee now.
479. HELEN.   Do! let me hear!
480. Thy talk is the sweet extract of all speech,
481. And holds mine ear in blissful slavery.
482. FESTUS. 'Twas on a lovely summer afternoon,

483. Close by the grassy marge of a deep tarn,
484. Nigh halfway up a mountain, that we stood,
485. I and the angel, when she told me this.
486. Above us rose the grey rocks, by our side
487. Forests of pines, and the bright breaking wavelets
488. Came crowding, dancing to the brink, like thoughts
489. Unto our lips. Before us shone the sun.
490. The angel waved her hand ere she began,
491. As bidding earth be still. The birds ceased singing
492. And the trees breathing, and the lake smoothed down
493. Each shining wrinkle, and the wind drew off.
494. Time leant him o'er his scythe and, listening, wept.
495. The circling world reined in her lightning pace
496. A moment; Ocean hushed his snow-maned steeds,
497. And a cloud hid the sun, as does the face
498. A meditative hand: then spake she thus: —
499. Scarce had the sweet song of the morning stars,
500. Which rang through space at the first sign of life
501. Our earth gave, springing from the lap of God
502. On to her orbit, when from Heaven
503. Came down a white-winged host; and in the east,
504. Where Eden's Pleasance was, first furled their wings,
505. Alighting like to snowflakes. There they built,
506. Out of the riches of the soil around,
507. A house to God. There were the ruby rocks,
508. And there, in blocks, the quarried diamonds lay;
509. Opal and emerald mountain, amethyst,
510. Sapphire and chrysoprase, and jacinth stood
511. With the still action of a star, all light,
512. Like sea-based icebergs, blinding. These, with tools
513. Tempered in Heaven, the band angelic wrought,
514. And raised, and fitted, having first laid down
515. The deep foundations of the holy dome
516. On bright and beaten gold; and all the while
517. A song of glory hovered round the work
518. Like rainbow round a fountain. Day and night
519. Went on the hallowed labour till 'twas done.
520. And yet but thrice the sun set, and but thrice
521. The moon arose; so quick is work divine.
522. Tower, and roof, and pinnacle, without,
523. Were solid diamond. Within, the dome
524. Was eyeblue sapphire, sown with gold-bright stars

525. And clustering constellations; the wide floor
526. All emerald, earthlike, veined with gold and silver,
527. Marble and mineral of every hue,
528. And marvellous quality, the meanest thing,
529. Where all things were magnificent, was gold, —
530. The plainest. The high altar there was shaped
531. Out of one ruby heartlike. Columned round
532. With alabaster pure was all. And now
533. So high and bright it shone in the midday light,
534. It could be seen from Heaven. Upon their thrones
535. The sun-eyed angels hailed it, and there rose
536. A hurricane of blissfulness in Heaven,
537. Which echoed for a thousand years. One dark,
538. One solitary and foreseeing thought,
539. Passed, like a planet's transit o'er the sun,
540. Across the brow of God; but soon he smiled
541. Towards earth, and that smile did consecrate
542. The temple to Himself. And they who built
543. Bowed themselves down and worshipped in its walls.
544. High on the front were writ these words — to God!
545. The heavenly built this for the earthly ones,
546. That in his worship both might mix on earth,
547. As afterward they hoped to do in Heaven.
548. Had man stood good in Eden this had been:
549. He fell and Eden vanished. The bright place
550. Reared by the angels of all precious things,
551. For the joint worship of the sons of earth
552. And Heaven, fell with him, on the very day
553. He should have met God and His angels there —
554. The very day he disobeyed and joined
555. The host of death blackbannered. Eden fell;
556. The groves and grounds, which God the Lord's own feet
557. Had hallowed; the all-hued and odorous bowers
558. Where angels wandered, wishing them in Heaven;
559. The trees of life and knowledge — trees of death
560. And madness, as they proved to man — all fell;
561. And that bright fane fell first. No death-doomed eye
562. Gazed on its glory. Earthquakes gulped it down.
563. The Temple of the Angels, vast enough
564. To hold all nations worshipping at once,
565. Lay in its grave; the cherubs' flaming swords
566. The sole sad torches of its funeral.

567. Till at the flood, when the world's giant heart
568. Burst like a shell, it scattered east and west,
569. And far and wide, among less noble ruins.
570. The fragments of that angel-builded fane,
571. Which was in Eden, and of which all stones
572. That now are precious, were; and still shall be,
573. Gathered again unto a happier end.
574. In the pure City of the Son of God,
575. And temple yet to be rebuilt in Zion;
576. Which, though once overthrown, and once again
577. Torn down to its foundations, in the quick
578. Of earth, shall soul-like yet re-rise from ruin —
579. High, holy, happy, stainless as a star,
580. Imperishable as eternity.
581. — The angel ended; and the winds, waves, clouds,
582. The sun, the woods, and merry birds went on
583. As theretofore, in brightness, strength and music.
584. One scarce could think that earth at all had fallen,
585. To look upon her beauty. If the brand
586. Of sin were on her brow, it was surely hid
587. In natural art from every eye but God's.
588. All things seemed innocence and happiness.
589. I was all thanks. And look! the angel said,
590. Take these, and give to one thou lovest best:
591. Mine own hands saved from them the shining ruin
592. Whereof I have late told thee; and she gave
593. What now are greenly glowing on thine arms.
594. Ere I could answer, she was up, star-high!
595. Winging her way through Heaven.
596. HELEN. How shall I thank thee
597. Enough, or that kind angel who hath made
598. The gift to me dear doubly? I shall be
599. Afraid almost to wear them, but would not
600. Part with them for the treasures of all worlds.
601. How shew my thanks?
602. FESTUS. Love me as now, dear beauty!
603. Present or absent always, and 'twill be
604. More than enough of recompense for me.
605. HELEN. Hast met that angel late-while?
606. FESTUS.   I have not.
607. Yet oft methinks I see her, catch a glimpse
608. Of her sun-circling pinions or bright feet

609. Which fitter seem for rainbows than for earth,
610. Or Heaven's triumphal arch, more firm and pure
611. Than the world's whitest marble; — see her seated oft
612. On some high snowy cloud-cliff, harp in hand,
613. Singing the sun to sleep as down he lays
614. His head of glory on the rocking deep:
615. And so sing thou to me.
616. HELEN. There, rest thyself. [*sings.*]
617.   Oh! not the diamond starry bright
618.   Can so delight my view.
619.   As doth the moonstone's changing light
620.   And gleamy glowing hue;
621.   Now blue as Heaven, and then anon
622.   As golden as the sun,
623.   It hath a charm in every change —
624.   In brightening, darkening, one.
625.   And so with beauty, so with love,
626.   And everlasting mind;
627.   It takes a tint from Heaven above,
628.   And shines as it's inclined;
629.   Or from the sun, or towards the sun,
630.   With blind or brilliant eye,
631.   And only lights as it reflects
632.   The life-light of the sky.
633. He sleeps! The fate of many a gracious moral
634. This, to be stranded on a drowsy ear.

SCENE 20

[*Home — Dusk*]
[*FESTUS, and HELEN at her Piano*]

1. HELEN. I cannot live away from thee. How can
2. A flower live without its root?
3. FESTUS.   I, too,

4.   Must love or die,
5.   HELEN.   But I must have. Attend!
6.   I am to say and do just as I please;
7.   I may command thee, may I? that I will.
8.   FESTUS. I love to be enslaved. Oh! I would rather
9.   Obey thee, beauty! than rule men by millions.
10.   HELEN. Near, as afar, I will have love the same —
11.   With a bright sameness, like this diamond,
12.   Which, wherever the light be, shines like bright.
13.   And thou shalt say all sorts of pretty things
14.   To me; mind, to me only: write love-songs
15.   About me, and I will sing them to myself;
16.   Perhaps to thee, sometime, as it were now,
17.   If I should happen to be very kind.
18.   FESTUS. Sing now!
19.   HELEN.   No!
20.   FESTUS.   Tyrant! I will banish thee.
21.   HELEN. Nay, if to sing and play would please thee, I
22.   Would die to music. It was very wrong
23.   To say I would deny thee anything;
24.   But be not angry with me; for though God
25.   Forgave me, I could ne'er forgive myself,
26.   If I brought sorrow to thee, could I love?
27.   FESTUS. As thou art empress of my bosom, No!
28.   HELEN. Nought fear I but an unkind word from thee.
29.   Dark death may frighten children, Hell the wretch
30.   Who feels that he deserves it; but for me,
31.   I know I cannot do nor say aught worthy
32.   Of the pure pain a frown of thine can cause,
33.   Or a cold, careless look. No! never frown.
34.   If I do wrong, forgive me, or I die;
35.   And thou wilt then be wretcheder than I; —
36.   The unforgiving than the unforgiven.
37.   FESTUS. I do absolve thee, beauty, of all faults,
38.   Past, present, or to come.
39.   HELEN.   Well, that will do.
40.   What was I saying? I love this instrument,
41.   It speaks, it thinks — nay, I could kiss it: look!
42.   There are three things I love half killingly; —
43.   Thee lastly, and this next, and myself first.
44.   FESTUS. Thou art a silly, tiresome thing, and yet
45.   I never weary of thee; but could gaze,

46. Sick with excess and not satiety,
47. Upon thy countenance, with the serious joy
48. With which we eye and eye the unbounded space
49. Which is the visible attribute of God,
50. Who makes all things within Himself; and thus
51. It is the Heaven we hope for, and can find
52. No point from which to take its altitude;
53. For the Infinite is upwards, and above
54. The highest thing created — upwards aye:
55. So I could, thinking on thy face, believe
56. An infinite expression, heightening still
57. The longer that I thought, and leaving thee,
58. Coming to thee, or being with thee, — love!
59. HELEN. I am so happy when with thee.
60. FESTUS.   And I.
61. They tell us virtue lies in self-denial.
62. My virtue is indulgence. I was born
63. To gratify myself unboundedly,
64. So that I wronged none else. These arms were given me
65. To clasp the beautiful, and cleave the wave;
66. These limbs to leap and wander where I will;
67. These eyes to look on every thing without
68. Effort; these ears to list my loved one's voice;
69. These lips to be divinised by her kiss:
70. And every sense, pulse, passion, power, to be
71. Swoln into sunny ripeness.
72. HELEN.   Virtue is one
73. With nature, or 't is nothing: it is love.
74. FESTUS. I come fresh from thee every time we meet,
75. Steeped in the still sweet dew of thy soft beauty,
76. Like earth at day-dawn, lifting up her head
77. Out of her sleep, star-watched, to face the sun —
78. So I, to front the world, on leaving thee.
79. Oh! there is inspiration in thy look;
80. Poesie, prophecy. Come hither, love;
81. The evening air is sweet.
82. HELEN.   It comes on us
83. Fresher and clearer through these dewy vine-leaves,
84. Fit for the forehead of the young wine-god.
85. FESTUS. A large, red egg of light the moon lies like
86. On the dark moor-hill and now, rising slow,
87. Beams on the clear flood, smilingly intent,

88. Like a fair face, which loves to look on itself,
89. Saying — 'There is no wonder that men love me,
90. For I am beautiful!' — as I heard thee.
91. HELEN. It was not right to overhear me that.
92. FESTUS. 'T was very wrong to do what I could not help;
93. But vanity speaks out.
94. HELEN.   Well, I don't mind;
95. I never knew that I was as I am
96. Till others told me.
97. FESTUS.   Now were soon enough.
98. HELEN. Ah, nothing comes to us too soon but sorrow.
99. FESTUS. For all were happiness, if all might live
100. Long, or die soon, enough: for even us.
101. HELEN. Dost not remember, when, the other eve,
102. Thy friend the student called, there was a tale
103. Upon thy tongue he interrupted?
104. FESTUS.   Was there? —
105. HELEN. A tale out of the poets, about love,
106. And happiness and sorrow, and such things.
107. FESTUS. But I forget such things when thou art by.
108. Besides, I asked him here again, to-night,
109. Here, at this hour; and he is punctual.
110. HELEN. In truth, then, I despair of hearing it.
111. He keeps his word relentlessly. With not
112. More pride an Indian shews his foeman's scalp
113. Than he his watch for punctuality.
114. FESTUS. But tales of love are far more readily
115. Made than remembered.
116. HELEN. Tell-tale, make one, then.
117. FESTUS. Love is the art of hearts and heart of arts.
118. Conjunctive looks and interjectional sighs
119. Are its vocabulary's greater half.
120. Well then, my story says, there was a pair
121. Of Lovers, once —
122. HELEN.   Once! nay, how singular!
123. FESTUS. But where they lived indeed I quite forget; —
124. Say anywhere — say here: their names were — I
125. Forget those, too; say any one's, say ours.
126. HELEN. Most probable, most pertinent, so far!
127. FESTUS. The lady was, of course, most beautiful,
128. And made her lover do just as she pleased;
129. And consequently, he did very wrong.

130. They met, sang, walked, talked folly, just as all
131. Such couples do, adored each other; thought,
132. Spoke, wrote, dreamed of and for nought on earth
133. Except themselves; and so on.
134. HELEN.   Pray proceed! —
135. FESTUS. That's all.
136. HELEN. Oh, no!
137. FESTUS. Well, thus the tale ends; stay!
138. No, I cannot remember nor invent.
139. HELEN.   Do think!
140. FESTUS.   I can't.
141. HELEN.   Oh then, I don't like that;
142. 'Tis not in earnest.
143. FESTUS. Well, in earnest, then.
144. She did but look upon him, and his blood
145. Blushed deeper even from his inmost heart;
146. For at each glance of those sweet eyes a soul
147. Looked forth as from the azure gates of Heaven;
148. She laid her finger on him, and he felt
149. As might a formless mass of marble feel
150. While feature after feature of a god
151. Were being wrought from out of it. She spake
152. And his love-wildered and idolatrous soul
153. Clung to the airy music of her words,
154. Like a bird on a bough, high swaying in the wind.
155. He looked upon her beauty and forgot,
156. As in a sense of drowning, all things else;
157. And right and wrong seemed one, seemed nothing; she
158. Was beauty, and that beauty everything.
159. He looked upon her as the sun on earth:
160. Until, like him, he gazed himself away
161. From Heaven so doing; till he even wept, —
162. Wept on her bosom as a Storm-charged cloud
163. Weeps itself out upon a hill, and cried —
164. I, too, could look on thee until I wept, —
165. Blind me with kisses! let me look no longer;
166. Or change the action of thy loveliness,
167. Lest long same-seemingness should send me mad! —
168. Blind me with kisses; I would ruin sight
169. To give its virtue to thy lips, whereon
170. I would die now, or ever live; and she,
171. Soft as a feather-footed cloud on Heaven,

172. While her sad face grew bright like night with stars,
173. Would turn her brow to his and both be happy; —
174. Numbered among the constellations they! —
175. Then as tired wanderer, snow-blinded, sinks
176. And swoons upon the swelling drift, and dies,
177. So on her dazzling bosom would he lay
178. His famished lips, and end their travels there.
179. Oh, happy they! not he would go to Heaven,
180. Not, though he might that moment.
181. HELEN.   Nor I now.
182. FESTUS. Helen, my love!
183. HELEN.   Yes, I am here.
184. FESTUS.   It has
185. Been such a day as that, thou knowest, when first
186. I said I loved thee; that long, sunny day
187. We passed upon the waters — heeding nought,
188. Seeing nought but each other.
189. HELEN. I remember.
190. The only wise thing that I ever did —
191. The only good, was to love thee, and therefore
192. I would have no one else as wise as I,
193. Didst thou not say that student would be here?
194. FESTUS. I think I hear him every minute come.
195. HELEN. It is not kind. We should be more alone.
196. There was a time thou wouldst have no one else.
197. FESTUS. Am I not with thee all day?
198. HELEN. Yes, I know;
199. But often and often thou art thinking not
200. Of me.
201. FESTUS. My good child! —
202. HELEN.   Well, I know thou lovest me;
203. And so I cannot bear thee to think, speak,
204. Or be with any but me.
205. FESTUS.   Then I will not.
206. HELEN. Oh! thou would'st promise me the clock round. Now
207. Promise me this — that I shall never die,
208. And I'll believe thee when I am dead — not till.
209. But let it pass. I am at peace with thee;
210. And pardon thee, and give thee leave to live.
211. FESTUS. Magnanimous!
212. HELEN.   When earth, and Heaven, and all
213. Things seem so bright and lovely for our sakes,

214. It is a sin not to be happy. See,
215. The moon is up, it is the dawn of night.
216. Stands by her side one bold bright, steady star —
217. Star of her heart, and heir to all her light,
218. Whereon she looks so proudly mild and calm,
219. As though she were the mother of that star,
220. And knew he was a chief sun in his sphere,
221. But by her side, in the great strife of lights
222. To shine to God, he had filially failed,
223. And hid his arrows and his bow of beams.
224. Mother of stars! the Heavens look up to thee.
225. They shine the brighter but to hide thy waning;
226. They wait and wane for thee to enlarge thy beauty!
227. They give thee all their glory night by night;
228. Their number makes not less thy loneliness
229. Nor loveliness.
230. FESTUS. Heaven's beauty grows on us;
231. And when the elder worlds have ta'en their seats,
232. Come the divine ones, gathering one by one,
233. And family by family, with still
234. And holy air, into the house of God —
235. The house of light He hath builded for Himself
236. And worship Him in silence and in sadness,
237. Immortal and immovable. And there,
238. Night after night, they meet to worship God.
239. For us this witness of the worlds is given,
240. That we may add ourselves to their great glory,
241. And worship with them. They are there for lights
242. To light us on our way through Heaven to God;
243. And we, too, have the power of light in us.
244. Ye stars, how bright ye shine to night; mayhap
245. Ye are the resurrection of the worlds, —
246. Glorified globes of light! Shall ours be like ye?
247. Nay, but it is! this wild, dark earth of ours,
248. Whose face is furrowed like a losing gamester's,
249. Is shining round, and bright, and smooth in air,
250. Millions of miles off. Not a single path
251. Of thought I tread, but that it leads to God.
252. And when her time is out, and earth again
253. Hath travailed with the divine dust of man,
254. Then the world's womb shall open, and her sons
255. Be born again, all glorified immortals.

256. And she, their mother, purified by fire,
257. Shall sit her down in Heaven, a bride of God,
258. And handmaid of the Everbeing One.
259. Our earth is learning all accomplishments
260. To fit her for her bridehood.
261. HELEN.   He is here.
262. FESTUS. Welcome.
263. STUDENT. I thought the night was beautiful,
264. But find the in-door scene still lovelier.
265. HELEN. Ah! all is beautiful where beauty is.
266. STUDENT. Night hath made many bards; she is so lovely.
267. For it is beauty maketh poesie,
268. As from the dancing eye comes tears of light
269. Night hath made many bards; she is so lovely.
270. And they have praised her to her starry face
271. So long, that she hath blushed and left them, often.
272. When first and last we met, we talked on studies;
273. Poetry only I confess is mine,
274. And is the only thing I think or read of: —
275. Feeding my soul upon the soft, and sweet,
276. And delicate imaginings of song;
277. For as nightingales do upon glow-worms feed,
278. So poets live upon the living light
279. Of nature and of beauty; they love light.
280. FESTUS. But poetry is not confined to books.
281. For the creative spirit which thou seekest
282. Is in thee, and about thee; yea, it hath
283. God's everywhereness.
284. STUDENT. Truly. It was for this
285. I sought to know thy thoughts, and hear the course
286. Thou wouldst lay out for one who longs to win
287. A name among the nations.
288. FESTUS.   First of all,
289. Care not about the name, but bind thyself,
290. Body and soul, to nature, hiddenly.
291. Lo, the great march of stars from earth to earth,
292. Through Heaven. The earth speaks inwardly alone.
293. Let no man know thy business, save some friend, —
294. A man of mind, above the run of men;
295. For it is with all men and with all things.
296. The bard must have a kind, courageous heart,
297. And natural chivalry to aid the weak.

298. He must believe the best of everything;
299. Love all below, and worship all above.
300. All animals are living hieroglyphs.
301. The dashing dog, and stealthy-stepping cat,
302. Hawk, bull, and all that breathe, mean something more
303. To the true eye than their shapes show; for all
304. Were made in love, and made to be beloved.
305. Thus must he think as to earth's lower life,
306. Who seeks to win the world to thought and love,
307. As doth the bard, whose habit is all kindness
308. To every thing.
309. HELEN.   I love to hear of such.
310. Could we but think with the intensity
311. We love with, we might do great things, I think.
312. FESTUS. Kindness is wisdom. There is none in life
313. But needs it and may learn; eye-reasoning man,
314. And spirit unassisted, unobscured.
315. STUDENT. Go on, I pray. I came to be informed.
316. Thou knowest my ambition, and I joy
317. To feel thou feedest it with purest food.
318. FESTUS. I cannot tell thee all I feel; and know
319. But little save myself, and am not ashamed
320. To say, that I have studied my own life,
321. And know it is like to a tear-blistered letter,
322. Which holdeth fruit and proof of deeper feeling
323. Than the poor pen can utter, or the eye
324. Discover; and that often my heart's thoughts
325. Will rise and shake my breast, as madmen shake
326. The stanchions of their dungeons, and howl out.
327. HELEN. But thou wast telling us of poesie,
328. And the kind nature-hearted bards.
329. FESTUS.   I was.
330. I knew one once — he was a friend of mine;
331. I knew him well; his mind, habits, and works,
332. Taste, temper, temperament, and every thing;
333. Yet with as kind a heart as ever beat,
334. He was no sooner made than marred. Though young,
335. He wrote amid the ruins of his heart;
336. They were his throne and theme; — like some lone king,
337. Who tells the story of the land he lost,
338. And how he lost it.
339. STUDENT. Tell us more of him.

340. HELEN. Nay, but it saddens thee.
341. FESTUS.   'Tis like enough;
342. We slip away like shadows into shade;
343. We end, and make no mark we had begun;
344. We come to nothing, like a pure intent.
345. When we have hoped, sought, striven, and lost our aim,
346. Then the truth fronts us, beaming out of darkness,
347. Like a white brow, through its overshadowing hair —
348. As though the day were overcast, my Helen!
349. But I was speaking of my friend. He was
350. Quick, generous, simple, obstinate in end,
351. High-hearted from his youth; his spirit rose
352. In many a glittering fold and gleamy crest,
353. Hydra-like to its hindrance; mastering all,
354. Save one thing — love, and that out-hearted him.
355. Nor did he think enough, till it was over,
356. How bright a thing he was breaking, or he would
357. Surely have shunned it, nor have let his life
358. Be pulled to pieces like a rose by a child;
359. And his heart's passions made him oft do that
360. Which made him writhe to think on what he had done,
361. And thin his blood by weeping at a night.
362. If madness wrought the sin, the sin wrought madness,
363. And made a round of ruin. It is sad
364. To see the light of beauty wane away,
365. Know eyes are dimming, bosom shrivelling, feet
366. Losing their spring, and limbs their lily roundness;
367. But it is worse to feel our heart-spring gone,
368. To lose hope, care not for the coming thing,
369. And feel all things go to decay with us,
370. As 'twere our life's eleventh month: and yet
371. All this he went through young.
372. HELEN. Poor soul! I should
373. Have loved him for his sorrows.
374. FESTUS. It is not love
375. Brings sorrow, but love's objects.
376. STUDENT. Then he loved.
377. FESTUS. I said so. I have seen him when he hath had
378. A letter from his lady dear, he blessed
379. The paper that her hand had travelled over,
380. And her eye looked on, and would think he saw
381. Gleams of that light she lavished from her eyes

382. Wandering amid the words of love there traced
383. Like glow-worms among beds of flowers. He seemed
384. To bear with being but because she loved him.
385. She was the sheath wherein his soul had rest,
386. As hath a sword from war: and he at night
387. Would solemnly and singularly curse
388. Each minute that he had not thought of her.
389. HELEN. Now that was like a lover! and she loved
390. Him, and him only.
391. FESTUS.   Well, perhaps it was so.
392. But he could not restrain his heart, but loved
393. In that voluptuous purity of taste
394. Which dwells on beauty coldly, and yet kindly,
395. As night-dew, whensoever he met with beauty.
396. HELEN. It was a pity, that inconstancy —
397. If she he loved were but as good and fair
398. As he was worthy of.
399. STUDENT.   It was his way.
400. FESTUS. There is a dark and bright to every thing:
401. To every thing but beauty such as thine,
402. And that is all bright. If a fault in him,
403. 'Twas one which made him do the sweetest wrongs
404. Man ever did. And yet a whisper went
405. That he did wrong: and if that whisper had
406. Echo in him or not, it mattered little;
407. Or right or wrong, he were alike unhappy.
408. Ah me! ah me! that there should be so much
409. To call up love, so little to delight!
410. The best enjoyment is half disappointment
411. To that we mean or would have in this world.
412. And there were many strange and sudden lights
413. Beckoned him towards them; they were wreckers' lights:
414. But he shunned these, and righted when she rose,
415. Moon of his life, that ebbed and flowed with her.
416. A sea of sorrow struck him, but he held
417. On; dashed all sorrow from him as a bark
418. Spray from her bow bounding; he lifted up
419. His head, and the deep ate his shadow merely.
420. HELEN. A poet not in love is out at sea;
421. He must have a lay-figure.
422. FESTUS.   I meant not
423. To screen, but to describe this friend of mine.

424. HELEN. Describe the lady, too; of course she was
425. Above all praise and all comparison.
426. FESTUS. Why, true. Her heart was all humanity,
427. Her soul all God's; in spirit and in form,
428. Like fair. Her cheek had the pale pearly pink
429. Of seashells, the world's sweetest tint, as though
430. She lived, one half might deem, on roses sopped
431. In silver dew; she spake as with the voice
432. Of spheral harmony which greets the soul
433. When at the hour of death the saved one knows
434. His sister angels near; her eye was as
435. The golden pane the setting sun doth just
436. Imblaze; which shews, till Heaven comes down again,
437. All other lights but grades of gloom; her dark,
438. Long rolling locks were as a stream the slave
439. Might search for gold, and searching find.
440. HELEN.   Enough! —
441. I have her picture perfect; — quite enough.
442. STUDENT. What were his griefs?
443. FESTUS.   He who hath most of heart
444. Knows most of sorrow; not a thing he saw
445. Nor did, but was to him, at times, a woe;
446. At times indifferent, at times a joy.
447. Folly and sin and memory make a curse
448. Wherewith the future fires may vie in vain.
449. The sorrows of the soul are graver still.
450. STUDENT. Where and when did he study? Did he mix
451. Much with the world, or was he a recluse?
452. FESTUS. He had no times of study, and no place;
453. All places and all times to him were one.
454. His soul was like the wind-harp, which he loved.
455. And sounded only when the spirit blew.
456. Sometime in feasts and follies, for he went
457. Life-like through all things; and his thoughts then rose
458. Like sparkles in the bright wine, brighter still.
459. Sometimes in dreams, and then the shining words
460. Would wake him in the dark before his face.
461. All things talked thoughts to him. The sea went mad,
462. And the wind whined as 't were in pain, to shew
463. Each one his meaning; and the awful sun
464. Thundered his thoughts into him; and at night
465. The stars would whisper theirs, the moon sigh hers.

466. The spirit speaks all tongues and understands;
467. Both God's and angel's, man's and all dumb things,
468. Down to an insect's inarticulate hum
469. And an inaudible organ. And it was
470. The spirit spake to him of everything;
471. And with the moony eyes like those we see,
472. Thousands on thousands, crowding air in dreams,
473. Looked into him its mighty meanings, till
474. He felt the power fulfil him, as a cloud
475. In every fibre feels the forming wind.
476. He spake the world's one tongue; in earth and Heaven
477. There is but one, it is the word of truth.
478. To him the eye let out its hidden meaning;
479. And young and old made their hearts over to him;
480. And thoughts were told to him as unto none
481. Save one who heareth said and unsaid, all.
482. And his heart held these as a grate its gleeds,[1]
483. Where others warm them.
484. STUDENT. I would I had known him.
485. FESTUS. All things were inspiration unto him;
486. Wood, wold, hill, field, sea, city, solitude,
487. And crowds and streets, and man where'er he was;
488. And the blue eye of God which is above us;
489. Brook-bounded pine spinnies where spirits flit:
490. And haunted pits the rustic hurries by,
491. Where cold wet ghosts sit ringing jingling bells;
492. Old orchards' leaf-roofed aisles, and red cheeked load;
493. And the blood-coloured tears which yew trees weep
494. O'er churchyard graves, like murderers remorseful.
495. The dark green rings where fairies sit and sup,
496. Crushing the violet dew in the acorn cup:
497. Where by his new-made bride the bride-groom sips,
498. The white moon shimmering on their longing lips;
499. The large o'erloaded wealthy-looking wains
500. Quietly swaggering home through leafy lanes,
501. Leaving on all low branches as they come,
502. Straws for the birds, ears of the harvest home.
503. Summer's warm soil or winter's cruel sky,
504. Clear, cold and icy-blue like a sea-eagle's eye;

---

1. Gleed: A live coal (*OED*). *Archaic. Festus* is the first known use.

505. All things to him bare thoughts of minstrelsy,
506. He drew his light from that he was amidst,
507. As doth a lamp from air which hath itself
508. Matter of light although it show it not. His
509. Was but the power to light what might be lit.
510. He met a muse in every lovely maid;
511. And learned a song from every lip he loved.
512. But his heart ripened most 'neath southern eyes,
513. Which sunned their sweets into him all day long:
514. For fortune called him southwards, towards the sun.
515. HELEN. Did he love music?
516. FESTUS.   The only music he
517. Or learned or listened to was from the lips
518. Of her he loved, and that he learned by heart.
519. Albeit, she would try to teach him tunes,
520. And put his fingers on the keys; but he
521. Could only see her eyes, and hear her voice,
522. And feel her touch.
523. HELEN. Why, he was much like thee.
524. FESTUS. We had some points in common.
525. STUDENT. Was he proud?
526. FESTUS. Lowliness is the base of every virtue:
527. And he who goes the lowest, builds the safest.
528. My God keeps all his pity for the proud.
529. STUDENT. Was he world-wise?
530. FESTUS.   The only wonder is
531. He knew so much, leading the life he did.
532. STUDENT. Yet it may seem less strange when we think back,
533. That we, in the dark chamber of the heart,
534. Sitting alone, see the world tabled to us;
535. And the world wonders how recluses know
536. So much, and most of all, how we know them.
537. It is they who paint themselves upon our hearts
538. In their own lights and darknesses, not we.
539. One stream of light is to us from above,
540. And that is that we see by, light of God.
541. FESTUS. We do not make our thoughts; they grow in us
542. Like grain in wood: the growth is of the skies,
543. Which are of nature, nature is of God.
544. The world is full of glorious likenesses.
545. The poet's power is to sort these out,
546. And to make music from the common strings

547. With which the world is strung; to make the dumb
548. Earth utter heavenly harmony, and draw
549. Life dear and sweet and harmless as spring water,
550. Welling its way through flowers. Without faith,
551. Illimitable faith, strong as a state's
552. In its own might, in God, no bard can be.
553. All things are signs of other and of nature.
554. It is at night we see heaven moveth, and
555. A darkness thick with suns. The thoughts we think
556. Subsist the same in God as stars in Heaven.
557. And as these specks of light will prove great worlds
558. When we approach them sometime free from flesh,
559. So too our thoughts will become magnified
560. To mind-like things immortal. And as space
561. Is but a property of God, wherein
562. Is laid all matter, other attributes
563. May be the infinite homes of mind and soul.
564. And thoughts rise from our souls, as from the sea
565. The clouds sublimed in Heaven. The cloud is cold,
566. Although ablaze with lightning — though it shine
567. At all points like a constellation; so
568. We live not to ourselves, our work is life;
569. In bright and ceaseless labour as a star
570. Which shineth unto all worlds but itself
571. HELEN. And were this friend and bard of whom thou
     speakest,
572. And she whom he did love, happy together?
573. FESTUS. True love is ever tragic, grievous, grave.
574. Bards and their beauties are like double stars,
575. One in their bright effect
576. HELEN.   Whose light is love.
577. STUDENT. Or is it poesie thou meanest?
578. FESTUS.   Both:
579. For love is poesie — it doth create;
580. From fading features, dim soul, doubtful heart,
581. And this world's wretched happiness, a life
582. Which is as near to Heaven as are the stars.
583. They parted; and she named Heaven's judgment-seat
584. As their next place of meeting: and 'twas kept
585. By her, at least, so far that no where else
586. Could it be made until the day of doom.
587. HELEN. So soon men's passion passes! yea, it sinks

588. Like foam into the troubled wave which bore it.
589. Merciful God! let me entreat Thy mercy!
590. I have seen all the woes of men — pain, death,
591. Remorse, and worldly ruin; they are little
592. Weighed with the woe of woman when forsaken
593. By him she loved and trusted. Hear, too, thou!
594. Lady of Heaven, Mother of God and man,
595. Who made the world His brother, one with God —
596. Maid-mother! mould of God, who wrought in thee
597. By model as He doth in the world's womb,
598. So that the universe is great with God —
599. Thou in whom God did deify Himself,
600. Betaking him into mortality,
601. As in Thy Son He took it into Him,
602. And from the temporal and eternal made
603. Of the soul-world one same and ever God!
604. Oh, for the sake of thine own womanhood,
605. Pray away aught of evil from her soul,
606. And take her out of anguish unto thee.
607. Always, as thou didst this one!
608. FESTUS.   Who doth not
609. Believe that that he loveth cannot die?
610. There is no mote of death in thine eye's beams
611. To hint of dust, or darkness, or decay;
612. Eclipse upon eclipse, and death on death;
613. No! immortality sits mirrored there
614. Like a fair face long looking on itself;
615. Yet thou shalt lie in death's angelic garb
616. As in a dream of dress, my beautiful!
617. The worm shall trail across thine unsunned sweets,
618. And fatten him on that men pined to death for;
619. Yea, have a further knowledge of thy beauties
620. Than ever did thy best-loved lover dream of.
621. HELEN. It is unkind to think of me in this wise.
622. Surely the stars must feel that they are bright,
623. In beauty, number, nature infinite;
624. And the strong sense we have of God in us
625. Makes me believe my soul can never cease.
626. The temples perish, but the God still lives.
627. FESTUS. It is therefore that I love thee; for that when
628. The fiery perfection of the world,
629. The sun, shall be a shadow and burnt out,

630. There is an impulse to eternity
631. Raised by this moment's love.
632. STUDENT.   I pray it may!
633. Time is the crescent shape to bounded eye
634. Of what is ever perfect unto God.
635. The bosom heaves to Heaven and to the stars;
636. Our very hearts throb upwards, our eyes look;
637. Our aspirations always are divine:
638. Yet is it in the gloom of soul we see
639. Most of the God about us, as at night.
640. For then the soul, like the mother-maid of Christ,
641. Is overshadowed by the Holy Spirit;
642. And in creative darkness doth conceive
643. Its humanized Divinity of life.
644. FESTUS. Think then God shews his face to us no less
645. In spiritual darkness than in light.
646. HELEN. But of thy friend? I would hear more of him.
647. Perhaps much happiness in friendship made
648. Amends for his love's sorrows.
649. FESTUS.   Ask me not.
650. HELEN. But loved he never after? Came there none
651. To roll the stone from his sepulchral heart,
652. And sit in it an angel?
653. FESTUS.   Ah, my life!
654. My more than life, my immortality!
655. Both man and womankind belie their nature
656. When they are not kind: and thy words are kind,
657. And beautiful, and loving like thyself;
658. Thine eye and thy tongue's tone, and all that speak
659. Thy soul, are like it. There's a something in
660. The shape of harps as though they had been made
661. By music: beauty's the effect of soul,
662. And he of whom thou askest loved again.
663. Could'st thou have loved one who was unlike men?
664. Whose heart was wrinkled long before his brow?
665. Who would have cursed himself if he had dared
666. Tempt God to ratify his curse in fire:
667. And yet with whom to look on beauty was
668. A need, a thirst, a passion?
669. HELEN.   Yes, I think
670. I could have loved him: but, no — not unless
671. He was like thee; unless he had been thee.

672. Tell me, what was it rendered him so wretched
673. At heart?
674. FESTUS.   I will not tell thee.
675. STUDENT.   But tell me
676. How and on what he wrote, this friend of thine?
677. FESTUS. Love, mirth, woe, pleasure, was in turn his theme.
678. And the great good which beauty does the soul;
679. And the God-made necessity of things.
680. And like that noble knight in olden tale,
681. Who changed his armour's hue at each fresh charge
682. By virtue of his lady-love's strange ring,
683. So that none knew him save his private page
684. And she who cried, God save him, every time
685. He brake spears with the brave till he quelled all —
686. So he applied him to all themes that came;
687. Loving the most to breast the rapid deeps
688. Where others had been drowned, and heeding nought
689. Where danger might not fill the place of fame.
690. And 'mid the magic circle of those sounds,
691. His lyre rayed out, spell-bound himself he stood,
692. Like a stilled storm. It is no task for suns
693. To shine. He knew himself a bard ordained,
694. More than inspired, of God, inspirited: —
695. Making himself like an electric rod
696. A lure for lightning feelings; and his words
697. Felt like the things that fall in thunder, which
698. The mind, when in a dark, hot, cloudful state,
699. Doth make metallic, meteoric, ball like.
700. He spake to spirits with a Spirit tongue,
701. Who came compelled by wizard word of truth,
702. And rayed them round him from the ends of Heaven.
703. For as be all bards he was born of beauty,
704. And with a natural fitness to draw down
705. All tones and shades of beauty to his soul,
706. Even as the rainbow-tinted shell, which lies
707. Miles deep at bottom of the sea, hath all
708. Colours of skies and flowers, and gems, and plumes,
709. And all by Nature which doth reproduce
710. Like loveliness in seeming opposites.
711. Our life is like the wizard's charmed ring:
712. Death's heads, and loathsome things fill up the ground;
713. But spirits wing about, and wait on us,

714. While yet the hour of enchantment is.
715. And while we keep in, we are safe, and can
716. Force them to do our bidding. And he raised
717. The rebel in himself, and in his mind
718. Walked with him through the world.
719. STUDENT.   He wrote of this?
720. FESTUS.   He wrote a poem.
721. STUDENT.   What was said of it?
722. FESTUS. Oh, much was said — much more than understood;
723. One said that he was mad; another, wise;
724. Another, wisely mad. The book is there.
725. Judge thou among them.
726. STUDENT. Well, but, who said what?
727. FESTUS. Some said that he blasphemed; and these men lied
728. To all eternity, unless such men
729. Be saved, when God shall rase that lie from life,
730. And from His own eternal memory:
731. But still the word is lied; though it were writ
732. In honeydew upon a lily leaf,
733. With quill of nightingale, like love letters
734. From Oberon sent to the bright Titania,
735. Fairest of all the fays — for that he used
736. The name of God as spirits use it, barely,
737. Yet surely more sublime in nakedness,
738. Statuelike, than in a whole tongue of dress.
739. Thou knowest, God! that to the full of worship
740. All things are worship-full; and Thy great name,
741. In all its awful brevity, hath nought
742. Unholy breeding in it, but doth bless
743. Rather the tongue that utters it; for me,
744. I ask no higher office than to fling
745. My spirit at Thy feet, and cry Thy name
746. God! through eternity. The man who sees
747. Irreverence in that name, must have been used
748. To take that name in vain, and the same man
749. Would see obscenity in pure white statues.
750. Call all things by their names. Hell, call thou hell;
751. Archangel, call archangel; and God, God.
752. STUDENT. And what said he of such?
753. FESTUS. He held his peace
754. A season, as a tree its sap till spring,
755. Preparing to unfold itself, and let

756. All rigor do its worst, which only served
757. To harden him, though nothing nesh[2] at first.
758. And then he said at last, what, at the first,
759. He deemed would have been seen by other men,
760. By men, at least, above low-water mark,
761. Who take it, they lead others; that it is they
762. Who set their shoulders to the stalled world's wheel,
763. And give it a hitch forwards.
764. HELEN. There were some
765. Encouraged him with goodwill, surely?
766. FESTUS. Many.
767. The kind, the noble, and the able cheered him;
768. The lovely, likewise: others knew he nought of.
769. And yet he loved not praise, nor sighed for fame.
770. Men's praise begets an awe of one's own self
771. Within us, till we fear our heart, lest it,
772. Magician-like, shew more than we can bear.
773. Nor was he fameless; but obscurity
774. Hath many a sacred use. The clouds which hide
775. The mental mountains rising nighest Heaven,
776. Are full of finest lightning, and a breath
777. Can give those gathered shadows fearful life,
778. And launch their light in thunder o'er the world.
779. STUDENT. And thought he well of that he wrote?
780. FESTUS. Perchance.
781. Perchance we suffer, and perchance succeed.
782. Perchance he would his tongue had perished ere
783. It uttered half he said, from childhood up
784. To manhood, and so on; for much I heard
785. From him required expiation, much
786. Soul sacrifice and penance for heart-deeds
787. Which passion had accomplished; yea, perchance,
788. He wished, how vain! that fruitful heart and breast
789. Had withered like a witch's ere he had trained
790. The parasites of feeling that he did
791. About it; and perchance, for all I know,
792. He would his brain had died ere it conceived
793. One half the thought-seeds that took life in it,
794. And in his soul's dark sanctuary dwelt.

---

2. Nesh: A British regionalism for 'to yield easily' (*OED*).

795. Yet his blue eye's dark ball grew greater with
796. Delight, and darker, as he viewed the things
797. He made; not monsters outside of the fane,
798. Grinning and howling, but seraphic forms —
799. Embodied thoughts of worship, wisdom, love,
800. Joining their fire-tipped wings across the shrine
801. Where his heart's relics lay, and where were wrought
802. Immortal miracles upon men's minds.
803. STUDENT. Take up the book, and, if thou understandest
804. Unfold it to me.
805. FESTUS.   What I can, I will.
806. Well I remember me of thee, poor book!
807. But there is consolation e'en for thee.
808. Fair hands have turned thee over, and bright eyes
809. Sprinkled their sparkles o'er thee with their prayers.
810. The poet's pen is the true divining rod
811. Which trembles towards the inner founts of feeling;
812. Bringing to light and use, else hid from all,
813. The many sweet clear sources which we have
814. Of good and beauty in our own deep bosoms;
815. And marks the variations of all mind
816. As does the needle an air-investing storm's.
817. STUDENT. How does the book begin, go on and
818. End? It has a plan, but no plot. Life hath none.
819. HELEN. Tell us, love; we will listen and not speak.
820. I wish I understood it, for I know
821. You would rather hear me than yourselves talk.
822. STUDENT. Surely.
823. I'd give up half the organs in my head,
824. Besides all undiscovered faculties,
825. To list to such a lecturer; and then
826. Have quite enough, perhaps, to comprehend.
827. HELEN. 'Twere needless that, to one half-witted now.
828. FESTUS. There is a porch, wherefrom is something seen
829. Of the main dome beyond. Though shadows cross
830. Each other's path, yet let us go through it
831. And lo! an opening scene in Heaven, wherein
832. The foredoom of all things, spirit and matter,
833. Is shewn, and the permission of temptation;
834. The angelic worship of the Trinity,
835. By God's name uttered thrice; the joys and powers
836. Of souls o'erblest, and the sweet offices

837. Of warden-angel told; and the complete
838. Well-fixed necessity and end of all things.
839. From Heaven we come to earth, and so do souls.
840. For next succeeds a soft and sunset scene,
841. Wherein is shown the collapsed, empty state
842. In which all worldly pleasures leave us; youth's
843. Though natural, fitful, unavailing, struggle
844. Against a great temptation come unlooked for:
845. And that to sin is to curse God in deed.
846. The soul long used to truth still keeps its strength,
847. Though plunged upon a sudden mid the false;
848. As hands, thrust into a dark room, retain
849. Their sunlent light a season. So with this.
850. The lines have under meanings, and the scene
851. Of self-forgetfulness and indecision
852. Breaks off, not ends. A starry, stirless night
853. Follows, which shadows out youth's barren longings
854. For goodness, greatness, marvels, mysteries.
855. Whence comes this dream of immortality,
856. And the resurgent essence? Let us think!
857. What mean we by the dead? The dead have life,
858. The changed; and, if they come, it is to show
859. Their change is for the better. The bait takes.
860. Man and his foe shake hands upon their bargain.
861. The youth sets out for joy, and 'neath the care
862. Of his good enemy, begins his course.
863. The next scene seems to promise fair; for sure
864. If that there be one scene in life, wherefrom
865. Evil is absent, it is pure early love.
866. HELEN. Alas! when beauty pleads the cause of virtue
867. The chief temptation to embrace it's wanting.
868. FESTUS. A man in love sees wonders. But not love
869. Makes the soul happy: so the youth gets hopeless.
870. To this comes on a stern and stormy quarrel
871. 'Tween the two foe friends — Youth demanding what
872. Cannot be; and the other withholding safe
873. And easy grants. They part and meet, as though
874. Nothing had happened, in the next scene: none
875. Know how we reconcile ourselves to evil.
876. But there they are, together, aiding each
877. The other, and abusing others.
878. HELEN.   I

879. Was waiting for an eloquential pause
880. In this mysterious, allegorical,
881. Mythical, theological, odd story.
882. So now, then, I shall ask myself to sing;
883. And granting that I agree to my request,
884. I think you ought to thank me.
885. STUDENT. That we will.
886. But not just now.
887. HELEN. Oh! yes, now; yes, this moment.
888. I'm in the humour.
889. STUDENT. We are not.
890. FESTUS. Yes, let her!
891. HELEN. What shall I sing?
892. FESTUS. Sing something merry, love.
893. HELEN. I won't: I'll sing the dullest thing I know;
894. One of thine own songs.
895. STUDENT. What a compliment!
896. FESTUS. Sing what thou lik'st, then.
897. HELEN. No; what thou lik'st.
898. STUDENT.   Well,
899. Something about love, and it can't be wrong.
900. For love the sunny world supplies
901. With laughing lips and happy eyes.
902. FESTUS. And 'twill be sooner over.
903. STUDENT.   And so better.
904. HELEN.
905.   Like an island in a river,
906.   Art thou, my love, to me;
907.   And I journey by thee ever
908.   With a gentle ecstasie.
909.   I arise to fall before thee;
910.   I come to kiss thy feet;
911.   To adorn thee and adore thee,
912.   Mine only one! my sweet!
913.   And thy love hath power upon me,
914.   Like a dream upon a brain;
915.   For the loveliness which won me,
916.   With the love, too, doth remain.
917.   And my life it beautifieth,
918.   Though love be but a shade,
919.   Known of only ere it dieth,
920.   By the darkness it hath made.

921. Was that addressed to me?
922. STUDENT. Well, now resume.
923. FESTUS. Trial alone of ill and folly gives
924. Clear proofs of the world's vanities; but little
925. Good comes of sermons, prophecies, or warnings,
926. Though from the steps of an old grey market-cross,
927. The Devil is holding forth to the faithless. There
928. A social prayer is offered up, too. This
929. Is followed by a bird's-eye view of earth,
930. A stirring-up of the dust of all the nations.
931. Then comes a village feast; a kind of home
932. Unto the traveller — where, with the world,
933. We mix in private, talking divers things;
934. A country merry-making, where all speak
935. According to their sorts, and the occasion.
936. Deeper than ever leadline went, behold
937. We search the rayless central sun within.
938. We penetrate all mysteries, but are
939. Unfitted long to dwell in the recess
940. Of our own nature, and we long for light.
941. True aspiration riseth from research.
942. Next, by the o'erthrown altar of a fane,
943. Foundation-shattered, like the ripened heart,
944. We find ourselves in worship. Let us hope
945. The spirit, form, and offering, grateful all.
946. In one of Earth's head cities, after this,
947. We tower-like rise, and with an eminent eye
948. Glance round society, insatiate; —
949. The high unknown as yet unrealized.
950. In less time than the twinkling of a star,
951. Insphered in air, the arch-fiend and the youth,
952. Like twilight and midnight, discourse and rise.
953. Thence to another planet, for the book,
954. Stream-like, doth steal the images of stars,
955. And trembles at its boldness, where we meet
956. The spirit of the first of night temptation;
957. And mix with many of those lofty musings
958. Which sow in us the seeds of higher kind
959. And brighter being. Heavenly poesie,
960. Which shines among the powers of our mind,
961. As that bright star she dwells in, mid the worlds
962. Which make the system of the sun, is there too.

963. But these high things are lost, and drowned, and dimmed,
964. Like a blue eye in tears, that trickle from it
965. Like angels leaving Heaven on their errands
966. Of love, behind them, in the scene succeeding; —
967. A scene of song, and dance, and mirth, and wine,
968. And damsels, in whose lily skin the blue
969. Veins branch themselves in hidden luxury,
970. Hues of the heaven they seem to have vanished from.
971. HELEN. Moonlight and music, and kisses, and wine,
972. And beauty, which must be, for rhyme-sake, divine.
973. FESTUS. Mere joys; but saddened and sublimed at close
974. By sweet remembrance of immortal ones
975. Once loved, aye hallowed. Still, in scenes like this,
976. Youth lingers longest, drawing out his time
977. As a gold-beater does his wire, until
978. 'Twould reach round the earth.
979. STUDENT. And be of no use then.
980. FESTUS. Blame not the bard for showing this, but mind
981. He wrote of youth as passionate genius,
982. Its flights and follies — both its sensual ends
983. And common places. To behold an eagle
984. Batting the sunny ceiling of the world
985. With his dark wings, one well might deem his heart
986. On heaven; but, no! it is fixed on flesh and blood,
987. And soon his talons tell it. Pass we on!
988. A brief and solemn parley o'er a grave
989. Follows, in which youth vows to trust in God,
990. Be the end what it may. A prescient view
991. Of what is true repentance to the soul,
992. Spirit-informed, expands; and over all
993. The spiritual harmonies of Heaven
994. By the raised soul are heard, and God's great rule
995. To creatures justified. And next we find
996. Ourselves in Heaven. Even man's deadly life
997. Can be there, by God's leave. Once brought to God,
998. The soul's foredoom is set before it brightly,
999. And Heaven's designs are seen to be brought to bear.
1000. A lightning revelation of the Heavens,
1001. And what is in them. Let it not be said
1002. He sought his God in the self-slayer's way,
1003. Whose highest aim was but to worship in
1004. All humbleness; for he was called thereto,

1005. To show the holy God, in three scenes, first
1006. And last in Threelihood, and midst in One:
1007. Although less hard to shape the wide-winged wind
1008. O'er the bright heights of air. He will forgive:
1009. For we, this moment, and all living souls —
1010. All matter, are as much within his presence,
1011. And known through, like a glass film in the sun,
1012. As we can ever be. Through sundry worlds
1013. The mortal wends, returning, and relates
1014. To her he loves — and joyously, they greet,
1015. As boat by breeze and billow backed by tide —
1016. His bright experience of celestial homes;
1017. Where spiritual natures, kind and high,
1018. Light-born, which can divine immortal things,
1019. Abide embosomed in Eternity.
1020. Something he tells, too, of the friendly fiend,
1021. Something of ancient ages, infant Earth.
1022. To this succeeds a scene explaining much,
1023. Of retrospective and prospective cast,
1024. Between the bard his beauty and his friend.
1025. Our story ties us here to earth again,
1026. And sea all aged. Evil is in love;
1027. And ever those who are unhappiest have
1028. Their hearts' desire the oftenest, but in dreams.
1029. Dreams are mind-clouds, high and unshapen beauties,
1030. Or but God-shaped, like mountains, which contain
1031. Much and rich matter; often not for us,
1032. But for another. Dreams are rudiments
1033. Of the great state to come. We dream what is
1034. About to happen to us.
1035. HELEN.   What may be
1036. The dream in this case?
1037. FESTUS.   It is one of death.
1038. HELEN. Of death! is that all? Well, I too have had,
1039. What every one hath once, at least, in life —
1040. A vision of the region of the dead;
1041. It was the land of shadows: yea, the land
1042. Itself was but a shadow, and the race
1043. Which seemed therein were voices, forms of forms,
1044. And echoes of themselves. And there was nought,
1045. Of substance seemed, save one thing in the midst,
1046. A great red sepulchre — a granite grave;

1047. And at the bottom lay a skeleton,
1048. From whose decaying jaws the shades were born;
1049. Making its only sign of life, its dying
1050. Continually. Some were bright, some dark.
1051. Those that were bright, went upwards heavenly.
1052. They which were dark, grew darker and remained.
1053. A land of change, yet did the half things nothing
1054. That I could see; but passed stilly on,
1055. Taking no note of other, mate or child;
1056. For all had lost their love when they put off
1057. The beauty of the body. And as I
1058. Looked on, the grave before me backed away;
1059. And I began to dream it was a dream;
1060. And I rushed after it: when the earth quaked,
1061. Opened and shut, like the eye of one in fits;
1062. It shut to with a shout. The grave was gone.
1063. And in the stead there stood a gleed-like throne,
1064. Which all the shadows shook to see, and swooned;
1065. For fiends were standing, loaded with long chains,
1066. The links whereof were fire, waiting the word
1067. To bind and cast the shadows into hell;
1068. For Death the second sat upon that throne,
1069. Which set on fire the air not to be breathed.
1070. And as he lifted up his arm to speak,
1071. Fear preyed upon all souls, like fire on paper,
1072. And mine among the rest, and I awoke.
1073. STUDENT. By Hades, 'twas most awful.
1074. FESTUS.   And when love
1075. Merges in creature-worship, let us mind:
1076. We know not what it is we love: perhaps
1077. It is incarnate evil. In the time
1078. It takes to turn a leaf, we are in Heaven;
1079. Making our way among the wheeling worlds,
1080. Millions of suns, half infinite each, and space
1081. For ever shone into, for ever dark,
1082. As God is, to and by created mind,
1083. Upheld by the companion spirit. There
1084. The nature of the all in one, and whence
1085. Evil; the fixed impossibility
1086. Of creatures' perfectness, until made one
1087. With God; and the necessity of ill
1088. As yet, are things all touched upon and proven.

1089. The next scene shows us hell, in the mad mock
1090. Of mortal revelry — the quelling truth
1091. That all life's sinful follies run to hell;
1092. That lies, debauches, murders never die,
1093. But live in hell forever; make, are hell.
1094. And truth is there too. Hell is its own moral.
1095. Perdition certain to the unrepentant;
1096. Redemption on a like scale with creation;
1097. And all creation needing it and having.
1098. What follows is of earth, and setteth forth
1099. God's mercy, and the mystery of sin;
1100. And a great gathering of the worlds round God,
1101. Told by the youth to his truthful, trustful, love;
1102. Who, light and lowly as a little glow-worm,
1103. Sheddeth her beauty round her like a rose
1104. Sweet smelling dew upon the ground it grows on.
1105. And then a rest in light, as though 'tween earth
1106. And Heaven there were a mediate spirit point,
1107. A bright effect original of God,
1108. Enlightening all ways, inwardly and round.
1109. Then comes a scene of passion, brought about
1110. By the bad spirit's means for his own ends,
1111. Whom we know not when come, so dark we grow;
1112. Making it but a blind for the next scene,
1113. Laid by the lonely seashore, as before,
1114. Where the great waves come in frothed, like a horse
1115. Put to his heart-burst speed, sobbing up hill,
1116. Wherein he works his victim's death, to clear
1117. His way, and keep his name of murderer;
1118. As he in other parts makes good his titles,
1119. Deceiver, liar, tempter, and accuser;
1120. Hater of man, and, most of all, of God.
1121. In the next scene we picture back our life,
1122. Contrasting the pure joys of earlier years,
1123. With the unsatedness of current sin;
1124. And the sad feel that love's own heart turns sick
1125. Like a bad pearl; but that the feeling still
1126. Is adamantine, though the splendid thing
1127. Whereon it writes its record, is of all
1128. Frailest; and though earth shows to good and bad,
1129. The same blind kindness, beautiful to see,
1130. Wherewith our lovely mother loveth us,

1131. The world in vain unbosometh her beauty,
1132. We have no lust to live; for things may be
1133. Corrupted into beauty; and that love,
1134. Where all the passions blend, as hues in white,
1135. Tires at the last, as day would, if all day
1136. And no night. So despair of heart increases.
1137. The last lure — power — is proffered, taken. All
1138. Hangs on the last desire, whatever it be.
1139. A scene of prescient solitude and soul
1140. Commune with heaven, repentance, prayer, faith,
1141. Which are all things inspired alone of God,
1142. Who signifies salvation, follows this.
1143. In the next scene, we feel the end draw nigh.
1144. A change is wrought on earth as great as that
1145. In its first ages, when the elements
1146. Less gross and palpable than air, were changed
1147. To mountainous and adamantine mass,
1148. Now 'neath the feet of nations; — figuring forth
1149. The fateful mind which is to govern all,
1150. Controlling the great evil; for it is mind
1151. Which shall rule and be ruled, and not the body,
1152. In the last age of human sway on earth; —
1153. Ambition ruined by its own success;
1154. Aims lost, power useless: love, pure love, the last
1155. Of mortal things that nestles in the heart.
1156. There is a love which acts to death, and through death,
1157. And may come white, and bright and pure, like paper,
1158. From refuse, or from clearest things at first;
1159. It is beyond the accidents of life.
1160. For things we make no compt of, have in them
1161. The seeds of life, use, beauty, like the cores
1162. Of apples that we fling away; — nought now
1163. Is left but trust in God, who tries the heart
1164. And saves it, at the last, from its own ruin —
1165. The parting spirit fluttering like a flag,
1166. Half from its earthy staff. The death-change comes.
1167. Death is another life. We bow our heads
1168. At going out, we think, and enter straight
1169. Another golden chamber of the king's,
1170. Larger than this we leave, and lovelier.
1171. And then in shadowy glimpses, disconnect,
1172. The story, flower like, closes thus its leaves.

1173.   The will of God is all in all. He makes,
1174.   Destroys, remakes, for His own pleasure, all.
1175.   After inferior nature is subdued,
1176.   The evil is confined. All elements
1177.   Conglobe themselves from chaos, purified.
1178.   The rebegotten world is born again.
1179.   The body and the soul cease; spirit lives:
1180.   And gloriously falsified are all
1181.   Earth's caverned prophecies of bodyhood.
1182.   Spirits rise up and rule and link with Heaven; —
1183.   The soul state is searched into; dormant Death,
1184.   Evil, and all the dark gods of the heart,
1185.   And the idolatrous passions, ruined, chained,
1186.   And worshipless, are seen; and there, the Word,
1187.   Heard and obeyed; — next comes the truth divine,
1188.   Redintegrative;[3] Evil's last and worst
1189.   Endeavour, vanquished — by Almighty good.
1190.   The last scene shews the final doom of earth,
1191.   Soul's judgment, and salvation of the youth,
1192.   As was fore-fixed on from and in the first:
1193.   The universe expurgated of evil,
1194.   And hell for aye abolished; all create,
1195.   Redeemed, their God all love, themselves all bliss.
1196.   We may say that the sun is dead and gone
1197.   For ever; and may swear he will rise no more;
1198.   The skies may put on mourning for their God,
1199.   And earth heap ashes on her head: but who
1200.   Shall keep the sun back, when he thinks to rise?
1201.   Where is the chain shall bind him? Where the cell
1202.   Shall hold him? Hell, he would burn down to embers;
1203.   And would lift up the world with a lever of light
1204.   Out of his way: yet, know ye, 'twere thrice less
1205.   To do thrice this, than keep the soul from God.
1206.   O'er earth, and cloud, and sky, and star, and Heaven,
1207.   It dwells with God uprisen as a prayer.
1208.   The spirit speaks of God in Heaven's own tongue,
1209.   No mystery to those who love, but learned,
1210.   As is our mother tongue, from Him, the parent;

---

3. Redintegrative: Of, relating to or tending to promote redintegration (*OED*). *Festus* is
    the first known use of this term, meaning something like revival of a previous whole.

1211. By whom created, fashioned, flesh and spirit,
1212. All forms and feelings of all kinds of beauty
1213. Are burned into our heart-clay, pattern like.
1214. Much too is writ, elsewhere and here, not yet
1215. Made clear, nor can be till earth come of age;
1216. Like the unfinished rudiments of light
1217. Which gather time by time into a star.
1218. Thus have I shown the meaning of the book,
1219. And the most truthful likeness of a mind,
1220. Which hath as yet been limned; the mind of youth
1221. In strengths and failings, in its overcomings,
1222. And in its short comings; the kingly ends,
1223. The universalizing heart of youth;
1224. Its love of power, heed not how had, although
1225. With surety of self-ruin at the end.
1226. Every thing urged against it proves its truth
1227. And faithfulness to nature. Some cried out
1228. 'Twas inconsistent; so 'twas meant to be.
1229. Such is the very stamp of youth and nature;
1230. And the continual losing sight of its aims,
1231. And the desertion of its most expressed
1232. And dearest rules and objects, this is youth.
1233. STUDENT. I look on life as keeping me from God,
1234. Stars, Heaven, and angels' bosoms. I lay ill;
1235. And the dark hot blood, throbbing through and through me;
1236. They bled me and I swooned; and as I died,
1237. Or seemed to die, a soft, sweet sadness fell
1238. With a voluptuous weakness, on my soul,
1239. That made me feel all happy. But my heart
1240. Would live, and rose, and wrestled with the soul,
1241. Which stretched its wings and strained its strength in vain,
1242. Twining around it as a snake an eagle.
1243. My eyes unclosed again, and I looked up,
1244. And saw the sweet blue twilight, and one star,
1245. One only star, in Heaven; and then I wished
1246. That I had died and gone to it; and straight
1247. Was glad I lived again, lo love once more.
1248. And so our souls turn round upon themselves
1249. Like orbs upon their axles: what was night
1250. Is day; what day, night. God will guide us on,
1251. Body and soul, through life and death, to judgment.
1252. FESTUS. Earth hath her deserts mixed with fruitful plains;

1253. The word of God is barren in some parts;
1254. A rose is not all flower, but hath much
1255. Which is of lower beauty, yet like needful;
1256. And he who in great makings doth like these,
1257. Doth only that which is most natural.
1258. Like life too it is boundlessly unequal,
1259. Now soaring, and now grovelling: at one time
1260. All harmony, and then again all harshness,
1261. With an ever-changing style of thought and speech.
1262. The work is still consistent with itself:
1263. As one part often bears upon another,
1264. Lifting it to the light, where most it needs.
1265. The thoughts we have of men are bold as men;
1266. Our thoughts of God are thin and fleet as ghosts;
1267. But it was not his meaning to draw men,
1268. Such as he heard they were in the old world
1269. And sometimes mixed with; he blessed God he knew
1270. But little of the world, that little good;
1271. While some sighed out that little was its all.
1272. So for the persons and the scenes he drew,
1273. Oft in a dim and dreamy imagery
1274. Shapen, half-shapen, mis-shapen, unshapen,
1275. They are the shadowy creatures which youth dreams
1276. Live in the world embodied, but are not,
1277. Save in the mind's, which is the mightier one.
1278. They are the names of things which we believe in,
1279. Ideas not embodied, alas, not!
1280. And the sad fate which many of those meet
1281. Whom the youth loves and quits, means nought so ill
1282. As the betrayer's sin, salvationless
1283. Almost: it is but desertion, not betrayal;
1284. And forced on him according to a promise.
1285. Made at the first unto him, and to be
1286. Wrought out in brief time; and the same fair souls
1287. Saved, stand for our desires made pure in Heaven.
1288. Let us work out our natures; we can do
1289. No wrong in them, they are divine, eterne:
1290. I follow my attraction, and obey
1291. Nature, as earth does, circling round her source
1292. Of life and light, and keeping true in Heaven,
1293. Though not perfect in round, which nothing is.
1294. 'Twas the heart-book of love, well nigh all grief.

1295. For the heart leaves its likeness best in that
1296. O'erwhelming sorrow which burns up and buries,
1297. Like to the eloquent impression left
1298. In lava, of Pompeian maiden's bosom.
1299. All passions, and all pleasures, and all powers
1300. Of man's heart, are brought in, and mind and frame.
1301. He made this work the business of his life;
1302. It was his mission; and was laid on him.
1303. He was a labourer on the ways of God,
1304. And had his hire in peace and power to work.
1305. He wrote it not in the contempt of rule.
1306. And not in hate; but in the self made rule
1307. That there was none to him, but to himself
1308. He was his sole rule, and had right to be.
1309. The faults are faults of nature, and prove art
1310. Man's nature, that a thing of art, like it,
1311. Should be so pure in kind.
1312. HELEN.   I do believe
1313. The world is a forged thing, and hath not got
1314. The die of God upon it. It will not pass
1315. In Heaven, I tell ye.
1316. STUDENT.   How shouldst thou know aught
1317. Of Heaven, unless by contrast?
1318. FESTUS.   Pray now cease;
1319. Ye two are jarring ever, though as with
1320. The bickering beauty of two swords, whose strife,
1321. Though deadly, maketh music, I could listen,
1322. Did not each stab, whichever way, pain me.
1323. HELEN. Oh, I could stand and rend myself with rage
1324. To think I am so weak, that all are so;
1325. Mere minims in the music made from us —
1326. While I would be a hand to sweep from end
1327. To end, from infinite to infinite,
1328. The world's great chord. The beautiful of old
1329. Had but to say some god had been with them,
1330. And their worst fault was hallowed to their best deed.
1331. That was to live. Could we uproot the past,
1332. Which grows and throws its chilling shade o'er us,
1333. Lengthening every hour and darkening it;
1334. Or could we plant the future where we would,
1335. And make it flourish, that, too, were to live.
1336. But it is not more true that what is, is,

1337. Than that what is not, is not. It is enough
1338. To bear the ever present, as we do.
1339. The city of the past is laid in ruins;
1340. Its echo-echoing walls at a whisper fall:
1341. The coming is not yet built; nor as yet
1342. Its deep foundations laid; but seems, at once,
1343. Like the air city, goodly and well watered,
1344. Which the dry wind doth dream of on the sands
1345. Where he dies away with his wanderings:
1346. While we enjoy the hope thereof, and perish;
1347. Not seeing that the desert present is
1348. Our end.
1349. FESTUS.   The brightest natures oft have darkest
1350. End, as fire smoke.
1351. STUDENT.   I will read the book in the hope
1352. Of learning somewhat from it.
1353. FESTUS.   Thou may'st learn
1354. A hearty thanksgiving for blessings here,
1355. And proud prediction of a state to come,
1356. Of love, and life, and power unlimited;
1357. And uttered in a sound and homely tongue,
1358. Fit to be used by all who think while speaking.
1359. With here and there some old, hard uncouth words
1360. Which have withal a quaint and meaning richness,
1361. As stones make more the power of the soil
1362. The world hath said its say for and against;
1363. And after praise and blame cometh the truth.
1364. Living men look on all who live askance.
1365. Were he a cold grey ghost, he would have honour;
1366. And though as man he must have mixed with men,
1367. Yet the true bard doth make himself ghost-like;
1368. He lives apart from men; he wakes and walks
1369. By nights; he puts himself into the world
1370. Above him; and he is what but few see.
1371. He knows, too, to the old hid treasure, truth:
1372. And the world wonders, shortly, how some one
1373. Hath come so rich of soul; it little dreams
1374. Of the poor ghost that made him. Yet he comes
1375. To none save of his own blood, and lets pass
1376. Many a generation till his like
1377. Turns up; moreover, this same genius
1378. Comes, ghost-like, to those only who are lonely

1379. In life and in desire; never to crowds:
1380. And it can make its way through every thing,
1381. And is never happy till it tells its secret;
1382. But pale and pressed down with the inward weight
1383. Of unborn works, it sickens nigh to death,
1384. Often; but who like happy at a birth?
1385. STUDENT. Say what a poet ought to do and be.
1386. FESTUS. Though it may scarce become me, knowing little.
1387. Yet what I have thought out upon that theme,
1388. And deem true, I will tell thee.
1389. HELEN.   Now I know
1390. You two will talk of nothing else all night;
1391. So I will to my music. Sweet! I come.
1392. Art thou not glad to see me? What a time
1393. Since I have touched thine eloquent white fingers.
1394. Hast thou forgot me? Mind, now? Know'st though not
1395. My greeting? Ah! I love thee. Talk away!
1396. Never mind me; I shall not you.
1397. STUDENT. Agreed!
1398. HELEN. By the sweet muse of music, I could swear
1399. I do believe it smiles upon me; see it
1400. Full of unuttered music, like a bird;
1401. Rich in invisible treasures, like a bud
1402. Of unborn sweets, and thick about the heart
1403. With ripe and rosy beauty — full to trembling.
1404. I love it like a sister. Hark! — its tones;
1405. They melt the soul within one like a sword,
1406. Albeit sheathed, by lightning. Talk to me.
1407. Lovely one! Answer me, thou beauty!
1408. STUDENT.   Hear her!
1409. FESTUS. Experience and imagination are
1410. Mother and sire of song — the harp and hand.
1411. The bard's aim is to give us thoughts: his art
1412. Lieth in giving them as bright as may be.
1413. And even when their looks are earthy, still
1414. If opened, like geoids, they may be found
1415. Full of all sparkling sparry[4] loveliness.
1416. They should be wrought, not cast; like tempered steel,
1417. Burned and cooled, burned again, and cooled again.

---

4. Sparry: Of lustre, etc.: resembling that of spar (*OED*).

1418. A thought is like a ray of light — complex
1419. In nature, simple only in effect.
1420. Words are the motes of thought, and nothing more.
1421. Words are like sea-shells on the shore; they show
1422. Where the mind ends, and not how far it has been.
1423. Let every thought, too, soldier-like, be stripped,
1424. And roughly looked over. The dress of words,
1425. Like to the Roman girl's enticing garb,
1426. Should let the play of limb be seen through it,
1427. And the round rising form. A mist of words,
1428. Like halos round the moon, though they enlarge
1429. The seeming size of thoughts, make the light less
1430. Doubly. It is the thought writ down we want,
1431. Not its effect — not likenesses of likenesses.
1432. And such descriptions are not, more than gloves
1433. Instead of hands to shake, enough for us.
1434. STUDENT. But is the power — is poesie inborn,
1435. Or is it to be gained by art or toil?
1436. FESTUS. It is underived, except from God; but where
1437. Strongest, asks most of human care and aid.
1438. Great bards toil much and most; but most at first,
1439. Ere they can learn to concentrate the soul
1440. For hours upon a thought to carry it.
1441. STUDENT. Why I have sat for hours and never moved,
1442. Saving my hands, clock-like, in writing round
1443. Day after day of thought, and lapse of life.
1444. FESTUS. Many make books, few poems, which may do
1445. Well for their gains, but they do nought for truth,
1446. Nor man, true bard's main aim. Perish the books,
1447. But the creations live. Some steal a thought,
1448. And clip it round the edge, and challenge him
1449. Whose 't was to swear to it. To serve things thus
1450. Is as foul witches to cut up old moons
1451. Into new stars. Some never rise above
1452. A pretty fault, like faulty dahlias;
1453. And of whose best things it is kindly said,
1454. The thought is fair; but, to be perfect, wants
1455. A little heightening, like a pretty face
1456. With a low forehead. Do thou more than such,
1457. Or else do nothing. And in poetry,
1458. There is a poet-worship, one of other
1459. Which is idolatry, and not the true

1460. Love-service of the soul to God, which hath
1461. Alone of His inbreathing, and is rendered
1462. Unto Him, from the first, without man's mean,
1463. By those whom He makes worthy of His worship;
1464. Who kneel at once to Him, and at no shrine,
1465. Save in the world's wide ear, do they confess them
1466. Of faults which are all truths; and through which ear,
1467. As the world says them over to itself,
1468. He heareth and absolveth; for the bard
1469. Speaks but what all feel more or less within
1470. The heart's heart, and the sin confessed is done
1471. Away with and for ever.
1472. STUDENT.   What of style?
1473. FESTUS. There is no style is good but nature's style.
1474. And the great ancients' writings, beside ours,
1475. Look like illuminated manuscripts
1476. Before plain press print; all had different minds,
1477. And followed only their own bents: for this
1478. Nor copied that, nor that the other; each
1479. Is finished in his writing, each is best
1480. For his own mind, and that it was upon;
1481. And all have lived, are living, and shall live;
1482. But these have died, are dying, and shall die;
1483. Yea, copyists shall die, spark out and out.
1484. Minds which combine and make alone can tell
1485. The bearings and the workings of all things
1486. In and upon each other. All the parts
1487. Of nature meet and fit: wit, wisdom, worth,
1488. Goodness and greatness; to sublimity
1489. Beauty arises, like a planet world,
1490. Labouring slowly, seemingly, up Heaven;
1491. But with an infinite pace to some immortal eyes.
1492. And he who means to be a great bard, must
1493. Measure himself against pure mind, and fling
1494. His soul into a stream of thought, as will
1495. A swimmer hurl himself into the water.
1496. But never swimmer on the stream, nor bird
1497. On wind, feels half so strong, or swift, or glad,
1498. As bard borne high on his mind above himself;
1499. As though he should begin a lay like this,
1500. Where spiritual element is all;
1501. Thought chafing thought, as bough bough, till all burn,

1502. Like the star-written prophecies of Heaven.
1503. The shattered shadow of eternity
1504. Upon the troubled world, even as the sun
1505. Shows brokenly on wavy waters, time;
1506. All time is but a second to the dead.
1507. The smoke of the great burning of the world
1508. Had trailed across the skies for many an age,
1509. And was fast wearing into air away,
1510. When a saint stood before the throne, and cried —
1511. Blessed be Thou, Lord God of all the worlds
1512. That have been, and that are, and are to be!
1513. For Thy destruction is like infinite
1514. With Thy creation, just and wise in both:
1515. Give me a world; and God said, Be it so:
1516. And the world was: and then go on to show
1517. How this new orb was made, and where it shone;
1518. Who ruled, abode, worshipped and loved therein;
1519. Their natures, duties, hopes: let it be pure,
1520. Wise, holy, beautiful; if not to be
1521. Without it, made so by constraint of God —
1522. Kindly forced good: we have had enough of sin
1523. And folly here to wish for and love change.
1524. Let him show God as going thither mildly,
1525. Father-like, blessing all and cursing none;
1526. And that there never will be need for them
1527. That He shall come in glory new to Himself,
1528. With light to which the lightning shall be shadow,
1529. And the sun sadness; borne upon a car
1530. With wheels of burning worlds, within whose rims
1531. Whole hells burn, and beneath whose course the stars
1532. Dry up like dew-drops. But of this enough;
1533. I mean that he must weigh himself as he
1534. Will be weighed after by posterity;
1535. After us all are critics, to a man.
1536. Write to the mind and heart, and let the ear
1537. Glean after what it can. The voice of great
1538. Or graceful thoughts is sweeter far than all
1539. Word-music; and great thoughts, like great deeds, need
1540. No trumpet. Never be in haste in writing.
1541. Let that thou utterest be of nature's flow,
1542. Not art's; a fountain's, not a pump's. But once
1543. Begun, work thou all things into thy work;

1544. And set thyself about it, as the sea
1545. About earth, lashing at it day and night
1546. And leave the stamp of thine own soul in it
1547. As thorough as the fossil flower in clay.
1548. The theme shall start and struggle in thy breast,
1549. Like to a spirit in its tomb at rising,
1550. Bending the stones, and crying, Resurrection!
1551. STUDENT. What theme remains?
1552. FESTUS. Thyself, thy race, thy love,
1553. The faithless and the full of faith in God;
1554. Thy race's destiny, thy sacred love.
1555. Every believer is God's miracle.
1556. Nothing will stand whose staple is not love;
1557. The love of God, or man, or lovely woman;
1558. The first is scarcely touched, the next scarce felt,
1559. The third is desecrated; lift it up;
1560. Redeem it, hallow it, blend the three in one
1561. Great holy work. It shall be read in Heaven
1562. By all the saved of sinners of all time;
1563. Preachers shall point to it, and tell their wards
1564. It is a handful of eternal truth;
1565. Make ye a heartful of it: men shall will
1566. That it be buried with them in their hands:
1567. The young, the gay, the innocent, the brave,
1568. The fair, with soul and body both all love,
1569. Shall run to it with joy; and the old man,
1570. Still hearty in decline, whose happy life
1571. Hath blossomed downwards, like the purple bell-flower,
1572. Closing the book, shall utter lowlily —
1573. Death, thou art infinite, it is life is little.
1574. Believe thou art inspired, and thou art.
1575. Look at the bard and others; never heed
1576. The petty hints of envy. If a fault
1577. It be in bard to deem himself inspired,
1578. 'T is one which hath had many followers
1579. Before him. He is wont to make, unite,
1580. Believe; the world to part, and doubt, and narrow.
1581. That he believes, he utters. What the world
1582. Utters, it trusts not. But the time may come
1583. When all, along with those who seek to raise
1584. Men's minds, and have enough of pain, without
1585. Suffering from envy, may be God-inspired

1586. To utter truth, and feel like love for men.
1587. Poets are henceforth the world's teachers. Still
1588. The world is all in sects, which makes one loathe it.
1589. STUDENT. The men of mind are mountains, and their heads
1590. Are sunned long ere the rest of earth. I would
1591. Be one such.
1592. FESTUS.   It is well. Burn to be great.
1593. Pay not thy praise to lofty things alone.
1594. The plains are everlasting as the hills.
1595. The bard cannot have two pursuits: aught else
1596. Comes on the mind with the like shock as though
1597. Two worlds had gone to war and met in air.
1598. And now that thou hast heard thus much from one
1599. Not wont to seek, nor give, nor take advice,
1600. Remember, whatsoe'er thou art as man,
1601. Suffer the world, entreat it and forgive.
1602. They who forgive most shall be most forgiven.
1603. Dear Helen, I will tell thee what I love
1604. Next to thee — poesie.
1605. HELEN.   Can any thing
1606. Be even second to me in thy love?
1607. Doth it not distance all things?
1608. FESTUS.   To say sooth,
1609. I once loved many things ere I met with thee,
1610. My one blue break of beauty in the clouds;
1611. Bending thyself to me as Heaven to earth.
1612. HELEN. My love is like the moon, seems now to grow,
1613. And now to lessen; but it is only so
1614. Because thou canst not see it all at once.
1615. It knows nor day, nor morrow, like the sun;
1616. Unchangeable as space it shall still be
1617. When yon bright suns, which are themselves but sands
1618. In the great glass of Time, shall be run out.
1619. FESTUS. Man is but half man without woman; and
1620. As do idolaters their heavenless gods,
1621. We deify the things which we adore.
1622. HELEN. Our life is comely as a whole; nay, more,
1623. Like rich brown ringlets, with odd hairs all gold.
1624. We women have four seasons, like the year.
1625. Our spring is in our lightsome girlish days,
1626. When the heart laughs within us for sheer joy;
1627. Ere yet we know what love is or the ill

1628. Of being loved by those whom we love not.
1629. Summer is when we love and are beloved,
1630. And seems short; from its very splendour seems
1631. To pass the quicker; crowned with flowers it flies.
1632. Autumn, when some young thing with tiny hands,
1633. And rosy cheeks, and flossy tendrilled locks,
1634. Is wantoning about us day and night.
1635. And winter is when these we love have perished;
1636. For the heart ices then. And the next spring
1637. Is in another world, if one there be.
1638. Some miss one season, some another; this
1639. Shall have them early, and that late; and yet
1640. The year wear round with all as best it may.
1641. There is no rule for it; but in the main
1642. It is as I have said.
1643. FESTUS.   My life with thee
1644. Is like a song, and the sweet music thou,
1645. Which doth accompany it.
1646. STUDENT.   Say, did thy friend
1647. Write aught beside the work thou tell'st of?
1648. FESTUS.   Nothing.
1649. After that, like the burning peak, he fell
1650. Into himself and was missing ever after.
1651. STUDENT. If not a secret, pray who was he?
1652. FESTUS. I.

SCENE 21

[Garden and Bower by the Sea]
[LUCIFER and ELISSA]

1. LUCIFER. Night comes, world-jewelled, as my bride
    should be.
2. The stars rush forth in myriads as to wage
3. War with the lines of Darkness; and the moon,
4. Pale ghost of Night, comes haunting the cold earth

5.   After the sun's red sea-death — quietless.
6.   Immortal Night! I love thee. Thou and I
7.   Are of one seed — the eldest blood of God.
8.   He makes; we mar together all things — all
9.   But our own selves. Love makes thee cold and tremble,
10.   And me all fire. Do off that starry robe;
11.   Catch me up to thee. Let us love, and die,
12.   And weld our souls together. Night! But here
13.   Cometh mine earthly. My Elissa! welcome.
14.   ELISSA. Is 't not a lovely, nay, a heavenly eve?
15.   LUCIFER. Thy presence only makes it so to me.
16.   The moments thou art with me are like stars
17.   Peering through my dark life.
18.   ELISSA. Nay, speak not so,
19.   Or I shall weep, and thou wilt turn away
20.   From woman's tears: yet are they woman's wealth.
21.   LUCIFER. Then keep thy treasures, lady! I would not have
22.   The world, if prized at one sad tear of thine.
23.   One tear of beauty can outweigh a world
24.   Even of sin and sorrow, heavy as this;
25.   But beauty cannot sin and should not weep,
26.   For she is mortal. Oh! let deathless things
27.   Alone weep. Why should aught that dies be sad?
28.   ELISSA. The noble mind is oft too generous,
29.   And, by protecting, weakens lesser ones;
30.   And tears must come of feeling though they quench
31.   As oft the light which love lit in the eye.
32.   LUCIFER. And thy love ever hangs about my heart
33.   Like the pure pearl-wreath which enrings thy brow.
34.   I meant not to be mournful. Tell me, now,
35.   How thou hast passed the hours since last we met?
36.   ELISSA. I have stayed the livelong day within this bower;
37.   It was here that thou did promise me to come —
38.   Watching from wanton morn to repentant eve,
39.   The self-same roses ope and close; untired,
40.   Listening the same birds' first and latest songs —
41.   And still thou camest not. To the mind which waits
42.   Upon one hour the others are but slaves.
43.   The week hath but one day — the day one hour —
44.   That hour of the heart — that lord of time.
45.   LUCIFER. Sweet one! I raced with light and passed the laggard

46. To meet thee — or, I mean I could have done —
47. Yea, have outsped the very dart of Death —
48. So much I sought; and were I living light
49. From God, with leave to range the world, and choose
50. Another brow than His whereon to beam —
51. To mark what even an angel could but covet —
52. A something lovelier than Heaven's loveliness —
53. To thee I straight would dart, unheeding all
54. The lives of other worlds, even those who name
55. Themselves thy kind; for oft my mind o'ersoars
56. The stars; and pondering upon what may be
57. Of their chief lording natures, man's seems worst —
58. The darkest, meanest, which, through all these worlds,
59. Drags what is deathless, may be, down to dust.
60. ELISSA. Speak not so bitterly of human kind;
61. I know that thou dost love it. Hast not heard
62. Of those great spirits, who, the greater grow,
63. The better we are able them to prize?
64. Great minds can never cease; yet have they not
65. A separate estate of deathlessness:
66. The future is a remnant of their life:
67. Our time is part of theirs, not theirs of ours:
68. They know the thoughts of ages long before.
69. It is not the weak mind feels the great mind's might;
70. None but the great can test it. Does the oak
71. Or reed feel the strong storm most? Oh! unsay
72. What thou hast said of man; nor deem me wrong.
73. Mind cannot mind despise — it is itself.
74. Mind must love mind: the great and good are friends;
75. And he is but half great who is not good.
76. And, oh! humanity is the fairest flower
77. Blooming in earthly breasts; so sweet and pure,
78. That it might freshen even the fadeless wreaths
79. Twined round the golden harps of those in Heaven.
80. LUCIFER. For thy sake I will love even man, or aught.
81. Spirit were I, and a mere mortal thou,
82. For thy sake I would even seek to die;
83. That, dead, or living, I might still be with thee.
84. But no! I'll deem thee deathless — mind and make,
85. And worthier of some spirit's love than mine;
86. Yea, of the first-born of God's sons, could he
87. In that sweet shade thy beauty casts o'er all,

88. One moment lay and cool his burning soul;
89. Or might the ark of his wide flood-like woe
90. But rest upon that mount of peace and bliss —
91. Thy heart inbosomed in all beauteousness.
92. Nay, lady! shrink not. Thinkest thou I am he?
93. ELISSA. Thou art too noble, far. I oft have wished,
94. Ere I knew thee, I had some spirit's love;
95. But thou art more like what I sought than man,
96. And a forbidden quest, it seems; for thou
97. Hast more of awe than love about thee, like
98. The mystery of dreams which we can feel,
99. But cannot touch.
100. LUCIFER. Nay, think not so! It is wrong.
101. Come, let us sit in this thy favourite bower,
102. And I will hear thee sing. I love that voice,
103. Dipping more softly on the subject ear
104. Than that calm kiss the willow gives the wave —
105. A soft rich tone, a rainbow of sweet sounds,
106. Just spanning the soothed sense. Come, nay me not.
107. ELISSA. Do thou lead out some lay; I'll follow thine.
108. LUCIFER. Well, I agree. It will spare me much of shame
109. In coming after thee. My song is said
110. Of Lucifer the star. See there he shines!
111. [*sings*] I am Lucifer, the star:
112.   Oh! think on me,
113.   As I lighten from afar
114.   The Heavens and thee!
115.   In town, or tower,
116.   Or this fair bower.
117.   Oh! think on me;
118.   Though a wandering star,
119.   As the loveliest are,
120.   I love but thee.
121.   Lady! When I brightest beam,
122.   Love! look on me!
123.   I am not what I may seem
124.   To the world or thee;
125.   But fain would love
126.   With thee above.
127.   Where thou wilt be.
128.   But if love be a dream,
129.   As the world doth deem,
130.   What is't to me?

131. ELISSA. Could we but deem the stars had hearts and loved,
132. They would seem happier, holier, even than now;
133. And ah! why not? they are so beautiful;
134. And love is part and union in itself
135. Of all that is in nature brilliant, pure —
136. Of all in feeling sacred and sublime.
137. Surely the stars are images of love:
138. The sunbeam and the starbeam doth bring love.
139. The sky, the sea, the rainbow, and the stream
140. And dark blue hill were all the loveliness
141. Of earth and Heaven, in sweet ecstatic[1] strife,
142. Seem mingling hues which might immortal be,
143. If length of life by height of beauty went:
144. All seem but made for love — love made for all:
145. We do become all heart with those we love:
146. It is nature's self — it is everywhere — it is here.
147. LUCIFER. To me there is but one place in the world,
148. And that where thou art; for where'er I be,
149. Thy love doth seek its way into my heart,
150. As will a bird into her secret nest:
151. Then sit and sing; sweet wing of beauty, sing.
152. ELISSA. Bright one! who dwellest in the happy skies,
153. Rejoicing in thy light as does the brave,
154. In his keen flashing sword, and his strong arm's
155. Swift swoop, canst thou from among the sons of men,
156. Single out those who love thee as do I
157. Thee from thy fellow glories? if so, star,
158. Turn hither thy bright front; I love thee, friend.
159. Thou hast no deeds of darkness. All thou dost
160. Is to us light and beauty: yea, thou art
161. A globe all glory; thou who at the first
162. Didst answer to the angels which in Heaven
163. Sang the bright birth of earth, and even now,
164. As star by star is born, dost sing the same
165. With countless hosts in infinite delight,
166. Be unto me a moment! Write thy bright
167. Light on my heart before the sun shall rise
168. And vanquish sight. Thou art the prophecy
169. Of light which he fulfils. Speak, shining star,
170. Drop from thy golden lips the truths of Heaven;

1. Ecstatic: 'Extatic' in the original.

171. First of all stars and favoured of the skies,
172. Apostle of the sun— thou upon whom
173. His mantle resteth—speak, prophetic beauty!
174. Speak, shining star out of the heights of Heaven,
175. Beautiful being, speak to God for man!
176. Is it because of beauty thou wast chosen
177. To be the sign of sin? For surely sin
178. Must be surpassing lovely when for her
179. Men forfeit God's reward of deathless bliss
180. And life divine; or, is it that such beauty,
181. Sometimes, before the truth, and sometimes after,
182. As is a moral or a prophecy,
183. Is ever warning? Why wast thou accorded
184. To the great Evil? Is it because thou art
185. Of all the sun's bright servants nearest earth?
186. And shall we then forget that Christ hath said
187. He is thyself, the light-bringer of Heaven?
188. Star of the morning! unto us thou art
189. The presage of a day of power. Like thee
190. Let us rejoice in life, then, and proclaim
191. A glory coming greater than our own.
192. All ages are but stars to that which comes,
193. Sunlike. Oh! speak, star! Lift thou up thy voice
194. Out of yon radiant ranks, and I on earth,
195. As thou in Heaven, will bless the Lord God ever.
196. Hear, Lucifer, thou star! I answer thee. [*sings*.]
197.   Oh! ask me not to look and love,
198.   But bid me worship thee;
199.   For thou art earthly things above,
200.   As far as angels be:
201.   Then whether in the eve or morn
202.   Thou dost the maiden skies adorn,
203.   Oh! let me worship thee!
204.   I am but as this drop of dew;
205.   Oh! let me worship thee!
206.   Thy light, thy strength, is ever new,
207.   Even as the angels' be:
208.   And as this dew-drop, till it dies,
209.   Bosoms the golden stars and skies,
210.   Oh! let me worship thee!
211. But, dearest, why that dark look?
212. LUCIFER.   Let it not

213. Cloud thine even with its shadow: but the ground
214. Of all great thoughts is sadness; and I mused
215. Upon past happiness. Well — be it past!
216. Did Lucifer, as I do, gaze on thee,
217. The flame of woe would flicker in his breast,
218. And straight die out — the brightness of thy beauty
219. Quenching it as the sun doth earthly fire.
220. ELISSA. Nay, look not on me so intensely sad.
221. LUCIFER. Forgive me: it was an agony of bliss.
222. I love thee, and am full of happiness.
223. My bosom bounds beneath thy smile as doth
224. The sea's unto the moon, his mighty mistress;
225. Lying and looking up to her, and saying —
226. Lovely! lovely! lovely! lady of the Heavens!
227. Oh! when the thoughts of other joyous days —
228. Perchance, if such may be, of happier times —
229. Are falling gently on the memory
230. Like autumn leaves distained with dusky gold,
231. Yet softly as a snowflake; and the smile
232. Of kindliness, like thine, is beaming on me —
233. Oh! pardon, if I lose myself, nor know
234. Whether I be with Heaven or thee.
235. ELISSA.   Use not
236. Such ardent phrase, nor mix the claim of aught
237. On earth with thoughts more than with hopes of
238. Heaven.
239. LUCIFER.   Hopes, lady I have none.
240. ELISSA.   Thou must have. All
241. Have hopes, however wretched they may be,
242. Or blest. It is hope which lifts the lark so high —
243. Hope of a lighter air and bluer sky:
244. And the poor hack which drops down on the flints —
245. Upon whose eye the dust is settling —
246. He hopes to die. No being is which hath
247. Not love and hope.
248. LUCIFER.   Yes — One! The ancient ill,
249. Dwelling and damned through all which is; that spirit
250. Whose heart is hate — who is the foe of God —
251. The foe of all.
252. ELISSA.   How knowest though such doth live?
253. Love is the happy privilege of mind —
254. Love is the reason of all living things.

255. A Trinity there seems of principles,
256. Which represent and rule created life —
257. The love of self, our fellows, and our God.
258. In all throughout one common feeling reigns:
259. Each doth maintain and is maintained by the other;
260. All are compatible — all needful; one
261. To life — to virtue one —and one to bliss;
262. Which thus together make the power, the end,
263. And the perfection of created Being.
264. From these three principles doth every deed,
265. Desire, and will, and reasoning good or bad, come;
266. To these they all determine — sum and scheme:
267. The three are one in centre and in round;
268. Wrapping the world of life as do the skies
269. Our world. Hail! air of love by which we live!
270. How sweet, how fragrant! Spirit, though unseen —
271. Void of gross sign — is scarce a simple essence,
272. Immortal, immaterial, though It be.
273. One only simple essence liveth — God —
274. Creator, uncreate. The brutes beneath,
275. The angels high above us, with ourselves,
276. Are but compounded things of mind and form.
277. In all things animate is therefore cored
278. An elemental sameness of existence;
279. For God, being Love, in love created all,
280. As He contains the whole, and penetrates.
281. Seraphs love God, and angels love the good:
282. We love each other; and these lower lives,
283. Which walk the earth in thousand diverse shapes,
284. According to their reason, love us too:
285. The most intelligent affect us most.
286. Nay, man's chief wisdom's love — the love of God.
287. The new religion — final perfect, pure —
288. Was that of Christ and love. His great command —
289. His all-sufficing precept — was 't not love?
290. Truly to love ourselves we must love God —
291. To love God we must all His creatures love —
292. To love His creatures, both ourselves and Him.
293. Thus love is all that's wise, fair, good, and happy.
294. LUCIFER. How knowest thou God doth live? Why did He not,
295. With that creating hand which sprinkled stars
296. On space's bosom, bidding her breathe and wake

297. From the long death-like trance in which she lay, —
298. With that same hand which scattered o'er the sky,
299. As this small dust I strew upon the wind,
300. Yon countless orbs, aye fixing each on Him
301. Its flaming eye, which winks and blenches oft
302. Beneath His glance, — with the finger of that hand
303. Which spangled o'er infinity with suns,
304. And wrapped it round about Him as a robe, —
305. Why did He not write out his own great name
306. In spheres of fire, that Heaven might alway tell
307. To every creature, God? If not, then why
308. Should I believe when I behold around me
309. Nought scarce, save ill and woe?
310. ELISSA.   God surely lives!
311. Without God all things are in tunnel darkness.
312. Let there be God, and all are sun — all God.
313. And to the just soul, in a future state,
314. Defect's dark mist, thick-spreading o'er this vale,
315. Shall dim the eye no more, nor bound survey;
316. And evil, now which boweth being down
317. As dew the grass, shall only fit all life
318. For fresher growth and for intenser day,
319. Where God shall dry all tears as the sun dew.
320. LUCIFER. Oh! lady, I am wretched.
321. ELISSA.   Say not so.
322. With thee I could not deem myself unhappy.
323. Hark to the sea! It sounds like the near hum
324. Of a great city.
325. LUCIFER.   Say, the city earth;
326. For such these orbs are in the realms of space.
327. ELISSA. I dreamed once that the night came down to me;
328. In figure, oh! too like thine own for truth.
329. And looked into me with his thousand eyes,
330. And that made me unhappy; but it passed,
331. And I half wished it back. Mind hath its earth
332. And Heaven. The many petty common thoughts
333. On which we daily tread, as it were, make one,
334. And above which few look; the other is
335. That high and welkin-like[2] infinity —
336. The brighter, upper half of the mind's world,

2. Welkin-like: A synonym for 'heavenly'.

337. Thick with great sun-like and constellate thoughts;
338. And in the night of mind, which is our sleep,
339. These thoughts shine out in dreams. Dreams double life;
340. They are the heart's bright shadow on life's flood;
341. And even the step from death to deathlessness —
342. From this earth's gross existence unto Heaven —
343. Can scarce be more than from the harsh hot day
344. To sleep's soft scenes, the moonlight of the mind.
345. The wave is never weary of the wind,
346. But in mountainous playfulness leaps to it
347. Always; but mind gets weary of the world,
348. And glooms itself in sleep, like a sweet smile,
349. Line by line, settling into proper sadness;
350. For sleep seems part of our immortality:
351. And why should any thing that dies be sad?
352. Last night I dreamed I walked within a hall —
353. The inside of the world. Long shroud-like lights
354. Lit up its lift-like dome and pale wide walls,
355. Horizon-like; and every one was there:
356. It was the house of Death, and Death was there.
357. We could not see him, but he was a feeling:
358. We knew he was around us — heard us — eyed us;
359. But where wast thou? I never met thee once.
360. And all was still as nothing; or as God,
361. Deep judging, when the thought of making first
362. Quickened and stirred within Him; and He made
363. All Heaven at one thought as at a glance.
364. Noise was there none; and yet there was a sound
365. Which seemed to be half like silence, half like sound.
366. All crept about still as the cold wet worms,
367. Which slid among our feet, we could not scape from.
368. Round me were ruined fragments of dead gods —
369. Those shadows of the mystery of One —
370. And the red worms, too, flourished over these,
371. For marble is a shadow weighed with mind;
372. Each being, as men of old believed, distinct
373. In form, and place, and power. But Oh! not all
374. The gathered gods of Eld shine like ours,
375. No more than all yon stars could make a sun.
376. But truly then men lived in moral night,
377. 'Neath a dim starlight of religious truth.
378. I felt my spirit's spring gush out more clear,

379. Gazing on these: they beautified my mind
380. As rocks and flowers reflected do a well.
381. Mind makes itself like that it lives amidst,
382. And on; and thus, among dreams, imaginings,
383. And scenes of awe, and purity, and power,
384. Grows sternly sweet and calm — all beautiful
385. With god-like coldness and unconsciousness
386. Of mortal passion, mental toil, until,
387. Like to the marble model of a god,
388. It doth assume a firm and dazzling form
389. Scarcely less incorruptible than that
390. It emblems: and so grew, methought, my mind.
391. Matter hath many qualities; mind one:
392. It is irresistible: pure power — pure god.
393. While wandering on I met what seemed myself:
394. Was it not strange that we should meet, and there?
395. But all is strange in dreaming, as in death,
396. And waking, as in life: nought is not strange.
397. Methought that I was happy, because dead.
398. All hurried to and fro; and many cried
399. To each other — Can I do thee any good?
400. But no one heeded: nothing could avail:
401. The world was one great grave. I looked, and saw
402. Time on his two great wings — one, night — one, day —
403. Fly, moth-like, right into the flickering sun;
404. So that the sun went out, and they both perished.
405. And one gat up and spake — a holy man —
406. Exhorting them; but each and all cried out —
407. Go to!— it helps not — means not: we are dead.
408. Death spake no word methought, but me he made
409. Speak for him; and I dreamed that I was Death;
410. Then, that Death only lived: all things were mixed;
411. Up and down shooting, like the brain's fierce dance
412. In a delirium, when we are apt to die.
413. Hell is my heir; what kin to me is Heaven?
414. Bring out your hearts before me. Give your limbs
415. To whom ye list or love. My son, Decay,
416. Will take them: give them him. I want your hearts,
417. That I may take them up to God. There came
418. These words among us, but we knew not whence;
419. It was as if the air spake. And there rose
420. Out of the earth a giant thing, all earth;

421. His eye was earthy, and his arm was earthy:
422. He had no heart. He but said, I am Decay;
423. And, as he spake, he crumbled into earth,
424. And there was nothing of him. But we all
425. Lifted our faces up at the word, God,
426. And spied a dark star high above in the midst
427. Of others, numberless as are the dead.
428. And all plucked out their hearts, and held them in
429. Their right hands. Many tried to pick out specks
430. And stains, but could not: each gave up his heart
431. And something — all things — nothing — it was Death,
432. Said, as before, from air — Let us to God!
433. And straight we rose, leaving behind the raw
434. Worms and dead gods, all of us — soared and soared
435. Right upwards, till the star I told thee of
436. Looked like a moon — the moon became a sun:
437. The sun — there came a hand between the sun and us,
438. And its five fingers made five nights in air.
439. God tore the glory from the sun's broad brow,
440. And flung the flaming scalp off flat to Hell.
441. I saw Him do it; and it passed close by us.
442. And then I heard a long, cold, skeleton scream,
443. Like a trumpet whining through a catacomb,
444. Which made the sides of that great grave shake in.
445. I saw the world and vision of the dead
446. Dim itself off — and all was life! I woke,
447. And felt the high sun blazoning on my brow
448. His own almighty mockery of woe,
449. And fierce and infinite laugh at things which cease.
450. Hell hath its light — and Heaven; he burns with both.
451. And my dream broke, like life from the last limb —
452. Quivering; so loth I felt to let it go,
453. Just as I thought I had caught sight of Heaven.
454. It came to nought, as dreams of Heaven on earth
455. Do always.
456. LUCIFER.   It is time we part again.
457. ELISSA. Farewell, then, gentle stars! To-night, farewell!
458. For we all part at once. It is thus the bright
459. Visions and joys of youth break up — but they
460. For ever. When ye shine again I will
461. Be with ye; for I love ye next to him.
462. To all, adieu! When shall I see thee next?

463. LUCIFER. Lady, I know not.

464. ELISSA. Say!

465. LUCIFER. Never! perchance.

466. ELISSA. There is but one immortal in the world

467. Who need say — never!

468. LUCIFER.   What if I were he?

469. ELISSA. But thou art not he; and thou shalt not say it.

470. Stars rise and set — rise, set, and rise again

471. In their sublime-like beauty through all time.

472. Why should not we, too, ever meet, like them?

473. LUCIFER. I see no beauty — feel no love — all things

474. Are unlovely.

475. ELISSA. O earth! be deaf; and Heaven!

476. Shut thy blue eye. He doth blaspheme the world.

477. Dost not love me?

478. LUCIFER.   Love thee? Ay! Earth and Heaven

479. Together could not make a love like mine.

480. ELISSA. When will thou come again? To-morrow?

481. LUCIFER.   Well.

482. And then I cross yon sea ere I return;

483. For I have matters in another land.

484. Fear not.

485. ELISSA.   When will our parting days be over?

486. LUCIFER. Oh! Soon — soon! think of me love, on the
      waters!

487. Be happy! and, for me, I love few things more

488. Than at night to ride upon the broad-backed billow,

489. Seeing along and plunging on his precipitous path;

490. While the red moon is westering low away,

491. And the mad waves are fighting for the stars,

492. Like men for — what they know not.

493. ELISSA. Scorner!

494. LUCIFER. Saint!

495. ELISSA. The world hath much that's great; and but one sea,

496. Which is her spirit; and to her it stands

497. As the mad monarch passion to the heart —

498. Fathomless, overwhelming, which receives

499. The rivers of all feeling; in whose depths

500. Lie wrecked the ruins of all nature. God,

501. When He did make thee, moved upon thee then,

502. And left His impress there, the same even now

503. As when thy last wave leapt from Chaos. — Hark!

504. Nay, there is some one coming.
505. [FESTUS *entering*]. It is I.
506. I said we should be sure to meet thee here:
507. For I have brought one who would speak with thee.
508. LUCIFER. Thanks! and where is he?
509. FESTUS. Yonder. He would not
510. Come up so far as this.
511. LUCIFER. Who is it?
512. FESTUS.   I know not
513. Who he may be, or what; but I can guess.
514. LUCIFER. Remain a moment, love, till I return.
515. ELISSA. Nay — let me leave!
516. LUCIFER. Not yet: do not dislike him.
517. He is a friend, and — more another time.
518. FESTUS. I am sorry, lady, to have caused this parting.
519. I fear I am unwelcome.
520. ELISSA.   We were parting.
521. FESTUS. Then am I doubly sorry; for I know
522. It is the saddest and the sacredest
523. Moment of all with those who love.
524. ELISSA.   He is coming
525. So I forgive thee.
526. LUCIFER.   I must leave thee, love:
527. I know not for how long; it rests with thee
528. If it seem long at all. Eternity
529. Might pass, and I not know it in thy love.
530. ELISSA. If to believe that I do love thee always
531. May make time fly the fleeter —
532. LUCIFER.   I'll believe it —
533. Trust me. I leave this lady in thy charge,
534. FESTUS. Be kind — wait on her — may he, love?
535. ELISSA. Thou knowest. I receive him as thy friend
536. Whenever he come.
537. FESTUS.   I ask no higher title
538. Than friend of the lovely and the generous.
539. ELISSA. Farewell!
540. FESTUS.   Lady! I will not forget my trust
541. [*Apart*] The breeze which curls the lake's bright lip but lifts
542. A purer, deeper, water to the light;
543. The ruffling of the wild bird's wing but wakes
544. A warmer beauty and a downier depth.
545. That startled shrink, that faintest blossom-blush

546. Of constancy alarmed! — Love! if thou hast
547. One weapon in that shining armoury,
548. The quiver on thy shoulder, where thou keep'st
549. Each arrowy eye-beam feathered with a sigh; —
550. If from that bow, shaped so like Beauty's lip
551. Strung with a string of pearls, thou wilt twang forth
552. But one dart, fair into the mark I mean, —
553. Do it, and I will worship thee for ever:
554. Yea, I will give thee glory and a name
555. Known, sunlike, in all nations. Heart, be still!
556. LUCIFER. This parting over —
557. ELISSA. Yes, this one — and then?
558. LUCIFER. Why, then another may be.
559. ELISSA.   No — no more.
560. I'll be unhappy if thou tell'st me so.
561. LUCIFER. Well then — no more.
562. ELISSA. But when wilt thou come back?
563. LUCIFER. Almost before thou wishest. He will know.
564. ELISSA. I shall be always asking him. Farewell!
565. [*goes*]
566. LUCIFER. Shine on, ye stars! and light her to her rest;
567. Scarce are ye worthy for her handmaidens.
568. Why, Hell would laugh to learn I had been in love.
569. I have affairs in Hell. Wilt go with me?
570. FESTUS. Yes, in a month or two: — not just this minute.
571. LUCIFER. I shall be there and back again ere then.
572. FESTUS. Meanwhile I can amuse myself: so, go!
573. But sometime I would fain behold thy home,
574. And pass the gates of fire.
575. LUCIFER.   And so thou shalt.
576. My home is everywhere where spirit is.
577. All things are as I meant them. Fare thee well. [*goes*]
578. FESTUS. The strongest passion which I have is honor:
579. I would I had none: it is in my way.

THE GUARDIAN ANGEL OF EARTH FLYING DISCONSOLATE
ROUND THE HEAVENS

SCENE 22

[*Everywhere*]
[*LUCIFER and FESTUS*]

1. FESTUS. Why, earth is in the very midst of Heaven!
2. And space, though void of things, feels full of God.
3. Hath space no limit?
4. LUCIFER.   None to thee. Yet, if
5. Infinite, it would equal God; and that
6. To think of is most vain.
7. FESTUS.   And yet if not
8. Infinite how can God exist therein?
9. LUCIFER.   I say not.
10. FESTUS. No. So soon when placed beside
11. The infinite the poor immortal fails.
12. LUCIFER. Space is God's space: Eternity is His
13. Eternity; His, Heaven. He only holds
14. Perfections which are but the impossible
15. To other beings.
16. FESTUS.   We are things of time.
17. LUCIFER. With God time is not. Unto Him all is
18. Present Eternity. Worlds, beings, years,
19. With all their natures, powers, and events,
20. The range whereof when making He ordains,
21. Unfold themselves like flowers. He foresees
22. Not, but sees all at once. Time must not be
23. Contrasted with Eternity: 't is not
24. A second of the everlasting year.
25. Perfections although infinite with God,
26. Are all identical; as much of Him —
27. And holy is His mercy, merciful
28. His wisdom, wise His love, and kind his wrath; —
29. As form, extension, parts, are requisites
30. Of matter. Spirit hath no parts. It is
31. One substance, whole and indivisible,
32. Whatever else. Souls see each other clear

33. At one glance, as two drops of rain in air
34. Might look into each other, had they life.
35. Death does away disguise. Even here I feel
36. Among these mighty things, that, as I am,
37. I am akin to God; — that I am part
38. Of the use universal, and can grasp
39. Some portion of that reason in the which
40. The whole is ruled and founded; — that I have
41. A spirit nobler in its cause and end,
42. Lovelier in order, greater in its powers,
43. Than all these bright immensities — how swift!
44. And doth creation's tide for ever flow,
45. Nor ebb with like destruction? World on world,
46. Are they for ever heaping up, and still
47. The mighty measure never full? To act
48. Is power's habit; alway to create,
49. God's; which, thus ever causing worlds, to Him
50. Nought cumbrous more than new down to a wing,
51. Aye multiplies at once my power and pain.
52. I have seen many frames of being pass.
53. This generation of the universe
54. Will soon be gathered to its grave. These worlds,
55. Which bear its sky-pall, soon will follow thine.
56. I, both. All things must die.
57. FESTUS.   What are ye orbs?
58. The words of God — the Scriptures of the skies?
59. For words with Him cannot he passing, nor
60. Less real, vast, or glorious than yourselves.
61. The world is a great poem, and the worlds
62. The words it is writ in, and we souls the thoughts.
63. Ye cannot die.
64. LUCIFER.   Think not on death. Here all
65. Is life, light, beauty. Harp not so on death.
66. FESTUS. I cannot help me, spirit! Chide no more.
67. As who dare gaze the sun, doth after see
68. Betwixt him and else a dark sun in his eye;
69. So I, once having braved my burning doom,
70. See nought beside — or that in everything.
71. Hark, what is that I hear?
72. LUCIFER.   An angel weeping—
73. Earth's guardian angel. She is ever weeping.
74. FESTUS. See where she flies, spirit-torn, round the heavens,

75. Like a fore-feel of madness about the brain.
76. ANGEL OF EARTH. Stars, stars!
77.   Stop your bright cars!
78.   Stint your breath —
79.   Repent ere worse—
80.   Think of the death
81.   Of the universe.
82.   Fear doom, and fear,
83.   The fate of your kin-sphere.
84.   As a corse in the tomb,
85.   Earth! thou art laid in doom:
86.   The worm is at thy heart.
87.   I see all things part: —
88.   The bright air thicken,
89.   Thunder-stricken:
90.   Birds from the sky
91.   Shower like leaves:
92.   Streamlets stop
93.   Like ice on leaves:
94.   The sun go blind:
95.   Swoon the wind
96.   On the high hill top —
97.   Swoon and die:
98.   Earth rear off her cities
99.   As a horse his rider;
100.   And still, with each death-strain,
101.   Her heart-wound tear wider:
102.   The lion roar and die
103.   With his eye-balls on the sky:
104.   The eagle scream
105.   And drop like a beam:
106.   Men crowd and cry,
107.   Out on this deathful dream!
108.   A low dull sound —
109.   'Tis the march of many bones
110.   Under ground;
111.   Up! and they fling
112.   Like a fly's wing,
113.   Off them the grey grave-stones;
114.   They sit in their biers —
115.   Father and mother,
116.   Man and wife,

117.   Sister and brother,
118.   As in life;
119.   Lady and lover —
120.   Love all over.
121.   Their flesh re-appears —
122.   Their hearts beat —
123.   Their eyes have tears:
124.   Woe! Woe!
125.   Do they speak?
126.   Stir? No!
127.   Tongues were too weak,
128.   Save to repeat
129.   Woe!
130.   But they smile
131.   In a while;
132.   For to wipe from His word
133.   The dust of years,
134.   He comes! he comes! the Lord,
135.   Man-God, re-appears;
136.   To bless, and to save
137.   From death and the grave —
138.   To redeem and deliver
139.   For ever and ever!
140.   The dead rise —
141.   Death dies.
142.   Go, Time, and sink
143.   Thy great thoughts in the sea!
144.   And quench thy red link!
145.   Let him flutter to rest
146.   On thy God-nursing breast,
147.   Eternity!
148.   Mother Eternity!
149.   What is for me?
150. FESTUS. Poor angel! Ah! it is the good who suffer.
151. Look! like a cloud, she has wept herself away.
152. What of this world we view and all yon worlds?
153. If God made not all things from nothing, how
154. Is He creator? Something must exist
155. If otherwise, eternal with Himself;
156. And all things had not origin in Him.
157. LUCIFER. He made all things of Him. The visible world
158. Is as the Christ of nature; God the maker

159. In matter made self manifest through time.
160. All things are formed of all things — all of God.
161. The world is made of wonders. Every day
162. Is born a new creation. Every orb
163. Hath its revealed word; and every race
164. Of Being hath its judgment, or shall have.
165. FESTUS. Are all these worlds, then, stocked with souls like man's —
166. Free, fallible, and sinful?
167. LUCIFER.   Ay, they are.
168. All creature-minds, like man's, are fallible.
169. The seraph who in Heaven highest stands
170. May fall to ruin deepest. God is mind —
171. Pure, perfect, sinless. Man imperfect is —
172. Momently sinning. Evil then results
173. From imperfection. The idea of good
174. Is owned in imperfection's lowest form.
175. God would not, could not, make aught wholly ill,
176. Nor aught not like to err. Man never was
177. Perfect nor pure, or he would be so now.
178. Thy nature hath some excellencies — these
179. Oft thwarted by low lusts and wicked wills.
180. What then? They are necessitate in kind,
181. As change in nature, or as shade to light.
182. No darkness hath the sun — no weakness God:
183. These only be the faulty qualities
184. Of secondary natures — planets, men.
185. God hath no attributes unless To Be.
186. Be one: 't would mix Him with the things He hath made.
187. God is all God, as life is that which lives.
188. I am a mighty spirit, and yet I
189. Am but to God what lightning is to light:
190. Lightning slays one thing — light makes all things live.
191. Bear, then, thy necessary ills with grace;
192. No positive estate or principle
193. Is Evil — debtor wholly for its form
194. And measure to defect — defect to good.
195. Good's the sole positive principle in the world;
196. It is only thus, that what God makes, He loves —
197. And must: the others are but off-shoots. Ill
198. Is limited. One cannot form a scheme
199. For universal evil; not even I.

200. FESTUS. Can imperfection from perfection come?
201. Can God make aught defective?
202. LUCIFER.   How aught else?
203. There are but three proportions in all things —
204. The greater — equal — less. God could not make
205. A God above Himself nor equal with —
206. By nature and necessity the Highest;
207. So, if He make, it must be lesser minds —
208. Little and less from angels down to men,
209. Whose natures are imperfect, as His own
210. Must be all-perfect. These two states are not,
211. Except as whole unto its parts, opposed;
212. And evil is itself no ill unless
213. Creation be.
214. FESTUS.   Is God the cause of evil?
215. LUCIFER. So far as evil comes from imperfection,
216. And imperfection from the things He hath made,
217. And what He hath made from His will to make.
218. FESTUS. Oh! let me rest, be it but a moment's pause!
219. This endless light-like journey wearies me.
220. Remember still my spirit toils in dust —
221. A dark close cloud.
222. LUCIFER.   Alight, then, on this orb.
223. I am not wearied: I will watch by thee.
224. He sleeps — he dreams. How far men see in dreams!
225. In dreams they can accomplish worlds of things:
226. The heart then suffers a fusion of all feeling
227. Back to its youthful hours of innocence.
228. And nakedness, and paradise; ere yet
229. The world had wound a perishing garb around it;
230. While yet its God came down and spake to it.
231. Such and so great are dreams. My might, my being
232. To him is but a dream's. And could a state
233. To come fill up their dream-stretched minds, they might
234. Be gods. And may it not be so? Then man
235. Is worth my ruining. What does he dream?
236. With all the sway his spirit now exerts
237. O'er time, space, thought, it is but a shadowy sway,
238. Light as a mountain shadow on a lake.
239. Mine is the mountain's self. A touch would shake
240. To nought whatever his soul now feels or acts;
241. But not a world-quake could touch aught of mine:

242. Thus much we differ. I will not envy man.
243. Power alone makes being bearable.
244. And yet this dream-power is mind-power — real:
245. All things are real: fiction cannot be.
246. A thought is real as the world — a dream
247. True as all God doth know — with whom all is true.
248. The deep dense sleep of half-dead exhaustedness!
249. Would I could feel it. Ah! he wakes at last.
250. FESTUS. Oh! I have dreamed a dream so beautiful!
251. Methought I lay as it were here; and, lo!
252. A spirit came and gave me wings of light,
253. Which thrice I waved delighted. Up we flew
254. Sheer through the shining air, far past the sun's
255. Broad blazing disk, — past where the great great snake
256. Binds in his bright coil half the host of Heaven, —
257. Past thee, Orion! who, with arm uplift,
258. Threatening the throne of God, dost ever stand
259. Sublimely impious; and thy mighty mace
260. Whirling on high, down from its glorious seat
261. Drops, crushed and shattered, many a shining world.
262. And so the brave and beautiful of old
263. Believed thou wast a giant made of worlds:
264. And they were right, if thus they bodied out
265. The immortal mind; for it hath starlike beauty,
266. And worldlike might; and is as high above
267. The things it scorns, and will make war with God,
268. Though He gave it earth and Heaven, and arms to win
269. Them both; and, spite of lust and pride, to earn them.
270. And now thy soul informs yon hundred stars,
271. As mine my limbs — well, 't is a noble end.
272. What now to thee be mortal maid or goddess?
273. Look! she who fled thee once, now loves and longs
274. To clasp thee to her cold and beamy breast.
275. Pine moon! thou art as far below him now,
276. As once she was above thee, thou of the world-belt!
277. And she who had thee, and who knew thee god,
278. Died of her boast, and lies in her own dust.
279. And she who loved thee, the young blushy Morning,
280. Who caught thee in her arms, and bore thee off
281. Far o'er the lashing seas to a lonely isle,
282. Where she might pleasure longer and in secret —
283. That love undid thee; and it is so now:

284. Whether the beauty seek, or flee, or have,
285. 'Tis a like ill — this beauty doubly mortal.
286. What though the moon with madness slew thee there,
287. Let me believe it was within the arms
288. That loved thee even in the stroke of death,
289. And that there snapped the lightning link of life.
290. Kill, but not conquer, man nor mind may gods.
291. Thou image of the Almighty error, man!
292. Banished and banned to Heaven, by a weak world,
293. Which makes the minds it cannot master gods
294. And thou, the first and greatest of half-gods,
295. Which they in olden time did star together
296. To an idolatrous immortality;
297. Who nationalized the Heavens, and gave all stars
298. Unto the spirits of the good and brave,
299. Forestalling God by ages — wonderous men!
300. And if — beguiled by wine, and the low wiles
301. Thou wouldst not creep to meet, and a drunken sleep,
302. Like to high noon in the midst of all his might,
303. Close by the brink of immortality —
304. The deep dominions of the sea-sire, thou
305. Didst lose thy light by kings who hate the great,
306. Thou only hadst to stand up to the sun,
307. And gain again thine eyes. So the great king,
308. The world, the tyrant we elect, in vain
309. Puts out the eyes of mind: it looks to God,
310. And reaps its light again. Wherefore, revenge!
311. Out with the sword! the world will run before thee,
312. Orion! belted giant of the skies!
313. Thou with the treble strain of godhood in thee!
314. March! there is nought to hinder thee in Heaven: —
315. Past that great sickle saved for one day's work,
316. When He who sowed it shall reap Creation's field; —
317. Past those high diademed orbs which show to man
318. His crown to come; — up through the starry strings
319. Of that high harp close by the feet of God,
320. Which He, methought, took up and struck, till Heaven,
321. In love's immortal madness, rang and reeled;
322. The stars fell on their faces; and, far off,
323. The wild world halted — shook his burning mane —
324. Then, like a fresh-blown trumpet blast, went on,
325. Or like a god gone mad. On, on we flew,

326. I and the spirit, far beyond all things
327. Of measure, motion, time and aught create;
328. Where the stars stood on the edge of the first nothing,
329. And looked each other in the face and fled, —
330. Past even the last long starless void, to God;
331. Whom straight I heard, methought, commanding thus:
332. Immortal! I am God. Hie back to earth,
333. And say to all, that God doth say — Love God!
334. LUCIFER. God visits men adreaming: I, awake.
335. FESTUS. And my dream changed to one of general doom.
336. Wilt hear it?
337. LUCIFER.   Ay, say on! It is but a dream.
338. FESTUS. God made all mind and motion cease; and, lo!
339. The whole was death and peace. An endless time
340. Obtained, in which the power of all made failed.
341. God bade the worlds to judgment, and they came —
342. Pale, trembling, corpse-like. To the souls therein
343. Then spake the Maker: Deathless spirits, rise!
344. And straight they thronged around the throne. His arm
345. The Almighty then uplift, and smote the worlds
346. Once, and they fell in fragments like to spray,
347. And vanished in their native void. He shook
348. The stars from Heaven like rain-drops from a bough;
349. Like tears they poured adown creation's face.
350. Spirit and space were all things. Matter, death,
351. And time, left even not a wake to tell
352. Where once their track o'er being. God's own light
353. Undarkened and unhindered by a sun,
354. Glowed forth alone in glory. And through all
355. A clear and tremulous sense of God prevailed,
356. Like to the blush of love upon the cheek,
357. Or the full feeling lightening through the eye,
358. Or the quick music in the chords of harps.
359. God judged all creatures unto bliss or woe,
360. According to their deeds, and faith, and His
361. Own will: and straight the saved upraised a voice
362. Which seemed to emulate eternity
363. In its triumphant overblessedness.
364. The lost leapt up and cursed God to His face —
365. A curse might make the sun turn cold to hear;
366. And thee, in all thy burning glory, tremble,
367. In front of all thy angels, like a chord

368. Rage writhed each brow into a changeless scowl.
369. Madly they mocked at God, and dared His eye,
370. Safe in their curse of deathlessness. To Hell
371. They hied like storms; and, cursing all things, each
372. Soul wrapped him in his shroud of fire for aye,
373. With one long loud howl which seemed to deafen Heaven —
374. And then I woke.
375. LUCIFER. A wild fantastic dream!
376. A mere mirage of mind! Come, let us leave:
377. We have seen enough of this world.
378. FESTUS. Lift me up, then!
379. World upon world how they come rolling on!
380. But none that I see are so fair as earth:
381. There is so much to love that is purely earth.
382. Now I could wander all day in the wood,
383. Where nature, like a sibyl, writes the fate
384. Of all that live on her red forest leaves:
385. And have no other aim than wandering
386. Within that wood, and wind my arms around
387. Its grey gaunt trunks, and think and feel to them;
388. While the wind, sinking, moans over the earth
389. Like a giant over some dead captive dame,
390. Whom death had saved from madness and his love; —
391. Could tramp across the brown and springy moor
392. And over the purple ling and never tire; —
393. Could look upon the ripple of a river,
394. Or on a tree's long shadow down a hill,
395. For a whole summer's day, wishing the sun
396. Would drink up my soul to him as he draws
397. Dew from the earth. These things are in my mind,
398. And suns and systems cannot drive them out.
399. Dost ravage all these worlds?
400. LUCIFER.   Ay, all mine own.
401. Where spirit is, there evil; and the world
402. Is full of me as ocean is of brine.
403. FESTUS. God is all perfect; man imperfect. Thou?
404. LUCIFER. I am the imperfection of the whole —
405. The pitch profoundest of the fallible.
406. Myself the all of evil which exists —
407. The ocean heaped into a single surge.
408. FESTUS. O God! why wouldst Thou make the universe?
409. LUCIFER. Child! Quench yon suns; strip death of its decay;

410. Men of their follies — Hell of all its woe!
411. These, if thou didst, thou couldst not banish me.
412. I am the shadow which Creation casts
413. From God's own light. — But here we are, at Hell.
414. Hark to the thunderous roaring of its fires!
415. Yet ere we further pass — stop! dost thou shrink?
416. FESTUS. At nought — not I! Come on, fiend! follow me!

SCENE 23

[*Hell*]
[*LUCIFER and FESTUS entering*]

1. LUCIFER. Behold my world! Man's science counts it not
2. Upon the brightest sky. He never knows
3. How near it comes to him; but, swathed in clouds,
4. As though in plumed and palled state, it steals
5. Hearse-like and thief-like round the universe
6. For ever rolling and returning not —
7. Robbing all worlds of many an angel soul —
8. With its light hidden in its breast, which burns
9. With all concentrate and superfluent woe.
10. Nor sun nor moon illume it, and to those
11. Which dwell in it, not live, the starry skies
12. Have told no time since first they entered there.
13. Worlds have been built, and to their central base
14. Ruined and rased to the last atom; they
15. Of neither know nor can — unconscious save
16. To agony — nought knowing even of God
17. But His omnipotence to execute
18. Torture on those He hath in wrath endowed
19. With Heaven's own immortality, to make
20. Them feel what woe the Almighty can inflict,
21. And the all-feeble suffer, and not be
22. Annihilated as they would. Be sure

23. That this is Hell. The blood which hath embrued[1]
24. Earth's breast, since first men met in war, may hope
25. Yet to be formed again and re-ascend,
26. Each drop its individual vein; the foam-bubble,
27. Sun-drawn out of the sea into the clouds,
28. To scale the cataract down which it fell,
29. Or seek its primal source in earth's hot heart;
30. But for the lost to rise to or regain
31. Heaven, or to hope it, is impossible.
32. FESTUS. Are all these angels then, or men, or both?
33. Or mortals of all worlds?
34. LUCIFER.   Immortals all.
35. FESTUS.   What numbers!
36. LUCIFER. All are spirits fallen through sin
37. At various periods of eternity;
38. And not by one offence, to one same doom,
39. And at one moment, did they down from Heaven
40. Like to the rapid droppings of a shower; —
41. No! each distinct as thunder-peals, they fell;
42. Save those that fell with me. With me began
43. Sin even in Heaven; with me but sin remains.
44. Once I alone was Hell. Behold my fruits!
45. FESTUS. What do yon fiends! some 'mong them look like mortals:
46. Their hearts shine through them like live coals through ashes.
47. They look like madmen gone delirious.
48. Oh! horror! Let me hence!
49. LUCIFER.   Nay, hear!
50. FESTUS.   I hear!
51. A strain incongruous as a merry dirge
52. Or sacramental bacchanal might be.
53. LUCIFER. Men are they not, but devils at the best;
54. And I would have thee mark them.
55. FESTUS.   I attend.
56. FIENDS. Fill the bow! It burns but blackly:
57. Fill it up with living fire:
58. Drunkard! hadst thou sipped as slackly
59. As thou pourest — pour it higher!
60. Then thou hadst ne'er with me been bound

1. Embrued: Sometimes given as 'imbrue': stained.

61. In Hell to dwell;
62. But let the burning health go round —
63. Drunkard! to Hell!
64. Fill! it drinks but cold and leadly;
65. Fill it up with bubbling fire:
66. Drink! 'tis nothing half so deadly
67. As thy soul when living, Liar!
68. Or thou hadst ne'er with me been bound
69. In Hell to dwell;
70. But let the burning health go round —
71. Liar! — to Hell!
72. Fill! it boils but sick and sadly;
73. Fill! some more immortal fire:
74. Murderer! drain it quickly, madly,
75. As the stab thou gavest thy sire!
76. Or thou hadst ne'er with me been bound
77. In Hell to dwell;
78. But let the burning health go round —
79. Murderer! — to Hell!
80. FESTUS. Nay, let me quit! now know I what Hell is.
81. What are they — drunkards, liars, murderers?
82. LUCIFER. Can wine destroy the soul? or Hell's fierce flames
83. Feed upon holy water, wherewith Priest
84. Baptiseth sinless babe? Can liar make
85. God lie? or cheat his neighbour of his soul?
86. No! God's salvation waiteth not on man's
87. Weak will nor ministry; nor man's perdition
88. Upon his brother's hatred or neglect.
89. Can murderer slay the soul? or suicide
90. Drug immortality? Their sin is great,
91. And is eternally condemned of God;
92. But of their nature, the which Death destroys,
93. Their own as well as victim's recompense.
94. When Time hath overcome the ruin wrought
95. Upon their hearts who loved the dead, that they
96. Who suffered most have most forgiven ill, —
97. Shall the dead slay the living ceaselessly? —
98. Shall God, who is all Love, reverse, reserve,
99. Here in Hell, ages afterwards, those crimes?
100. And because man hath sinned a moment, crown
101. All crime in instituting punishment
102. Unending for an instantaneous wrong?

103. Shall that be justice? It were more than vengeance.
104. Yet such the Deity men fable, such
105. The Hell whereto they doom themselves.
106. FESTUS.   No more.
107. The world is all sufficient for itself;
108. And Hell and Heaven are not the equivalents
109. Of earth's iniquities and righteousness.
110. LUCIFER. Can those who are idolaters defraud
111. God of His worship? who adore the world,
112. Gold, or as savages, the stars and Heaven,
113. And Elements of Earth? None worship Him,
114. But with and in His spirit. Naught attains
115. His love but that proceedeth from it first.
116. His praise is everlasting in all worlds
117. And starry ages of eternity.
118. Can they who covet the world's worthiest goods,
119. Wealth, honour, power, knowledge, rank, or aught
120. Merit eternal torment for a sin
121. Wherewith is bound the world's prosperity
122. And human glory? Naught eternal is
123. But that which is of God. All pain and woe
124. Are therefore finite. Can the robber steal
125. From God or Heaven a thing or from the soul?
126. Or the deflowerer desecrate and undo
127. The espousals of the spirit with its Lord?
128. How weak is virtue, then, and vice, how vain!
129. How wretched human righteousness — and sin,
130. How despicable to the soul assured,
131. Since neither hath a recompense. The one
132. By Him destroyed who can alone unmake
133. That He hath made; the other perfected,
134. United, Deified in God the son
135. With His own nature. Infinite Universe!
136. Thou hast no like, no second favourite
137. To mortal man of God's.
138. FESTUS. What mean the words
139. Of yonder fiendish chant, there?
140. LUCIFER.   Words and shapes
141. Are equally as soon assumed by spirits.
142. What mean my words to thee?
143. FESTUS. In sooth, I know not.
144. I am constrained to hear them.
145. LUCIFER. As for these! —

146. It is a fire of soul in which they burn,
147. And by which they are purified from sin —
148. Rid of the grossness which had gathered round them,
149. And burned again into their virgin brightness.
150. All things work round like worlds. The orb of Hell
151. Hath yet its place in Heaven as thine and all.
152. But, as a spiritual quality,
153. As spirit is the substance of all matter —
154. Hidden or open, heat-like doth inhere
155. In all existence — or for good or ill.
156. Look at yon spirit.
157. FESTUS. What was it brought thee hither?
158. SPIRIT. I was an angel once, ages agone;
159. But doing good and glorifying not
160. God, who empowered me, He sent me here
161. To fire the proud spot from my heart.
162. FESTUS.   And when
163. Wilt thou do this, and own thou hast wronged God?
164. SPIRIT. I do repent me, and confess it now.
165. I will not ask God now to let me be
166. What once I was; but might I only sit
167. A footstool for some other worthier far
168. Who owneth now my throne, I should be happy —
169. Far happier than I was in my proud prayers,
170. That God would give me worlds on worlds to govern,
171. And in receiving all their prayers and blessings.
172. O God! remember me! O save me!
173. FESTUS.   See!
174. I do believe there is an angel coming
175. This way from Heaven.
176. SPIRIT. He comes to me — to me!
177. ANGEL. Hail, sufferer!
178. SPIRIT. Sinner.
179. ANGEL. God hath bade me bring thee
180. Away to Heaven; thy throne is kept for thee;
181. And all the hosts of Heaven are on the wing
182. To welcome thee again.
183. SPIRIT. I dare not come:
184. I am not worthy of Heaven.
185. ANGEL. But God will make thee.
186. FESTUS. Spirit — farewell! and may we meet again
187. In better time and place.
188. SPIRIT.   Glory to God!

189. I go — farewell! — and I will speak of thee.
190. But, oh! repent! Be humble, and despair not.
191. [*Angel and Spirit rise*]
192. LUCIFER. Oh! think, when all are judged, what hosts of
     souls
193. Will then be mine at last! — what wings of fire!
194. Deemest thou yet as mortal?
195. FESTUS.   This is not
196. As thou didst speak of Hell, nor as I judged.
197. LUCIFER. Hell is the wrath of God — His hate of sin.
198. God hates man's nature; be it said of his
199. As of all beings!
200. FESTUS.   How hate that He hath made?
201. LUCIFER. The infinite opposition of Perfection
202. To imperfection leaves nor choice nor mean.
203. Thus the demeanour of thy world grieved God,
204. Till its destruction pleased Him, and its name
205. Was struck out of the starry scroll; thus all
206. Creation worketh infinite grief in Time.
207. When human nature is most perfect, then
208. Its fall is nearest, as of ripest fruit.
209. Man's pleasure in the world — to both of which
210. His nature is made fit — is not of God,
211. Save theirs on whom His spirit He bestows,
212. As in a twilight between earth and Heaven,
213. A promissory Being unfulfilled —
214. But still how glorious to the stone-blind world.
215. This is in time, but in eternity.
216. He raises, remakes, adds to all He made
217. His own immortalizing love and grace,
218. Which keeps them ever pure as is the sea,
219. And incorruptible in godly will.
220. The bliss of God and man originates,
221. Unites, and ends in self — in Deity:
222. To whom is neither motive — good — nor end
223. Greater or less or other than Himself.
224. FESTUS. But how can the Creator glory find
225. In Hell, or creature, good — if God be Love,
226. Or man a being salvable? Oh, say!
227. But who comes hither?
228. LUCIFER. It is the Son of God! —
229. Omnipotent! before whose steadfast feet

230. The thrones of Heaven, which hoped to have o'erthrown
     thine,
231. But now all strengthless, hopeless, Godless here,
232. Rose once and ebbed forever, even these
233. Deep in their fiery abyss of woe
234. Unbent, unbettered will again rush forth
235. In all the might of madness and despair,
236. To prove their hatred of Thee and Thy love.
237. Salvation is the scorn of Angels here.
238. What dost Thou here, not having sinned?
239. SON OF GOD.   For men
240. I bore with death — for fiends I bear with sin;
241. And death and sin are each the pain I pay
242. For the love which brought me down from Heaven to save
243. Both men and devils; and the Father makes
244. And orders every instant what is best.
245. FESTUS. This is God's truth: Hell feels a moment cool.
246. SON OF GOD. Hell is His justice — Heaven is His love —
247. Earth His long suffering: all the world is but
248. A quality of God; therefore come I
249. To temper these — to give to justice, mercy;
250. And to long-suffering, longer. Heaven is mine
251. By birthright. Lo! I am the heir of God:
252. He hath given all things to me. I have made
253. The earth mine own, and all yon countless worlds,
254. And all the souls therein; yea, soul by soul,
255. And world by world, have I redeemed them all —
256. One by one through eternity, or given
257. The means of their salvation: why not, then, Hell?
258. FESTUS. Every spirit is to be redeemed.
259. SON OF GOD. Mortal! it has: the best and worst need one
260. And same salvation. There is nothing final
261. In all this world but God; therefore these souls
262. Whom I see here, and pity for their woes —
263. But for their evil more — these need not be
264. Inhelled for ever; for although once, twice, thrice,
265. On earth or here they may have put God from them,
266. Disowned His prophets — mocked His angels — slain
267. His Son in his mortality — and stormed
268. His curses back to Him; yet God is such,
269. That He can pity still; and I can suffer
270. For them, and save them. Father! I fear not,

271. But by Thy might I can save Hell from Hell.
272. Fiends! hear ye me! Why will ye burn for ever?
273. Look! I am here all water: come and drink,
274. And bathe in me! baptize your burning souls
275. In the pure well of life — the spring of God.
276. I come to save all souls who will be saved.
277. Come, ye immortal fallen! rise again!
278. There is a resurrection for the dead,
279. And for the second dead. And though ye died,
280. And fell, and fell again, and again died —
281. There is a life to come, a rise for all, —
282. A life to come for ever, and a rise
283. Perpetual as the spring is in the year.
284. A FIEND. Thou Son of God! what wilt thou here with us?
285. Have we not Hell enough without Thy presence?
286. Remorse, and always strife, and hate of all,
287. I see around me: is it not enough?
288. Why wilt Thou double it with Thy mild eyes?
289. SON OF GOD. Spirit! I come to save thee.
290. FIEND.   How can that be?
291. SON OF GOD. Repent! God will forgive thee then: And I
292. Will save thee: and the Holy One shall hallow.
293. Repent thou, for thy judgment is at hand;
294. But if thou slurrest over thee means and times,
295. Which have been given thee for repentance here —
296. Tremble! This Hell is nothing to thy next.
297. Believest thou I can save thee?
298. FIEND.   Son of God!
299. I do, believe it. Let me worship.
300. SON OF GOD.   Come!
301. Come to me! Lo! I will but touch thy brow,
302. And make thee bright as morning is in Heaven.
303. SPIRIT. Angel of light I am again! Look here!
304. This — this is to be saved!
305. LUCIFER. I like it not.
306. SON OF GOD. Hear! ye immortals dead! this I can do.
307. Repent! and be all angels.
308. SPIRIT.   Oh, believe!
309. He is God. Worship Him! He comes to save us.
310. LUCIFER. Stand thou beside me: I will speak to them;
311. Or they will sure believe Him. Hell! oh Hell!
312. Powers of perdition! thrones of darkness! — hear!
313. Wrath, ruin, torment! — hear me! It is I!
314. Thanks, fiends! I know ye hate me well, and may:

315. I tempted, ruined, damned ye every one.
316. Were ye not proud, now, to be conquered by me?
317. But wherefore so supine? Am I your lord?
318. Me do ye doubt? or dare ye Him believe?
319. What is an angel dressed in shiny white?
320. Can I not make ye angels? Ay! and more:
321. I cannot make ye less — nor ye yourselves —
322. Nor God — nor Son of God. But hark to me!
323. Be still, ye thunderblasts and hills of fire!
324. Hell doth out-din itself. — Hell-hearted slaves!
325. What are ye that I thus should toil for ye?
326. Who hardly earn the fire that burns ye up?
327. Power I have proffered, but ye have refused:
328. Nothing is for ye but your fiery fate.
329. Kingdoms I have prepared, and ye have spurned.
330. Slaves! slaves! ye are too much at ease! Ye leave
331. Me single in the work of woe. I, sole,
332. Go forth to sow destruction: I, alone,
333. Reap ruin. Had ye been as I, ere now
334. The universe had been all Hell; and, for
335. A pit, each fiend had had a world to rule.
336. Rise! Yet we'll play all hell against all Heaven.
337. Up! up! and then at once we will battle God;
338. And hurling each his orb against the throne,
339. Strange if we will not scatter it like sand.
340. To reign is nothing half like to dethrone!
341. Dethrone! and each is greater then than God.
342. And will ye, then, give up your hopes of Heaven,
343. And entrance as young conquerors fresh from spoil,
344. And choice of thrones won by your death-red hands,
345. For pitiful repentance, like him yonder?
346. Forbid it! all the prowess, pride, and pain
347. Of Hell that we have borne with! do ye not?
348. Meanwhile man's world is straight to be destroyed.
349. Be glad! be glad! Earth's sons may soon be here.
350. And here, as earnest of the truth I tell,
351. Behold this earthling standing by my side!
352. Speak to them, Festus.
353. FESTUS.   Nay, I dread them.
354. LUCIFER.   Speak!
355. Great spirits! he scarce is worthy to address ye,
356. In that I cannot say he yet is damned.
357. FESTUS. But I am here; what recks it how or why?
358. Ye care not and I know not. It is fate:

359. The will of God and him who sets me here;
360. And which I question not. It must be good,
361. Whether decreed that I be saved or lost.
362. But I have poor pretensions for this place;
363. And none, I hope, have worse that are to come.
364. For I have never mocked the word of God,
365. Nor torn it into fuel for my scorn:
366. Nor doubted, saving tremblingly, His being: —
367. His love to man — His right to be adored, —
368. Never have hated, never wronged my race, —
369. Deluded nor rejoiced in their delusion;
370. Never have beckoned off the good from good —
371. Never have mocked nor scattered hopes — nor e'er
372. Have wasted hearts, nor desolated hearths;
373. And if I have once, twice, as who hath not?
374. Toyed with temptation, yet even he will say
375. Who standeth there, that I have never given
376. Up to his burning dalliance my soul.
377. And yet he is my friend, the Evil one.
378. And why is wondrous; judge ye wherefore too.
379. I have no malice, envy, nor revenge;
380. None of those petty passions which bad hearts
381. Scourge red into themselves — for passions are
382. Sufferings — and which to nourish is his want;
383. Wherein doth lie his power: these I have not.
384. And save enjoying earth, I have done never
385. Aught that he could take part in. But he came
386. From God he said, to give; and I believed; —
387. Great spirits lie not — doubt not.
388. LUCIFER.   He says truth.
389. But it is not for him nor you to know
390. The reason of my doings: it is the thing
391. Unfeared and unforethought which tempts, betrays.
392. It is I who bait the world to do its will.
393. As to this mortal, God hath sanctioned all
394. That I have done, or may do to the end;
395. Which I have nought to do with. Son of God!
396. Go on redeeming! — I will go on damning.
397. God! go on making! — I will go on marring.
398. Go on believing, man! — I go on tempting.
399. Saint! Angel! Cherub! seraph! and archangel!
400. Go ye on blessing! — I will go on cursing!
401. I now retrack my course to earth; therein

402. To work out what remaineth of the fate
403. Of this man, and await his world's destruction.
404. What next may hap I care not.
405. FESTUS.   Let us hence!
406. LUCIFER.   Where is He?
407. FESTUS. There — see many do believe.
408. Orb of perdition! thou too shalt die out,
409. And thy red sheeted flames shall fail for aye.
410. Thy palpitating piles of ruin, hot
411. With ever active agony, and quick
412. With soul immortal, down whose midnight heights
413. The wrath of God in cataracts of fire
414. Precipitates itself unceasingly,
415. Shall rush into destruction as a steed
416. Rushes into the battle, there to die.
417. Thy quivering hills of black and bloody hue,
418. Death-breathing, shall collapse like lifeless lungs.
419. And end in air and ashes. Thou shalt be
420. Dashed from creation spark-like from a hand
421. Scarless: pass like a rolled syllable
422. Of midnight thunder from the coming day.
423. The river of all life, which flows through Heaven,
424. Shall yet reach thee and overflood thy flames! —
425. Thou shalt no more vex God nor man; nor all
426. The seekings of the soul shall hunt thee out.
427. Thy day is sometime over. Be it soon!
428. And thou the lost world which the world hath lost!

SCENE 24

[*Colonnade and Lawn*]
[*FESTUS and CLARA*]

1. CLARA. What is it thou wilt tell me?
2. FESTUS.   I have seen
3. What ne'er again may be, nor e'er till now hath been.
4. CLARA. Where didst thou see — and what?

5.   FESTUS. In space. He took me there.

6.   Of whom I oft have told thee. Midst in air

7.   Was God. I'll tell thee that he told the spheres;

8.   For the great family of the universe

9.   Round Him were gathered as a fire: but we

10.   Held back; and, saving God, none did us see.

11.   Though round his throne in sunny halo rolls

12.   A ceaseless, countless throng of sainted souls.

13.   CLARA. Say on, love! Let me hear.

14.   FESTUS.   A sound, then, first

15.   I heard as of a pent-up flood just burst:

16.   It was the rush of God's world-winnowing wing;

17.   Which bowed the orbs as flowers are bowed by breath of spring.

18.   And then a voice I heard, a voice sublime —

19.   To which the hoarded thunders of all time

20.   Pealing earth's death-knell shall a whisper be —

21.   Saying these words — Where will ye worship me?

22.   Ay, where shall be your Maker's holy place?

23.   The Heaven of Heavens is poor before His face.

24.   How shall ye mete my temple, ye who die?

25.   Look! can ye span your God's infinity?

26.   Hear, mighty universe, thy Maker's voice!

27.   Let all thy myriad, myriad worlds rejoice!

28.   Lo! I, your Maker, do amid ye come,

29.   To choose my worship and to name my home.

30.   This heard each sphere; and all throughout the sky

31.   Came crowding round. Our earth was rolling by,

32.   When God said to it — Rest! and fast it stood.

33.   With voice like winds through some wide olden wood,

34.   Thus spake the One again: Behold, O Earth!

35.   Thy parent, God! it is I who gave thee birth.

36.   With all my love I did thee once endow;

37.   With all my mercy — and thou hast them now.

38.   But hear my words! thou never lovedst me well,

39.   Nor fearedst my wrath: dreadst thou no longer Hell?

40.   Dream'st thou that guilt shall always mock those fires?

41.   That deathless death which Hell for aye expires?

42.   Should all creation its rebellion raise,

43.   I speak, and this broad universe doth blaze —

44.   Pass like a dew-drop 'neath mine angry rays —

45.   Blaze like the fat in sacrificial flame:

46. And that burned offering, when I come to claim,
47. Its scorching, quenchless mass, all, I will pour
48. Upon thy naked soul: — canst thou endure?
49. He spake; and, as the fear-fraught words flew past,
50. Earth fluttered like a dead leaf in their blast.
51. Am not I God? Answer me! Hope not thou,
52. Impenitent, to ward my righteous blow.
53. Yet, come again! my proffered mercy hear!
54. Rejoice and sing! sweet music in thine ear
55. And peace I speak: seek but to be forgiven:
56. Repent! and thou shalt meet thy God in Heaven.
57. Go! cleanse thy brow from blood, thy heart from crime,
58. And on thy Saviour call while yet is time!
59. Now to this universe of pride and sin
60. I speak, ere yet I call mine angels in.
61. Draw nigh, ye worlds! — and, lo! their light did seem
62. Before His eye paled to a pearl's dull beam.
63. Attend! said God — o'er all He lift his hand. —
64. Where will ye set my tent? where shall my temple stand?
65. And all were dumb. Distracting silence spread
66. Throughout that host as each were stricken dead.
67. I made ye. I endowed ye. Ye are mine.
68. Then trembled out each orb: Thine, God! for ever Thine!
69. All that ye have, within myself have I;
70. God, am complete; full inexhaustibly.
71. I dwell within myself, and ye in me,
72. Not in yourselves; I have infinity.
73. The everything in all things is my throne;
74. Your might is my might, and your wealth mine own:
75. 'Tis by my power and sufferance that ye shine:
76. I live in light and all your light is mine.
77. Be dark! said God. Night was. Each glowing sphere
78. Dulled. Night seemed everything and everywhere,
79. Save that in utter space a feeble flare
80. Told that the pits of hell were sunken there.
81. Shuddered in fear the universe the while,
82. Till God again embraced it with a smile.
83. And all things made were glad. Come now and hear,
84. Ye worlds! said God, the truth I thus make clear:
85. My words are mercy, wherefore should ye fear?
86. And straight, obedient to his sacred will,
87. One great concentrate globe they crowd to fill;

88. Systems and suns pour forth their glowing urns;
89. Full in the face of God the glory burns.
90. Hearken, thou host! thy trembling hope to raise,
91. I to all Being thus make plain my ways; —
92. God, the creator, bade creation rise,
93. And matter came in void like clouds in skies;
94. Lifeless and cold it spread throughout all space,
95. And darkness dwelt and frowned upon its face:
96. Chaos I bade depart this work of mine,
97. And straight the mighty elements disjoin.
98. Then light I lit; then order I ordained
99. And put the dance of atoms to an end.
100. Matter I brake, and scattered into globes,
101. And clad ye each in green and growing robes:
102. Your sizes, places, forms, I fixed with laws,
103. And wrought the link between effect and cause.
104. Then formed I lives for each, which might inherit
105. Will, reason, form, and power — not deathless spirit.
106. Then I made spirits, things of Heavenly worth,
107. Deathless, Divine. Round these, from every earth,
108. I gathered forms and features fit for love,
109. Trust, pleasure, power, and all I could approve.
110. To every spirit I disclosed my name,
111. My love, my might, and whence all Being came:
112. To deathless souls I righteously decreed
113. Accountability for thought, word, deed.
114. Then every orb complete, along the sky,
115. In glory, beauty, order, harmony,
116. I launched. Souls, worlds did every thing possess
117. Which could a mortal and immortal bless.
118. To all the hope of happier state was given —
119. For all I keep one common boundless Heaven.
120. Ye all have freedom, and ye all do sin,
121. For ye are creatures: but ye all may win
122. Life everlasting — everlasting joy,
123. If ye do but the love of sin destroy:
124. This only is offence; for sin ye must
125. Not by my will; but weakness dwells with dust
126. Unless ye have sinned ye cannot enter Heaven.
127. How shall a sinless creature be forgiven?
128. And by forgiveness only can ye claim
129. Hope in my mercy, trust upon my name.

130. I knew that ye would all to sin be given;
131. But I, even God, have paid your price to Heaven:
132. And if ye will not journey on that way —
133. The truth — the life — what do ye merit? say!
134. Death is the gate of life, and sin, of bliss:
135. Mark the dread truth! but mourn your deeds amiss.
136. Cast off your guilt! abandon folly's path!
137. Turn to the Lord your God ere hell His wrath!
138. Turn from your madness, wicked ones, and live!
139. Take, take the bliss which God alone can give.
140. God, the Creator, me all beings own —
141. God, the Redeemer, I will still be known —
142. God, too, the Judge — the each — the three — the one.
143. Again the Everlasting cried — Repent!
144. To bless or curse I am Omnipotent.
145. And what art thou, created Being? Round
146. That world of worlds His arm the Almighty wound;
147. The bright immensity He raised, and pressed,
148. All trembling, like a babe, unto His breast.
149. There, in the Father's bosom rose again,
150. Of filial love, the universal strain;
151. Strong and exultant — blissful, pure, sublime,
152. It rolled, and thrilled, and swelled in notes unknown to time.
153. Think ye that I, who thus do ye maintain;
154. Thus always cherish ye, or all were vain —
155. Ye all would drop into your native void,
156. If by my hand ye were not held and buoyed:
157. Think ye that I cannot uphold in Heaven,
158. In righteous state, the souls I have forgiven?
159. Is this a weightier task? with God, 'tis one
160. To guide a sunbeam or create a sun —
161. To rule ten thousand thousand worlds or none.
162. Go, worlds! said God, but learn, ere ye depart,
163. My favoured temple is an humble heart;
164. Therein to dwell I leave my loftiest skies —
165. There shall my holy of all holies rise!
166. He spake; and swiftly, reverent to His will,
167. Sprang each bright orb on high its sphere to fill.
168. Glory to God! they chanted as they soared —
169. Father Almighty! be Thou all-adored.
170. Thou art the glory — we, Thine universe,
171. Serve but abroad Thy lustre to disperse.

172. Unsearchable, and yet to all made known!
173. The world at once Thy kingdom and Thy throne —
174. Pity us, God! nor chase us quite away
175. Before Thy wrath, as night before the day.
176. In Thee, our God, we live; from Thee we came —
177. The feeble sparks of Thine eternal flame.
178. Thy breath from nothing filled us all at first,
179. And could again as soon the bubble burst.
180. In Thee, like motes in the sunbeam, we move;
181. Glow in Thy light, and gladden in Thy love.
182. And midst this praise, earth was the only one
183. Sullen remained in that grand union
184. Of joy and harmony. Word spake she none.
185. CLARA. Earth only had been chidden.
186. FESTUS.   Not alone.
187. High o'er all height, God sat[1] upon His throne.
188. Downwards He bent; and, as a grain of sand,
189. He lifted up our globe. Then from His hand,
190. As 't were in pity, bowled the ingrate sphere,
191. Which rushed like ruin down its dark career.
192. And high the airs blue billows rolled and swelled
193. On many an island world mine eye beheld.
194. CLARA. And where and what is he, this mighty friend,
195. Who to thee, human, thus his might doth lend?
196. Who bore thee harmless, as thou sayst, through space,
197. And brought thee front before thy Maker's face?
198. FESTUS. I know not where he is. It is but at times
199. That he is with me; but he aye sublimes
200. His visits thus, by lending me his might
201. O'er things more bright than day, more deep than night.
202. And he obeys me — whether good or ill
203. His or my object, he obeys me still.
204. CLARA. O Festus! I conjure thee to beware
205. Lest thus the Evil one thy soul ensnare.
206. FESTUS. What! may not a free spirit have preferred
207. A mortal to his heart — as thou thy bird
208. Lovest, because it singeth of the sky,
209. Although it is as far below thy soul
210. As I 'neath an archangel's majesty?

---

1. Sat: 'Gat' is in the original, probably a printer's error.

211. God will protect the atom as the whole.
212. CLARA. Him, then, I pray: the spirit full must share
213. The truths it feels with God Himself in prayer.
214. So guide us, God! in all our works and ways,
215. That heart may feel, hand act, mouth shew Thy praise;
216. That when they meet, who love, and when they part,
217. Each may be high in hope, and pure in heart:
218. That they who have seen, and they who have but heard
219. Of Thy great deeds, may both obey Thy word!
220. FESTUS. Unto the wise belongs the sphere of light,
221. And to the spirit world-compelling might
222. Yon sun, now setting in the golden main,
223. Shall count me his ere next he rise again.
224. Would that the earth had nothing fair to lure,
225. Nor being more to answer or endure!
226. But I foresee, fore-suffer. Bound to earth,
227. Wrecked in the deeps of Heaven, in Death's expiring birth!

SCENE 25

[*The Sun*]

1. FESTUS. Soul of the world, divine Necessity,
2. Servant of God, and master of all things!
3. Here, in the Heaven of light's eternal noon,
4. First see I all things clear: from end to end
5. The divine cycle of the soul of man;
6. How spirit, soul, mind, life, flesh, feeling, mix,
7. And how, withal they each reciprocate,
8. As ocean, earth, air, fire and wind; how flow
9. The streams of feeling, and the cataracts
10. Of passion; mine and mountain, this of pride,
11. And that of covetousness. Man I know;
12. The human universe, and the divine
13. And central fate; know all must be fulfilled

14.   Of nature that there is; of sin and strife,

15.   Peace, righteousness, change, self-delusion, self-

16.   Destruction, ere the earth can take new life,

17.   Or man become the minister of God.

18.   The world and man are just reciprocal,

19.   Yet contrary. Spirit invadeth sense

20.   And carries captive Nature. Be this true,

21.   All good is Heaven, and all ill is Hell.

22.   All things are means for greater good. Thou, Sun,

23.   Art just a giant slave, a god in bonds.

24.   The summit-flower of all created life

25.   Is its unition with Divinity,

26.   In essence, yet existence separate.

27.   High o'er my own existence, here then I

28.   Look down upon the nature and the earth,

29.   Yet mine, whose separate and combined ends

30.   Have still to be evolved. How wide men miss,

31.   While in the lower world of soul and sense,

32.   In aiming even at life-ruling Truth —

33.   Formless as air, simple and one as Death.

34.   If Heaven and all its stars depend on earth,

35.   Then may eternity on time; — not else.

36.   But since now earth is as a crumb of Heaven,

37.   And time an atom of eternity.

38.   Neither depends upon the other, both

39.   One essence being emanant from God,

40.   Whose flowings forth are aye and infinite,

41.   And radiant as the rivers of the skies.

42.   One only truth hath consequence. God's truth

43.   Inspirited in man. Mere human truth

44.   Or falsehood matters not. The world may act,

45.   Believe, or bless, or curse, as best it lists.

46.   Yet men expend life, solemnizing points

47.   Uncertain as the site of Paradise

48.   And area of Hades. Not the less,

49.   There is no disappointment we endure

50.   One half so great as that we are to ourselves.

51.   We make our hearts the centres of all hopes,

52.   All powers, all rewards, remembering not

53.   That centres are imaginary points.

54.   Imaginary circles only too

55.   Are perfect; therefore, draw life as we may,

56. Round as a world, or as an atom round,
57. And pure as virgin visionary's dream,
58. Or perfect faith's regenerative wave —
59. It fails to match the true invisible
60. Whereof we labour. It is come to this.
61. One state of life with me hath passed away.
62. Aught henceforth that may matter be of doubt
63. To me is matter of indifference. I
64. Love only that is certain. Me no more
65. The spirits of the bright invisible
66. Shall throng round as the winds some mountain-top;
67. Nor watery lightfulness of ghostly eyes,
68. Belonging heavenly forms informed with light,
69. Impose their spell of record under pain.
70. The inspiration quits me — it is gone —
71. Like a retreating army from the land
72. Which it hath wasted — the long gleaming mass,
73. Snakelike, at last hath wound itself away,
74. And left me weak and wretched. None again
75. Of all the starry tribes of shining mien —
76. Swifter than undulations of the light,
77. A million in a moment, multiform
78. As atomies of air, shall visit me;
79. Their word of leave is taken back — henceforth,
80. Restricted to perfection, earth they quit.
81. True, albeit, I loved them more than life;
82. I felt myself made sacred by their touch: —
83. But they are gone, and there is nought on earth
84. Left acceptable. Fiery shadows, hence!
85. I have outbraved ye once. It matters not.
86. I have left all for one; Truth's countless rays
87. For Truth itself; the mean for the supreme,
88. The dubitable for the throned power.
89. Yet thus I cannot rest. The mightiest sphere
90. Is not for man. The elements of mind
91. And matter are proportioned in all worlds;
92. The father they and mother of all things.
93. And earth hath favour over crowds of stars.
94. I must reseek earth. Still what boots it now,
95. To plunge in pleasure or to passion bow.
96. The very lion-honey of the heart
97. Which dwelleth in corruption? Yet, perchance

98. 'T were wisdom to extract it while we may.
99. The oak, as lily, feels the lightest breeze.
100. The ineradicable seed is sown
101. Of love in life, and tide-like 't will have way
102. O'er the impalaced prisoner of the breast.
103. The thirst for power and knowledge still exist,
104. And meet with dizzy mixture in the brain.
105. If suffering could expiate offence,
106. They who have most enjoyed have most atoned,
107. It may be, humanly; — but it cannot.
108. Earth-like, the heart must undergo all change
109. Ere the superior life be formed therein,
110. The chastity of heart which loves but God.
111. Life's sensuous warmth, the spirit's holy chill,
112. Time's week-day work, have yet to be gone through.
113. The hortus siccus of a Paradise
114. Is all earth now can boast. To God belongs
115. The autumn of all nature. But, alas!
116. Not yet can we o'ercome our nature here,
117. Would we. If therefore passion strike the heart,
118. Let it have length of line and plenteous play.
119. The safety of superior principles
120. Lies in exhaustion of the lower ones,
121. However vast or violent. Men and angels
122. Obey the order of existence. Fate!
123. Who seeks thee everywhere, will find thee there.

SCENE 26

[*A Drawing Room*]
[*FESTUS and ELISSA*]

1. FESTUS. Who says he loves and is not wretched, lies;
2. Or that love is madness came mad from his mother.
3. 'T is the most reasonable thing in nature.

4.   What can we do but love? It is our cup.
5.   Love is the cross and passion of the heart,
6.   Its end — its errand. In the name of God,
7.   What made us love, Elissa?
8.   ELISSA.   I know not.
9.   I am not happy. I have wept all day.
10.   FESTUS. 'T was thine own fault. What wouldst thou have
        of me?
11.   I tell thee we must — no, I cannot tell thee.
12.   Nor can I bear those tears. Thou know'st I love thee,
13.   Worship thee; oh! It's a world more than worship.
14.   The cold obedience which we give to God.
15.   Elissa! turn to me!
16.   ELISSA.   I cannot. Go! —
17.   FESTUS. Thou hadst no need, no business to have loved me.
18.   One loved thee well.
19.   ELISSA.   I could not help his loving
20.   Me, nor my loving thee. It was our fate.
21.   FESTUS. Then Fate hath fee'd the passion for our death,
22.   And we are sold.
23.   ELISSA.   Well! Let us die together.
24.   Together we will quit our bodies here.
25.   FESTUS. Together will we go to God and judgment.
26.   ELISSA. Festus! I will, I can love none but thee.
27.   FESTUS. Thou must not.
28.   ELISSA.   But I must. I cannot help it.
29.   Look at me — heart and arms, I am thine own.
30.   Thou knowest I am and have been. Wilt not love me?
31.   Festus! mine own and only! wilt thou not?
32.   Have I done nothing, suffered and abandoned
33.   Nothing for thee? Oh! I was happy once;
34.   Ere I knew thee. Why wast thou kind to me?
35.   Cruelly kind — or this had never been.
36.   But now thou mayst be cruel if thou wilt.
37.   Hate me! still I am thine: disown me, thine!
38.   Desert me! no — thou canst not. I am thine;
39.   I am! look at me, Festus! look at me!
40.   I am half blind with weeping; and mine eyes
41.   Have not a tear left in them. But I know
42.   How it will end. Thou wilt leave me as I am —
43.   Loveless and lonely.
44.   FESTUS.   Nay, not so; my love

45.   Shall aye be with thee, and my soul with both.
46.   But we must part! Think that I come again.
47.   ELISSA. Not be again with thee! nor thou with me!
48.   It is too much. Let me go mad or die.
49.   FESTUS. Live, mine Elissa! and thou shalt live with me,
50.   And I will love thee ever as I now love.
51.   Wilt thou?
52.   ELISSA.   Oh! make me happy! say I may
53.   Believe thee.
54.   FESTUS.   May? Thou must.
55.   ELISSA.   Say it again!
56.   I cannot know too often of my bliss.
57.   But dost thou love me? tell me — wilt thou love me?
58.   FESTUS. Since I have known thee I have done nought else.
59.   All hours not spent with thee are blanks between stars.
60.   I love thee! love thee! love thee! madly love thee!
61.   Oh! thou hast drank my heart dry of all love!
62.   It will be empty to aught after thee.
63.   Come, dry thine eyes. Blessings on those sweet eyes!
64.   By Heaven! they might a moment win the glance
65.   Of any seraph gazing not on God.
66.   ELISSA. No wonder they drew thine. There is a tear!
67.   FESTUS. Ay; strange and startling is the first hot tear
68.   That we have shed for years; and which hath lain
69.   Like to a water-fairy in the eye's
70.   Blue depths — spell-bound in the socket of the soul.
71.   Death brought it not — pain brought it not — nor shame;
72.   Nor penitence — nor pity —nor despair:
73.   Nothing but love could. For a fearful time
74.   We can keep down the floodgates of the heart,
75.   But we must draw them sometime; or it will burst
76.   Like sand this brave embankment of the breast,
77.   And drain itself to dry death. When pride thaws —
78.   Look for floods!
79.   ELISSA.   Now, thou wilt be very kind
80.   When next we meet? Our time will soon be gone.
81.   FESTUS. I cannot think of time: — there is no time!
82.   Time! time! I hate thee — with the hate of Hell
83.   For aught that's good— but thou art infamous.
84.   I will give thee half my immortality
85.   To keep back for one hour. Leave me, to-night;
86.   And wither me, to-morrow, like a weed!

 87. ELISSA. Where is he now?
 88. FESTUS.   In Hell, — I hope.
 89. ELISSA.   What mean'st thou?
 90. He wronged thee never. Say, when cometh he?
 91. FESTUS. To-night.
 92. ELISSA.   He comes to sever us, like fate.
 93. But shall he part us?
 94. FESTUS.   Never! Let him part
 95. The sun in two first.
 96. ELISSA.   It was ever thus:
 97. I am made to make unhappy all around me.
 98. FESTUS. I will not hear of thy being wrong, — it is I.
 99. I am the false usurper. And since one
100. Out of the three must be a sacrifice,
101. Let it be me. It shall be.
102. ELISSA.   Thou didst swear,
103. Even now, to love me ever.
104. FESTUS.   Be it so.
105. I have sworn — and now and then I keep my oath —
106. I will not give thee up, so save me, God!
107. ELISSA. Oh! we have been too happy, have we not?
108. But, now I think of it, we might have known
109. It could not last. Woe follows bliss as close
110. As death does life — as naturally, may be.
111. We might have thought —
112. FESTUS. I never thought about it.
113. My love — Elissa! ah, how cold thy hand is!
114. Here — warm it on my heart. Nay, let it be,
115. The hand that is on the heart is on the soul
116. And it is thus some moments take the wheel,
117. And steer us through eternity. Believe me,
118. Could I but crowd life, love too, in one throb,
119. I would beat it out, this moment, in thy hand,
120. And would die blessing.
121. ELISSA.   Give me my hand back!
122. FESTUS. My sweet one! if this heart hath warmed thy hand,
123. It hath not beaten in vain — it but returns
124. A pleasure, and a passion, and a power:
125. For oft at touch of thine this bosom burns.
126. ELISSA. Love hath no end except itself. We only
127. Felt we loved and were happy.
128. FESTUS.   Ah! It was so.

129. ELISSA. Our sole misfortune is, we have been happy:
130. We never shall be happy here again.
131. FESTUS. Nay, say not so. Let us be happy now.
132. Happy? To fling aside thy wavy locks,
133. And feed mine eyes on thy white brow — to look
134. Deep in thine eyes till I feel mine have drank
135. Full of that soft wet fire which floats in thine —
136. Eyes which I ne'er would leave — yet when most near,
137. Then most astray I — oh! to lay my cheek
138. Upon thy sweet and swelling bosom thus;
139. Where midst upon the beauty of thy breast
140. Sits love like God between the cherubim —
141. To crop the red budding kisses from thy lips —
142. To name thee, make thee, but one moment, mine—
143. Delights me more than all that earth can lend
144. The good or bad — or Heaven can give the saved.
145. One long wild kiss of sunny sweets, till each
146. Lack breath, the lips half bleed, and, come — thou knowest!
147. I ask but one such — let it last for ever!
148. ELISSA. Now, Festus! this is wrong.
149. FESTUS.   What? — what is wrong?
150. Shall my blood never bound beneath beauty's touch,
151. Heart throb, nor eye thaw with hers — when her tears
152. Drop, quick and bright, upon the glowing brow
153. Plunged in her bosom — because, forsooth, it is wrong?
154. Let it be wrong! it is wrong, it is wretchedness
155. That I would lose both sense and soul to suffer.
156. ELISSA. How dare we love each other as we do?
157. FESTUS. Give me some wine! more — more, love!
158. ELISSA.   Drink and drain
159. The bowl! the vintage of a hundred years
160. Would never slake the memory of shame;
161. Nor quench the thirst of folly.
162. FESTUS.   Fill again!
163. My beauty! sing to me, and make me glad.
164. Thy sweet words drop upon the ear as soft
165. As rose-leaves on a well: and I could listen,
166. As though the immortal melody of Heaven
167. Were wrought into one word — that word a whisper,
168. That whisper all I want from all I love.
169. ELISSA. I am not happy, and I cannot sing.
170. Thou lookest happy. I wish I were so.

171. FESTUS. They tell us that the body of the sun
172. Is dark, and hard, and hollow; and that light
173. Is but a floating fluid veiling him.
174. Ah! how oft, and how much, the heart is like him!
175. Despite the electric light it lives and hides in.
176. SERVANT. [*entering*]. A singer who was told to come is here.
177. FESTUS. Wilt hear him?
178. ELISSA.   Yes, love — gladly.
179. FESTUS.   Shew him in.
180. What have you there?
181. SINGER.   Oh! I think, everything.
182. FESTUS. Well, anything will be enough this once.
183. The last new song?
184. SINGER.   Certainly; here it is. [*Sings*].
185.   Oh! let not a lovely form
186.   With feeling fill thine eye;
187.   Oh! let not the bosom warm
188.   At love-lorn lady's sigh —
189.   For how false is the fairest breast;
190.   How little worth, if true:
191.   And who would wish possessed,
192.   What all must scorn or rue?
193.   Then pass by beauty with looks above;
194.   Oh! seek never — share never — woman's love!
195.   Oh! let not a planet-like eye
196.   Imbeam its tale on thine;
197.   In truth 'tis a lie — though a lie
198.   Scarce less than truth divine.
199.   And the light of its look on the young
200.   Is wildfire with the soul;
201.   Ye follow and follow it long,
202.   But find nor good nor goal.
203.   Then pass by beauty with looks above;
204.   Oh! seek never — share never — woman's love!
205.   ELISSA. Methinks I must have heard that voice before.
206. FESTUS. And I.
207. ELISSA.   Where?
208. FESTUS.   I forget.
209. ELISSA.   And so do I.
210. SINGER. Oh! let not a wildering tongue

211. Weave bright webs o'er thine ear;
212. Nor thy spirit be said nor sung
213. To the air of smile or tear.
214. And say it hath melody far
215. More than the spheres of Heaven,
216. Though to man and the Morning star
217. They sang, Ye be forgiven!
218. Yet pass by beauty with looks above;
219. Oh! seek never — share never — woman's love!
220. Oh! let not a soft bosom pour
221. Itself in thine! It is vain.
222. Love cheateth the heart, oh! be sure,
223. Worse even than wine the brain.
224. Then snatch up thy lip from the brim,
225. Nor drain its dreamlike death;
226. For Love loves to lie down and dim
227. The bright soul with his breath.
228. Then pass by beauty with looks above;
229. Oh! seek never — share never— woman's love!
230. FESTUS. Come hither, man! I wish to look at thee,
231. A moment. No! it can't be. Yet I have seen
232. Some one much like thee.
233. ELISSA. It was a brother, may be?
234. SINGER. I have none, lady. Have ye done with me?
235. FESTUS. Yes — go! and we will take your song of you.
236. SERVANT. Here, follow me! [*They go.*]
237. FESTUS. Weeping again, my love?
238. Thou art, by turns, the proudest and the humblest
239. Creature I ever met with. The least thing
240. Dints thy soft heart. Come, cheer thee, sweet one — do!
241. Oh! if to say, I love, laid all the sins
242. Of all the worlds upon me, I would say it
243. Till I was out of breath: and will, till I die.
244. ELISSA. If Love be blind, it must be by his tears;
245. For love and sorrow alway come together —
246. Love with his sister, sorrow, by the hand.
247. FESTUS. Nay, I will conquer thee again to smile,
248. Or lose my right to love thee. Let me kneel!
249. Come! I will have no other gods but thee;
250. To none but thee will I bow down and worship;
251. Thy bosom is mine altar — and thine eyes
252. Are the divinity that preys upon me.

253. Oh! cruel as the week-day gods of old,
254. Thou wilt have human victims; not content
255. With tears and kisses — fire and water — thou
256. Wilt have the subtler element of life;
257. Thou needs must live on immortality!
258. Here — take me then! I offer up myself
259. A sacrifice to thee.
260. ELISSA.   Thou foolish boy!
261. Where will thy passionate folly end? I love thee.
262. FESTUS. Well then, let me conjure thee! let me swear
263. By some sweet oath that shall to both be holy: —
264. By arms which hold, by knees which worship thee!
265. By that dark eye, the dark divine of beauty,
266. Yet trembling o'er its lid all tears and light —
267. Glory and eye of eyes which yet have shone!
268. By this lone heart, which longeth for a mate!
269. By love's sweet will, and sweeter way! by all
270. I love — by thyself, myself! let me, let me,
271. Let me — but draw the lightning from thine eye: —
272. Kisses are my conductors: do not frown;
273. Nor look so temptingly angry. I was but trifling.
274. The cold calm kiss which cometh as a gift,
275. Not a necessity, is not for me.
276. Whose bliss, whose woe, whose life, whose all is love.
277. ELISSA. We both wrong whom we love, love whom we
         wrong.
278. FESTUS. But I am as a dog that fondles o'er
279. And licks the wound he dies of. Would I could
280. Suffer or feel enough of love to kill!
281. ELISSA. Thou lovest one whom thou oughtst not to love.
282. FESTUS. And what of that? Love hath its own belief,
283. Own worship — own morality — own laws:
284. And it were better that all love were sin
285. Than that love were not. It must have by-laws —
286. Exceptions to the rules of earth and Heaven —
287. For it means not the good it doth nor ill.
288. ELISSA. It is wrong — it is unjust — unkind.
289. FESTUS.   It is.
290. But I am half mad and half dead with it.
291. I have loved thee till I can love nought beside.
292. My heart is drenched with love as with a cloud.
293. I have too much of life that I scarce can live.

294. I hate all things but thee — shun men, like snakes —
295. Women, like pits. To me thou art all woman —
296. All life — all love and more than all my kind.
297. I love thee more than I shall love and look for
298. Death, if he takes thee from me. But who dreams
299. Of death and thee together!
300. ELISSA.   I do oft:
301. And as oft wish dreams would, for once, come true.
302. The best of all things are dreams realised.
303. FESTUS. Dreams such as gods may dream thy soul possess.
304. For ever in the Hadean Eden — Death:
305. But bless thy lover with reality!
306. Then, thou shalt live for ever, and with me.
307. I have gone round the compass of all life.
308. And can find nought worthy of thee. I but feel,
309. That were I — as I ought to be — a god,
310. I would just sacrifice the sun to thee,
311. In bright and burning honour of thy love.
312. Miracles are not miracles with gods.
313. ELISSA. Dearer thou canst not be to me, unless
314. I die in telling how dear.
315. FESTUS.   My Elissa!
316. I — I am bewildered: open but thine arms!
317. And make me happy and all wise of thee.
318. My soul is stung with thy beauty to the quick.
319. Oh! but thou art too good, or else too bad:
320. Be colder or be warmer!
321. ELISSA.   Leave, me!
322. FESTUS.   Well;
323. It is most cruel — first, to light the heart
324. With love completely — boundlessly; and then
325. Moonlike, slowly to edge aside, and leave
326. One only little line of all so bright,
327. Once — teach and unteach — nay, to use more arts
328. Than would outdo the devil of his throne,
329. To make us ignorant of all we know: —
330. To take the heart to pieces carefully —
331. For it is love alone can build the heart —
332. To root the tree up neath whose shade we have lived,
333. And give us back a sliver. Let it die!
334. ELISSA.   Hark! he is coming.
335. FESTUS. No! He cannot come;

336. For I have driven an oath into his heart,
337. And I have hung a curse about his neck
338. Might sink the prince of air into the centre.
339. ELISSA. All I have done, I have done to save ourselves.
340. FESTUS. Then let us perish! But unless we sin
341. We cannot perish. Have! Have! cries a voice,
342. As of a crowd, within me. I would do aught
343. To throw this dark desire which wrestles with me.
344. It answers not to hold it at arms-length:
345. It must be hurled, dashed, trampled down. — I can't.
346. Lady! how long am I to love thee thus?
347. Never did angel love its Heaven — nor God
348. Man, as I thee.
349. ELISSA.   I feared how it would end.
350. Can nothing less than sinning sate the soul?
351. Can nothing but perdition serve to nest
352. Our hearts, after so sweet a flight of love?
353. FESTUS. The might and truth of hearts is never shewn
354. But in loving those whom we ought not to love —
355. Or cannot have. The wrong, the suffering is
356. Its own reward.
357. ELISSA.   Let me not wrong thee, Festus.
358. Let me not think I have thought too well of thee.
359. Be as thou wast. What will become of us?
360. FESTUS. Be mine! be me! be aught but so far from me!
361. Give me thyself! It is not enough for me,
362. That I have gazed and doted on thee till
363. Mine eye is dazzled and my brain is dizzied:
364. Thou must exhaust all senses; not enough
365. That in long dreams my soul hath spread itself
366. Like water over every living line
367. Of this sweet make, dreaming thou wast all lips;
368. Nor that it now sinks in the face of thee,
369. Like a sea-sunset, hot and tired with the long,
370. Long day of love; — it is not enough. I must
371. Have more — have all! For I have sworn to fill
372. Mine arms with bliss — thus — thus — thus!
373. ELISSA.   Festus!
374. LUCIFER.   Friend!
375. Did ye not know me? It was I sang.
376. ELISSA.   It was he!
377. FESTUS.   Thou —

378. LUCIFER. Hush! thou art not to utter what
379. I am. Bethink thee; it was our covenant.
380. I said that I would see thee once again.
381. ELISSA. Thou didst; and I must thank thee.
382. LUCIFER.   Hear me now!
383. Thou knowest well what once I was to thee:
384. One who for love of one I loved — for thee —
385. Would have done or borne the sins of all the world;
386. Who did thy bidding at thy lightest look;
387. And had it been to have snatched an angel's crown
388. Off her bright brow as she sat singing, throned,
389. I would have cut these heartstrings that tie down,
390. And let my soul have sailed to Heaven, and done it —
391. Spite of the thunder and the sacrilege,
392. And laid it at thy feet. I loved thee, lady!
393. I am one whose love was greater than the world's,
394. And might have vied with God's; a boundless ring,
395. All pressing on one point — that point thy heart.
396. And now — but shall I call on my revenge? —
397. It is at hand in armies. Thou art a woman;
398. And that is saying the best and worst of thee.
399. I know that vengeance is the part of God:
400. And can make myself almighty for the moment.
401. For what? For nothing. Thou art utter nothing.
402. Thus it was always with me when with thee;
403. And I forget my purpose and my wrongs,
404. In looking and in loving. But I hate thee.
405. To say that thou didst love me! Curse the air
406. That bore the sound to me! Forgive me, God!
407. If I blaspheme, it is not at Thee, but her.
408. I'd not believe her were she saved in Heaven!
409. There is no blasphemy in love but doubt;
410. No sin, but to deceive.
411. FESTUS.   Then is she sinless.
412. She loved thee first — then me. What wouldst thou more?
413. Thy heart's embrace, though close, was snake-like cold;
414. And mine was warm, and what is more, was welcome.
415. LUCIFER. Patience! I spake not, cared not, thought not, of thee. —
416. Now I forgive thy having loved another;
417. And I forgive — but never mind it now;

418. I have forgiven so much, there is nothing left
419. To make more words about; but, for the future,
420. I will as soon attempt to entice a star
421. To perch upon my finger, or the wind
422. To follow me like a dog, as think to keep
423. A woman's heart again. Answer me not!
424. Let me say what I have to say and go.
425. Thou art all will and passion; that is thine
426. Excuse and condemnation.
427. ELISSA.   While that will
428. Was love to thee, I saw no harm, nor thou.
429. And if my heart hath gained, it was not I
430. Who put it on — nor could it help going wrong.
431. LUCIFER. Oh! I have heard, what rather than words, have heard,
432. I would have stopped mine ears with thunder:
433. That have gone singing through my soul, like arrows
434. Through the air.
435. ELISSA.   I never will defend myself.
436. For I despise defence like accusation —
437. And now look down on them and thee together.
438. LUCIFER. Now let us part, or I shall die of wrath.
439. Be my estrangement perfect as my love!
440. ELISSA.   Part then!
441. LUCIFER. Thank God it is for eternity!
442. ELISSA.   I do. Away.
443. LUCIFER.   Festus! I wait for thee.
444. FESTUS. Come, thou art not the first deceived in love;
445. Yet love is not so much love as a dream,
446. Which hath, it seems, like guerdon with the thing —
447. The staring madness when we wake and find
448. That what we have loved, must love, is not that
449. We meant to love. Perhaps I profited
450. Too much by thy good lessons. Go! I follow.
451. LUCIFER. [going]. Now therefore would I wager, and I might,
452. The great archangel's trump to a dog-whistle,
453. That whatsoever happens, worse ensues.
454. FESTUS. Forgive me, love, for having brought this on thee.
455. ELISSA. The love which giveth all, forgiveth aught.
456. And thou art more to me than earth, or Heaven;

457. They have but given life: thou gavest me love,
458. The lord of life — thou, my life! love, and lord!
459. Take me again! my kindest — dearest — best!
460. Him who hath gone I never loved like thee.
461. There was a desolation in his eye
462. I could not brook to look on; for it seemed
463. As though it ate the light out of mine own.
464. I think that thou dost love me.
465. FESTUS.   And I think,
466. For perfect love there should be but one god —
467. One worshipper.
468. ELISSA.   We know the gods of old
469. Worshipped each other — equal deities.
470. For the sweet poets surely spake the truth
471. About the gods; they dare not speak but truth.
472. FESTUS. Who but thyself would speak of poetry,
473. While thou art by? who art the very breathing
474. Beauty which bards may seek ideally.
475. And dost thou, then, believe the gods of old —
476. Those toys and playthings of an infant world?
477. ELISSA. If I do not believe, I do not scorn them.
478. Nay, I could mourn for them and pray for them.
479. I can scorn nothing which a nation's heart
480. Hath held, for ages, holy: for the heart
481. Is alike holy in its strength and weakness:
482. It ought not to be jested with, nor scorned.
483. All things, to me, are sacred that have been.
484. And, though earth, like a river, streaked with blood,
485. Which tells a long and silent tale of death,
486. May blush her history and hide her eyes,
487. The past is sacred — it is God's: not ours.
488. Let her and us do better if we can.
489. FESTUS. There are whole veins of diamonds in thine eyes,
490. Might furnish crowns for all the Queens of earth.
491. Oh! I could sooner set a price on the sun,
492. My love, than on thy lightest look. Look on me!
493. Speak! if it only be to say thou wilt not.
494. Look! I would rather look on thee one minute,
495. Than paradise for a whole day — such days
496. As are in Heaven. I love thee more and more.
497. ELISSA. To love, and say we love — to suck the sting

498. Out of the heart, and put its poison on
499. The tongue.
500. FESTUS.   Yet it is luxury to feel
501. Inflamed — to glow within ourselves, like fire-opals.
502. Now, stay thy pretty little tuneful tongue,
503. Nor silver o'er thy syllables! They will not
504. Pass. No, not one more word! I must away;
505. I have staid too long, already, for my word.
506. ELISSA. I cannot part with thee: nay, sit again!
507. Parted from thee I feel like one half riven,
508. And my soul acheth to spring to — as thus!
509. FESTUS. There! let me leave love! let me loose these arms.
510. Another time and, ah! well — never mind!
511. We shall be happier — I know we shall.
512. Thou hast been mine — thou art mine — and thou shalt be!
513. ELISSA. My life is one long loving thought of thee.
514. If any ask me what I do, I could say
515. I love, and that is all.
516. FESTUS.   It is enough.
517. One kiss! another! one more — there! farewell! [*goes.*]
518. ELISSA. And he is gone! and the world seems gone with
      him.
519. Shine on, ye Heavens! why can ye not impart
520. Light to my heart? Have ye no feeling in ye?
521. Why are ye bright when I am so unhappy?
522. But oh! I would not change my woes for thrice
523. The bliss of others, since they are for thee, love.
524. Our very wretchedness grows dear to us
525. When suffering for one we love. Sweet stars!
526. I cannot look upon your loveliness
527. Without sadness, for ye are too beautiful;
528. And beauty makes unhappy: so men say.
529. Ye stars! it is true — we read our fate in ye.
530. Bright through all ages, are ye not happy there?
531. With years, many as your light-rays are ye not
532. Immortal? Space-pervading, oh! ye must be,
533. Spirit-like, infinite. All-being God!
534. Who art in all things, and in whom all are! —
535. And it is thus we worship Thee the most;
536. When heart to heart with one we love we are gods; —
537. Let us believe that if Thou gavest earth

538. For our bodies, then the stars were for our souls;
539. For perfect beauty and unbounded love!
540. Let us believe they look upon us here
541. As their inheritors, and save themselves
542. For us, as we for Thee, and Thou for all!

SCENE 27

[*Garden and bower by the sea*]
[*ELISSA and LUCIFER*]

1. ELISSA [*alone*]. Come, Festus, let me think on thee, my love!
2. And fold the thought of thee unto my soul,
3. Until it fills it, and is one with it.
4. Ah! these poor arms are far from where they should be;
5. And this heart farther still. Mine only love!
6. Why art thou thus so long away from me?
7. I have whispered it unto the southern wind
8. And charged it with my love: why should it not
9. Carry that love to thee as air bears light?
10. And thou hast said I was all light to thee.
11. The stars grow bright together, and for aye,
12. Lover-like, watch each other; and though apart,
13. Like us, they fill each other's eyes with love
14. And beauty: and mine only fill with tears.
15. Oh! life is less than nothing without love!
16. And what is love without the embrace of love?
17. I would give worlds for one more ere I die.
18. Festus! come to me. I do think I am dying.
19. Let me bequeath my life to thee, that so,
20. In doubling thine, I may live alway with thee.
21. I know that I am dying. It is my heart
22. Which makes me live that kills me. But I want
23. To see him ere I do die. Oh! he will come!
24. He must know how I love him. It is long —

25.   Long since I saw him: I am ill with waiting.
26.   And I will fancy him coming to me now —
27.   Now he is thinking of me, loving me —
28.   He sees me — flies to me, half out of breath —
29.   His hand is on my arm — he looks on me —
30.   And puts my long locks backwards — God! Thy ban
31.   Lies upon waking dreams. To weep and sleep —
32.   Dream; — wake, and find one's only one hope false, —
33.   Is what we can bear, for we do endure it,
34.   And bear with Heaven still. Just one year ago,
35.   I watched that large bright star where it is now: —
36.   Time hath not touched its everlasting lightning,
37.   Nor dimmed the glorious glances of its eye —
38.   Nor passion clouded it — nor any star
39.   Eclipsed — it is the leader still of Heaven.
40.   And I who loved it then can love it now;
41.   But am not what I was, in one degree.
42.   Calm star! who was it named thee Lucifer,
43.   From him who drew the third of Heaven down with him?
44.   Oh! it was but the tradition of thy beauty!
45.   For if the sun hath one part, and the moon one,
46.   Thou hast the third part of the host of Heaven —
47.   Which is its power — which power is its beauty!
48.   LUCIFER. It was no tradition, lady, but of truth!
49.   ELISSA. I thought we parted last to meet no more.
50.   LUCIFER. It was so lady; but it is not so.
51.   ELISSA. Am I to leave, or thou, then?
52.   LUCIFER.   Neither, yet.
53.   I mean that thou should'st fear me and obey.
54.   ELISSA. And who art thou that I should fear and serve?
55.   LUCIFER. I am the morning and the evening star.
56.   The star thou lovest and thy lover too;
57.   I am that star! as once before I told thee,
58.   Though thou wouldst not believe me, but I am
59.   A spirit, and a star — a power — an ill
60.   Which doth outbalance being. Look at me!
61.   Am I not more than mortal in my form?
62.   Millions of years have circled round my brow
63.   Like worlds upon their centres; — still I live;
64.   And age but presses with a halo's weight.
65.   This single arm hath dashed the light of Heaven;
66.   This one hand dragged the angels from their thrones: —

67. Am I not worthy to have loved thee, lady?
68. Thou mortal model of all Heavenliness!
69. And yet I have abandoned all these spoils,
70. Cowered my powers, and becalmed my course,
71. And stooped from the high destruction of the skies
72. For thee, and for the youth who loveth thee —
73. And is lost with ye: ye are both, both — lost!
74. Thou hast but served the purpose of the Fiend.
75. And thou art but the vessel of the sin
76. Whose poison hath made drunk a soul to death;
77. And he hath drunk; and thou art useless now.
78. And it is for this I come; to bid thee die!
79. ELISSA. I said that I was dying. God is good.
80. The Heavens grow darker as they grow the purer:
81. And both, as we do near them; so, near death,
82. The soul grows darker and diviner, hourly.
83. Could I love less I should be happier!
84. But it is always to that mad extreme,
85. That death alone appears the fitting finish
86. To bliss like that my spirit presses for.
87. LUCIFER. Thy death shall be as gentle as thy life.
88. I will not hurt thee, for I loved thee once.
89. And thy sweet love, upon my burning breast
90. Fell like a snowflake on a fevered lip.
91. Thy soul shall pass out of thee like a dream.
92. One moment more, and thou shalt wake in Heaven!
93. ELISSA. I ever thought thee to be more than mortal.
94. And if thou art thus mighty, grant me this! —
95. Since now we love no more — as friend to friend —
96. Bring him I love, one moment, ere I die.
97. LUCIFER. Thou judgest well; I am all but almighty.
98. And I have stretched my strength unto its limits
99. To satisfy the heart of him who loves thee:
100. In proof whereof, did I not give up thee,
101. Because he loved thee? I have given him all things
102. Body or spirit could desire or have.
103. And even, at this moment, now he reigns
104. King of the sun, and monarch of the seven
105. Orbs that surround him — leaving earth alone—
106. The earth is in good keeping as it is.
107. I know that he is hasting hither now;
108. But may not see thee living.

109. ELISSA.   It is not thou
110. Who takest life: it is God, whose I shall be! —
111. And his, with God, whom here my heart deifies.
112. I glory in his power as in his love.
113. But I will, will see him while I am alive.
114. I hear him — he is come — it is he! it is he!
115. LUCIFER. Die! thou shalt never look on him again.
116. ELISSA. My love! haste, Festus! I am dying —
117. LUCIFER.   Dead!
118. A word could kill her. She hath gone to Heaven.
119. FESTUS. Fiend! what is this? Elissa — she is not dead.
120. LUCIFER. She is. I bade her die, as I had reason.
121. FESTUS. Now do I hate thee and renounce for ever! —
122. Abhor thee — go!
123. LUCIFER.   Who seeks the other first?
124. I am gone.
125. FESTUS.   Away, Fiend! Leave me! My Elissa!

SCENE 28

[*A Library and Balcony — A Summer Night*]

1. FESTUS. [*alone*]. The last high upward slant of sun on the
   trees,
2. Like a dead soldier's sword upon his pall,
3. Seems to console earth for the glory gone.
4. Oh! I could weep to see the day die thus;
5. The death-bed of a day, how beautiful!
6. Linger, ye clouds, one moment longer there;
7. Fan it to slumber with your golden wings!
8. Like pious prayers ye seem to soothe its end.
9. It will wake no more till the all-revealing day;
10. When, like a drop of water, greatened bright
11. Into a shadow, it shall shew itself
12. With all its little tyrannous things and deeds,

13.   Unhomed and clear. The day hath gone to God, —
14.   Straight, like an infant's spirit, or a mocked
15.   And mourning messenger of grace to man.
16.   Would it had taken me too on its wing!
17.   My end is nigh. Would I might die outright!
18.   And slip the coil without waiting its unwind.
19.   Who that hath lain lonely on a high hill,
20.   In the imperious silence of full noon,
21.   With nothing but the dear dark sky about him,
22.   Like God's hand laid upon the head of earth —
23.   But hath expected that some natural spirit
24.   Should start out of the universal air —
25.   And gathering his cloudy robe around him,
26.   As one in act to teach mysterious things,
27.   Explain that he must die? — that having got
28.   As high as earth can lift him up — as far
29.   Above that thing, the world, as flesh can mount —
30.   Over the tyrant wind, and the clouded lightning,
31.   And the round rainbow — and that having gained
32.   A loftier and a more mysterious beauty
33.   Of feeling — something like a starry darkness
34.   Seizing the soul — say he must die — and vanish?
35.   Who hath not, at such moments, felt as now
36.   I feel, that to be happy we must die?
37.   And here I rest — above the world and its ways;
38.   The wind, opinion — and the rainbow, beauty —
39.   And the thunder, superstition — I am free
40.   Of all: — save death, what want I to be happy?
41.   And shall I leave no trace, then, of my life?
42.   The soul begetteth shadows of itself
43.   Which do outlive their author: and are more
44.   Substantial than all nature, and the red
45.   Realities of flesh and blood, as echo
46.   Is longer, louder, further than the voice
47.   Of man can thunder, or his ear report.
48.   And oft the world hath Deified its echoes.
49.   A year! — and who shall find them? Can it be
50.   The mind's works have been deathless — not the mind?
51.   Or will the world's immortals die with me? —
52.   The sages, and the heroes, and the bards, —
53.   Whose verse set to the thunder of the seas,
54.   Seems as immortal as their ceaseless music!

55. O God! I fain would deem Thou livest not:
56. And that this world hath sprung up from chance seed,
57. Unknown to thee; and is not reckoned on.
58. Hell solves all doubts. — Come to me, Lucifer!
59. LUCIFER. Lo! I am here: and ever prompt
60. When called for.
61. How speed thy general pleasures?
62. FESTUS.   Bravely! joys
63. Are bubble-like — what makes them, bursts them too.
64. And like the milky way, there! dim with stars,
65. The soul that numbers most will shine the less.
66. LUCIFER. No matter — mind it not!
67. FESTUS. Yet, joys of earth!
68. That ye should ruin spirits is too hard.
69. Who can avoid ye? who can say ye nay?
70. Or take his eyes from off ye? who so chaste?
71. LUCIFER. They have well-nigh unimmortalized myself.
72. FESTUS. Yet have they nought to sate the pining spirit
73. Which doth enamour immortality.
74. No! they are all base, impure, ruinous —
75. The harlots of the heart. Forgive me, God!
76. I am getting too forlorn to live — too waste.
77. Aught that I can or do love, shoots by me,
78. Like a train upon an iron road. And yet
79. I need not now reproach mine arm or aims;
80. For I have winged each pleasure as it flew,
81. How swift or high soever in its flight.
82. We cannot live alone. The heart must have
83. A prop without, or it will fall and break.
84. But nature's common joys are common cheats.
85. As he who sails southwards, beholds, each night,
86. New constellations rise all clear, and fair;
87. So, o'er the waters of the world, as we
88. Reach the mid zone of life, or go beyond,
89. Beauty and bounty still beset our course;
90. New beauties wait upon us every where;
91. New lights enlighten and new worlds attract.
92. But I have seen and I have done with all.
93. Friendship hath passed me like a ship at sea;
94. And I have seen no more of it. I had
95. A friend with whom, in boyhood, I was wont
96. To learn, think, laugh, weep, strive, and love, together;

 97. For we were always rivals in all things —
 98. Together up high springy hills, to trace
 99. A runnel to its birthplace — to pursue
100. A river — to search, haunt old ruined towers,
101. And muse in them — to scale the cloud-clad hills
102. While thunders murmured in our very ear;
103. To leap the lair of the live cataract,
104. And pray its foaming pardon for the insult;
105. To dare the broken tree-bridge across the stream;
106. To crouch behind the broad white waterfall,
107. Tongue of the glen, like to a hidden thought —
108. Dazzled, and deafened, yet the more delighted;
109. To reach the rock which makes the fall and pool;
110. There to feel safe, or not to care if not;
111. To fling the free foot over my native hills,
112. Which seemed to breathe the bracing breeze we loved
113. The more it lifted up our loosened locks,
114. That nought might be between us and the skies;
115. Or, hand in hand, leap, laughing, with closed eyes,
116. In Trent's death-loving deeps;[1] yet was she kind
117. Ever to us; and bare us buoyant up.
118. And followed our young strokes, and cheered us on —
119. Even as an elder sister bending above
120. A child, to teach it how to order its feet —
121. As quick we dashed, in reckless rivalry,
122. To reach, perchance, some long green floating flag —
123. Just when the Sun's hot lip first touched the stream,
124. Reddening to be so kissed; and we rejoiced,
125. As breasting it on we went over depth and death,
126. Strong in the naked strife of elements,
127. Toying with danger in as little fear
128. As with a maiden's ringlets. And oft, at night,
129. Bewildered and bewitched by favourite stars,
130. We would breathe ourselves amid unfooted snows,
131. For there is poetry where aught is pure;
132. Or over the still dark heath, leap along, like harts,
133. Through the broad moonlight; for we felt where'er
134. We leapt the golden gorse, or lowly ling,

---

1. The River Trent, third longest river in the United Kingdom, known for flooding and deaths.

135. We could not be from home. — That friend is gone.
136. There's the whole universe before our souls.
137. Where shall we meet next? Shall we meet again?
138. Oh! might it be in some far happy world,
139. That I might light upon his lonely soul,
140. Hard by some broad blue stream, where high the hills,
141. Wood-bearded, sweep to its brink — musing, as wont,
142. With love-like sadness, upon sacred things;
143. For much in youth we loved and mused on them.
144. To say what ought to be to human wills,
145. And measure mortals sternly; to explore
146. The bearings of men's duties and desires;
147. To note the nature and the laws of mind;
148. To balance good with evil; and compare
149. The nature and necessity of each;
150. To long to see the ends and end of things;
151. Or, if no end there be, the endless, then,
152. As suns look into space; these were our joys —
153. Our hopes — our meditations — our attempts.
154. And, if I have enjoyed more love than others,
155. It is but superior suffering, and is more
156. Than balanced by the loss of one we love.
157. And love, itself, hath passed. One fond fair girl
158. Remains; one only, and she loves me still.
159. But it is not love I feel: it is pure kindness.
160. How shall I find another like my last?
161. The golden and the gorgeous loveliness —
162. A sunset beauty! Ah! I saw it set.
163. My heart, alas I set with it. I have drained
164. Life of all love, as doth an iron rod
165. The Heavens of lightning; I have done with it,
166. And all its waking woes, and dreamed-of joys.
167. No more shall beauty star the air I live in;
168. And no more will I wake at dead of night,
169. And hearken to the roaring of the wind,
170. As though it came to carry one away —
171. Claiming for sin. Ah! I am lost forever.
172. To earn the world's delights by equal sins.
173. Seems the great aim of life — the aim succeeds.
174. Here it is madness, and perdition there.
175. And, but for thee, I had renounced these joys —
176. These cursed joys my soul now writhes among,

177. Like to a half-crushed reptile on a rose: —
178. Ay, but for thee, I might have now been happy!
179. LUCIFER. Why charge, why wrong me thus?
180. When first I knew thee,
181. I deemed it thine ambition to be damned.
182. Thine every thought, almost, had gone from good,
183. As far as finite is from infinite;
184. And then thou wast as near to me as now.
185. Thou hadst declined in worship, and in wish
186. To please thy God; nor wouldst thou e'er repent.
187. What more need I to justify attempt?
188. Have I shrunk back from granting aught I promised?
189. Thy love of knowledge — is that satisfied?
190. FESTUS. It is. Yet knowledge is a doubtful boon —
191. Root of all good and fruit of all that's bad.
192. I have caused[2] face to face with elements,
193. Yea, learned the luminous language of the skies,
194. And the angelic kindred of high Heaven;
195. The bright articulations of all spheres, —
196. Impetuous hearted orbs, and mountain-maned,
197. Aye circling onwards breathless through the air —
198. And wisest stars which speak themselves in signs
199. Too sacred to be explicable here;
200. And now what better am I? — nearer God?
201. When the void finds a voice mine answer know.
202. LUCIFER. What better or what worse thou canst not tell.
203. For, good and evil! Wherein differ they?
204. Do they not both accrue from the same cause, —
205. As ripeness and decay? Light, light alone
206. Of hues, how contrary soever, is
207. The common cause.
208. FESTUS. Distracter of God's truth!
209. Shall not His word suffice the living world?
210. LUCIFER. Thou canst not have lacked joys?
211. FESTUS.   We seek them oft
212. Among our own delusions, pains and follies.
213. LUCIFER. Hath not care perished from thy heart, as did
214. The viper flung from the apostle's hand?

---

2. Caused: From the French *causer*: to speak familiarly, to chat (*OED*). *Festus* is the first known English use.

215. FESTUS. Ay; and, like that, all care will cease in fire;
216. Dark wretched thoughts like ice-isles in a stream,
217. Choke up my mind and clash; — and to no end.
218. In spite of all we suffer and enjoy,
219. There comes this question, over and over again,
220. Driven into the brain as a pile is driven —
221. What shall become of us hereafter? what
222. Is it we shall do? how feel, how be?
223. And there are times when burning memory flows
224. In on the mind, that saving it would slay,
225. As did the lava-floods which choked of joys
226. The Cyclopean[3] cities — brimming up
227. Brasslike their mighty moulds. And shall the past
228. Thus ruinously perfect aye remain;
229. Or present, past, and coming, all be one,
230. In natural mystery? Like snow, which lies
231. Down-wreathed round the lips of some black pit,
232. Thoughts which obscure the truth accumulate,
233. And those which solve it in it lose themselves;
234. And there is no true knowledge till descent,
235. Nor then till after. What shall make the truth
236. Visible? Through the smoky glass of sense
237. The blessed sun would never know himself.
238. All truth is one. All error is alike.
239. The shadow of a mountain hath no more
240. Substance than hath a dead and moss-mailed pine's;
241. But only more gigantic impotence.
242. LUCIFER. Hast thou not had thine every quest?
243. FESTUS.   Save one.
244. LUCIFER. I proffer now the power which thou dost long for.
245. Say but the word, and thou shalt press a throne
246. But less than mine — the scarcely less than God's; —
247. A throne, at which earth's puny potentates
248. May sue for slavedoms — and be satisfied.
249. FESTUS. I have had enough of the infinities:
250. I am moderate now. I will have the throne of earth.
251. LUCIFER. Thou shalt. Yet, mind! — with that, the world
     must end.

---

3. Cyclopean: Referring to an ancient masonry style featuring massive, irregular blocks
   of stone.

252. FESTUS. I can survive.
253. LUCIFER. Nay, die with it must thou.
254. FESTUS. Why should I die? I am egg-full of life:
255. And life's as serious a thing as death.
256. The world is in its first young quarter yet;
257. I dare not, cannot credit it shall die.
258. I will not have it, then.
259. LUCIFER.   It matters not;
260. I know thou wilt never have ease at heart
261. Until thou hast they soul's whole, full desire;
262. Whenever that may happen, all is done.
263. FESTUS. Well, then — be it now! I live but for myself —
264. The whole world but for me. Friends, loves, and all
265. I sought, abandon me. It is time to die.
266. I am yet young; yet have I been deserted,
267. And wronged, by those whom most I have loved and served.
268. Sun, moon, and stars! may they all fall on me,
269. When next I trust another — man or woman.
270. Earth rivals Hell too often, at the best.
271. All hearts are stronger for the being hollow,
272. And that was why mine was no match for theirs.
273. The pith is out of it now. — Lord of the world!
274. It will not directly perish?
275. LUCIFER. Not, perhaps. —
276. Thou wilt have all fame, while thou livest, now.
277. FESTUS. I care not: fame is folly; for it is, sure,
278. Far more to be well known of God than man.
279. With all my sins I feel that I am God's.
280. LUCIFER. Farewell, then, for a time!
281. FESTUS.   I am alone. —
282. Alone? He clings around me like the clouds
283. Upon a hill. When will the clouds roll off?
284. When will sun visit me? Oh! Thou great God!
285. In whose right hand the elements are atoms —
286. In whose eye, light and darkness but a wink —
287. Who, in Thine anger, like a blast of cold,
288. Dost make the mountains shake like chattering teeth —
289. Have mercy! Pity me! For it is Thou
290. Who hast fixed me to this test. Wilt Thou not save?
291. Forgive me, Father! but I long to die: —
292. I long to live to Thee, a pure, free mind.
293. Take again, God! and thou, fair Earth, the form

294. And spirit which, at first, ye lent me.
295. Such as they were, I have used them. Let them part.
296. I weary of this world; and, like the dove,
297. Urged o'er life's barren flood, sweep, tired, back
298. To thee who sent'st me forth. Bear with me, God!
299. I am not worthy of thy wrath, nor love! —
300. Oh! that the things which have been were not now
301. In memory's resurrection! But the past
302. Bears in her arms the present and the future;
303. And what can perish while perdition is?
304. From the hot, angry, crowding courts of doubt
305. Within the breast, it is sweet to escape, and soothe
306. The soul in looking upon natural beauty.
307. Oh! earth, like man her son, is half divine.
308. There is not a leaf within this quiet spot,
309. But which I seem to know; should miss, if gone.
310. I could run over its features, hour by hour.
311. The quaintly figured beds — the various flowers —
312. The mazy paths all cunningly converged —
313. The black yew hedge, like a beleaguering host,
314. Round some fair garden province — here and there,
315. The cloud-like laurel clumps sleep, soft and fast,
316. Pillowed by their own shadows — and beyond,
317. The ripe and ruddy fruitage — the sharp furs'
318. Fringe, like an eyelash, on the faint-blue west —
319. The white owl, wheeling from the grey old church, —
320. Its age-peeled pinnacles, and tufted top —
321. The oaks, which spread their broad arms in the blast,
322. And bid storms come, and welcome; there they stand,
323. To whom a summer passes like a smile: —
324. And the proud peacock towers himself there, and screams,
325. Ruffling the imperial purples of his neck.
326. O'er all, the giant poplars, which maintain
327. Equality with clouds half way up Heaven;
328. Which whisper with the winds none else can see,
329. And bow to angels as they wing by them; —
330. The lonely, bowery, woodland view before —
331. And, making all more beautiful, thou, sweet moon,
332. Leading slow pomp, as triumphing o'er Heaven!
333. High riding in thy loveless, deathless brightness,
334. And in thy cold, unconquerable beauty,
335. As though there were nothing worthy in the world

336. Even to lie below thee, face to God.
337. And Night, in her own name, and God's again,
338. Hath dipped the earth in dew; — and there she lies,
339. Even like a heart all trembling with delight,
340. Till passion murder power to speak — so mute.
341. Young maiden moon! just looming into light —
342. I would that aspect never might be changed;
343. Nor that fine form, so spirit-like, be spoiled
344. With fuller light. Oh! keep that brilliant shape;
345. Keep the delicious honour of thy youth,
346. Sweet sister of the sun, more beauteous thou
347. Than he sublime. Shine on, nor dread decay.
348. It may take meaner things; but thy bright look,
349. Smiling away an immortality,
350. Assures it us — nay, it seems, half, to give.
351. Earth may decease. God will not part with thee,
352. Fair ark of light, and every blessedness!
353. Yes, earth, this earth, may foul the face of life,
354. Like some swart[4] mole on beauty's breast — or dead,
355. Stiff, mangled reptile, some clear well — while thou
356. Shalt shine, aye brilliant, on creation's corse,
357. Like to a diamond on a dead man's hand;
358. Whence God shall pluck thee to His breast, or bid
359. Beam 'mid His lightning locks. What are earth's joys
360. To watching thee, tending thy bright flock over
361. The fields of Heaven? Thy light misleadeth not,
362. Though eyes which image Heaven oft lure to Hell; —
363. Thy smile betrayeth not — though sweet as that
364. Which wins and damns. Mother, and maid of light!
365. That, like a God, redeems the world to Heaven —
366. Making us one with thee, and with the sun,
367. And with the stars in glory — lovely moon!
368. I am immortal as thyself; and we
369. Shall look upon each other yet, in Heaven,
370. Often — but never, never more on earth.
371. Am I to die so soon? This death — the thought
372. Comes on my heart as through a burning glass.
373. I cannot bend mine eyes to earth, but thence
374. It riseth, spectre-like, to mock — nor towards

4. Swart: Malignant, ugly. *Archaic.*

375. The west, where sunset is, whose long bright pomp
376. Makes men in love with change — but there it lowers
377. Eve's last, still lingering, darkening, cloud; and on
378. The escutcheon of the morn, it is there — it is there!
379. But fears will come upon the bravest mind,
380. Like the white moon upon the crimson west.
381. I have attractions for all miseries:
382. And every course of thought, within my heart,
383. Leaves a new layer of woe. But it must end.
384. It will all be one, hereafter. Let it be!
385. My bosom, like the grave, holds all quenched passions.
386. It is not that I have not found what I sought —
387. But, that the world — tush! I shall see it die.
388. I hate, and shall outlive the hypocrite.
389. Stealthily, slowly, like the polar sun,
390. Who peeps by fits above the air-walled world —
391. The heavenly fief, he knows and feels his own,
392. My heart o'erlooks the Paradise of life
393. Which it hath lost, in cold, reluctant joy.
394. I live and see all beauteous things about me,
395. But feel no nature prompting from within
396. To meet and profit by them. I am like
397. That fabled forest of the Apennine,
398. Which leafless lives; whereto the spring's bright showers,
399. Summer's heat breathless, autumn's fruitful juice,
400. Nothing avail; — nor winter's killing cold.
401. Yet have I done, said, thought, in time now past,
402. What, rather than remember, I would die,
403. Or do again. It is the thinking on't,
404. And the repentance, maddens. I have thought
405. Upon such things so long and grievously,
406. My lips have grown like to a cliff-chafed sea,
407. Pale with a tidal passion; and my soul,
408. Once high and bright and self-sustained as Heaven,
409. Unsettled now for life or death, feels like
410. The grey gull balanced on her bowlike wings,
411. Between two black waves seeking where to dive.
412. Long we live, thinking nothing of our fate,
413. For in the morn of life we mark it not —
414. It falls behind; but as our day goes down
415. We catch it lengthening with a giant's stride,
416. And ushering us unto the feet of night.

417. Dark thoughts, like spots upon the sun, revolve
418. In troops for days together round my soul,
419. Disfiguring and dimming. Death! oh death!
420. The past, the present, and the future, like
421. The dog three-headed, by the gates of woe
422. Sitting, seem ready to devour me each.
423. I dare not look on them. I dare not think.
424. The very best deeds I have ever done
425. Seem worthy reprobation, have to be
426. Repented of. But have I done aught good?
427. Oh that my soul were calmer! Grant me, God!
428. Thy peace; that added, I can smile and die.
429. Thy Spirit only is reality:
430. All things beside are folly, falsehood, shame.

SCENE 29

[*Elsewhere*]

1. FESTUS. [*alone.*] I feel as if I could devour the days
2. Till the time came when I shall gain mine end;
3. God shall have made me ruler, and all worlds
4. Signed the sublime recognizance. Till then, —
5. Even as a boat lies rocking on the beach,
6. Waiting the one white wave to float it free,
7. Wait I the great event; — too great it seems.
8. Yet, Lord, thou knowest that the power I seek
9. Is but for others' good and Thine own glory,
10. And the desire for it inspired by Thee.
11. So use me as I use it. Thou hast passed
12. Thy word that such I shall enjoy, and then
13. My mission is accomplished in this world.
14. I go unto another, where all souls
15. Begin again, or take up life from where
16. Death broke it at. I cannot think there will be

17. Like disproportion there between our powers
18. And will, as here; if not, I shall be happy.
19. I feel no bounds. I cannot think but thought
20. On thought springs up, illimitably, round,
21. As a great forest sows itself; but here
22. There is nor ground nor light enough to live.
23. Could I, I would be every where at once,
24. Like the sea, for I feel as if I could
25. Spread out my spirit o'er the endless world,
26. And act at all points: — I am bound to one.
27. I must be here, and there, and everywhere,
28. Or I am nowhere. Sense, flesh, feeling, fail
29. Before the feet of the imperious mind.
30. To which they are but as the dust she treads, —
31. Windlike treads o'er, uplifts and leaves behind.
32. How mind will act with body glorified
33. And spiritualized, and senses fined,
34. And pointed brilliantwise, we know not. Here
35. Even, it may be wrong in us to deem
36. The senses degradations, otherwise
37. Than as fine steps, whereby the Queenly soul
38. Comes down from her bright throne to view the mass
39. She hath dominion over, and the things
40. Of her inheritance; and reascends,
41. With an indignant fiery purity,
42. Not to be touched, her seat. The visible world,
43. Whereby God maketh Nature known to us,
44. Is not derogatory to Himself
45. As the pure Spirit Infinite. A world
46. Is but, perhaps, a sense of God's, by which
47. He may explain His nature, and receive
48. Fit pleasure. But the hour is hard at hand,
49. When Time's grey wing shall winnow all away,
50. The atoms of the earth, the stars of Heaven;
51. When the created and Creator mind
52. Shall know each other, worlds and bodies both
53. Put off for aye; man and his Maker meet
54. Where all, who through the universe do well,
55. Embrace their heart's desire; what things they will,
56. And whom remember; live, too, where they list;
57. And with the beings they love best, and God,
58. Inherit and inhabit boundless bliss.

59. Hear me, all-favouring God! my latest prayer;
60. Thou unto whom all nations of the world
61. Lift up their hearts, like grass-blades to the sun;
62. Thou who hast all things and hast need of nought;
63. Thou who hast given me Earth and all it holds,
64. Give me, from out Thy garner stored with good,
65. Some sign, Lord! while I live, in proof to earth
66. My prayers are with Thee; that they rend the clouds,
67. And, rising through the sightless dark of space,
68. Reach to Thy central throne. Oh! let me feel,
69. What was my constant dream in my young years,
70. And is in all my better moments now, —
71. My hope, my faith, my nature's sum and end,
72. Oneness with Thee and Heaven. Lord! make me sure
73. My soul already is in unison
74. With the triumphant. Ah! I surely hear
75. The voices of the spirits of the saints,
76. And witnesses to the Redeeming Truth;
77. Not, as of old, in scanty scattered strains,
78. Breathed from the caves of earth and cells of cities, —
79. Nor as the voice of martyr choked with fire —
80. But in one solemn Heaven-pervading hymn
81. Of happiness impregnable, as when
82. From the bright walls of the Son's city they
83. Looked on the war of Hell, host upon host,
84. Foiled by God's single sword before their gates
85. Of perfect pearl; — nearer and nearer now!
86. This is the sign, O God! which Thou hast given,
87. And I will praise Thee through Eternity.
88. THE SAINTS FROM HEAVEN.
89.   Call all who love Thee, Lord, to Thee!
90.   Thou knowest how they long
91.   To leave these broken lays, and aid
92.   In Heaven's unceasing song;
93.   How they long, Lord, to go to Thee,
94.   And hail Thee with their eyes, —
95.   Thee in Thy blessedness, and all
96.   The nations of the skies;
97.   All who have loved Thee and done well,
98.   Of every age, creed, clime,
99.   The host of saved ones from the ends

100.   And all the worlds of time:
101.   The wise in matter and in mind,
102.   The soldier, sage, and priest,
103.   King, prophet, hero, saint, and bard,
104.   The greatest soul and least;
105.   The old and young and very babe,
106.   The maiden and the youth,
107.   All re-born angels of one age —
108.   The age of Heaven and truth;
109.   The rich, the poor, the good, the bad,
110.   Redeemed, alike, from sin;
111.   Lord! close the book of time, and let
112.   Eternity begin.
113. FESTUS.   Will ye away, ye blessed ones? To God
114. I then commend ye, and my soul with yours.
115. And midst the light in which ye live, oh! mind
116. Of all the sunless days and starless nights
117. Which myriads pass on earth, and pray for them!
118. Oh! pray for those who in the world's dark womb
119. Are bound, who know not yet their Father, God! —
120. Lord of all earth, all worlds, all Heaven! lift up
121. My spirit to Thy glory! Let me share
122. The comfort of Thy love, and while ordained
123. To the great task I have to go through, let
124. No more misgivings, fears, nor mortal doubts,
125. With the cold dew of darkness chill the soul
126. Which Thou hast hallowed with Thy love, and which,
127. Like molten gold within its mould, hath made
128. The thing that holds it precious; — or if, Lord!
129. For Thine own purpose, Thou wilt suffer such,
130. May they pass quick and perish tracelessly;
131. So, too, all thoughts of earth and pangs of death
132. May I o'ercome at last, and with Thy chosen,
133. Seraphs and saints, and all-possessing souls
134. Which minister unto the universe,
135. Enthroned in spirit and intensest bliss,
136. Succeed to Heaven for ever.
137. GUARDIAN ANGEL. Mortal, hear!
138. The soul once saved shall never cease from bliss,
139. Nor God lose that He buyeth with His blood.
140. She doth not sin. The deeds which look like sin,

141. The flesh and the false world, are all to her
142. Hallowed and glorified. The world is changed.
143. She hath a resurrection unto God
144. While in the flesh, before the final one,
145. And is with God. Her state shall never fail.
146. Even the molten granite which hath split
147. Mountains, and lieth now like curdled blood
148. In marble veins, shall flow again when comes
149. The heat which is to end all; when the air
150. Is as a ravening fire, and what at first
151. Produced, at last consumeth; but the soul
152. Redeemed is dear to God as His own throne,
153. And shall no sooner perish. Hearken, man!
154. Wilt thou distrust God? Doubt on doubt no more.
155. Prepare thee for the power and lot sublime
156. Whereto the Lord hath called thee. He hath heard
157. The prayers with which thou hast entreated Him,
158. And bids me tell thee, shrink not, doubt not. He
159. Will comfort and uphold thee at the end;
160. For after God the Chooser, God the Slain,
161. Cometh the God of Comfort to the heart,
162. Whose action and effect is ministrant
163. For ever after — consummating all.
164. FESTUS. I fear, I fear this miracle of Death
165. Is something terrible. But go to God,
166. Thou angel, and declare that I repent
167. Of all misdeeds; that but for His own grace
168. I should repent of my whole life; that on
169. That grace, which now hath sanctified the whole,
170. I trust for all the rest of it, and then
171. For ever; that I am prepared to act
172. And suffer as He bids, and in all things
173. To do His will rejoicing.
174. ANGEL.   It is done.
175. FESTUS. Oh! I repent me of a thousand sins,
176. In number as the breaths which I have breathed.
177. Am I forgiven?
178. ANGEL.   Child of God, thou art.
179. It is God prompts, inspires and answers prayer;
180. Not sin, nor yet repentance, which avails:
181. And none can truly worship but who have
182. The earnest of their glory from on high —

183. God's nature in them. The world cannot worship.
184. And whether the lip speak, or in inspired
185. Silence we clasp our hearts as a shut book
186. Of song unsung, the silence and the speech
187. Is each His; and as coming from and going
188. To Him, is worthy of Him and His Love.
189. Prayer is the spirit speaking truth to Truth;
190. The expiration of the thing inspired.
191. I go. Thy God is with thee. We shall meet
192. Again in Heaven, no more to part.
193. FESTUS. Thou art gone!
194. 'T is sweet to feel we are encircled here
195. By breath of angels as the stars by Heaven;
196. And the soul's own relations, all divine,
197. As kind as even those of blood; — and thus
198. While friends and kin, like Saturn's double rings,
199. Cheer us along our orbit, we may feel
200. We are not lone in life, but that earth's part
201. Of Heaven and all things. Praise we, therefore, God!
202. O all ye angels, pray and praise with us! —

FESTUS THRONED OVER THE EARTH

SCENE 30

[A Gathering of Kings and Peoples]

1. FESTUS. [*throned*] Princes and Peoples! Powers once, of
    earth!
2. It suits not that I point to ye the path
3. By which I reached this sole supreme domain —
4. This mountain of all mortal might. Enough,
5. That I am monarch of the world — the world.
6. Let all acknowledge loyally my laws,
7. And love me as I them love! It will be best.
8. No rise against me can stand. I rule of God;
9. And am God's sceptre here. Think not the world
10. Is greater than my might — less than my love —
11. Or that it stretcheth further than mine arm!
12. Kings! ye are Kings no longer. Cast your crowns
13. Here — for my footstool. Every power is mine.
14. Nobles! be first in honour. Ye, too, lose
15. Your place, in place: retrieve yourselves in good.
16. Peoples! be mighty in obedience.
17. Let each one labour for the common weal.
18. Be every man a people in his mind.
19. Kings — nobles — nations! love me and obey.
20. I need no aid — no arms. Burn books — break swords!
21. The world shall rest, and moss itself with peace.
22. Stand forth, and speak, sole servant of my throne!
23. If aught thou hast to settle and explain —
24. Or send away these nations to their homes.
25. LUCIFER. Ye mighty once — ye many weak, give ear!
26. I and my god — for god he sure must be,
27. In human form, who sitteth there enthroned —
28. For readier rule, and for the good of all,
29. Have cast again the dynasties of earth
30. According to the courses of the air: —
31. Therefore from east, and west, and north, and south.
32. Four element-like ministers shall bend

33.   Before his feet. Hearken, thou unkinged crowd!
34.   Ye have not sought the good of those ye governed.
35.   The people only for the people care.
36.   Ye seem to have thought earth but a ball for kings
37.   To play with: rolling the royal bauble, empire,
38.   Now east — now west. Your hour and power is past
39.   Ye are the very vainest of mankind,
40.   As loftiest things weigh lightest. Ye are gone!
41.   Nations, away with them! Nor do ye boast!
42.   Ye find that power means not good, not bliss.
43.   But ye would wed delusion: — now, ye know her.
44.   And she is yours for life — and death — and judgment.
45.   There is no power, nor majesty, save his:
46.   His is the kingdom of the world and glory.
47.   His throne is founded centre-deep by Heaven;
48.   And the whole earth doth bless him. Unto all
49.   He hath laid out one perfect level law —
50.   His will. For as the people cannot rule
51.   Themselves, so neither may a crowd of kings:
52.   And hence hath been the evil of the earth —
53.   Now ceased for ever. War will be no more.
54.   His is the sway of social sovereign peace:
55.   His tyranny is love and good to all: —
56.   His is the vice-royed, vouched-safe sway of God: —
57.   And he will turn the world, at will; as light
58.   Turneth the world round. Greet your Lord, and go!
59.   Depart, ye nations!
60.   FESTUS.   Hark! thou fiend! dost hear?
61.   LUCIFER. Ay! it is the death groan of the sons of men —
62.   Thy subjects — King!
63.   FESTUS. Why hadst thou this so soon?
64.   LUCIFER. It is God who brings it all about — not I.
65.   FESTUS. I am not ready — and — it shall not be!
66.   LUCIFER. I cannot help it, monarch! and — it is!
67.   Hast not had time for good!
68.   FESTUS.   One day — perchance.
69.   LUCIFER. Then hold that day as an eternity.
70.   FESTUS. All around me die. The earth is one great death-bed.
71.   CLARA. Oh! save me, Festus! I have fled to thee,
72.   Through all the countless nations of yon dead —
73.   For well I knew it was thou who sattest there,
74.   To die with thee, if that thou art not Death:

75. And, if thou wert, I would not shrink from thee.
76. I am thine own, own Clara!
77. FESTUS.   Thou art safe!
78. Here in the holy chancel of my heart —
79. The heavenly end of this our fleshly fane,
80. I hold thee to communion. Rest thee safe!
81. CLARA. Men thought I was an angel, as I passed;
82. And caught up at my feet — but I 'scaped all.
83. I knew — I was sure, that I should die by thee.
84. The heart is a true oracle — I knew it!
85. FESTUS. Then there is faith among these mortals yet.
86. Thy beauty cometh first, and goeth last —
87. Willow-like. Welcome!
88. CLARA. Oh! I am so happy!
89. FESTUS. I speak of thee as of the dead; the dead
90. Are alway faithful.
91. CLARA.   I will stay with thee —
92. Though angels beckon — may I? Let me, love!
93. I dare not — cannot, take mine eyes from thee,
94. For fear of looking on the dead. Dear Festus!
95. FESTUS. Thou art the only one hast answered me,
96. Love to love — life to life.
97. CLARA.   Oh! I am dying!
98. Give me one kiss — the kiss of life and death —
99. The only taste of earth I will take to Heaven.
100. Here! let me die, die in it. [*dies.*]
101. FESTUS. Last and best!
102. Now am I one, again. Oh! memory runs
103. To madness, like a river to the sea.
104. Happy as Heaven have I been with thee, love!
105. Thine innocent heart hath passed through a pure life,
106. Like a white dove, wing-sunned through the blue sky.
107. A better heart God never saved in Heaven.
108. She died as all the good die — blessing — hoping.
109. There are some hearts, aloe-like, flower once, and die:
110. And hers was of them. Ah! all life hath ceased.
111. And silence reads the dead world's burial tale.
112. And Death sits quivering, there, and watering,
113. His great gaunt jaw at me. When must I die?
114. LUCIFER. Say! dost thou feel to be mortal, or immortal?
115. FESTUS. Away! — and let me die alone.
116. LUCIFER.   I go:

117. And I will come again: but spare thee, now.
118. One hour to think — [*goes.*]
119. FESTUS. On all things. God, my God!
120. One hour to sum a life's iniquities!
121. One hour to fit me for eternity —
122. To make me up for judgment and for God!
123. Only one hour to curse thee! Nay, for that,
124. There may be endless hours. God! I despair, —
125. And I am dying. Let me hold my breath!
126. I know not if I ever may draw another.
127. I feel Death blowing hard at the lamp of life.
128. My heart feels filling like a sinking boat;
129. It will soon be down — down. What will come of me?
130. It is as I always wished it; — I shall die
131. In darkness, and in silence, and alone.
132. Even my last wish is petted. God! I thank Thee;
133. It is the earnest of Thy coming — what?
134. Forgiveness? Let it be so: for I know not
135. What I have done to merit endless pain.
136. Is pleasure crime? Forbid it, God of bliss!
137. Who spurn at this world's pleasures, lie to God;
138. And shew they are not worthy of the next.
139. What are Thy joys we know not — nor can we
140. Come near Thee, in Thy power, nor truth, nor justice;
141. The nearest point wherein we come towards Thee,
142. Is loving — making love — and being happy.
143. Thou wilt not chronicle our sandlike sins;
144. For sin is small, and mean, and barren. Good,
145. Only, is great, and generous, and fruitful.
146. Number the mountains, not the sands, O God!
147. God will not look as we do on our deeds;
148. Nor yet as others. If He more condemn,
149. Shall He not more approve? A few fair deeds
150. Bedeck my life, like gilded cherubs on
151. A tomb, beneath which lie dust, decay, and darkness.
152. But each is better than the other thinks.
153. Thank God! man is not to be judged by man: —
154. Or, man by man, the world would damn itself.
155. What do I see? It is the dead. They rise
156. In clouds! and clouds come sweeping from all sides.
157. Upwards to God: and now they are all gone —
158. Gone, in a moment, to eternity.

159. But there is something near me.
160. SPIRIT.   It is I.
161. FESTUS. Go on! I follow, when it is my time.
162. There is no shadow on the face of life:
163. It is the noon of fate. Why may not I die?
164. Methinks I shall have yet to slay myself.
165. I am calm now. Can this be the same heart
166. Which, when it did sleep, slept from dizziness,
167. And pure rapidity of passion, like
168. The centre circlet of the whirlpool's wheel?
169. The earth is breaking up; all things are thawing.
170. River and mountain melt into their atoms;
171. A little time, and atoms will be all.
172. The sea boils; and the mountains rise and sink
173. Like marble bubbles, bursting into death.
174. O thou hereafter! on whose shore I stand—
175. Waiting each toppling moment to engulf me —
176. What am I? Say, thou Present! — say, thou Past!
177. Ye three wise children of Eternity!
178. A life? — a death? — and an immortal? — all?
179. Is this the threefold mystery of man?
180. The lower, darker Trinity of earth?
181. It is vain to ask. Nought answers me — not God.
182. The air grows thick and dark. The sky comes down.
183. The sun draws round him streaky clouds, like God
184. Gleaning up wrath. Hope hath leapt off my heart,
185. And overturned it. I am bound to die.
186. God, why wilt Thou not save? The great round world
187. Hath wasted to a column beneath my feet.
188. I will hurl me off it, then; and search the depth
189. Of space, in this one infinite plunge! — Farewell,
190. To earth, and Heaven, and God! Doom! spread thy lap!
191. I come — I come!
192.   GOD.
193.   Forbear!
194. FESTUS.   I am God's!
195.   GOD.
196.   Man, die!

MILLENNIAL EARTH. FAITH, HOPE AND LOVE DESCEND

SCENE 31

[*The Skies*]
[*GOD, ANGELS, ANGEL OF EARTH, LUCIFER*]

1. GOD.
2. The age of matter consummates itself.
3. All things that are shall end, save that is mine.
4. As with one world, so shall it be with all;
5. For all are human, fallible, and false, —
6. As creature towards Creator must be aye.
7. But for the whole prepare ye, not the less
8. Grade upon grade of glory, sons of God!
9. And Earth shall live again, and like her sons
10. Have resurrection to a brighter being:
11. And waken like a bride, or like a morning,
12. With a long blush of love to a new life.
13. Another race of souls shall rule in her,
14. Creatures all loving, beautiful, and holy.
15. Go, angel! guide her as before through Heaven.
16. ANGEL OF EARTH. On! on! my world again!
17.   Away we fly
18.   Through Heaven's blue plain,
19.   Like thought through the eye.
20.   Ye angels keep your Heaven!
21.   I, Earth!
22.   For that with God I have striven,
23.   And have prevailed.
24.   I come once more,
25.   I come to thee, Earth!
26.   Like a ship to shore.
27. LUCIFER. Have not I triumphed o'er the earth that was?
28. GOD.
29. Prince of the powers of air! thy doom is nigh.
30. The prison place of spirits is for thee —
31. As for all others thou hast wronged, for a time —
32. But those who by my favour die not. Him
33. Conduct, ye angels, into Hades; there
34. To wait my will while the world's Sabbath lasts.

SCENE 32

The Millennial Earth
[SAINTS and ANGELS worshipping; FESTUS]

1. ANGEL. The Earth is all one Eden. Pity, sure,
2. That it should ever end.
3. SAINT. I say not so;
4. Although I have a thousand plans in hand,
5. Some interwoven with the farthest stars —
6. Each one of which might ask a year of years
7. To perfect.
8. ANGEL.   True; our Maker knoweth best
9. What thought or deed may best belong to time
10. Or to eternity.
11. SAINT.   All prophecy
12. Hath said the earth shall cease, and that right soon.
13. FESTUS. 'Tis like enough. Beauty's akin to Death.
14. ANGEL. Behold, our sister Graces of the skies,
15. Faith, Hope, and Love, descend! Methinks of late
16. Ye chiefly dwell on earth.
17. LOVE.   Where lives and reigns
18. The Son of God, there are we ever seen,
19. Successive, as the seasons to the sun.
20. SAINTS. Well are ye known and welcome in all.
21. Wherever lofty thought or godly deed
22. Is lodged or compassed, there your blessings rest.
23. HOPE. How sweet, how sacred now, this earth of man's!
24. The prelude of a yet sublimer bliss! —
25. I marked it from the first, while yet it lay
26. Lightless and stirless; ere the forming fire
27. Was kindled in its bosom, or the land
28. Lift its volcanic breastwork up from sea.
29. The deluge, and idolatries of men
30. I viewed, though shuddering, and with faltering eye,
31. E'en to the incarnation of Heaven's Lord,
32. And dawning of His faith; that faith which was

33. An infant and anon a giant; was
34. A star, and grew a Heaven-fulfilling sun;
35. Which was an outcast, and became, ere long,
36. A dweller in all palaces; which hid
37. Its head in dens of deserts, and sat throned,
38. After, in richest temples high as hills;
39. Which was poured out in mortal blood, and rose
40. In an immortal spirit; as a slave
41. Was sold for gold and prostrated to power; —
42. And now that lowly bondmaid is a Queen;
43. And lo! she is beloved in earth and Heaven;
44. And lieth in the bosom of her Lord,
45. The Bride of the all-worshipped, one with God.
46. LOVE. We even of divinest origin
47. In infinite progression view all worlds;
48. And we are happy.
49. FAITH.   The dead sleep as yet;
50. But their time cometh, and the bonds of death
51. Already slacken round the living soul;
52. The mortal sleep of ages, which began
53. When Time sank down into his slumberous west,
54. Thins even now o'er the reviving eyes
55. Gathering their Heaven-lent light, no more to wane
56. In woe or age; never be quenched in tears
57. Like a star in the sea. 'Tis as I ever knew;
58. My life is to receive and to believe
59. The Word and words of God.
60. LOVE.   I, who am Love
61. And Grace and Charity, rejoice with you;
62. Whither ye wend I with ye; whether here,
63. Or on the utmost rim of Light's broad reign —
64. The least and last of stars which even seems
65. To tremble at its insignificance
66. In presence of Infinity; where yet
67. No angel's wing hath waved, nor foot of fiend
68. Left its hot imprint; — still, in all do we
69. Find fit delight and honour, as now here.
70. Now earth and Heaven hold commune, day and night;
71. There's not a wind but bears upon its wing
72. The messages of God; and not a star
73. But knows the bliss of earth.
74. FESTUS. The earth hath God

75. Remade, and all its elements refined,
76. Fit for sublimer Being. Flesh hath passed
77. Its fiery baptism, and come forth clear
78. As crystal gold: all that of vile or mean
79. Pertained to it hath perished atomless.
80. Earth, like a diamond, basks in her own free light;
81. Unfed, unaided, unrequiring aught.
82. All now is purity and power and peace.
83. The first-born of creation, they who hail
84. Archangels as their brethren, mountainlike
85. Reign o'er the plains of men, converting all;
86. Reaping the fields of immortality,
87. Each one his sheaf for Him the Harvest-Lord,
88. To whom belongs earth's whole estate and life
89. And every world's.
90. ANGEL.   And He shall garner all.
91. The awful tribes which have in Hades dwelt,
92. Past count of time, await their rising. God's
93. Great day, the sabbath of the world's long week,
94. Is at high noon; and Christ hath yet to come
95. To judge and save the living and the dead.
96. SAINT. The shadows of Eternity o'ercast
97. Already Time's bright towers. The Heavens shall come
98. Down like a cloud upon a hill, and sweep
99. Their spirit over earth, and the whole face
100. And form of things shall be dissolved and change.
101. Nothing shall be but essence, perfect, pure,
102. And void of every attribute but God's.
103. This even is too gross for that which is
104. To come. The holy have both earth and Heaven.
105. FESTUS. Nor pain, nor toil of mind or frame, nor doubt,
106. Nor discontent, nor enmity to God,
107. Disturb the steady joy the spirit feels;
108. Nor element can torture, nor time tire;
109. Nor sea nor mountain make or bar or fear;
110. Sickness and woe and death are things gone by;
111. Destroyed with the destruction of the world: —
112. Shadows of things which have been, never more
113. To waste the world's bright hours, nor grate the heart
114. Of mighty man; now fit for thrones and wings;
115. Ruler of worlds, main minister of Heaven,

116. Inheritor of all the prophecies
117. Of God fore-uttered through the tongues of Time,
118. Ages of ages. Evil is no more.
119. ARCHANGEL. And does earth satisfy thee now?
120. FESTUS.   As earth.
121. There is a brighter, loftier life for man
122. Even yet, the very union with God.
123. ARCHANGEL. God works by means. Between the two extremes
124. Of earth and Heaven there lies a mediate state, —
125. A pause between the lightning lapse of life
126. And following thunders of eternity; —
127. Between eternity and time a lapse,
128. To soul unconscious, though agelasting where
129. Spirit is tempered to its final fate;
130. When every interfulgent¹ conscious state
131. Within or between worlds, repose or bliss,
132. Divested, man shall mix with Deity,
133. And the Eternal and Immortal make
134. One Being. As in earth's first paradise
135. God's Spirit walked with man, and commune made
136. With him, so in the second, after death,
137. Man's spirit walks with God in an elect
138. Existence, and a vigil of the great,
139. The holy day which is to break in Heaven.
140. Thither the Lord of Life went, in the hour
141. That Hell by Earth revenged itself on Heaven,
142. With one soul penitent accompanied; —
143. Nor long remained He there, yet long enough
144. To cheer earth's faithful, who received Him then
145. In silent unknown blessedness of soul,
146. With time-outwearing hope that yet in Him
147. They should partake the Godhood of His love.
148. And with Him rose then, in prophetic proof
149. Of His Divinity, many a deathless ghost,
150. Triumphant o'er that blind revenge which wrought,
151. Hell! thy destruction — thy salvation. Earth!
152. FESTUS. That such will be, the just well know; and all

---

1. Interfulgent: Shining between. *Rare.*

153. Earth's great events and changes tend thereto;
154. Its fiery dissolution in the past,
155. And supernatural recommencement now
156. Under the universal creed of Christ.
157. The chosen and the world-redeemed partake
158. His personal and spiritual reign.
159. ARCHANGEL. And this shall last, till, like the setting sun
160. Deserting earth, He shall retire to Heaven,
161. With all His captive victors in His train,
162. Triumphant, and translated evermore
163. Into the hierarchical skies. Wilt see,
164. While yet time is, earth's shadowy world within —
165. The inward living death she bears about
166. Her hearty hath ever borne — and, augur-like,
167. Explore the ominous bowels of the earth?
168. To me are given the secrets of the centre,
169. The keys of earth, to lock and to unlock,
170. Coffer-like. I, it was who seized and bound,
171. At His behest who wills and it is done —
172. Even on their thrones, the mighty thou wilt see.
173. FESTUS. Angel of Heaven! I would view these things.
174. ARCHANGEL. Nor these alone, but other wonders yet.
175. The valley where Death's dark wings brooded o'er,
176. A God-offending night, unvisited
177. By sun or star, where but the fatuous fire
178. Of man's weak judgement wandered, till God's Son
179. Laid o'er the black abyss a bridge of light,
180. And married earth to the mainland of Heaven —
181. This shalt thou see. Death's grave; and over him,
182. And over it, that monument of light,
183. Enlightening earth. The gods and fields of old,
184. And all the fictions of the heart of man.
185. Imagined of the future past for aye,
186. Thou shalt inspect. Behold this mountain! We
187. Must pass through it; for under lie the gates
188. Of the invisible regions whereunto
189. We tend, for a brief season.
190. FESTUS.   On then!
191. ARCHANGEL.   Bare
192. Thy marble breast, O mountain, to its depths!
193. An angel and a man divine demand

194. A way through these foundations.
195. FESTUS.   And the rocks
196. Open like mists before thee.
197. ARCHANGEL. Follow me!

SCENE 33

[Hades]
[ARCHANGEL, FESTUS, DEATH, LUCIFER]

 1. FESTUS. Almighty God! sustain me. This is Death; —
 2. And this — I knew not, angel! he was here —
 3. Is Lucifer — the fallen, like a bolt
 4. Of thunder forged in intramundane[1] air,
 5. Self-buried in the centre. Lucifer!
 6. Wake from thy sealike sleep; in peace or wrath,
 7. Rouse from thine age-long trance; arise and see;
 8. The representatives of earth and Heaven
 9. Stand by thee. As for me, I blame no more
10. The part thou tookest in my mortal life;
11. 'T is gone, — nor spurn thee for delusions dead.
12. The blood that hath been spilled is sunk in earth,
13. And run into the rivers, and dried up
14. Into the air; — and there's an end of it.
15. What good hath come of it alone I bear
16. At heart. And we have both offended God.
17. Let me, though not in nature to forget,
18. Forgive, what every one hath sometime felt —
19. The Devil's burning gripe upon his heart.
20. I see thee with compassion, half with hope.
21. LUCIFER. Mortal! I bow to thee, and would do to

---

1. Intramundane: Situated in the created world. *OED* gives *Festus* as the first known use.

22. The least and lowest spirit God hath made:
23. But still the curse that I am cursed with
24. Outlasts the elements — outlives all time.
25. FESTUS. All curses cease with time; all woe.
26. Blessings star forth for ever; but a curse
27. Is like a cloud — it passes.
28. LUCIFER. 'T was by him —
29. Yon angel, only not almighty, there!
30. As with a chain of mountains I was bound
31. And hurled into this unformed nebulous life;
32. Stripped of all might when mightiest, struck down
33. While triumphing the loftiest, — enslaved
34. When most a monarch o'er both earth and hell,
35. And made a shadow among shadows here.
36. It recks not. Let the impenetrable soul
37. Be ground as through a mill, I only know
38. In action or inaction equal woe —
39. Suffering, doing, being, one extreme.
40. Pass on! we meet again!
41. FESTUS. And when we do,
42. May God forgive, as I! —
43. ARCHANGEL. Behold there, Death!
44. Throned on his tomb — entombed in his throne;
45. Just as he ceased he rests for aye — his scythe,
46. Still wet out of its bloody swathe, one hand
47. Tottering sustains; the other strikes the cold
48. Drops from his bony brow: his mouldy breath
49. Tainteth all air.
50. FESTUS.   I dread him now no more,
51. Nor hate. He is a vanquished enemy.
52. ARCHANGEL. Listen! he speaks.
53. DEATH. To you, ye sons of God,
54. My latest words I utter. Unto him
55. Who ever lives, and hath for aye destroyed
56. Me and my reign, give ye this crown usurped,
57. And lay it at His feet; and this dulled dart
58. Which was my sceptre. To the conqueror
59. Belong these trophies. All the progeny
60. Of time will soon cease. Lo! the end's at hand.
61. ARCHANGEL. Thus shall it be, O Death! and thus it is.
62. FESTUS. And who are these gigantic awful shades
63. Which fill the midst — the present of the place?

64.   ARCHANGEL. These are the mighty nothings man
65.   Made; the dread unrealities by whom
66.   He swore, to whom he prayed, and at whose shrines of old
67.   He sacrificed a thousand times a day: —
68.   His brother falsehoods these, men like himself,
69.   Which mere imagination changed to gods,
70.   Some for their good deeds, others for their bad:
71.   Bel,[2] Odin, Bramh[3] and Zeus, the Lords of death
72.   And fire, and judgment, waiting here their death
73.   And fiery judgment — Time and Titan — war —
74.   Beauty, and strength, and Light, and the long roll
75.   Of creatural powers and passions Deified; —
76.   Who gave their names to stars which still roam round
77.   The skies, all worshipless, even from climes
78.   Where their own altars once topped every hill.
79.   JOVE. Before the Christian cross and Moslem mosque
80.   My marble fanes have fallen, and my shrines
81.   Shrunk like a withered hand ages ago.
82.   But now all signs and sacred domes for gods
83.   To dwell in are extinct. The world is all
84.   One Temple of the Truth.
85.   BRAMH. The ages feigned
86.   That made Time groan to think how old he was,
87.   And Deities in millions are no more.
88.   Ageless eternity and God the sole,
89.   The royalty of Heaven, is at hand.
90.   BOODH.[4] All things that are shall nothing be at last,
91.   Save what's resolvable in Deity.
92.   FESTUS.   And all these lesser shades, which move like moons
93.   Half-darkened by the greater — half-illumed —
94.   Are priests and prophets of the mightier ones?
95.   ARCHANGEL. They are; — and further round thine eye can mark,
96.   The myriads of adorers of each god,
97.   Confused and prostrate, as their souls awake

2. Bel: A synonym for 'Lord', Bel was used to refer to Marduk, the chief god of the city of Babylon.
3. Brahm: Brahma, the supreme god of post-Vedic Hindu mythology.
4. Boodh: Buddha, fifth-/sixth-century mystic, given here as founder of Buddhism.

98. To the demoniac madness of their creeds.
99. Behold! they kneel to those they hailed on earth
100. As makers — as omnipotent — eterne —
101. And cry for help, for comfort; none have they
102. To give to others or themselves. The false,
103. The base, the brutish Deities give way,
104. And all their sacred follies in their train,
105. Before the earthquake truth, engulphing all.
106. Woe to the false gods, woe! to prophet, priest,
107. And worshipper, all woe!
108. FESTUS.   Hark! round the earth
109. Each soul hath found a tongue and uttereth woe.
110. Lo! from their thrones the man-made gods descend,
111. And rend their robes and trample on their crowns,
112. And hurl away their sceptres. Woe to all
113. The gods and idols of the heart of man!
114. Their sun is set for ever in the night
115. Which was ere Light was. Surely it is more
116. To be true man or woman than false god
117. And falser prophet. God alone the true,
118. The God of Heaven, shall be witnessed to
119. And worshipped.
120. ARCHANGEL. Witnessed, worshipped, too,
121. By all: the faithful and the faithless — saint
122. And sinner.
123. FESTUS.   Lo! the nations of the dead,
124. Which do outnumber all earth's races, rise,
125. And high in sunless myriads over head
126. Sweep past us in a cloud, as 't were the skirts
127. Of the Eternal passing.
128. A VOICE. Souls, arise
129. To deathless life!
130. ARCHANGEL. 'T is God speaks. Let us hence.
131. The general judgment is in hand, — God's hand.
132. The souls of those whom God loves circle us.
133. For thee, thy lot thou knowest. As a seed
134. Buried in earth doth multiply itself
135. Full fifty fold, so will thy nature when
136. Changed, it lifts head in the air divine of Heaven.
137. FESTUS. Out of the depths of earth and the world's womb
138. Thine unborn angels seek thee, God, all Love!
139. Now is Thine hour for which all hours were made,

140. All life created, all things else ordained;
141. Be it the hour of mercy, Lord! to all,
142. For Thy Son's sake, who, for the sake of man,
143. Came down from Heaven into the pit of earth,
144. And lived as one of us and died; — He died
145. The death of all at once of every age;
146. The world's accumulated weight of woe,
147. From its first life unto its last, which none
148. But the Omnipotent could bear — He bore;
149. And all for us. God became man that man
150. Might become God. Oh, favour infinite!
151. Now reap the righteous, righteous but in Him
152. Any, their guerdon. Evil to repay
153. With good was Christ's command, and earth with Heaven
154. Is thus the great example of His word.
155. Enough for sinners this, for all which live.
156. Do Thou, Lord! be with us. In Thee we live;
157. Our treasure, trust and triumph is in Thee.
158. Behold the day of our salvation come
159. Unto the countless all Thou hast redeemed!
160. The ages sweep around me with their wings
161. Like angered eagles cheated of their prey.
162. The ages of all time: the glowing Heavens
163. Are rushing to receive us. Oh, rejoice
164. All ye that are immortal — and whate'er
165. Hath been predestined to eternal end,
166. The day determined ere all time was dawns!

DESCENT OF AZREAL

SCENE 34

[Earth]

[ANGELS and SAINTS — An Angel descending; FESTUS]

1. SAINT. Whence art thou?
2. ANGEL. I? from Heaven, and thither tend; —
3. One moment here to bid ye to prepare.
4. Our Lord the Eternal Son comes hither, girt
5. With His victorious hosts, to judge the world.
6. SAINT. What victory hath our Almighty gained?
7. ANGEL. One final, over Death and Hell. Shout, earth!
8. Thy freedom is accomplished, and thy foes
9. Brought down to endless ruin.
10. SAINT.   Angel, speak!
11. We burn to learn the tidings of this war,
12. Whereof thou tell'st, and doubtless wast a part.
13. ANGEL. Hot from the fight I come. This lightning blade
14. Hath holpen well to thin the infernal rout,
15. Which back hath fled to hell, howling like winds.
16. But let me, at your will, ye peaceful saints,
17. Relate what happed to us from first to last.
18. The time was come in Heaven when God the Son
19. Bowing his head before the Omnipotent,
20. Who doubled every blessing infinite
21. Wherewith he had enriched His Only One
22. From first, rose from his glorious throne, and stepped
23. Into His sun-bright car, calling aloud
24. His angels to attend Him while He went
25. To judge the earth, as fore-ordained of old:
26. That Heaven and earth might view the majesty
27. And mercy of the God of all. We came,
28. Selectest spirits, countless — crowded bright
29. As the great stream of stars which flows through Heaven
30. Fast by the foot of God, each wave a world —
31. Eager to the eye this act of glory long
32. Talked of in Heaven, and now to be achieved.

33.   Forth from the starry towers, and world-wide walls,
34.   Of Heaven, we set in high and silent joy,
35.   And journeyed half our way through Heaven, when lo!
36.   A sight which checked the foremost flaming ranks,
37.   That halted frontwise, working doubt at first,
38.   But triumph after. Shielded and drawn up close,
39.   Behind a broken and decaying world,
40.   From which the light had vanished like the light
41.   Out of a death-shrunk eye, sat Lucifer —
42.   Midst in the powers of darkness, and the hosts
43.   Of hell, enthroned sublime; and all were still
44.   As ambushed silence round the Foe of God.
45.   But oh! how changed from him we knew in Heaven,
46.   Whose brightness nothing made might match nor mar;
47.   Who rose, and it was morn; — who stretched his wing,
48.   And stepped from star to star; — so changed he shewed
49.   Most like a shadowy meteor, through which
50.   The stars dim glint — woe-wasted, pined with pain.
51.   And by his side there sat or shrank a shape
52.   We angels knew not, but the Son of God
53.   Knew him, and called him Death; whom, when he saw,
54.   Arousing, after, out of sleep intense,
55.   That unrealmed tyrant drew his mortal dart,
56.   And drave it through himself, — a shade, shade-quelled.
57.   Then to that chief of mischief and his fiends,
58.   Who, thick as burning stones that from the throat
59.   Of some volcano foul the benighted sky,
60.   Shot up triumphant into air as they
61.   Beheld our ranks move on, thus spake our Lord, —
62.   Not wrathfully, but sternly pitying:
63.   Hell's wretched remnant! wherefore crouch ye here?
64.   Is it to sue destruction, or to bar
65.   My passage? If it be, in both ye err.
66.   And will ye trust yourselves again to war
67.   With me Almighty? Have I not overcome
68.   Ye separately, both? Speak, brutal Death!
69.   Fit follower and fellow to all woes, —
70.   Wherefore this instantaneous haste from hell,
71.   And both from Hadëan bondage, thus again
72.   So soon to compass mightiest wickedness,
73.   And tempt extremest wrath? Speak, head of hell!
74.   To Him thus Lucifer: Almighty Son!
75.   Thy power I defy not; but in peace

76. I war with fate. My life is to destroy.
77. Evil hath more activity, if good
78. More strength: and one must wear the other out.
79. The more august the sin, so much the more
80. Is my necessity. Yon earth hath been
81. The battle-plain of Heaven and hell. From Thee,
82. Who knowest all things, it were vain to hide
83. My purpose, which for a thousand years, the years
84. Of bondage, hath grown in me and lived on,
85. Toad-like within a rock — vital where all
86. Beside was death — to seize the nascent souls
87. Of men as they rerose from death to life,
88. And sweep them off in midst of all these hosts,
89. Assembled for that cause here as Thou seest,
90. To hell; — the universal race of man.
91. But if ordained that not on them, but Thee
92. And Thine, old hate shall satisfy itself,
93. Approach no nearer; for we live by death; —
94. Or turn the tide of fate, Thou sole who canst!
95. Ceasing thereat, his host upraised a shout
96. Which shook the stars, and made them ring again.
97. Our Lord to him then spake thus, mild as Spring,
98. Addressing earth when smiling she lets fall
99. All flowerets from her lips — 'Tis well there is a God!
100. Lo! to what base extremes infernal pride
101. Can push a princely spirit once in Heaven.
102. Thee we will not destroy now, for thine hour
103. Hath yet to come — when least thou thinkest it.
104. God's wrath thou hast endured in punishment,
105. Not yet His power. Away! I warn ye hence
106. Ere wrath ride forth again. To Him the Fiend
107. Answered: God rules not us the unordered damned,
108. Nor recks of hell. For ages past belief,
109. Unless by those who like ourselves denied
110. Thine own eternity — by creature mind,
111. However lofty, hardly compassed — we
112. Have borne our pain without remorse, or sign
113. Of pity from our Maker. Shall we now
114. Believe, while thus confronting Him again,
115. He means us better? Never worse than now.
116. Therefore I say to ye, on! mightiest fiends,
117. On! Let us reap companions for our woes,
118. Or earn annihilation! At the word,

119. His fiery phalanx rushed to bar the way
120. Of Him whose ways are over all His works.
121. A million spears blazed forth their answer bright,
122. As of as many tongues. Serene our ranks
123. Stood as the stars o'er thunder. God the Son
124. Sate in His orbed car, and breathed on them;
125. And they were rolled up like the desert sands
126. Before the burning wind, — throne wrecked on throne.
127. All ruined and foredone. Pursue! He cried,
128. Nor let them near the earth I go to judge.
129. And we pursued, as many as He chose,
130. And chased from sphere to sphere that wretched wreck
131. Of falsest fiends: — and I, it seems, am first
132. Of all my victor brethren to declare
133. The triumph past and coming, and to cheer
134. Your hearts with tidings of our Lord, to whom
135. Be glory for His universal deeds,
136. And to him, only God!
137. SAINT. Behold where comes
138. Another warrior-angel from on high;
139. Like angels, always singly or in hosts.
140. ANGEL. It is the most dread Azrael, unto whom
141. The sword of Death is given as a boon.
142. SAINT. What sayst thou, heavenly one?
143. AZRAEL.   To the extreme bound
144. Of Light's domain we chased the flying foe,
145. Who on the confines of the lower air
146. Once rallied at their leader's stern command,
147. Whom more they fear, or seem to fear, than God.
148. They halted, formed, and faced us. I and mine,
149. As on we came in order, full career,
150. Exalted by success, hoped ardently
151. One more convincing contest; but in spite
152. Of future woe or the tempestuous threats
153. Of the great Fiend who marshalled them, each eyed
154. His neighbour pale; their trembling shook all air;
155. And each one lift his arm, but no one struck.
156. Awhile in dead throe-like suspense they stood,
157. Or like the irresolution of the sea
158. At turn of tide — then wheeled and fled amain.[1]

---

1. Amain: With full force. *Archaic.*

159. And in one mass immense broke down from Heaven,
160. Cliff-like; — there let them lie! such fate have fiends.
161. And we returned, hoping to meet, as charge
162. To all was given, the Lord our glory here.
163. ARCHANGEL. Let all the dead rejoice! their Saviour comes.

SCENE 35

[*The Judgment of Earth*]
[*THE SON OF GOD, THE ARCHANGEL, SAINTS and ANGELS*]

1. ARCHANGEL. Let all the dead rejoice! their Saviour comes;
2. With clouds of angels circled like a sun.
3. Belted with light, and brighter than all light,
4. Lo! He descends and seats Him on His throne,
5. Alighting like a new made sun in Heaven.
6. The world awaits Thee, Lord! Rise, souls of men,
7. Buried beneath all ages from the first;
8. Ye numbered and unnumbered, loathed and loved,
9. Awake to judgment! Rise! the grave no more
10. Hath power upon ye than the ravening sea
11. Upon the stars of Heaven. Ye elements!
12. Give back your stolen dead. He claimeth them
13. Whose they both were and are, and aye shall be.
14. SON OF GOD.
15. I come to repay sin with holiness,
16. And death with immortality; man's soul
17. With God's Spirit; all evil with all good.
18. All men have sinned; and as for all I died,
19. All men are saved. Oh! not a single soul
20. Less than the countless all can satisfy
21. The infinite triumph which to me belongs,
22. Who infinitely suffered. Ye elect!
23. And all ye angels, with God's love informed,
24. Who reign with me o'er earth and Heaven, assume

25.   Your seats of judgment. Judge ye all in love,
26.   The love which God the Father hath to you —
27.   For His Son's sake, and all shall be forgiven.
28.   SAINTS. Lord! let us render back to Thee the love
29.   Which is Thine own: none else is worthy Thee.
30.   SON OF GOD.
31.   Behold this day I dwell with thee on earth,
32.   E'en to the last; the next shall be in Heaven,
33.   Where ye shall meet the Father, and remain
34.   In the Eternal presence, He through me
35.   Blessing all spirits overflowingly.
36.   SAINTS. Dear Lord, our God and Saviour! for Thy gifts
37.   The world were poor in thanks, though every soul
38.   Were to do naught but breathe them, every blade
39.   Of grass and every atomie of earth
40.   To utter it like dew. Thy ways are plain
41.   Only in Thine own light. And this great day
42.   Unveils all nature's laws and miracles —
43.   All to Thee all as one. Thy death was life;
44.   Thy judgment is all mercy, Lord of Love!
45.   The world's incomprehensible no more
46.   To man, but all is bright as new-born star.
47.   SON OF GOD.
48.   The Book of Life is opened. Heaven begins.

LUCIFER RESTORED TO HIS ANGELIC STATE

SCENE 36

[The Heaven of Heavens]
[THE RECORDING ANGEL, LUCIFER, FESTUS, ANGELS]

1.   THE RECORDING ANGEL. All men are judged save one.
2.   SON OF GOD.
3.   He too is saved.
4.   Immortal! I have saved thy soul to Heaven.
5.   Come hither. All hearts bare themselves to me,
6.   As clouds unbind their bosoms to the sun,
7.   And thine was wealthy in the gifts of good.
8.   And, if its guilt and glory lay in love,
9.   Let light outweigh the darkness! Thou art saved.
10.   SAINTS.   Rejoice! Rejoice!
11.   FESTUS. Could I, Lord! pour my soul out,
12.   In thanks, even as a river rolling ever,
13.   'Twould be too scant for what I owe to Thee.
14.   SON OF GOD.
15.   Nay; immortality is long enough,
16.   As life, or as a moment is, to shew
17.   Thy love of good, thy thanks to me and God.
18.   One heart-throb sometimes earneth Heaven — one tear.
19.   FESTUS. My Maker! let me thank Thee, I have lived,
20.   And live a deathless witness of Thy grace.
21.   And Thee, the Holy One, who hast chosen me,
22.   From old eternity, while yet I lay
23.   Hid, like a thought in God, unuttered — Thou,
24.   Who makest finite full with the Infinite,
25.   As is a womb with an immortal spirit,
26.   Oh! let me thank Thee that I witness to Thee.
27.   And Thou, mid-God! my Saviour, and my Judge!
28.   Sun of the soul, whose day is now all noon —
29.   Who makest of the universe one Heaven —
30.   I praise Thee. Heaven doth praise Thee. God doth praise Thee.

31.   The Holy Ghost doth praise Thee. Praise Thyself!
32.   LUCIFER. Is he not mine?
33.   GOD.
34.   Evil! away for aye!
35.   In the beginning, ere I bade things be —
36.   Or ever I begat the worlds on space,
37.   I knew of him, and saved him in my Son,
38.   Who now hath judged; for, fraught with God-hood, He
39.   Yet feels the frailties of the things He has made;
40.   And therefore can, like-feelingly, judge them.
41.   For I abide not sin; and in my Son
42.   There is no sin —not that He takes away.
43.   It is destroyed for ever and made nothing.
44.   SON OF GOD.
45.   Spirit, depart! this mortal loved me.
46.   With all his doubts, he never doubted God:
47.   But from doubt gathered truth, like snow from clouds,
48.   The most, and whitest, from the darkest. Go!
49.   LUCIFER. I leave thee, Festus. Here thou wilt be happy.
50.   To be in Heaven is to love forever
51.   God — and thou must love here. Here thou wilt find
52.   All that thou canst and oughtst to love: for souls,
53.   Re-made of God, and moulded over again
54.   Into his sun-like emblems, multiply
55.   His might and love: the saved are suns, not earths;
56.   And with original glory shine of God,
57.   While I shall keep on deepening in my darkness,
58.   With not one gleam across the gloom of being.
59.   FESTUS. Let us part, spirit! it may be, in the coming,
60.   That as we sometime were all worth God's making.
61.   We may be worth forgiving; taking back
62.   Into His bosom, pure again — and then,
63.   All shall be one with Him, who is one in all.
64.   LUCIFER. It may be, then, that I shall die. Farewell.
65.   Forgive me that I tempted thee!
66.   FESTUS.   I am glad.
67.   GOD.
68.   Stay, spirit! all created things unmade
69.   It suits not the eternal laws of good
70.   That Evil be immortal. In all space
71.   Is joy and glory, and the gladdened stars,
72.   Exultant in the sacrifice of sin,

73. And of all human matter in themselves,
74. Leap forth as though to welcome earth to Heaven —
75. Leap forth and die. All nature disappears.
76. Shadows are passed away. Through all is light.
77. Man is as high above temptation now, —
78. And where by Grace he alway shall remain
79. As ever sun o'er sea; and sin is burned
80. In hell to ashes with the dust of death.
81. The worlds themselves are but as dreams within
82. Their souls who lived in them, and thou art null,
83. And thy vocation useless, gone with them.
84. Therefore shall Heaven rejoice in thee again,
85. And the lost tribes of angels, who with thee
86. Wedded themselves to woe, and all who dwell
87. Around the dizzy centres of all worlds,
88. Again be blessed with the blessedest.
89. Lo! ye are all restored, rebought, rebrought
90. To Heaven by Him who cast ye forth, your God.
91. Receive ye tenfold of all gifts and powers.
92. And thou who cam'st to Heaven to claim one soul,
93. Remain possessed by all. The sons of bliss
94. Shall welcome thee again, and all thy hosts,
95. Whereof thou first in glory as in woe —
96. In brightness as in darkness erst — shalt shine.
97. Take, Lucifer, thy place. This day art thou
98. Redeemed to archangelic state. Bright child
99. Of morning, once again thou shinest fair
100. O'er all the starry ornaments of light.
101. LUCIFER. The highest and the humblest I of all
102. The beings Thou hast made, Eternal Lord!
103. ANGEL. Behold they come, the Legions of the lost,
104. Transformed already by the bare behest
105. Of God our maker to the purest form
106. Of seraph brightness.
107. THE RESTORED ANGELS. His be all the praise!
108. And ours submissive thanks. When evil had done
109. Its worst, then God most blessed us and forgave.
110. Oh, He hath triumphed over all the world,
111. In mercy, over death and earth and hell!
112. SON OF GOD.
113. All God hath made are saved. Heaven is complete.
114. GUARDIAN ANGEL. Hither with me!

115. FESTUS. But where are those I love?

116. ANGEL. Yon happy troop!

117. FESTUS. Ah! blest ones, come to me!

118. Loves of my heart, on earth; and soul in Heaven!

119. Are ye all here, too, with me?

120. ALL.   All!

121. FESTUS. It is Heaven.

122. ANGEL. Come, let us join our souls into the song

123. Of glory, which the Saved all sing, to God.

124. THE SAVED. Father of goodness,

125.   Son of love,

126.   Spirit of comfort,

127.   Be with us!

128.   God who hast made us,

129.   God who hast saved,

130.   God who hast judged us.

131.   Thee we praise.

132.   Heaven our spirits,

133.   Hallow our hearts;

134.   Let us have God-light

135.   Endlessly.

136.   Ours is the wide world,

137.   Heaven on Heaven;

138.   What have we done, Lord,

139.   Worthy this?

140.   Oh! we have loved Thee;

141.   That alone

142.   Maketh our glory,

143.   Duty, meed.

144.   Oh! we have loved Thee!

145.   Love we will,

146.   Ever, and every

147.   Soul of us.

148.   God of the saved,

149.   God of the tried,

150.   God of the lost ones,

151.   Be with all!

152.   Let us be near Thee

153.   Ever and aye;

154.   Oh! let us love Thee

155.   Infinite!

156. FESTUS. So, soul and song, begin and end in Heaven,

157. Your birth-place and your everlasting home.
158. THE HOLY GHOST.
159. Time there hath been when only God was all:
160. And it shall be again. The hour is named,
161. When seraph, cherub, angel, saint, man, fiend,
162. Made pure, and unbelievably uplift
163. Above their present state — drawn up to God,
164. Like dew into the air — shall be all Heaven;
165. And all souls shall be in God, and shall be God,
166. And nothing but God, be.
167. SON OF GOD.
168. Let all be God's.
169. GOD.
170. World without end, and I am God alone;
171. The Aye, the Infinite, the Whole, the One.
172. I only was — nor matter else, nor mind,
173. The self-contained Perfection unconfined.
174. I only am— in might and mercy one;
175. I live in all things and am closed in none.
176. I only shall be — when the worlds have done,
177. My boundless Being will be but begun.

L'ENVOI

1.   READ this world! He who writes is dead to thee,
2.   But still lives in these leaves. He spake inspired:
3.   Night and day, thought came unhelped, undesired,
4.   Like blood to his heart. The course of study he
5.   Went through was of the soul-rack. The degree
6.   He took was high: it was wise wretchedness.
7.   He suffered perfectly, and gained no less
8.   A prize than, in his own torn heart, to see
9.   A few bright seeds: he sowed them — hoped them truth.
10. The autumn of that seed is in these pages.
11. God was with him, and bade old Time, to the youth,
12. Unclench his heart, and teach the book of ages.
13. Peace to thee, world! — farewell! May God the Power,
14. And God the Love — and God the Grace, be ours!

Appendix:

Contemporary Reviews from the Press

'English literature has no example of daring equal to *Festus*.'

- Arthur Mee

'There is matter enough in it to float a hundred volumes of the usual prosy poetry. It contains some of the most wonderful things I ever read.'

- S. C. Hall

'There is no more enthusiastic admirer of *Festus* than myself.'

- Mary Howitt

'In inspiration, in prophecy, in those flashes of the sacred fire which reveal the secret places where time is elaborating the marvels of nature, [*Festus*] stands alone. This book is a precious, even a sacred book . . . . England has now only two poets that can be named near him.'

- Margaret Fuller Ossoli

'There are passages of this work, figures of speech, images of tenderness and sublimity, thoughts of grandeur, expressions of fervor and reverence, alive with the very soul of poetry, instinct with celestial fire, strong, deep, intense—worthy of the masters of song.'

- *United States Magazine and Democratic Review*

'There will, doubtless, be many dull, cold, every-day souls, who will look upon *Festus* as a mere rhapsodical effusion; but all those who love to trace the thousand changeful and sparkling streams that spring from the fountain of the human mind, to enrich with their jewelled sands the waste of life, will read *Festus* with intense interest and delight.'

- Edward Mammatt

'I can scarcely conceive any degree of poetical eminence which this author, starting with so much richness of imagination and force of expression, may not be expected to attain.'

- Lord Francis Egerton

'What power! What fire of imagination, worth the stealing of Prometheus! A true poet indeed.'

- Elizabeth Barrett Browning

'A most remarkable and magnificent production.'

- Lord Lytton

'His place will be among the first, if not the first, of our native poets.'

- W. Harrison Ainsworth

'There is great exuberance of thought and imagery throughout this work, and a profuse expenditure of both, fearless of exhaustion of the author's stores.'

- James Montgomery

'It contains poetry enough to set up fifty poets.'

- Ebenezer Elliott

'I know no poem in any language that can be compared with it in copiousness and variety of imagery. The universe is as rife with symbols to this Poet as it is with facts to the common observer. His illustrations, sometimes bold and towering as the mountains, are at others soft, subtle, and delicate as the mists that veil their summits. But better than this, with a truth, force, and simplicity seldom paralleled, we have here disclosed the very inmost life of a sincere and energetic mind. Metaphysical and psychological speculations are, so to speak, actualized and verified by the earnestness and passion of the writer. There are few books in which what is so profound in its essence is rendered so familiar in its exposition.'

- J. Westland Marston

'Might such a simile be allowed, I should say honestly, that this book is in a modern library what the Garden of Eden was in the old world—a glory and perfection, in the midst of comparative sterility.'

- Charles Hooten

'With nothing are we more impressed on the whole than with the sacred character of this poem.'

- *Monthly Magazine*

'It is long since we have read any human composition, with equal interest.'

- *Birmingham Advertiser*

'We know of no book in our time so subordinated to nature. Do not consider it as a book, or as a work of art at all, but as a leaf out of the book of life. In boldness of conception and delicate touches of nature— wild passion, *Festus* is unsurpassed.'

- *The Dial, U.S.*

'This is one of those books which we read with throbbing of the heart, and with wonder, and almost amazement at the far-reaching thoughts that fill it. *Festus* is one of the greatest, if not the greatest of modern poems.'

- *Leeds Times*

'The volume before us is emphatically the production of the true poet; not the offspring of rules and systems, but nature's own child, and higher gifted with a wondrous power of song. Owning no guide but the impulse of his own genius, the poet has given us the musings of an earnest and well-balanced mind upon the great problem of human destiny. The struggle of good and ill for mastery in the mind of man, and the ultimate triumph of the former, are the subject matter of the poem. This is ground which he occupies with all true poets; Schiller in his "Wallenstein," Goethe in his "Faust," Byron in his "Cain," and Shakespeare have trodden it before. The great distinction between this poem and those to which we have alluded, is that here we have brought out more fully the all-pervading, all-governing power of Deity. God is all in all—the existence of evil and the operation of evil, are but parts of the vast machinery by which he is producing the fabric of universal good.'

- *Norfolk News*

'The book abounds in original conceptions of the sublimest cast, powerfully and magnificently wrought out.'

- *Cork Constitution*

'A poem remarkable for sustained power, glowing fancy, sublimity of language and high toned purity of purpose.'

- *Dublin Evening Packet*

'A great poem, and would have been thought an extraordinary production at any period of our literary history. Its characteristic is power—power of thought, and power of language. The poem is strongly imbued with the character of the time in which it is written, and is a gauge of the feeling of this age in its science, learning, and aspirings: but the hero has no place or time.'

- *The Nonconformist*

'The poem before us evolves a system of truth. The author evidently regards his picture and his scheme with all its allegorical evolution as including his theory of the universe, so that here we have not so much an artistic plot of a poem, as a theologic [*sic*] plan of the world; but it is a work of faith, and the poetry great and diversified as it is, is so subservient to the religion and philosophy, that we might fitly style the whole as a book of spiritual truth, edited by the muses. Our poet's fable is the man's creed; it is a song of belief, in object the noblest, in execution ranking with the completest of any in the whole range of modern productions. The work is making way, as all genuine workers must, with no questionable result, both at home and in the United States, where especially it seems to have attracted universal interest. If not the perfect poem of the country, *Festus* certainly abounds with some of the finest poetry in our language.'

- *The Metropolitan*

'We confidently declare there is no poem in existence, which makes such glorious use of the physics and metaphysics of the universe as *Festus*. It furnishes more profound views of man, the universe, Providence, and God, than can be found in any other work of genius.'

- *MacPhail's Ecclesiastical Journal*

'Mr. Bailey, like the Arab who employs his sword blade as a mirror, has first studied his own heart as seen by the poetic faculty, before girding on that weapon to capture the hearts of his fellows with it. He has thus secured truthfulness, a quality not to be attained by genius itself without some such effort. Sometimes indeed his ornaments are so numerous as almost to impart an air of stiffness to portions of the poem, just as a necklace will not hang gracefully if too many beads are placed on the string. The gorgeous creation like a cave of stalactites glistens everywhere with the wealth of many successive formations. It is as pleasant as it is rare to read a modern poem which is crowded like the present with fine thoughts. The author is one of those who understand that the thoughts of poetry, star-like, should be about the earth, but also above it. The great poet does not spend life in executing microscopic copies of small parts of nature. He makes the universe the scaffolding for his ideal.'

- *British Quarterly*

'The subject of *Festus* is the love of God and the love of man; the first more infinite than sin, and faithful to its purpose; the last finite as defect, and tainted with all manner of infidelities. The poem is in harmony with the age in which it has been produced; herein lies its significance, its justification and its greatness. The world-spirit of the time present, is enshrined in this magnificent book.'

- *The New Quarterly*

'Who that has ever read Festus has forgotten that prodigious poem: You find in it all contradictions reconciled—all improbabilities accomplished—all opposites paired—all formulas swallowed—all darings of thought and language attempted. In *Festus*, "silver is of no account." Golden images are even more plentiful than words. The pictures of nocturnal scenes—of the glories of the stars, are in our judgment unsurpassed in the compass of poetry.'

- *Tait's Magazine*

'In richness of imagery and aptness of illustration, we venture to affirm, the author has no competitor in modern times. His learning is profound and various, and lies beneath many an expression carelessly thrown over it, and needing the raising of the heart to extract it fully. Of the poetical spirit he is full to overflowing. The beauties of nature, art, and character, clasp him with mingled radiance like a rainbow; and the influence of an exalted morality touches and tinges every thing which passes before him, till the scenery he paints glows with the heavenly warmth of an Italian sunset.'

- *Dublin University Magazine*

'In the poem of *Festus* there is a wonderful commingling of the love-liness of nature, with all that is lovely in religion and morals. The dreamings of the minstrel, and the wisdom of the philosopher are here interlaced like star mingling its light with star. The lyrical skill of the author is wonderful, when we consider the grander attainments of his muse; yet the characteristic of the song dwells with him equally with the quality of the drama. The female characters in *Festus* are supremely charged with the ethereal and quick sensibility of womanliness; each one is a breathing history of her sex. Festus in his own person shews the triumph of good over evil.'

- *The Critic*

'*Festus* is a poem of great but unequal power. It abounds with passages, which, in all the elements of genuine poetry, are unsurpassed, we con-ceive, by any living writer. It is redolent with rich poetry, deep passion, and beautiful imagery. There is nothing in the mode of treating the subject at all calculated to shock the feelings of the orthodox; on the contrary, a strong religious feeling pervades the whole. The graphic power and spirit with which each form and character in this drama [is] delineated, and the thrilling interest which like a chain of electric fluid flashes with startling vividness through every vein, hold the "prisoned soul" of the reader captive, as if spellbound by some magic power.'

- *Liverpool Chronicle*

'This work may in truth be considered an extraordinary production, and is evidently the offspring of a glorious and surpassing genius. There is so much in it of the pure and exalted spirit of poesy, and so many of those bright scintillations that only flash from a glowing intellect, that it engages and at once absorbs our strongest sympathies. The book must be diligently and attentively read in order to find a just estimate of its value. There is a rich vein of metaphor which like a golden thread, is interwoven throughout the whole texture of the work; much rich imag-ery and lofty conception, and a considerable acquaintance with the philosophy of man. The writer appears to have a most acute perception and appreciation of the sublime and beautiful. Those who love to trace the thousand changeful and sparkling streams that spring from the fountain of the human mind, to enrich with their jewelled sands the waste of life, will read *Festus* with intense interest and delight.'

- *Analyst*

'The man who can write upon *Festus* without enthusiasm, is unworthy to read it: the richness and melody of the versification are a complete study, and form one of the most artistical exhibitions the world has witnessed . . . . This work is one of the wonders of literature; throughout it contains passage upon passage, that philosophy may esteem as texts, and the world as oracles.'

- *Sunbeam*

'Its design or story is excellent: its morals are orthodox. It contains many beautiful passages. The perusal of many of its detached portions will give great pleasure. The volume, like all which come from Mr. Pickering's establishment, is finely got up, worthy of the Aldine Anchor.'

- *Morning Advertiser*

'A poem evincing uncommon vigour of imagination; penned in a daring but not irreverent spirit; rich and graceful in its poetical garniture, and abounding in bold, subtle, and original thought. That the author is one who thinks and feels for himself is evident in every page. His conception of Lucifer, who is represented as a grand and thoughtful intelligence, remorse-striken [*sic*], is a thousand times loftier than Goëthe's vulgar, callous, Mephistopheles, with his eternal jokes and still worse sarcasms. There are many passages of a high and rare order of beauty, in which we are at a loss which most to admire, the boldness and grandeur of the conceptions, or the incomparable ease and simplicity of expression.'

- *Sun*

'*Festus* we heartily recommend to the lovers of poetic genius. Fancy, feeling, and vivid powers of illustration are a few of the many excellencies which abound in this admirable production.'

- *Bury St. Edmunds Herald*

'*Festus*—The author may be classed among the first poets of the day.'

- *Chester Gazette*

'Yielding to the inducement created by a desire for something new, we ran through this poem, and readily ascertained that it was the production of a young and enthusiastic writer, whose very soul and spirit seemed to flow through his pen . . . . We might select many passages of great force and wonderful imagining. It may be said that there is extravagance, but it is the extravagance of nature in its loveliness. The author possesses a power of intellect and tone of feeling eminently calculated to place him amongst the most esteemed poets of his native land.'

- *Nottingham Mercury*

'Here is a poem which will startle the critics throughout the kingdom, and give them pause before they venture to utter their opinions, so much there is of daring both in the conception and execution.'

- *Manchester Times*